DIVINANIMALITY

TRANSDISCIPLINARY THEOLOGICAL COLLOQUIA

Theology has hovered for two millennia between scriptural metaphor and philosophical thinking; it takes flesh in its symbolic, communal, and ethical practices. With the gift of this history and in the spirit of its unrealized potential, the Transdisciplinary Theological Colloquia intensify movement between and beyond the fields of religion. A multivocal discourse of theology takes place in the interstices, at once self-deconstructive in its pluralism and constructive in its affirmations.

Hosted annually by Drew University's Theological School, the colloquia provide a matrix for such conversations, and Fordham University Press serves as the midwife for their publication. Committed to the slow transformation of religiocultural symbolism, the colloquia continue Drew's long history of engaging historical, biblical, and philosophical hermeneutics, practices of social justice, and experiments in theopoetics.

Catherine Keller, *Director*

DIVINANIMALITY

Animal Theory,
Creaturely Theology

EDITED BY STEPHEN D. MOORE

FORDHAM UNIVERSITY PRESS ❧ NEW YORK ❧ 2014

Photographs of Jan Harrison's paintings in the Epilogue are by Nancy Donskoj.

Library of Congress Cataloging-in-Publication Data

Divinanimality : animal theory, creaturely theology / edited by Stephen D. Moore. — First edition.
   pages cm — (Transdisciplinary theological colloquia)
   Includes bibliographical references and index.
   ISBN 978-0-8232-6319-6 (cloth : alk. paper) — ISBN 978-0-8232-6320-2 (pbk. : alk. paper)
   1. Animals—Philosophy.   2. Animals—Religious aspects.   3. Ecotheology.
I. Moore, Stephen D., 1954– editor.
   BI05.A55D58 2014
   202'.4—dc23

2014013004

Printed in the United States of America
16 15 14   5 4 3 2 1
First edition

In memory of Helen Tartar

(1951–2014)

CONTENTS

FOREWORD

The present volume, which resulted from the eleventh Transdisciplinary Theological Colloquium held at Drew Theological School in 2011, was anticipated by *Ecospirit*, which resulted from the fifth Transdisciplinary Theological Colloquium held at Drew Theological School in 2005.[1] The specter of Jacques Derrida's cat Lutece hovered around the edges of the earlier colloquium that focused on conversations emerging in the field of religion and ecology, as did the feline peeking around the human face in Jan Harrison's painting that graced the cover of *Ecospirit*. Other-than-human animals were always present in our discussions.

The present volume's engagement with Derrida's *The Animal That Therefore I Am* is a significant contribution to the challenge to Cartesian philosophy and Western theology.[2] But this volume goes far beyond the discussion of Derrida. It includes wide-ranging contributions to animal studies, animality studies, the study of religion and animals, anthrozoology, and the myriad other names for the emerging transdisciplinary conversations about humans and other animals. It takes heed of Derrida's critique of philosophy for speaking of "'the animal' as of a single set that can be opposed to 'us,' 'humans,' subjects" in its engagement with the breadth of what *animal* means, from microbes to magpies.[3] Recognizing that humans are animals does not deny differences throughout the spectrum of animality. Some of the contributors also take heed of what Donna Haraway observed—that on the cusp of this moment of new awareness, Derrida "failed a simple obligation of companion species: he did not become curious about what the cat might actually be doing, feeling, thinking, or perhaps making available to him in looking back that morning."[4] This volume's authors are indeed curious about what other-than-humankind might contribute, indeed have contributed, to a changed way of thinking and acting in the world. Some of the chapters continue in a philosophical and symbolic engagement with the animal/animals, whereas others grapple with encounters with animals, be it their own or those of others. This range makes reading this volume both stimulating and a real joy.

Divinanimality is a welcome invitation into the conversations that have grown as a result of the rich interactions between the sciences, social sciences, and humanities, disciplinary distinctions that make less sense in the light of animal studies. *Divinanimality* beckons us to listen once again to the more-than-human world. I say "once again," for we know all too well that dominant strands of our Western culture, manifest in our religious traditions, science, politics, legal codes, philosophies, and worldviews, have been busy silencing that world, telling us that other-than-human animals cannot speak and, if they can, that we should shut our ears. The essays in this book give us glimpses throughout the Hebrew and Christian writings, and Christian history, of tales and saints and rituals where animals' ability to speak has been recognized. Roman Catholicism and Eastern Orthodoxy have more tales of saints interacting with animals, of talking animals, than do Protestants, as Laura Hobgood-Oster's work in this volume and elsewhere illustrates—too many to have insisted too strongly on the vastness of difference between *imago dei* humans and fallen animals/nature. Yet communication between animals and humans has sometimes been labeled evil: for example, in the witch trials and their condemnation of familiars; in the colonial impulse, everywhere Europeans went, to demonize those who could still listen, still communicate, who still in some way had not cut themselves off; and in the efforts of some contemporary conservative Protestants to vilify and label pagan most religious and spiritual environmentalism.

Hand in hand with this disenchantment of the world, as Max Weber would have it, is the line of thought, most familiar to us through Descartes, that indeed animals cannot communicate because they cannot think, they cannot feel, they cannot know, and, therefore, would have nothing to communicate. As Derrida and others remind us, animals were silenced because we stopped listening: "Men would be first and foremost those living creatures who have given themselves the word that enables them to speak of the animal with a single voice and to designate it as the single being that remains without a response, without a word with which to respond."[5]

Divinanimality continues the conversation about all who are "othered" and "silenced" in Western thought, an othering and silencing that has animated the whole Transdicisplinary Theological Colloquia series. *Divinanimality* focuses on the swirling dynamics unleashed by this human/animal dualism that has operated throughout Western thought, a sledgehammer force often used to shift racial, ethnic, sexual, or religious others, women, children, and the ill and disabled out of the category of *human* and into the category of *Other*. As Other, they are designated as deserving less respect, less justice, and less acknowledgment, and they are often named animals, beasts, brutes, and vermin to indicate a less than fully human condition. Much work has been done to undo such descending hierarchies, but the larger human/animal divide has often been left untouched, seemingly entrenched. These destructive dynamics illustrate how complex and difficult it is to open space for understanding humans as animals, for challenging this human/animal divide, when so many have worked so hard to climb back over the distinction, demanding to be recognized as fully human, as having civil and sacred worth and rights.

For many marked as less-than human and animal-like the discourse of humans as animals is hardly viewed as positive. Often it seems that there is so much other work to be done to assure justice among humans, that this distinction, this hierarchy, is of less importance. But this hierarchy is foundational to our human hubris, anthropocentrism, and elitism. It makes some exceptional and more worthy than others, and it degrades the ecosphere of all life. Thus it is of utmost importance, and many who work on behalf of various liberation movements have recognized that. James Cone, the preeminent black liberation theologian, declared in the opening sentence of "Whose Earth Is It Anyway?" that "the logic that led to slavery and segregation . . . and the rule of white supremacy . . . is the same one that leads to the exploitation of animals and the ravaging of nature."[6]

Others may not welcome such an undoing of the human/animal dualism through their lens of human exceptionalism, particularly Protestants, who may see it as demoting humans, taking the *imago dei* out of "us" by daring to spread it around. This fear, of course, is a result of amnesia about the work of the many founding figures of the Reformation. John Wesley commented that "God is in all things, and that we are to see the Creator in the face of every creature." He goes on to state that not to do so is, "indeed, a kind of practical atheism."[7] Martin Luther commented that "God is substantially present everywhere, in and through all creatures, in all their parts and places, so that the world is full of God."[8] If God is to be seen in the face of every creature, then much of contemporary Protestantism has a very limited notion of *imago dei*, and the question of whether animals have sacred worth seems silly to be asking in retrospect. But asked it is, and the answers have vast consequences.

Many of the contributors to this volume are reformers themselves, taking on traditional theological and biblical scholarship and thus opening wide spaces for reimagining. Others approach the conversation as part of the broad interdisciplinary field of religion and ecology that has taken on the human/nature divide, as if humans weren't "natural" or a part of "nature," and in doing so, have often directly, or indirectly, taken on the human/animal, as if humans were not animals, were not creatures. Within the growing world of religion and ecology, however, it has not been the gaze of Derrida's cat that has animated discussion so much as the dying of the fierce green fire in the eyes of a wolf that then bounty hunter Aldo Leopold had shot:

> We reached the old wolf in time to watch a fierce green fire dying in her eyes. I realized then, and have known ever since, that there was something new to me in those eyes—something known only to her and to the mountain. I was young then, and full of trigger-itch; I thought that because fewer wolves meant more deer, that no wolves would mean hunters' paradise. But after seeing the green fire die, I sensed that neither the wolf nor the mountain agreed with such a view.[9]

The continuing loss of the fierce green fire that died in this wolf and in so many others, leading almost to the extinction of a species, did help light a fire that grew into the green/blue environmental movement. The movement has motivated us to rethink our religious and philosophical traditions and change our attitude toward the more-than-human world, to both recover and rethink, to deconstruct and reconstruct, theology, philosophy, history, ritual, epistemologies, and sociocultural patterns. Many parts of that movement, particularly those with roots in religion and spirituality, connect with all the movements aimed at redressing inequality and hierarchies between humans for a full vision of ecojustice.

Aldo Leopold's work stands in a long line of confessional writing of reconceiving the human / nature / animal assumptions that have come to dominate Western theology and thought. Leopold joins a long line of figures who realized how our sociocultural presumptions limit us. Animal studies and animality studies are based on that epistemological insight that what we "know" is limited by the presumption that only humans know and speak.

The growing fields of animal cognition, emotions, culture, language, and ethology / behavior, in dialogue with the humanities and social sciences, are turning many philosophical, theological, and sociocultural presumptions on their head. What happens to epistemological understandings when we take into account how much animals know that we don't know without technological extensions—dogs who know an epileptic seizure is coming or who smell cancer, or birds, fish, turtles, and others who find their way over long distances to the places where they were born by using navigational means yet to be understood by humans? How does an octopus completely blend into its surroundings in a split second, changing not just the coloration but also the textured appearance of its skin to mimic sand or rock? How do migrating birds know the route? How do elephants communicate with each other from miles away? How does a spider or a silkworm spin a thread that is so thin, so light, and yet so strong? How does an abalone build a shell that is so light, so strong, and so hard to break? In the light of such abilities, humans are rather limited in some respects. Those scientists and observers who have spent their time learning from other-than-human animals are helping us realize how much we don't know and perhaps, in the process, undermining our human exceptionalist hubris and assumptions that are hurting all of us, the whole planet.

At the very moment when we are realizing the destructive silencing that our Western philosophical, theological, mechanistic, and reductionist worldviews accomplished, a time when many are seeking to relearn what our ancestors, and those more indigenous than most of us, know / knew, the terms are changing fast as we try to learn that we are not separate selves removed from "nature" and distinct from "animal." And learn we must, as ecosystems are irrevocably altered, affecting who can live where. Viruses, insects, plants, and animals, including humans, are affected by changes in the environment. Some become ecological opportunists, and others are climate-change refugees. Our animal bodies, and indeed all animal bodies, also participate in a vast experiment of chemicals engineered by humans and industrial wastes that are disrupting life processes. Finally, just as we are learning to understand the genetic code, that essential form of communication, as Haraway and others remind us, it is being manipulated and engineered into new code that is perhaps the most unsettling hybridizing. Science/bioengineering is creating previously unthought-of hybrids, no longer symbols or figures of our imaginations, erasing boundaries, and forcing new genetic language that is propelling us into new realms much faster than we collectively can think. Thus the question is no longer human/animal, but the continuum of animal, human, and machine, and if we aren't open to rethinking the first two, then how can we address the ethical questions our machines and technologies have raised about how they affect the world and all of us animals within it?

Laurel Kearns

ACKNOWLEDGMENTS

This volume had its origins in the proceedings of the eleventh Transdisciplinary Theological Colloquium, titled "Divinanimality: Creaturely Theology," which was held at Drew Theological School in Madison, New Jersey, from September 20 to October 2, 2011. There would have been no eleventh TTC, or even a first TTC, without Catherine Keller, Professor of Constructive Theology at Drew, whose vision birthed the colloquium series and who has now nursed it into its second decade. Strapping and rambunctious though TTC is, it would not have lasted this long without Catherine's unflagging energy and steady guidance. TTC XI, specifically, would not have come about without the additional leadership of Laurel Kearns, Associate Professor of Sociology and Religion and Environmental Studies at Drew. Laurel's exemplary ecological scholarship and activism has long provided (green) power, whether directly or indirectly, for all other ecological work at Drew Theological School. She served on the planning committee for TTC XI, along with Catherine Keller and Stephen Moore, and also graciously agreed to contribute a foreword to this volume. Special gratitude is owed to Mary-Jane Rubenstein and Mark Wallace, who provided splendid critical assessments of the volume in its chrysalis stage, and to copy editor Teresa Jesionowski and managing editor Eric Newman, who ably equipped it for flight. Helen Tartar, Editorial Director of Fordham University Press, created the TTC series, and her own passion for animality studies serendipitously closed the loop in the conception and production of the present contribution to the series. Helen died tragically in an automobile accident while the volume was in production. She was admired and loved by many of the contributors to the volume. We dedicate it to her memory.

Two Drew PhD students, Beatrice Marovich and Terra Rowe, expertly organized the organizers of the Divinanimality colloquium, along with every practical aspect of its operations, ensuring that it ran smoothly from beginning to end, and ensuring in particular that the dread words of John 2:3, "They have no wine," would never be heard during it. A third Drew PhD student, Karri Whipple, later prepared the index for the volume with astonishing expeditiousness.

In addition to the colloquium participants whose essays appear in this volume, a vibrant cast of other participants—moderators, respondents, discussants, and student presenters—enriched the proceedings. They included Edward Baring, Whitney Bauman, Chris Boesel, Marc Boglioli, Virginia Burrus, Christy Cobb, Brianne Donaldson, Danna Nolan Fewell, Antonia Gorman, Amy Beth Jones, Catherine Keller, Elias Ortega-Aponte, Stephanie Day Powell, Mayra Rivera, Mary-Jane Rubenstein, Althea Spencer-Miller, and Carol Wayne White.

The colloquium proper was prefaced by public lectures delivered by Jay McDaniel, Laura Hobgood-Oster, and Kate Rigby. Laura also led a workshop, as did Fletcher Harper from GreenFaith. Heather Murray Elkins designed an animal chapel service and delivered the sermon, and the service was also graced by Norman Lowrey and his amazing singing animal masks.

Last but not least, Jan Harrison, whose extraordinary animal art is the topic of the final essay in this collection, consented not only to exhibiting her paintings at the colloquium but also to surrounding the colloquium space with them and thereby rendering it numinous.

DIVINANIMALITY

❧ Introduction: From Animal Theory to Creaturely Theology

STEPHEN D. MOORE

Then the ahuman . . . —in a word—divinanimality, . . . would be the excluded, foreclosed, disavowed, tamed, and sacrificed foundation of . . . the human order, law and justice.
—JACQUES DERRIDA, *The Animal That Therefore I Am*

Critters are always relationally entangled rather than taxonomically neat.
—DONNA HARAWAY, *When Species Meet*

Transfixed by multiple animal eyes: This was the condition in which the participants in the colloquium of which this collection is the product found themselves. Those absent eyes were made piercingly present in the luminous animal paintings of Jan Harrison that ringed the proceedings—eyes more and other than human eyes, eyes demanding a justice more and other than that which human law provides.

TURNING TO MEET THE ANIMAL GAZE

A "turn to the animal" has been under way in the humanities for more than a decade, most evidently in philosophy, literary studies, cultural studies, and the fertile interstitial spaces between these and other contiguous fields. It is tempting to consider this turn to the animal that is occurring in the opening decades of the twenty-first century in relationship to other turns or overturnings—or, at any rate, interrogations—that occurred in the closing decades of the twentieth century. Specifically, it is tempting to set the interrogation of the human / animal hierarchy entailed in the turn to the animal in a continuous line with the interrogations of the male/female, masculine/feminine, heterosexual/homosexual, white/nonwhite, and colonizer/colonized hierarchies entailed in feminist studies, gender studies, queer studies, racial/ethnic studies, and postcolonial studies. It is tempting, but it might also be misleading. "Can the subaltern speak?" is a vexed question, but the subaltern at least speaks human languages, whereas "those who constitute the objects of animal studies," as Kari Weil observes, "cannot speak . . . any of the languages that the academy recognizes as necessary for . . . self-representation. Must they then be forever condemned to the status of objects?"[1]

The interdisciplinary enterprise we are considering flies, trots, slithers, and crawls under a variety of names: animal studies, human-animal studies, critical animal studies, animality studies, posthuman animality studies, zoocriticism. What's in a name? Quite a lot, according to Marianne DeKoven: "There is disagreement in the field over terminology. In general, those primarily motivated by animal advocacy and by the human-animal relation favor *animal studies*, while theorists of the posthuman, who want to move beyond the human-animal distinction, often prefer *animality studies*."[2] The present introduction will tip its theoretical hat by favoring *animality studies*, although without implying any disregard for the crucial work of animal advocacy. The prehistory of animality studies, in any case, is so thoroughly heterogeneous as to render any unitary account of it impossible and any high partition between it and animal studies artificial. That prehistory importantly includes such diversely situated endeavors as Dian Fossey's and Jane Goodall's ethological work with primates; Peter Singer's and Tom Regan's work on behalf of animal liberation and animal rights; and J. M. Coetzee's animal-attuned fiction, notably *The Lives of Animals*.[3] It also includes Lynn White Jr.'s "The Historical Roots of Our Ecologic Crisis," which famously charged Christianity with responsibility for the modern decimation of the natural world.[4] "What did Christianity tell people about their relations with the environment?" asked White,[5] answering in effect, "Be anthropocentric and multiply, and subdue and desacralize the earth." The final pages of White's manifesto are a paean to Francis of Assisi, "the greatest radical in Christian history since Christ,"[6] and the animals that have featured periodically in the article since its opening page now move to the fore. Many of the essays in the present volume can be conceived as a continuation of the conversation provocatively begun by White,[7] even if in theoretical dialects that he would likely have found strange.

Both in its origins and certain of its signal moments, the recent "turn to the animal" in the humanities has been a turn to meet an animal gaze. One animal, one gaze, and one human response to that gaze proved particularly catalytic for the emerging field of animality studies. The moment in question was an ultramundane one. It was not an encounter with, say, a male mountain gorilla in his native habitat, à la Dian Fossey, an encounter also characterized by an exchange of gazes, as it happens ("The expression in his eyes was unfathomable. Spellbound, I returned his gaze"),[8] and culminating in an iconic touch (he "extended his hand to touch his fingers against my own for a brief instant"),[9] Michelangelo's *The Creation of Adam* effectively updated for a post-Darwinian age: The Creator, now deanthropomorphized as ape, touches the hand of his human creation. The catalytic moment for animality studies was rather less thrilling. A middle-aged philosopher padded naked across his bedroom floor to his bathroom one morning and was caught in the gaze of his little black cat. This unremarkable encounter set in motion Jacques Derrida's remarkable "L'animal que donc je suis (à suivre)."

Derrida's 1997 conference paper was published in French in 1999[10] and in English in 2002 in the high-profile cultural studies journal *Critical Inquiry*, under the title "The Animal That Therefore I Am (More to Follow)."[11] In 2008, four years after Derrida's death, the essay was herded together with three others to form a book, also titled *The Animal That Therefore I Am*.[12] In 2008 and 2010, two further animals books appeared in French under the name of the posthumously prolific Derrida, and in English with dizzying speed as *The Beast and the Sovereign*, volumes 1 and 2.[13] By now, more than eight hundred pages singlemindedly devoted to the animal had appeared in Derrida's name—even apart from all of the less sustained engagements with the animal that had marked his writing from the beginning ("the innumerable critters that . . . overpopulate my texts")—making animality one of his central and most enduring philosophical themes.[14] Yet it was "The Animal That Therefore I Am (More to Follow)" that served as a catalyst for the emergent field of animality studies. Cary Wolfe, in the course of a magisterial survey of the field in 2009, claimed that Derrida's article "([along with the] book that shares its title) is arguably the single most important event in the brief history of animal studies."[15]

ANIMALS IN THEORY

Arguably too, however, the history of animal(ity) studies is not quite as brief as Wolfe implies, particularly if it is reconceived as "animal theory," taking "theory" to mean what it has generally meant in the humanities since the 1980s: a congeries of critical and philosophical discourses intimately or loosely intertwined with poststructuralism, although not identical with it.[16] Animal theory has had a moderately long history. One of its signal instances would be the "becoming-animal" sequence in Gilles Deleuze and Félix Guattari's *A Thousand Plateaus*, now enjoying a vigorous (if controversial) afterlife in the literature of animality studies.[17] But animal theory would also include much of Julia Kristeva's *Powers of Horror*, to which Kelly Oliver devotes a chapter in her *Animal Lessons*;[18] Emmanuel Levinas's "The Name of a Dog," with which Ken Stone engages in his essay in the present volume;[19] the selections from Georges Bataille, Michel Foucault, and Luce Irigaray in the anthology *Animal Philosophy*;[20] certain sequences in Hélène Cixous's writings, such as the one that impels Erika Murphy's essay in the present volume; Gloria Anzaldúa's ruminations on animality and *mestizaje*, which animate An Yountae and Peter Mena's essay in the present volume; and other examples too numerous to list.[21]

DERRIDANIMALITY

The most suggestive example of animal theory, however, for most of the contributors to the present collection has been Derrida's "The Animal That Therefore I Am" or the book of the same name. Because of this immediate relevance, and also because of the importance of the article and book for the diffuse field of animality studies in general, some account of them, necessarily brief and partial, is in order.[22]

The article and book derive their significance from the biopolitical ramifications of their common theme.[23] That theme is the cruelly sharp wedge that the Western philosophical tradition has driven between the human and the animal. For Derrida, this tradition is epitomized by five names: Descartes, Kant, Heidegger, Levinas, and Lacan, "summits of a mountain range" over which Derrida will fly "in the hope of sighting the animal" consigned to this bleak environment.[24] For Derrida, all five philosophers think that in contrast to us humans—a difference that is determined by this fact—the animal neither speaks nor responds, that its capacity to produce signs is foreign to language. . . . Not one of them has taken into account, in a serious and determinate manner, the fact that we hunt, kill, exterminate, eat, and sacrifice animals, use them, make them work or submit them to experiments that are forbidden to be carried out on humans. . . . Not one of them really integrates progress in ethological or primatological knowledge into his work.[25]

Furthermore (and here Derrida's critique becomes distinctive), all five philosophers "speak of 'the animal' as of a single set that can be opposed to 'us,' 'humans,' subjects . . . of an 'I think,' 'I am,' along the line of a single common trait and on the other side of a single, indivisible limit"[26]—and always "in spite of the infinite space that separates the lizard from the dog, the protozoon from the dolphin, the shark from the lamb, the parrot from the chimpanzee, the camel from the eagle, the squirrel from the tiger, the elephant from the cat, the ant from the silkworm, or the hedgehog from the echidna."[27]

Not unexpectedly, Derrida deconstructs the human/animal opposition—but not in quite the same way that he has previously deconstructed other hierarchical binary oppositions, which is to say by demonstrating how each term of the opposition is joined to its companion by an invisible network of arteries. After Darwin, there would be nothing novel in a demonstration of the arbitrariness or provisionality of the human/animal opposition.[28] Hence, perhaps, Derrida's declaration: "Everything I'll say will consist, certainly not in effacing the limit, but in multiplying its figures, in complicating, thickening, delinearizing, folding, and dividing the line precisely by making it increase and multiply"—a strategy he terms "limitrophy."[29] Derrida is less interested in effacing, or even questioning, the human-animal distinction than in complicating it, and complicating it infinitely. "Beyond the edge of the *so-called* human," he writes, "beyond it but by no means on a single opposing side, rather than 'The Animal' or 'Animal Life' there is already a heterogeneous multiplicity of the living, or more precisely . . . a multiplicity of organizations of relations between living and dead."[30]

Since "the animal" no longer suffices to name that abyssal other-than-human heterogeneity, Derrida spawns a further neologism—*animot*—

which, like so many of his neologisms, is designed to multitask. When read, *animot* serves as a graphic reminder that the French word for animal—*animal*—is merely that: a *mot* or "word." When spoken, *animot* is aurally indistinguishable from *animaux*, "animals." The grammatically singular word *animot* enunciates the multiplicity that *animal* conceals. "I would like to have the plural *animals* heard in the singular," he explains.[31] The *mot* in *animot* also signifies what the philosophical tradition has held to be the limit dividing the human from the animal, namely, the word. "It would not be a matter of 'giving speech back' to animals but perhaps of acceding to a thinking . . . that thinks the absence of the name and of the word otherwise, and as something other than a privation."[32]

UNPLUGGING THE ANIMAL MACHINE

Derrida's article (and now book) title, "The Animal That Therefore I Am," is, of course, a riposte to Descartes's "I think, therefore I am"—"a summons issued to Descartes," as he himself puts it.[33] Descartes is, indeed, something of a bête noire for animality studies in general. Particularly when the field is termed "posthuman animality studies," the term "posthuman" is frequently a synonym for "post-Cartesian." Descartes absolutized philosophical and theological conceptions of the animal with deep roots in antiquity. Aristotle in his copious writings on animals distinguished them from humans by their alleged lack of reason, speech, and upright posture. The Stoics built on and extended Aristotle's ideas on animals, and their ideas in turn were adapted by Jews such as Philo and Christians such as Augustine.[34] Aquinas was a particularly important channel for the Aristotelian stream that Descartes harnessed. Descartes's work on human-animal relations, then, was a labor of inflection and intensification rather than outright invention. Yet Descartes was also the prime creator of the animal in the peculiarly modern sense of the term. So devoid are animals of mind, reason, and language, for Descartes, that their behavior is purely mechanistic and as such altogether unlike human behavior. His philosophical redescription of the nonhuman animal is commonly termed his *bête-machine* ("animal machine") doctrine for its equation of animals with clocks and other mechanisms with automatic moving parts.[35]

The preceding paragraph is not intended to suggest that Descartes, invoked by name and with a target affixed to his chest, is a ubiquitous figure in animality studies. As significant a contribution to the field as Giorgio

Agamben's *The Open* explicitly invokes Descartes only once. Agamben cites Linnaeus's testy dismissal of the *bête-machine* doctrine: "Surely Descartes never saw an ape."[36] Donna Haraway's yet more significant *When Species Meet* makes no explicit mention of Descartes at all.[37] From the very first sentences of her book, however, Haraway is busily dismantling the fence that Descartes worked harder than anybody to erect and that his eighteenth- and nineteenth-century successors, most notably Kant, worked so diligently to maintain. "Whom and what do I touch when I touch my dog?" is one of two questions that guide Haraway's book, as she informs us in her first sentence,[38] and soon thereafter we encounter her exuberant, much-quoted declaration:

> I am a creature of the mud, not the sky. . . . I love the fact that human genomes can be found in only about 10 percent of all the cells that occupy the mundane space I call my body; the other 90 percent of the cells are filled with the genomes of bacteria, fungi, protists, and such, some of which play in a symphony necessary to my being alive at all, and some of which are hitching a ride and doing the rest of me, of us, no harm. I am vastly outnumbered by my tiny companions; better put, I become an adult human being in company with these tiny messmates. To be one is always to *become with* many.[39]

Part 1 of her book is titled "We Have Never Been Human," and the book itself is a volume in a series titled "Posthumanities." In combination, this is less "a summons issued to Descartes" (Derrida's description of his own animality project, as we saw) than a stake through the heart of Descartes.

CATS AND GODS

Yet Haraway, who is thoroughly familiar with Derrida's animality work, is also deeply critical of it. She gives him credit for much, not least that when he encountered that little black cat in his bathroom, it was not as a Cartesian that he appraised her: "Derrida knew he was in the presence of someone, not of a machine reacting. 'I see it as *this* irreplaceable living being that one day enters my space, enters this place where it can encounter me, see me, see me naked.'"[40] The philosopher faced with the cat, however, was able, apparently, only to philosophize. For Haraway, "Derrida failed a simple obligation of companion species; he did not become curious

about what the cat might actually be doing, feeling, thinking."[41] In this regard, Derrida, for all his philosophical profundity, fell short of "a Gregory
Bateson or Jane Goodall . . . or many others [who] have met the gaze of
living, diverse animals and in response undone and redone themselves and
their sciences."[42] Unlike Levinas, "Derrida, to his credit, recognized in his
small cat 'the absolute alterity of the neighbor.'"[43] Nevertheless,

> Derrida's full human male frontal nudity before an Other, which was
> of such interest in his philosophical tradition, was of no consequence
> to [the cat], except as the distraction that kept her human from giving
> or receiving an ordinary polite greeting. I am prepared to believe that
> he did know how to greet this cat and began each morning in that mu-
> tually responsive and polite dance, but if so, that embodied mindful
> encounter did not motivate his philosophy in public. That is a pity.[44]

Yet Derrida might not have been entirely taken aback by Haraway's
critique. At one point in *The Animal That Therefore I Am*—one of it most
"theological" moments, as it happens—he seems to anticipate that critique: "When I feel so naked in front of a cat, facing it, and when, meeting
its gaze, I hear the cat or God ask itself, ask *me*: Is he going to call me, is
he going to address me? What name is he going to call me by, this naked
man, before I give him woman?"[45] Derrida here fades back into Adam, au-
thorized to assign names to all the animals (Gen. 2:19–20),[46] while the cat,
paradoxically, fades back into God, through a certain implacable Levinasian logic. If, for Levinas, God is in principle indistinguishable from the human other,[47] for "later" Derrida, that distinguished (and critical) Levinasian
disciple,[48] the little black cat, as a Levinasian absolute other,[49] is in principle
indistinguishable from God (although it would not have been for Levinas
himself). Hence Derrida's earlier comment: "The cat that looks at me . . .
and to which I seem—but don't count on it—to be dedicating a negative
zootheology."[50] As the constitutive others of the human, the divine and the
animal are (for the human, at least) not clearly or cleanly separable. Derrida defines the "ahuman," which he also names "divinanimality," as "the
excluded, foreclosed, disavowed, tamed, and sacrificed foundation of what
it founds, namely, the symbolic order, the human order, law and justice."[51]
The human in turn, of course, will not manage to stay cleanly separate or

separable from the divinanimality that founds it. In *The Beast and the Sovereign* we read: "There are gods and there are beasts, there is, there is only, the theo-zoological, and in the theo-anthropo-zoological, man is caught, evanescent, disappearing, at the very most a simple mediation, a hyphen between the sovereign and the beast, between God and cattle."[52]

HUMANIMALITY

All of the preceding is singularly un-Cartesian, and as such uncreates the animal. Prior to the epochal changes in European culture synecdochically signified by the name "Descartes," there were no "animals" in the modern sense. There were "creatures," "beasts," and "living things," a bionomic arrangement reflected in, and reinforced by, the early vernacular Bibles. As Laurie Shannon notes, "*Animal* never appears in the benchmark English of the Great Bible (1539), the Geneva Bible (1560), or the King James Version (1611)."[53] The term *animal* could be used, moreover, without implying stark opposition to *human*. Susan Crane cites an illuminating medieval evocation of human animality or bestial humanity:

> John Trevisa's fourteenth-century translation of Bartholomaeus Anglicus places the human within the animal category: "All that is compounded of flesh and spirit of life, and so of body and soul, is called *animal*, a beast, whether it be of the air like birds, or of the water like fish that swim, or of the earth such as beasts that go on the ground and in fields, *like men* and wild and tame beasts."[54]

Even Trevisa's subsequent theological qualification of "man" does not deanimalize him. Trevisa cites Isidore of Seville's sixth-century *Etymologies*, which "says that a man is a beast that resembles God."[55]

Creature was a more encompassing term than *beast*. In addition to "men" and beasts, the continuum evoked by "creature" also included angels and demons. Absent in the pre-Cartesian era, argues Shannon, was "the fundamentally modern sense of the animal or animals as humanity's persistent, solitary opposite."[56] Cartesianism catalyzed a philosophical erasure of the animal, but it also catalyzed a corresponding physical erasure of the animal, one whose effects are manifested with unprecedented starkness in our own time. As Shannon notes:

The disappearance of the more protean *creatures* into the abstract nominalizations of *animal, the* animal, and *animals* parallels livestock's banishment to a clandestine, dystopian world of industrial food production, where the unspeakable conditions of life depend on invisibility. It mirrors, too, the increasing confinement of wildlife in preserves as wild spaces disappear with alarming speed.[57]

CRITTERLY THEOLOGY

What would it take to coax the creature back out of the abstract nominalization of the animal? Specifically, what would it take in theology and other contiguous fields? What are the prospects for a creaturely theology—or a "critterly theology," as Haraway might quip? "Critters are always relationally entangled rather than taxonomically neat," she observes,[58] which is why she uses "critter" for human and nonhuman animals alike.

"And say the animal responded?" muses Derrida,[59] pushing back against the philosophical tradition that denies language to the animal. "And say the philosopher responded?" replies Haraway, perturbed, as we saw, by Derrida's insufficient response to the animal in question. "And say the theologian also responded?" many of the contributors to the present volume might add, perturbed that a field predicated on a response to the other-and-more-than-human should, so systemically and so abysmally, have failed to respond—or respond responsibly—to the more-and-other-than-human animal.

Of course, to level this criticism is to sketch theology and its associated fields in broad historical strokes. With the blossoming of ecotheology, biblical ecocriticism, and other related developments in religious studies, animals are now receiving various forms of theological attention.[60] Even a brief survey of that multidisciplinary and multifaceted phenomenon is beyond the scope of the present introduction[61] but would prominently include such developments as the establishment in 2003 of a (still thriving) Animals and Religion program unit at the annual meeting of the American Academy of Religion and the landmark publication in 2006 of *A Communion of Subjects*, the first comparative study of the conceptualization of animals in world religions.[62]

What distinguishes the present collection from other book-length theological engagements with the animal? It is the extent of its engagement (sometimes critical) with *animal theory*, as that term was defined above.[63]

This is what distinguishes it from the sibling collection *Creaturely Theology: On God, Humans and Other Animals*,[64] in particular, whose ethics and politics are so similar to its own. The interdisciplinary field of animal(ity) studies, as fleshed out in the present introduction, does not feature in the introduction to *Creaturely Theology*, and only one of its thirteen essays engages with animal theory.[65] The present collection seems to share more common ground with certain self-described "postsecular" appropriations of the creaturely (the term *creature* no longer being theologically trademarked) than with *Creaturely Theology*.[66]

Creaturely theology in the theory-anima(la)ted mode of the present collection—so far as it is possible to generalize its diverse contents—begins with the recognition that the concepts of the human and the animal inherited from the early modern *épistémè* are best construed as the epiphenomenal products of a particular historical moment—albeit the formative moment for almost every aspect of Western culture, including the academic discipline of theology itself—bracketed by a pre- and posthumanism that think the human-animal distinction differently.[67] But if the animal-human distinction is being rethought and retheorized, then the animal-human-divine distinctions must be rethought, retheorized, and retheologized along with it. The resources for creaturely theology, critterly theology, or zootheology (both positive and negative) are considerable, moreover, and far exceed animality studies or even animal theory. All Christian scriptures and most Christian theologies predate the Cartesian realignment of human-animal relations in terms absolutely oppositional and hierarchical, as do most Jewish, Muslim, Buddhist, and Hindu scriptures, theologies, or philosophies.

Let us preview how the contributors to the present volume have engaged the creaturely, whether in therological, theological, or therotheological mode.

Glen A. Mazis, in his "Animals, before Me, with Whom I Live, by Whom I Am Addressed: Writing after Derrida," descends deeply into *The Animal That Therefore I Am* and *The Beast and the Sovereign*, writing after Derrida but also with and beyond Derrida. In this task, Mazis is aided by Jean-Christophe Bailly and Maurice Merleau-Ponty. In the second half of his essay, Mazis takes up Derrida's discourse on the wolf as a traditional figure of human rapacity and pushes beyond that discourse to engage with the history of human predation on the wolf. That horrific history, for Mazis, is emblematic of a systematic misrecognition that has turned the animal world into a world that humans no longer know how to inhabit or even to see.

With Ken Stone's essay, the focus shifts from the wolf to another member of the Canidae family. Stone's "The Dogs of Exodus and the Question of the Animal" takes one dog in particular as its point of departure, that in Emmanuel Levinas's "The Name of a Dog," an essay that has acquired unprecedented significance with the emergence of animality studies. Stone notes how Levinas's tale of Bobby, the Nazi labor-camp dog, begins and ends with reference to two differently positioned groups of dogs in the book of Exodus. Stone picks up where Levinas leaves off, following the intricate tracks of the dogs and other nonhuman animals though Exodus and other biblical literature, aided by Derrida, and demonstrating how complex, and occasionally nonanthropocentric, are biblical representations of "the animal."

With Erika Murphy's "Devouring the Human: Digestion of a Corporeal Soteriology" we run with a different dog, the one that bit Hélenè Cixous as a child. This deep bite was an epiphany of "the meat we are," yet also emerged out of the animal's suffering. The dog becomes Job and Christ for Cixous. For Murphy, Cixous's reflections open up crucial aspects of the Johannine Jesus' corporality as flesh to be devoured and sacrificial animal. Murphy proceeds to add layer upon complex layer to this corporeal Christology, concluding that the call to consume Christ is an invitation to recognize the shared vulnerability of human and animal flesh, a vision that takes us to the brink of transcendence. Consumed by the animal, the human develops a taste for the divine.

What kind of creaturely theology might arise from reflection on microbial and bacterial interactions, such as in the human digestive system, rather than on the interactions of large-scale organisms (Derrida and his cat; Haraway and her dog)? Denise Kimber Buell's "The Microbes and Pneuma That Therefore I Am" argues that reflecting on invisible or near-invisible agencies, such as pneuma and microbes, has the potential to catalyze a creaturely theology that is also a relational ontology, one that conceives of all living beings as complex interacting systems. Buell finds theological models for such viscously porous ontologies in certain ancient Christian texts (the Gospels of John, Philip, and Thomas; Irenaeus's

Against Heresies), notwithstanding the apparently contradictory fact that these texts also evince anxiety about the boundaries of the human.

Jacob J. Erickson's "The Apophatic Animal: Toward a Negative Zootheological *Imago Dei*" picks up Derrida's passing reference to "a negative zootheology" and runs with it. At issue, for Erickson, is the traditional theological insistence on treating human beings as the privileged revelation of the divine ("created in the image of God"). Erickson contests this human exceptionalism by proposing a negative zootheology that does not cordon off nonhuman animality in order to image the divine. He follows Derrida in refusing to think "the animal" in undifferentiated terms, leading to a wild profusion of creaturely singularities that enable a radical reimagining of the biblical and theological trope of "wilderness." The Spirit becomes a wild immanence in creaturely life, and God becomes a creaturely imaging of the "divine wilderness" of the Spirit.

We remain in the wilderness with Terra Rowe's "The Divinanimality of Lord Sequoia," which begins with a letter from John Muir written from what would become Yosemite National Park. Muir's doxology to "Lord Sequoia" prompts Rowe, aided by Derrida, Laurel Schneider, and others, to propose a posthumanist Christ. This would be a Christ whose incarnation would no longer be exclusively human but multiplied across all species of creation. It would be a limitrophic Christ, sprouting at the limit and overrunning every limit, complicating every border between human and animal, human and divine, and divine and other-than-human in all its limitless variety. As "divinanimal," this Christ would be left as a trace on every wholly other that has been deemed necessary and then discarded, whether human, animal, or tree.

Kate Rigby's "Animal Calls" extends Donna Haraway's "respectful curiosity" to undomesticated animal others, epitomized for Rigby by the magpie, a familiar sight and sound in her corner of Australia. Throughout her essay, Rigby urges human attention to the semiosis of the more-than-human world. Ultimately she asks us to ponder how nonhuman animals might be considered to be calling on humans in the context of the current humanly engendered mass extinction event. She notes that animal oracles, not least bird oracles, have abounded in many traditional cultures, and she narrates a dream in which a magpie plays an ecoprophetic role. The magpie's call, summoning human beings out of solipsistic self-enclosure, sounds on behalf of the innumerable voiceless or silenced creatures who are in the front line of environmental devastation.

Beatrice Marovich's "Little Bird in My Praying Hands: Rainer Maria Rilke and God's Animal Body" brings Derrida's animal philosophy into dialogue with Rilke's animal theology as crafted in his *Stories of God* and *Book of Hours*. For Rilke, animals have a privileged relationship to a space-time he termed *The Open* and through it to the divine, whereas humans can neither perceive nor enter The Open. Marovich explores the oblique relationship between Rilke's Open and Derrida's divinanimality—another extrahuman space-time coinhabited by gods and animals. The creaturely God that emerges in The Open finds consummate expression as the fragile bird wriggling in the praying hands of a child, signifying to the child that God is real, even though God must disappear when the prayer is over.

The Open, now transformed into Giorgio Agamben's book of that name, also informs Eric Daryl Meyer's "The Logos of God and the End of Humanity: Giorgio Agamben and the Gospel of John on Animality as Light and Life." Meyer rereads the Johannine prologue, the locus classicus for the doctrine of the Incarnation, with Agamben and Derrida. Meyer contests the traditional assumption that the divine *Logos* (Word) of the prologue is aligned with human discourse. Instead, the prologue's identification of the *Logos* with *zōē* (life) aligns it with *to zōon* (the animal). The human rejection of the *Logos* that the prologue narrates is the human refusal to acknowledge the animality of the divine. The prologue does not endorse the human as a categorically exceptional creature but subverts humanity from within.

An Yountae and Peter Anthony Mena's "Anzaldúa's Animal Abyss: *Mestizaje* and the Late Ancient Imagination" explores Gloria Anzaldúa's potential contributions to animality studies and creaturely theology. The essay falls into two parts. Mena shows how Anzaldúa's concept of a *mestiza* identity forged in the arid spaces of the U.S.-Mexican borderlands, and transcending and transforming ethnic difference and human/animal difference, can travel to a different desert in which human-animal hybrids also abound, that of Jerome's fourth-century *Life of Paul*. An extends Mena's reflections into a more direct exploration of the significance of the animal for Anzaldúa. He argues that Anzaldúa's animal images figure the multiple layers of her *mestizaje*. These images also express a dialectical tension between Anzaldúa's decolonial vision of freedom and the abyssal groundlessness of creaturely existence.

Jennifer Koosed and Robert Paul Seesengood's "Daniel's Animal Apocalypse" plunges us into one of the most animal-populous books of the Bible. The first half of the essay ponders various encounters that the book's eponymous hero has with animals. Each encounter entails transformation from human to animal either enacted (Nebuchadnezzar into grazing animal; empires into hybrid monsters) or denied (Daniel into lion), and each entails a revelation of what Derrida terms divinanimality. The second half of the essay brings postcolonial themes into dialogue with animality themes across the catastrophe-ridden space of the book of Daniel. Aided by Giorgio Agamben and Donna Haraway, the authors reflect on how this apocalypse consigns entire human populations to the category of the killable in a logic that relies on the dispensability of the animal.

Imperial Rome is figured in the book of Revelation as a *thērion*, a "beast" or "wild beast." Stephen D. Moore's "Ecotherology" begins by reading Derrida's *The Beast and the Sovereign* together with *The Animal That Therefore I Am* as commentary on Revelation's theological bestiary: its Beast, its beastlike God, its animal Christ. Moore then considers the interspecies intimacy of the Lamb and its Bride, and ponders the Bride's transformation into a heavenly megalopolis that is a continent-sized shopping mall with a single stream and a token tree. Throughout, Moore attempts to relate what Revelation has to say about nonhuman animals—and category-crossing creatures that are neither human, animal, nor divine—to the plight of nonhuman animals in our apocalyptically theriocidal world.

Laura Hobgood-Oster's "And Say the Animal Really Responded: Speaking Animals in the History of Christianity" contests the assumption, embedded in Christian theology and Western philosophy, that words position humans as superior to animals. A corrective to that assumption is provided by sacred stories of speaking animals—stags, asses, dogs, lions—who break into the closed human circle of the word. They demonstrate an animal connection to the divine that has no need of human intermediaries. When such animals speak, divine-animal-human voices merge in a moment of what Derrida might call divinanimality. Yet Hobgood-Oster also takes Derrida to task, following Haraway, for not being curious about what his cat was communicating to him, in contrast to Peter and Paul in the speaking-animal tales in which they feature.

Critique of Derrida, and of continental philosophy generally, is a yet more prominent theme in Jay McDaniel and J. Aaron Simmons's "So Many Faces: God, Humans, and Animals." In the first part of the essay, Simmons raises two major objections to continental philosophy's ability to address animal welfare, what he terms the *secondary status objection* (epitomized by Levinasian philosophy) and the *inadequate activism objection* (epitomized by Derridean philosophy), before highlighting what he regards as more animal-positive developments in continental thought. McDaniel continues by setting out in terms of six core ideas the potential of A. N. Whitehead's process thought to foster a postanthropocentric sensitivity to the subjectivity, beauty, spirituality, and intrinsic value of animals, and to encourage the ethical treatment of them.

Matt Riley's "A Spiritual Democracy of All God's Creatures: Ecotheology and Lynn White Jr.'s Animals" returns to the beginnings of ecotheology, but only to tell the tale differently and expose the overlooked place of the animal in it. Ecotheology in its early stages largely coalesced in response to the accusations leveled at Christianity by White in his 1967 article, "The Historical Roots of Our Ecologic Crisis." Riley argues, however, that the White of the popular ecotheological imagination is a reductionistic construct. Reading White's seminal article in the context of his larger body of work reveals a profound theological vision of "a spiritual democracy of all God's creatures," human and nonhuman. White was not just a critic of Christianity, Riley contends, but a prophetic Christian voice.

The volume ends with an epilogue by Jay McDaniel that reflects on the animal art of Jan Harrison—those haunting animal paintings referred to at the outset of this introduction, which ringed the participants in the Divinanimality colloquium, transfixing us in a many-eyed animal gaze. Yet Harrison's animals are not merely looking at us, as McDaniel observes. They are also flowing and causing us to flow. They are bearing witness to *the witness of the body*, and hence inviting a knowing with rather than a knowing about. They are teaching us to fold into their singularity in our difference. They are telling us that their flesh does not simply belong to us, nor does our flesh simply belong to us. They are impelling us to ask, How far does flesh go down? And they are prompting us to answer, Deep enough to show that your bodies are also our bodies, and so your futures are also our futures.

Animals, before Me, with Whom I Live, by Whom I Am Addressed: Writing after Derrida

GLEN A. MAZIS

In the opening essay of *The Animal That Therefore I Am*, Jacques Derrida reverses the usually assumed order between humans and animals—assumed, that is, within European and American cultures, in a long line of Western philosophical, ethical, and theological discourses. Humans have been taken to come first in rank of value, ethical worth, and ethical behavior and first in reflecting more purely the divine and holding the first level in Being of earthly beings. Derrida tries to imagine beyond these discourses how we are actually linked with varied animals and declares that in almost all respects we "follow after" them. This critique of Derrida's concerning Western metaphysics and its assumption about animals interestingly plays off a later text by Jean-Christophe Bailly, *The Animal Side*. This text begins with an experience that Bailly has with a deer in the night that leads him to feel as if he "were skidding over the surface of the world transformed."[1] Forced to follow after the deer who is trapped within the boundaries of the road he is traveling in his car, forced to slow down, Bailly is "taken aback, overcome" in following the deer and seeing it disappear when it finally finds a gap in the hedgerow to return to its world of the forest that he could never enter. He could not enter that unique world that he suddenly sees with "the clarity, the violence, of an image in a dream."[2] In his following after the deer, Bailly sees the world of this animal as "something from which as a human being, I shall be forever excluded." However, rather than seeing it as a trivial world, a mere curiosity or an inferior world, instead the strangeness of the forest world expresses "a different posture, a different impetus, and quite simply a different modality of being." What struck

Bailly that night was that the "strangeness lay in the opportunity I was given to follow the animal for a while: that is, at bottom the chance to accompany it in spite of itself," which gave him the dizzying "fragment that might have been dislodged from the whole" of a world "right within the field of vision"[3] that he cannot see. Bailly's sense, however, is like Bataille's, whom he quotes, that beyond the human "social forms" of "a continuous distancing" lies a "lost intimacy" in that other world.[4]

FOLLOWING AFTER, BEING SEEN

This openness to other worlds marks Bailly's discourse as one that Jacques Derrida would classify as within a scant minority discourse in the long tradition of Western ethics, philosophy, and theology. In *The Animal That Therefore I Am*, Derrida finds two ongoing philosophical discourses: one a human-centered enclosed speech and the other a dialogue with the more than human world. Descartes, Kant, Heidegger, Lacan, and Levinas, all fall into the dominant discourse in regard to animals, which is more of an *imposed* monologue. It is a monologue as regards the world of animals, because the members of this discourse community can be addressed only by other humans, and actually only certain other humans at that and not all humanity. The dominant discourse was written by those who, when addressed by an animal,

> took no account of it. They neither wanted nor had the capacity to draw any systematic consequences from the fact that an animal could, facing them, look at them, clothed or naked, and in a word, without a word, address them. They have taken no account of the fact that what they call "animal" could look at them, and address them from down there, from a wholly other origin.[5]

In fact, in some sense for those who promulgated this dominant traditional discourse in Western philosophy, there is no animal as a fellow being; or, as Derrida says, "They made of the animal a theorem, something seen and not seeing."[6] The animal was devoid of a gaze. The place of the human or rather *of men* in this long tradition, for it is a male tradition, are the observers who are not observed by most others and certainly not by animals. It is as if instead of an encounter with them, animals merely parade before them: "It is as if the men of this configuration had seen without being seen, seen the animal without being seen by it."[7] This passage reminds us of Derrida's discussion in *The Beast and the Sovereign* of the first zoological garden, the Ménagerie de Versailles, where for his pleasure, the Sun King could gaze on the beasts and "where sovereignty is marked by the power to see, by being-able-to see *without* being seen."[8] Derrida calls this sort of gaze "autopsic" and "de-vitalizing."[9] The only vision of such a gaze is that turned inward at the only self who matters, whom one feels certain about and can control and display to others. Its lack of reciprocity is taken as a norm. It is devitalizing since it renders all the beings whom it could encounter as other kinds of existence; the lifeblood and vitality-infusing encounter and existence have been transformed into a landscape of inert presences, a wasteland.

Derrida's implication is that vision has other possibilities of reciprocity that he himself explores in the famous pages on the encounter with his cat. It is clarifying in regard to vision to remember Merleau-Ponty's description of the kind of vision of a prereflective seeing as "folded into" the "flesh of the world" that would underlie such imperial and alienating constructed modes (what Merleau-Ponty would call "institutions") of seeing in European and American cultures. Merleau-Ponty describes at length the vision of the human as an encompassed creature such that "he who sees cannot possess the visible unless he is possessed by it, unless he is of it, unless . . . he is one of the visibles, capable, by a singular reversal, of seeing them—he who is one of them."[10] For Merleau-Ponty, then, vision comes about only by a reversal in which we are exposed to the world of beings as embodied, within the world, and are seen, and it is only in joining up with this encompassing current of seeing among all beings that we can see. He continues: "As soon as I see, it is necessary that the vision (as is so well indicated by the double meaning of the word) be doubled with a complementary vision or with another vision: myself seen from without, such as another would see me, installed in the midst of the visible, occupied in considering it from a certain spot."[11] Merleau-Ponty's point is that it is a constitutive possibility of seeing that may be covered over by cultural constructs, but it is always possible to cultivate again, as artists are wont to do; vision only takes place among the beings of the world by joining up with a general "Visibility."[12] As he says, both in French and in English, the word that denotes the power of seeing, *vision*, also denotes the rendering of something by sight. To see is to be seen, unless one attempts to escape from the round of encompassing fleshly beings to a disembodied mental or spiritual vantage point that asserts it can leave behind or hover above the enfleshed realm.

In other words, I can see only because as an embodying being I return to myself from the vantage points of everything else with which I am in relation in my surround, as seeing through the things, creatures, and others who are part of a dimension of visibility. Of course, Merleau-Ponty points out that this reversibility is imperfect or asymmetric: I am always "more on my side," yet I can't avoid taking in the vantage of the other as part of vision. Yet it is as if the philosophers of this dominant tradition saw themselves as residing on some other plane of existence, provided by the elevation of spirit and reason that fueled them, as if their vision emanated from some other origin, and not as Merleau-Ponty put it: "The visible can thus fill me and occupy me only because I who see it do not see it from the depths of a nothingness, but from the midst of itself: I the seer am also visible."[13] To be in the midst of the visible and its interrelated creatures through fleshiness is to be called beyond oneself as the very way of returning to oneself. Yet the other discourse could be only a self-contained monologue, as is the speech of the sovereign as detailed in *The Beast and the Sovereign*, whose word comes from above the law to guide it from without, and has no place in the dialogue of the community, and so safeguards its assumption of power and invulnerability. Yet to return to Bailly's experience, his time of literally following the deer makes him acutely aware that "human beings are to be defined precisely . . . by the fact that that they have managed to get themselves out of these enclosures, leaving behind *bestiality*—condemned as disgraceful—and *animality*, deeply feared, as if these were stages in a journey and bad (though haunting) memories."[14] All humans in this tradition have assumed the same sovereignty over animals by assuming that animals are left in the world of exposure to the regard of other beings, whereas humanity has escaped being addressed by the regard of the other.

Derrida traces this attempt to come before all others, to come before the animals, to be above the creatures of the earth as on a different plane of existence back to the Bible and Genesis. Here is the beginning of sovereignty and a profound loneliness that is first told in the tale of Adam's naming the creatures, a performance accomplished as the first "I," as Derrida puts it, and before Adam has a partner. Adam "would begin to see them and name them without allowing himself to be seen or named by them . . . these living things that came into the world before him but were named after them, on his initiative."[15] This is the beginning of a powerful discourse of human priority and sovereignty, a placing that which is most distinctly human outside the law and above the earth, which is the reference point of Derrida's title to the essay, "The Animal That Therefore I Am (More to Follow)." The title protests that rather than coming before the other creatures in rank and ontological privilege, "man is in both senses of the word after the animal. He follows after the animal. He follows him. This 'after,' which determines a sequence, a consequence, or a persecution, is not in time, nor is it temporal: it is the very genesis of time."[16] This placing of the human before, at the origin, at the source, at one with the source, with Being, the supreme Being, generates a succession of events as the sense of time of this dominant discourse. Time in this discourse, within philosophy, within the Judeo-Christian texts and within the tales we will tell of animals (to which we will come), is a succession, a causality that begins with the word spoken, the birth of reason and naming, as a telos and excellence that the human insists makes all the rest of the beings on this planet come after us, not in a linear sense of time, but as after that which is prior in rank, in being, in knowing. And yet, as Derrida will challenge us, are these the significant predicates—speaking, reasoning, naming? Are they the right language and the right questions?

Instead, we may come to see that we come after, we follow the animal, who is the before of who we are, who continues to come to be as what was not yet, in the temporality of the trace, not as simple origin either, but as "unreadable, undecidable, abyssal and secret . . . found in such intolerable proximity that I do not feel qualified to call it my fellow, even less my brother."[17] It comes "before me, here next to me, there in front of me. . . . And also, therefore, since it is before me, it is behind me, it surrounds me."[18] There is this blatant contradiction in that we all attempt to name ourselves as masters, to grant ourselves "human exceptionalism," as if what came before us both in time and as the basis for who we are does not count, does not matter, can be usurped and extirpated. All our human names for ourselves, whether the "rational animal," the "speaking animal," the "narrating animal," or other names tend to acknowledge that we are after, we follow, the animals, and yet we overlook, literally, this debt, this owing of ourselves to others. What if, as merely among the world of animals, the wider world of beings, humans were not special, were not even always the focus of the gaze? This is what Bailly begins to ponder after his encounter with the deer, thinking of Rilke's line in the eighth of the *Duino Elegies*: "And yet, sometimes a silent animal looks up at us and silently looks through us."[19] This looking through us is not a failure to take in the meaning of the world, but as Bailly remembers the opening of the poem, it is a look beyond the human to the more encompassing, or as Rilke says, "All eyes, the creatures of the World look out, into the open." Rather than being closed to the other and to the Being of the world, its unfathomable meaning, as Heidegger will say of animals and their closure to the Open, asserting their impoverished sense of world, Rilke asserts the power of their gaze.

To recall the power of the animal gaze returns us to the scene of Derrida and the cat that begins the narration of *The Animal That Therefore I Am*. If the animal's gaze is toward the open of the world, then Derrida is not caught in the Sartrean look by this cat, not ashamed of his body before the cat's regard as somehow objectifying him as another human might be apt to do, so he is not naked in that sense for which Sartre is so famous, even though this is the sense in which this encounter between Derrida and his cat has often been interpreted. Rather, Derrida is addressed, brought back to the history of the discourse of humans toward animals. The history of this discourse cannot help but be palpable in their unspoken dialogue: "It is as if the cat had been recalling itself and recalling that, recalling me and reminding me of this awful tale of Genesis, without breathing a word. Who was born first, before the names? . . . Who has remained the despot for so long now?"[20] What is so disconcerting about the address of the cat, or the address of any of the animals, is that this despotism—"the unprecedented proportions of this subjection of the animal,"[21] as Derrida calls it—this denial of filiation has been proclaimed in the name of ethics, spirit, philosophy, and religion. This history of usurpation, of domination, and of the negation of the felt overlapping bond of embodiment, passion, and overlapping is within the regard, the address of the cat. Notice, too, how this address of the cat to Derrida differs from the address of the face of the other or the neighbor for Levinas, which immediately stands in as a cipher for the presence of the divine other in the otherness of the neighbor, the stopping short of being involved in the immediate plane of embodiment as a plane of appropriation and self, called to the sacrificial plane of higher spirit. Rather, Derrida is called back by the thousands of years of criss-crossing of blood and flesh, of cruel practices, of myriad forms of despotism and our companion species' histories on this planet, as Haraway would call them, back to an immediate, but deeper than mundane, felt compassion.

THE DISCOURSES ABOUT ANIMALS AND HUMAN SELF-HATRED

Derrida is passionate in *The Animal That Therefore I Am* in a way that surpasses perhaps any other lecture or written piece of his. But, of course, he has warned us of his passion for animals in this work and claimed in *The Beast and the Sovereign* that his work is full of animals. However, before I quote his passionate condemnation of the anthropocentric tradition, I must agree wholeheartedly with Derrida's comment on the human naming *of the realm of "the animal"*: "The animal, what a word! The animal is a word, it is an appellation that men have instituted, a name they have given themselves the right and authority to give to the living other."[22] With the myriad of life-forms, the multiplicity of kinds of existence, to which this name is supposed to refer and yet humans dare to name in general as if a singular, *the animal*.[23] It is for this reason that I prefer Derrida's locution, that of *animot*, which I will now adopt as a red flag that we cannot use the word *animal* without this domination being in effect, that we have adopted a word to name myriad beings in such a way as to keep them outside, below, as if they are a (lower) "nature" that shores up our human "nature" held in opposition to it. *Animot* is a word that points to the fact that it is a "word" (*mot*) meant to refer to one whom we follow after and cannot catch up to, that is, properly fathom, especially in the old categories, phrases, and discourse.

In the later essay, "But as for me, who am I (following)?" Derrida denounces both Kant's and Levinas's ethics, as well as the supposed concern of Heidegger and Lacan to undermine an oppressive rule of embedded authority and alienation in social structures that prevent authentic ethical action. All display for him a disguised Cartesianism; and, like Descartes, all follow a path of domination and cruelty. He says of each of their Cartesian observational stances toward the world, oblivious to the address of the *animot*: "I think that Cartesianism belongs, beneath its mechanist indifference, to the Judeo-Christian-Islamic tradition of a war against the animal, of a sacrificial war as old as Genesis."[24] The Kantian ethic, like the Judeo-Christian, locates morality in reason, in the higher spirit, the recognition of the law, and the further legislation of the law in terms of the innate light of reason; and in less obvious ways contemporary philosophers place these attributions before the findings of science or other transformations of relations with living beings that Derrida embraces. I agree with him that the contemporary ethics of Heidegger, Lacan, and Levinas follow the same exclusive predications of the human versus the rest of living beings; or as Derrida states, "It is a matter of putting the animal outside the ethical circuit."[25] If this is the case, then I also agree with Derrida that to claim an exclusive property for humanity as being what gives humans both rights and obligations, that is, an ethical dimension to their existence, is itself a hostile act toward all other living beings:

> One could say, first, that in the end such a bellicose hatred in the name of human rights, far from rescuing man from the animality that he claims to rise above, confirms the waging of a kind of species war and confirms that the man of practical reason remains bestial in his defensive and repressive aggressivity, in his exploiting the animal to death. One could also say, second, that bad will, even a perverse malice, inhabits and animates so-called good moral will.[26]

War can be a stealth war, and for Heidegger the animal doesn't die, is wordless, is impoverished in not really encountering others; whereas for Levinas, the animal is not called to the higher realm of spirit and "does not have a face,"[27] is not really a neighbor, and is not capable of hospitality and sacrifice; and for Lacan, animals are without a superego and without relation to the Law; they only react but do not respond, are not capable of a symbolic order, express no true communication, but only "codes," and cannot be seen as fellows or similars to whom one could be cruel or against whom commit a crime or even genocide.[28]

Not only are there these attributions of the poverty of animals, but if they are part of a self-enclosed discourse—as they must be since they lack the sense of being addressed—without entering into a dialogue, then like the discourse of the sovereign who is addressing only himself, seeing only himself, the attributions to the *animot* are more about us, about who we are, or at least feign to be (part of the *bêtise* much discussed by Derrida). What is this need to assert our superiority, if we are not defensive about who we are—the human? It seems that much of this discourse about the *animot* is a disguised self-loathing (or at least loathing for aspects of who we are), or as Derrida states it, "The Kantian has nothing but hate for the animality of the human."[29] If we loathe ourselves, as in the long tradition in philosophy inaugurated by Plato's condemnation of our body and our passions as nails that pin us down in enslavement to the perceptible world (*Phaedo* 83D), to "this earth and all the stones and all the places here corrupted and corroded . . . infinite mud and slime . . . things worth nothing" (*Phaedo* 109E), then this discourse about the "animal" and its inferior place makes more sense as being a symptom of the *ressentiment* so aptly described by Nietzsche in the *Genealogy of Morals*. If Derrida is correct, and I believe he is, that beneath the supposed emotional neutrality of Kant's ethics, or of Heidegger, Levinas, and Lacan and their discourses (still indebted to Descartes and Kant) on more authentic or liberatory community, is a hatred of the *animot*, then there is a hostility at work here against other life-forms as well as toward aspects of human beings, and there is much dissimulation and projection of the evils of the world. If we are to think of the *animot* as abject, as focus of disgust in a realm of projection about what is perceived as disgusting about ourselves, then it is an easy step to Derrida's suggestive pondering about how hatred of the "animal" might be related to the hatred of the Jew, femininity, and childhood.[30] He leaves the question open for us to ponder. Derrida points out that every question we pose to the *animot*—such as whether it has reason, whether it mourns, whether it has language—are all questions used to impose an attribution about ourselves that seeks to place us outside what surrounds us.

To ask whether thought about the status of the "animal" is really about the status of the human makes us question by what right we make the classical attributions about ourselves as human—and also ask with what dishonesty we may be naming the other. In both *The Animal That Therefore I Am* and in *The Beast and the Sovereign* Derrida asks the same question:

> It is less a matter of wondering whether one has the right to refuse the animal such and such a power (speech, reason, experience of death, mourning, culture, institution, politics, technique, clothing, lying, feigned feint, effacement of the trace, gift, laughter, tears, respect, etc.—the list is necessarily indefinite, and the most powerful philosophical tradition in which we have lived has refused *all of that* to the "animal"). It is more a matter of wondering whether what one

calls man has the right, for his own part, to attribute in all rigor to man, to attribute to himself, then, that which he refuses to the animal, and whether he has a concept of it that is *pure, rigorous, indivisible, as such.*[31]

This is a stratagem: To fail to see in the other what one could not see in oneself nor could see anywhere else, since it is a chimera, but to use this blindness as a way to see oneself as superior, when the region to which one is pointing is only a lacuna. Derrida asks what is the status of this impossible "as such." Reason "as such," laughter "as such," or whatever as "such" in its purity—what could it be like and how could it ever be attributed to humans, since it never has been encountered? These attributes of the human "would not simply consist in unfolding, multiplying, leafing through the structure of the 'as such,' or the opposition between 'as such' and 'not as such' . . . ; it would obey the necessity of asking oneself whether man, the human itself, has the 'as such.'"[32] Humans certainly have any of these attributes in fitful moments, sometimes absent, always partial, and always intermixed. This means that the attributions of these qualities to ourselves are idealizations toward which we aspire. If the attributions of the human are ambiguous, then the discourse concerning these attributions in regard to the animot should show the same ambiguity, if we had the good taste of which Nietzsche speaks to be more honest about ourselves. Yet to implicitly claim pure being or pure goodness by using the discourse of the "as such" of these qualities as being intrinsic to the human versus the animot is an imposition of a chimerical standard, like using a yardstick to beat so-called belligerent children. It is to flail out at myriad beings as the expression of a suppressed self-flagellation in punishment for our impure earthiness. On some level, humans know this a hollow self-attribution. This ongoing discourse of "the good" (as such) or "the holy" (as such) seems rather petulant behavior for the "rational animal," or, as Derrida would say, a *bêtise.*

Derrida points to this ambivalence about what the human is in the contradictory terms we use to name and describe aspects of animals: "The dominant discourse of man on the path of hominization imagines the animal in the most contradictory and incompatible generic terms: absolute (because natural) goodness, absolute innocence, prior to good and evil, the animal without fault or defect (that would be its superiority as inferiority), but also the animal as absolute evil, cruelty, murderous savagery."[33] The ways we name animals and their attributes, or the lack of them, constitute "hominization"—predications in human terms, human attributes, exclusions. And the contradictoriness of attribution is more about our own suppressed awareness of the mixture of human behaviors and ways of being with others; some laudatory and many rather malicious. Of course, both the extremes of description are chimeras of what should be more truthfully expressed as ambiguities in that we do not have these qualities in any pure form, but instead continually excuse human lapses from the "as such" as being accidents of history and not indicative of what the human is.

THE ACTUAL LYCONOMY: HUMAN VIOLENCE UNLEASHED

One extreme is the image of bestiality so often represented by the wolf, as discussed at length in *The Beast and the Sovereign*, as rapacious, as cruel, as unrestrained violence.[34] The wolf is the image of the terror that humans inflict on one another. Man (the gendering here is part of the constitution of the male's role) is said "to be the wolf for man" insofar as humans are rapacious and require the beast of a sovereign to inspire fear in them. Humans are taken to be the rapacious wolf that will back down only in face of a more rapacious wolf. This empowers the sovereign to be the one "to terrorize the terrorists," as Derrida puts it (giving a pertinent current example), according to the Hobbesian and Machiavellian logic of the sovereign who is outside and above the law. Like the beast who is "below" the law, the sovereign "above" the law terrorizes, but the sovereign draws on human ingenuity to terrorize for the good of the whole and the survival of the law.[35] On one side of our ambivalence about animals as beasts, humans are said to require unrestrained violence from the sovereign as our chief warrior to be kept within the law. What we require of the sovereign is the savagery of the human, but which is attributed only to the wolfish or bestial inferior linkage of the human to the animal, here turned to the good of the state by the sovereign. On the other side of our ambivalence about animals as "naturally good," we incorporate this idea of natural goodness into our notion of animality. What is best about the superior human in some way comes "from below," from the inferior animal. This natural proclivity as applied both to the sovereign and to the sovereignty within all humans is our proclivity to self-legislate for the overall good. However, the ambivalence is still there in the human claim that, despite their natural goodness, we locate beasts outside and below the law, needing our sovereign legislating power to order them. The true good becomes actualized only "from above."

When we realize that such discourses are discrepant with characterizations based on actual observations of wolves, for example, by ethologists who have spent decades in their presence (and Derrida, too, stops his discourse on two or three occasions in his seminar and says we must pay attention to such scientific findings) and have found them to be among the most social animals on the planet and also among the least aggressive, we have to wonder with Derrida about what kind of discourses these are, and where to turn for alternatives:

> In short, I was dreaming of inventing an unheard-of grammar and music in order to create a scene that was neither human, nor divine, nor animal, with a view to denouncing all discourses on the so-called animal, all the anthropo-theomorphic or anthropo-theocentric logics and axiomatics, philosophy, religion, politics, law, ethics, with a view to recognizing in them animal strategies, precisely in the human sense of the term, stratagems, ruses, war machines, defensive or offensive maneuvers, search operations, predatory, seductive, indeed exterminatory operations as part of pitiless struggle between what are presumed to be species.[36]

Before we seek a new discourse, Derrida is correct that we need to recognize that the historical discourses on "the animal" are themselves vital to the war machine. Now, the discourses about animals are part of the seduction of others to the reign and use of terror supposed as the only way to fight terror, to the manipulative power of all sorts of stratagems in which the law is transgressed in the name of defending the possibility of law, and finally to exterminating ruses and practices against the very creatures enlisted as tools of discourse for this terror turned against them. It is this cruel logic that Derrida calls *lyconomy* (drawing on the Greek root for wolf, *lykos*) in *The Beast and Sovereign*: "The law (*nomos*) is always determined from the place of some wolf."[37] That is because the law is invoked from within the opposition to the other: "It is always a matter of the law and of placing the other outside of the law."[38] Yet if the discourse on the wolf is not about animals, but is rather about the human as disowned and projected onto the other—the abject inspiring terror and disgust—what in the human is the source of the law, and for whom, and in order to subject whom? It is interesting that ethologists find the social bonding, the caregiving, the need for community, the strength of cooperation among wolves to be very much like that of both humans and primates,[39] and so there is a strong resemblance among these species. Yet there is also a strange dissimilarity in the lack of any concerted aggression among wolves or against any other creatures. According to Adolf Murie, "A second characteristic of wolf personality is the animal's basic aversion to fighting."[40] He related the anecdote of a wolf "frantically upset" at a dog fight and breaking it up by pulling the aggressor dog by the tail off of the other dog. The wolf is an animal that will not attack a human being, even if the human were to take its pups from its den or remove the prey that it had hunted down and was in the midst of devouring.[41] As a matter of fact, Lee Smits, who looked over all available historical records, came to the same conclusion as previous researchers who have made this search: "No wolf, except a wolf with rabies, has been ever known to make a deliberate attack on a human being in North America."[42] Of course, the tales often claimed otherwise. Are these tales not also *bêtises*, not only silly ways to distance humans from the world and themselves, but also awkward, gauche attempts to disown responsibility for violence and project it onto the other?

It seems that for much of prehistory and even recorded history, human and wolf coexisted, and helped one another as the two predators of large mammals: "Until about four hundred years ago the wolf was second only to man as the most successful and widespread mammal in North America. There is extensive evidence to show that far from being at enmity, the wolf and hunting man enjoyed globally something approaching symbiosis, whereby the existence of each benefited the existence of the other."[43] Wolves near human encampments were believed to have served as a warning system for humans of the approach of adversaries with the wolves' sensory acuity and tendency to communicate by howling. For many of the Native American peoples of North America, the wolf was an object of veneration for its strong loyalty and affection for its family, its skill as a hunter, and its role in maintaining the health of its prey by culling the weak, sick, and decrepit.[44] As is common knowledge, however, the state of affairs between wolves and humans changed in the Middle Ages (although scapegoating wolves is more ancient, as Derrida notes) and in North America with the arrival of European settlers: "Of the twenty-four wolf subspecies and races inhabiting North America at the beginning of the European invasion, seven are now extinct and most of the remainder are endangered. The wolf has been effectively exterminated in all of the south-central portions of Canada, in Mexico, and in almost all of the United States south of Alaska."[45] To concentrate on North America, especially the United States, it is estimated that *since the first settlers arrived, two million wolves have been killed.*[46] This is the actual lyconomy of European-inspired American culture: the slaughter of a species pursued with religious fervor in the name of human superiority and goodness.

The fervor of this lyconomy is quite evident. Not only were wolves killed to the point of extinction, but they were slaughtered with a vehemence that is shocking:

> Wolves were shot, poisoned, trapped, bludgeoned, and tortured. Wolves were infected with mange and then released to spread the deadly disease across the plains. Wolves were staked down and torn apart by dogs. Wolves had their jaws shut so they could not eat, ensuring a long slow agonized death by starvation. Wolves were blown to bits by set guns or poisoned by wolf getters, devices that when bitten fired sodium cyanide into a wolf's mouth. Wolves were poisoned by the thousands by strychnine strewn carelessly across the prairies. Wolf pups were dragged from their dens and either beaten to death or shot.[47]

Wolves were killed with a kind of zeal and self-righteousness by humans throughout European and American history waging a particular kind of war to which I have given a specific name: *speciocide* (a term I have used specifically regarding wolves).[48] The justification for this speciocide toward wolves was their supposed savagery! Just as Derrida documents in *The Beast and the Sovereign* how the Europeans demonized the wolf, of all the wild creatures within the New World, the wolf epitomized a peculiar threat seen as "the Devil, Red tongued, sulfur breathing and yellow eyed."[49] The wolf's tearing creatures limb from limb was seen as symptom of its depravity, as well as its attacks on the livestock the Europeans brought with them that were seen as innocent creatures. These animals were innately good and the wolf was innately evil—a murderer.[50] That these discourses survive and wolf slaughter continues is rather fantastic behavior on the part of humans who feel morally called upon to do this killing while being "the only animal that habitually preys upon prime, mature animals"[51] and who shocks cows with massive voltage for slaughter, slits their throats, and lets them bleed to death hanging upside down. Yet in the discourse of political force as a lyconomy, the human stands as the guardian of order aspiring toward an inherent good, undermined by a lingering animality, and especially, the savage wolfishness that tears from within.

This discourse will remain obfuscating and disowning of human responsibility until as Derrida puts it, "the signifier requires another locus— the locus of the Other, the Other witness, the witness Other than any of the partners."[52] The excluded Other, that locus which has been extirpated, is the true gaze of the animal, its witnessing of a wider context of which we are part, and from which there could be an encounter, rather than the mere projection of those aspects of our viciousness that humans would rather not see. Bailly's meeting with the deer and Derrida's address by his cat point to a lacuna, a blind spot, that requires another discourse. Derrida says that we need to find a radical place that will "break with the identification of the image of self" and this place can only be the truly other. Derrida asks of us, "Must not this place be ahuman?" The animot is our poor construction, and yet in an encounter with the animal in its world and its context, Derida continues, "then the ahuman or some figure of some—in a word—divinanimality, would be the quasi-transcendental referent, the excluded, foreclosed, disavowed, tamed, and sacrificed foundation of what it founds, namely, the symbolic order, the human order, law and justice."[53] This place outside our current discourse inspired by allowing a witnessing of the animal, its gaze to fall upon us and beyond us to a wider context, might allow us to escape from a discourse of sovereignity and animality that is a self-enclosure and projection of our transgressions. There might be an encounter with a larger community inspiring an inclusiveness of the other and inspiring more self-reflexively the founding of an order of inclusiveness of otherness within the human community.

ANIMAL PHILOSOPHERS OF HOSPITALITY

If we are so blind to animals with our looking inward and then projecting outward, it is a formidable project to once again make contact. As Bailly points out in his night of making contact with another world, with the other: "The contact is always unsettled, for the encounter relates and even stipulates difference."[54] Yet we need to find ways out of this blindness and ways to cease fighting our own demons in the shape of the other whose regard no longer addresses us in our naming of them as inferior beings without this capacity. Bailly tells us that the boundaries are vacillating always and a contact is always there between human and animal as almost formed, as always nascent. Part of this almost is our troubled affects regarding animals. Right before Derrida tells us that he dreams of another set of questions in regard to the *animot* and another sort of discourse and another sort of music, he says, "I wish to indicate a tonality."[55] The tonality is connected to his praise of Bentham as asking the only relevant question about the *animot*: "Is there suffering?"[56] The tonality has to include compassion, "a feeling with," felt from within a slippage between our place and that of the *animot*. We might then not only feel the suffering of animals but also the distinctive joys, affections, concerns, curiosities, fears, and so on, of the myriad kinds. There is music and a use of language that comes from the overlap, the in-between, suggested by Derrida's newer questions: "Does animality participate in every concept of the world, even of the human world? Is being-with-the-animal a fundamental and irreducible structure of being-in-the-world, so much that the idea of the world without animals could not even function as a methodological fiction?"[57] These questions move us into affects and imaginings that might get humans beyond the self-enclosure of their reasoned narratives. These questions not only move us toward real encounter with the animal as other, but with the human as open-ended interchange and hybrid with a larger context of beings and as itself other to traditional notions of the human.

If we follow Derrida's lead here, we might wonder where in our love for children, in our love for our mate, in our love of the sky above, in our love of the feel of our bodies moving, in our fear of the thunderstorm, in our fear of hunger, in our loyalty to our group, in our need for belonging and home, in our patience with repetition, in the frolic of play, in the fierce defense of the group, in the mourning for those killed is the voice and address of the animals or the world that is just out of our field of vision currently, that nonplace to which Bailly points. To listen to such "voices of silence" was the lifelong task of Derrida's predecessor, Merleau-Ponty. It meant a painstaking attention, like that practiced by the artist, to how seeing the world means to be seen by and through the world—to be found within layers of our own perceiving, feeling, dreaming, imagining, remembering, and speaking. It requires a silence and a poetic rendering if this hearkening is to occur—a loosening of our integration as "I think, therefore I am." Merleau-Ponty, in thinking about how vision is not from us toward the world as a surveying, but is rather a coming together of realms of gazes that intersect and interweave that we might enter, questioned this disjunction of worlds among humans and animals: "Why would not synergy exist among different organisms, if it is possible within each? Their landscapes interweave, their actions and their passions fit together exactly: this is possible as soon as we make belongingness to one same 'consciousness' the primordial definition of sensibility, and as soon as we rather understand it as the return of the visible upon itself."[58] It may be that human and animals are both dispersed within the world in such a way that the forest as not our forest, but the world of the deer and its modes of being, is not entirely closed to us, if we can abandon our Cartesian identities and allow that other force we feel in a world of gazes to affect us. Bailly calls this "the pensivity of animals."[59] He cautions us with regard to this other sort of gaze that "this force may not need to be named, but where it is exercised it is as though we were in the presence of a different form of thought, a thought that could only have ahead of it, and overwhelmingly, the pensive path."[60] We need not stay imprisoned in the binaries in which we are the rational ones and they the irrational ones but rather recognize different modes of being, feeling, and being pensive.

Merleau-Ponty in his lectures about animality at the end of his life was moving toward this new sort of use of language, a philosophy as a non-philosophy or "a-philosophy," as he called it. I think Derrida also sees this as a possibility:

> I suppose a historian of philosophy might one day wonder, as a historian of painting or sculpture might, whether within the classification of genres there existed the category of animal philosopher. There are animal painters and sculptors. One also speaks of animal literature, as though animality not only defined a kingdom, species, or genus, but an artistic genre.[61]

I think humans need and the planet needs *animal philosophers*—or else the kind of hospitality at the heart of what ethics and spirituality were supposed to engender remains impossible. That place outside the discourses of human and animal, outside the sphere of sovereignty as excuse for violence, requires the play that is Derrida's legacy and is the wolf's continual activity. So *divinanimality* may appear in another place.

A place where *divinanimality* is there for an instant and then lost is in D. H. Lawrence's poem "The Snake," which Derrida discusses at length in *The Beast and the Sovereign*. He gives it as his example of how we miss hospitality and fellowship in the pettiness of discourse that is actually a cruelty. The poem draws the picture of a scene in which the owner of property comes down to his water trough and finds a great dark snake has arrived at the trough before him and is taking a drink of water on this hot day. The man resents waiting for a snake to have his water. Even more representative of the human regard for snakes, he suddenly admits, "The voice of my education said to me / He must be killed. . . . If you were a man / You would take a stick and break him now, and finish him off."[62] The speaker in the poem is convinced earlier that he is being "civilized" and exercising his proper "rights," and only later does he come to see his actions in an entirely new light by moving outside the customary discourse of rights. Suddenly, he sees that his place is not the first place because of a higher rank than the snake, and that he should come after it: "The drinker knew in his compassion, in his bones, that 'someone was before me at my water-trough / And I, like a second comer, waiting.'"[63] The drinker's education, his discourse, told him he was first in line, even though coming after in time. This line of thought would have led him to attack the snake, asserting his priority, his authority over the other. Yet in the stillness after this, he realizes his mistake, the mistake of the discourses that have deceived him. Other feelings dawn, telling him that actually he follows after this snake, this "honored visitor, this fellow," whom he is following in the creaturely ways of the country on a hot afternoon. He feels then that he should have felt the address of the snake. And if he had done so, then he would have been "honored still more / That he should seek my hospitality / From out of the dark door of the secret earth."[64] At that instant, which he later destroys, by still following his education just enough to at least scare off the snake. Yet, too late, he wishes he would have shown the hospitality befitting the creature, the human, that he knows he comes after the snake in a deeper way.

Derrida is struck by the lines in the poem describing the snake: "For he seemed to me again like a king / Like a king in exile, uncrowned in the underworld, / now due to be crowned again."[65] Derrida admits he likes these lines because they place sovereignty back in the realm of animals and in the realm of the world that Bailly felt he got a glimpse of after following the deer. It restores a sense of autonomy that is before us, yet we seem to only see it as an afterthought. We have exiled the worlds we can only glimpse and made those that inhabit those worlds into exiles. This is why Derrida ends the lecture series of that year calling for a biopolitics or a zoopolitics that would allow those whom we follow after but are now exiled to return to their sovereignty. I think that is what Bailly feels is the only answer to the gaze of animals. He states that his pointing to the "pensivity of animals" is not an attempt "to credit animals with access to thought," but rather "what it establishes is that the world in which we live is gazed upon by other beings, that the visible is shared among creatures, and that a politics should be invented on this basis, if it is not too late."[66] To see is to be seen, but not as an object, but rather to be among a plurality of gazes that together are the open of the world.

❧ The Dogs of Exodus and the Question of the Animal

KEN STONE

How might we reread biblical texts in the light of what Jacques Derrida calls "the question of the animal"? "The question of the animal" is not a single question, and those who approach it do so from many points of view. Derrida's particular exploration of the question, however, focuses on the ways in which a tradition of philosophical thought has defined "the human" partly by contrasting it with, and excluding, something else called "the animal."[1]

It has, of course, become common within contemporary critical theory to criticize homogenous representations of "the human." Once the attempt to describe the properly human gets under way, individuals who fail to conform to that description may be denounced as inhuman, indeed, as "beastly." Distinctions can be made between what Cary Wolfe calls the "humanized human" and the "animalized humans," those individuals and populations who, falling short of hegemonic notions of humanity, are marked for treatment like animals.[2] Partly for that reason, many contemporary thinkers interrogate the exclusionary moves by which normalizing views of the human are constituted. To cite only one influential example, Judith Butler has throughout her work brought considerable energy to the critical analysis of "normative schemes of intelligibility," including schemes organized around gender, sexuality, race, religion, and nation, that "establish what will and will not be human." As she notes, these schemes "differentiate among those who are more and less human" and "produce images of the less than human, in the guise of the human."[3]

Derrida, however, follows a less conventional path when he interrogates just as insistently that co-implicated sign, "the animal."[4] The use of this singular, homogenizing sign, with definite article, obscures significant differences among diverse life-forms while hiding the fact that some of those life-forms are positioned much more closely than others to human existence. Close attention to the multiple modes of life found among nonhuman animals thus has the paradoxical effect of pluralizing "the animal" while destabilizing the boundary constructed between humans and other animals. Once one begins to examine carefully the particular characteristics of a wide range of living creatures, routine appeals to such traditional criteria as language, self-consciousness, and reason no longer lead easily to absolute distinctions between "the human" as such and "the animal" as such. As Derrida puts it, "There is not one opposition" between the human and the animal. Rather, "There are, between different organizational structures of the living being, many fractures, heterogeneities, differential structures."[5]

Derrida's goal, then, is also not to insist on "some homogeneous continuity" between humans and other animals. Indeed, while criticizing the traditional philosophical distinctions between "Man" and "the Animal," he explicitly distances himself, rhetorically, from any suggestion that he is interested in effacing altogether the line between human and animal. Although a few of Derrida's readers criticize him for retaining some version of the distinction between humans and other animals, Derrida points out that a simple erasure of this distinction would be untrue to his long "attention to difference, to differences, to heterogeneities and abyssal ruptures as against the homogeneous and the continuous."[6] In his approach to the distinction between humans and animals, Derrida expresses an interest instead "in multiplying its figures, in complicating, thickening, delinearizing, folding, and dividing the line precisely by making it increase and multiply."[7] That last turn of phrase cannot help catching the attention of the biblical scholar. If God, in Genesis, calls on both animals and humans to "increase and multiply" upon the earth (1:22, 28), so also Derrida calls on his audience to "increase and multiply" our awareness or acknowledgment of the many differential relations that structure both the distinctions between humans and other animals, and the distinctions among innumerable species of animals, across that same earth.

But apart from such rhetorical allusions, what does this "multiplying" and "complicating" project have to do with biblical interpretation? Although Derrida is focused primarily on philosophical texts that appear in what he calls "a certain 'epoch' . . . from Descartes to the present,"[8] he positions this philosophical discourse within a larger chronological and cultural framework, signaled by such phrases as "a Greco-Judeo-Christiano-Islamic tradition"[9] and, more graphically, "the Judeo-Christiano-Islamic tradition of a war against the animal, of a sacrificial war that is as old as Genesis."[10] As that last reference indicates, the opening chapters of Genesis play an important role in *The Animal That Therefore I Am*. Derrida's interest in Genesis and occasional references to other biblical passages might therefore be taken as an indication that additional opportunities exist for bringing biblical interpretation to bear on the question of the animal and for using the question of the animal to reread biblical texts. Such opportunities would ideally take forms other than survey-like examinations of animals in the Bible, although such examinations can themselves be quite valuable.[11] They might also include explorations of the possibility that biblical literature, originating as it does prior to the modern humanist division between human and animal, actually multiplies, complicates, and divides lines of association and difference not only between humans and other animals but also among humans, animals, and the divine.

To explore this possibility, I take as my biblical point of departure a couple of passages found outside Genesis that Derrida mentions almost in passing. In the context of a longer discussion of Emmanuel Levinas and the question of the animal, Derrida devotes several pages to a short piece by Levinas that has, in turn, captured the attention of a number of philosophically inclined contributions to the contemporary "animal studies" literature. In that essay, titled "The Name of a Dog, or Natural Rights," Levinas cites two rather obscure texts from the book of Exodus.[12] As a way into my own reflection on those texts, it may be useful to recall briefly how they function within the rhetoric of Levinas.

Levinas opens his essay with a quotation from Exodus 22:31 (22:30 in Hebrew): "You shall be people consecrated to me; therefore you shall not eat any meat that is mangled by beasts in the field; you shall throw it to the dogs."[13] Taking this commandment as his point of departure, Levinas moves quickly through a paragraph that references meat-eating, Adam's vegetarianism, hunting, and a kind of comparison between "the horrors of war" and "the butchery that every day claims our 'consecrated' mouths" before exclaiming, "But enough of this theology! It is the dog mentioned at the end of the verse that I am especially interested in. I am thinking of Bobby."[14] Rather than telling us immediately who "Bobby" is, however, Levinas next works his way through several figures of speech that he calls "allegories"—"a dog's life," "raining cats and dogs," the "wolf" that hides under "dogged faithfulness," and so on—only to arrive at another passage from Exodus. As Levinas notes, Jewish tradition interprets the reference to dogs eating meat in Exodus 22 by recalling other dogs in Exodus 11. There, Moses, recounting a word from God, speaks to the Israelites about the night of the last plague, a night when the firstborn throughout Egypt shall die. Although there will be much wailing in Egypt on that night, Moses tells the Israelites in 11:6 that "not a dog shall growl at any of the Israelites—not at people, not at animals—so that you may know that the LORD makes a distinction between Egypt and Israel" (11:6). As Levinas observes, certain Jewish texts find in this verse in chapter 11 a rationale for giving torn flesh to dogs in Exodus 22. According to this tradition, the carrion in Exodus 22 is God's reward to the dogs for having held their tongues in Exodus 11.[15] Using this interpretation as a way to shift his focus from the dogs of Exodus 22 to the dogs of Exodus 11, Levinas notes that these dogs' silent recognition of the Israelites takes place just as the Israelites are being freed from bondage. This is the moment, according to Exodus, that "not a dog shall growl." By holding their tongues, the dogs mark the liberation of Israelite slaves. And here, Levinas observes, we see what it means to say that dogs are the friends of humanity, for "with neither ethics nor *logos*, the dog will attest to the dignity of its person."[16]

This reference to the dog who attests to human dignity, however, serves as a transition in the short piece by Levinas, for it is only after his meditation on Exodus 11 that Levinas turns to another dog who attested to human dignity. Levinas finally introduces us to Bobby, the friend of whom he has been "thinking." The setting for this introduction is another scene of bondage. In a Nazi camp for Jewish prisoners of war, Levinas and his fellows are being dehumanized. In the eyes of the Germans, Levinas says, "We were subhuman, a gang of apes" (153). And yet in this desolate location, where it was easy to forget "our essence as thinking creatures," for several weeks "a wandering dog entered our lives":

One day he came to meet this rabble as we returned under guard from work. . . . We called him Bobby, an exotic name, as one does with a cherished dog. He would appear at morning assembly and was waiting for us as we returned, jumping up and down and barking in delight. For him there was no doubt that we were men.

A contrast is drawn by Levinas between Bobby the dog and the German masters. But the contrast, ironically, makes Bobby seem humane and the Germans more beastly. If the Nazis dehumanize their Jewish prisoners by treating them like animals ("We were subhuman, a gang of apes"), this animal happily recognizes those prisoners as human ("For him there was no doubt that we were men"). Like the dogs of Exodus 11, according to the interpretation of Levinas, Bobby "attests to the dignity" of humans in captivity. Thus Levinas concludes:

This dog was the last Kantian in Nazi Germany, without the brain needed to universalize maxims and drives. He was a descendant of the dogs of Egypt. And his friendly growling, his animal faith, was born from the silence of his forefathers on the banks of the Nile. (153)

So this extraordinary little essay with a dog in its title, which opens with one reference to dogs in Exodus 22, closes with a reference to other dogs in Exodus 11.

Now discussions of animals are rare enough in Levinas's work that Derrida refers to this essay at one point as "a sort of hapax."[17] Partly because of its unusual focus, "The Name of a Dog" has been the object of numerous readings that reflect on the possible implications or limitations of Levinasian thought for contemporary animal ethics.[18] Such readings frequently wrestle with paradox in the piece by Levinas. What should one do with a canine Kantian who nevertheless lacks "the brain needed to universalize maxims and drives"? How should one respond to a piece that juxtaposes the violence of humans against animals, the violence of animals against animals, and the violence of humans against humans, all in the troubling context of the Shoah? And what, if anything, does this piece tell us about the possibilities for a different approach to animal ethics, an approach that might allow us to see the "face" of our animal others?

Not surprisingly, readers of Levinas have been unable to reach agreement about these questions. The diverse readings of such a short piece seem, in fact, to be grounded in divergent currents at work within the essay itself. As David Clark observes, "The enigma of the animal evokes contradictory thoughts and feelings in Levinas."[19] After all, the rhetorical drift of "The Name of a Dog" moves from a reflection on eating animals, a reflection that evokes "the horrors of war" and the carnivorous "butchery" that could "make you a vegetarian again" (151), to the horrors of a war camp for Jewish prisoners who are reduced by the Nazis to "beings entrapped in their species . . . beings without language," whose attempts to express themselves are treated as nothing more than "monkey talk" (153). Reflecting on this movement, it is hard to disagree with John Llewelyn when he notes in a frequently quoted statement that Levinas here "all but proposes an analogy between the unspeakable human Holocaust and the unspoken animal one."[20] As if to keep that analogy in check, however, Levinas also gestures clearly toward distinctions between humans and animals: Bobby may be a Kantian, but he lacks "the brain needed to universalize maxims and drives," the brain, that is, of a rational, dutiful humanity. We do well to remember the context for Levinas's refusal, here, to obliterate distinctions between humans and other animals. The racism of the Nazi regime, which turned Levinas and his fellows into a "gang of apes" reduced to "monkey talk," serves as a stark reminder that, in Clark's words, "the animalization of human beings leads directly to . . . horrific consequences."[21] And yet the moving invocation of this dog Bobby, of whom Levinas has been thinking all these years, and who, with "animal faith" and "friendly growling," recognizes humanity in the faces of the prisoners, suggests to many readers that Levinas comes tantalizingly close in this essay to breaking out of his self-professed agnosticism about the extent to which an animal has "the right to be called 'face.'"[22]

Ultimately, most readers of the essay, including Derrida, conclude that Levinas remains corralled within an anthropocentric ethics that relies on a clear distinction between humans and animals, a distinction that excludes animals from serious ethical consideration by Levinas. Such readers adopt different positions, however, about the ease with which, or whether, Levinas's ethical framework could be extended in such a way as to make room for our responsibility for other animals. But it is striking to note that, even as their responses diverge from one another both in their styles of reading and in their conclusions about Levinas and animal ethics, nearly all commentators on "The Name of a Dog" share one characteristic that cannot fail to catch the attention of the biblical scholar. They generally show far more interest in Bobby than in the unnamed dogs of Exodus who both open and close Bobby's tale.[23]

Now if most readers of Levinas who are interested in animal ethics seem disinclined to follow Levinas down the path toward biblical interpretation, biblical scholars have not done a great deal to lure them there. "The question of the animal" has not been high on the list of research priorities for biblical scholarship. To be sure, a few studies have started to appear that investigate the material and symbolic roles of animals in the Hebrew Bible and in ancient Israel.[24] Moreover, scholars have long been curious about the criteria used by biblical writers to decide which animals were appropriate objects for eating and sacrifice.[25] These studies are often insightful and are surely relevant for a reading of Exodus 22, with its distinction between meat that can be eaten by Israelites and meat that is given to dogs. Nevertheless, the dogs of Exodus themselves receive little attention from biblical scholars. Indeed, commentators on Exodus sometimes discuss the verses in which dogs appear without referring explicitly to dogs at all.[26]

In modern scholarship, moreover, the dogs of Exodus 11 and the dogs of Exodus 22 are, for methodological reasons, seldom placed in relation to one another as they are by Levinas. After all, the dogs of Exodus 11 appear in the narrative account of the Israelite exodus from Egypt. The dogs of Exodus 22, however, show up in legal material constituting the book's latter half. Apart from the fact that these two passages provide us with the only two references to dogs in the book of Exodus, they may seem to have little in common.

But what might readers who are interested in biblical interpretation and the question of the animal find if we pursue the path taken by Levinas when, following Jewish exegetical tradition, he links these two sets of dogs, and hence different sets of texts, in Exodus to each other? Instead of asking whether the philosophy of Levinas offers a sufficient framework for handling the question of the animal, I am more interested here in taking a cue from a passing comment by Derrida, who, immediately after quoting a reference by Levinas to the dogs of Exodus, remarks that "there would be much to say concerning this allusion to Egypt."[27] Derrida then says relatively little about it, although significantly, on the next page, he directs his reader's attention to two important verses that immediately precede the admonition to throw torn meat to the dogs, verses that I examine below. But if Clark observes, toward the end of his moving essay on "The Last Kantian in Nazi Germany," that the dog Bobby "traces and retraces the oppositional limits that configure the human and the animal,"[28] perhaps the dogs of Exodus, who according to Levinas are Bobby's silent ancestors, can point us toward certain biblical ways of dealing with, and sometimes complicating, those same "oppositional limits."[29]

The verse from Exodus 22 with which Levinas opens his essay is one of a series of biblical texts in which references to dogs are sometimes understood as having "bad connotations."[30] These negative connotations are often taken for granted by biblical scholars who discuss references to dogs in the Hebrew Bible. Many such scholars follow in the tracks of D. Winton Thomas, who suggested in an influential article published in 1960 that the Israelites and their neighbors considered the dog a "vile and contemptible animal . . . the scavenger *par excellence*."[31] Although the consensus that subsequently formed around this position has recently been challenged, it is worth recalling the types of texts that led Thomas to his conclusion.[32] Several of these texts use canine references rhetorically to insult human beings by comparing them to dogs or, in some cases, dead dogs (e.g., 1 Sam. 23:14; 2 Sam. 3:8, 9:8, 16:9; Pss. 22:16, 20; 59:6; Prov. 26:11; Isa. 56:10–11). Biblical characters can also refer to themselves as dogs in a self-deprecating fashion (2 Kings 8:13). In other passages, however, including Exodus 22, negative connotations are derived rather from the fact that dogs eat food that humans will not eat. Indeed, in a number of these passages, dogs eat human flesh or drink human blood (e.g., 1 Kings 16:4; 21:19, 23–24; 22:38; 2 Kings 9:10, 36; Ps. 68:22–23; cf. Jer. 15:3). The specification of blood in several of these passages is worth underscoring. The Hebrew Bible famously prohibits the human ingestion of blood, in which the "life" (*nephesh*) of living creatures was thought to reside (e.g., Lev. 17:10–16). Any negative connotations associated with dogs as creatures who not only eat human bodies but drink human blood may have been intensified by such a prohibition. But more important for my purposes here, we see already that the dogs' search for food across biblical literature results in a blurring of the boundary between humans and other creatures, for it exposes the fact that our bodies and the bodies of other animals are equally useful as edible meat.

The dogs in Exodus 22, however, are not eating human meat, but rather meat that humans should not eat, meat that has been killed by other animals. As Walter Houston notes, these dogs serve what was likely one of their common functions as scavengers who "get rid of unclean and uneatable refuse." Yet this function "puts them into an ideologically ambiguous position."[33] On the one hand, the willingness of dogs to eat corpses (human and otherwise) differentiates them from other domestic animals and appears to place them closer to wild animals, which in the Hebrew Bible are often conceptualized separately from domesticated animals.[34] On the other hand, dogs are certainly not wild animals but domesticated animals, with "the longest history of human domestication of any animal by several thousand years."[35] They have evolved in complex relationships with human beings, over many centuries and under circumstances that are still in several respects debated.[36] They are found primarily inside rather than outside human communities, or perhaps just on the boundaries of those communities; for the dogs referred to most often in the Hebrew Bible are probably not "pets" in the modern sense of that term but rather so-called pariah dogs or, to borrow a category from the influential book on dogs by Raymond and Lorna Coppinger, the ubiquitous "village dogs."[37] Thus dogs exist in an unusual space of their own, which leads Houston to refer to them as "anomalous" animals in the sense given to that word by Mary Douglas.[38] In Exodus 22 it is precisely dogs who eat meat killed by wild animals, dogs in distinction from wild animals, but dogs also in distinction from either human beings (who live in proximity to the dogs but do not eat the meat in question) or other domesticated animals (who for the most part do not eat meat at all). We can thus see already that the category of "the animal" is differentiated within the Hebrew Bible in several respects: There are domestic animals; there are wild animals; and there are dogs who do not fit neatly into either category.

The meat that is given to dogs is often read as food fit only for a dog. Yet the rhetoric of Levinas turns this meat into something positive, something to which the dogs have a "right." Levinas accomplishes this transvaluation by following his rabbinic sources, which, as noted above, interpret the meat in chapter 22 as the dogs' reward for actions taken by other dogs in chapter 11. Such a jump between contexts is hardly unusual in rabbinic hermeneutics, and we might assume that the presence of dogs in both passages is the only point of connection between chapters 11 and 22. If we look carefully at the larger literary contexts for each verse, however, we may notice other links as well, links that Levinas does not mention. And some of these links complicate the question of the animal by increasing and multiplying the ways in which humans are, and are not, differentiated from other animals.

The stipulation that carrion should be given to dogs is not actually located among the biblical laws on clean and unclean animals, laws that differentiate among animals in other ways. Animals do appear, however, in several of the laws that are found in the same section of Exodus as the verse in question. So, for example, in 23:4 we read that one should return a stray ox or donkey even if it belongs to one's enemy. In 23:5 we read that one should relieve a donkey lying under its burden even if it belongs to a person one hates. Several verses later, we find a commandment to let fields, vineyards, and olive orchards rest every seventh year, accompanied by a specification that both poor Israelites and animals may eat from the land during that year (23:11). The very next commandment describes the seventh day as a day of rest not only for humans, but also for ox and donkey. Thus, concern for the well-being of others, which comes to expression in numerous laws from this section of Exodus, does not stop at the line between human and animal.

That line is blurred in a more unsettling way, however, in the two verses that immediately precede the stipulation about giving food to dogs. Those verses specify that "you shall not delay to make offerings from the fullness of your harvest and from the outflow of your presses. The firstborn of your sons you shall give me. You shall do the same with your oxen and with your sheep; seven days it shall remain with its mother; on the eighth day you shall give it to me" (22:29–30). This is not the only place where Pentateuchal law requires the Israelites to offer firstborn sons along with firstborn animals and the first fruits of the field. In distinction from other passages, however, this chapter does not provide any means for substituting animal sacrifices for human ones. Thus it is possible to find in this chapter evidence that some Israelites considered child sacrifice acceptable to God. Indeed, several biblical scholars have argued, on the basis of this passage and other evidence, that the prohibition on child sacrifice as something displeasing to Yhwh developed only late in the history of Israel.[39] Biblical literature as we have it thus speaks to both sides of this controversial issue: Some texts condemn child sacrifice while others seem to allow it or even, as in Exodus 22, command it. Ezekiel 20:25–26, strangely, tries to have it both ways, indicating that child sacrifice could be understood even by a prophet who opposed it as having been required at some point by certain of God's commandments, perhaps the very ones from Exodus that we are reading, which, however, are actually "laws that were not good," used by God to make Israel unclean and desolate. This strand of biblical thought therefore blurs the line between human and animal even at the point of sacrifice.

Now Derrida, in his discussion of "The Name of a Dog" in *The Animal That Therefore I Am*, explicitly calls attention to the fact that these verses, not quoted by Levinas, appear immediately prior to the biblical admonition to throw torn meat to the dogs.[40] Although Derrida does not elaborate on the significance of this contiguity, we may discern some of the implications of it when we recall that sacrifice has already appeared in his discussion of Levinas. Derrida notes a few pages earlier that, in spite of the Levinasian emphasis on the biblical command "Thou Shalt Not Kill," which Levinas associates with a prohibition on murder, Levinas restricts the scope of the command to "the face of the other, my neighbor, my brother, the human, or another human. Putting to death or sacrificing the animal, exploiting it to death . . . are not forbidden by 'Thou shalt not kill.'"[41] We may recall here Derrida's reference a few pages earlier to "a war against the animal, a sacrificial war that is as old as Genesis."[42] And the matter of sacrifice is also raised by Derrida in connection with Levinas and animals in "Eating Well," a published interview with Jean-Luc Nancy on the deconstruction of the modern Western subject. There Derrida argues that the philosophies of Levinas and Heidegger "remain profound humanisms *to the extent that they do not sacrifice sacrifice*."[43] "Sacrifice," here, refers not simply to literal sacrifices but also to what Derrida calls the "sacrificial structure" of Western philosophical and religious discourses, in which one finds "a place left open . . . for a noncriminal putting to death." The most obvious and perhaps foundational examples of this "noncriminal putting to death" involve animals, which, as Derrida, notes, Western culture permits to be killed, most notably when we eat them. However, Derrida also suggests that it may be "very difficult, truly impossible to delimit" the "operation" of this permitted "noncriminal putting to death" to animals but not to humans.[44] Indeed, both symbolically and literally, we put other humans to death all the time. And when Derrida refers to this sacrificial structure and the subjectivity that it enables with such phrases as "carnivorous viril-ity" and "carno-phallogocentrism,"[45] we begin to suspect that the exclu-sion of the animal from ethical consideration cannot be separated from the exclusion of others, for example women and feminized men,[46] from Western subjectivity and ethics. Although it is not possible here to explore this complex argument (the implications of which continue to be debated by philosophers attempting to take seriously the question of the animal),[47] recalling it serves to underscore the potential importance of recognizing that the Hebrew Bible, in spite of popular misconceptions to the contrary, does not consistently use sacrifice to draw a line between the permitted killing of animals and the forbidden killing of humans. Rather, biblical discourses of sacrifice such as that found in Exodus 22, which sometimes permit or even command the sacrifice of humans, highlight the difficulty of using the distinction between human and animal to define clearly the difference between sacrifice and murder.

Given Derrida's association between carnivorous subjectivity and the distinction between male and female, it may also be useful to recall the un-easy similarities and differences between the story in Genesis 22 of the male character Isaac, whose sacrifice God famously commands and then prevents via the substitution of an animal, and the story in Judges 11 of Jephthah's daughter, whose sacrifice God permits. The different fates of these two characters underscore the importance of taking gender into ac-count when examining more thoroughly than I can do here the Hebrew Bible's "sacrificial structures." Yet gender lines alone will not permit us to make sense of the multiple biblical ways of construing this issue. After all, in Exodus 22:28 it is explicitly firstborn sons who must be given to God, along with firstborn animals.

Moreover, lines between human and animal are obscured even in bibli-cal passages where provision is made for the substitution of animals in place of firstborn humans as objects of sacrifice. Exodus 13:13 and 34:19–20, for example, allow the Israelites to substitute a sheep in order to redeem a firstborn human. Yet both of these passages also specify that the Israelites may substitute a sheep to redeem a firstborn donkey. This specification is sometimes understood as a consequence of the donkey's unclean status; and although neither passage in Exodus gives this rationale for the sub-stitution, a passage from Numbers 18 on redemption does make such an explanation plausible. Yet it is strange that the donkey alone of all unclean animals is singled out for redemption in Exodus, with no mention of its unclean status, in distinction, say, from Leviticus 27:27, which allows all unclean animals to be redeemed without mentioning the donkey or any other species in particular.[48] Whatever explanation we supply for these peculiarities, one effect of the substitution of a sheep for a donkey in Exodus is to set up a strange kind of equivalence in the book between human and donkey, which is differentiated as a consequence from other animals whose firstborn are not explicitly redeemed. Indeed, the unusual association of donkeys and humans may be strengthened by the fact that the donkey is the only animal other than the snake in the Garden of Eden who talks with humans in the Hebrew Bible (Num. 22:22–35).[49] Thus, these passages on sacrifice simultaneously make divisions among animals while aligning some animals more closely with humans than others.

The reference to the firstborn in Exodus 22:29–30 also provides us with another link between this chapter, where dogs are given meat, and Exodus 11, where no dog will growl. The book of Exodus itself explains the requirement to give the firstborn to God by referring to the deliverance from Egypt. As Exodus 13 notes, when the Israelite children ask their parents about the reason for giving the firstborn, the Israelites should respond by recalling God's slaughter of "all the firstborn in the land of Egypt, from human firstborn to the firstborn of animals" (13:15). And this is precisely the event being foretold in chapter 11 when Exodus first refers to dogs.

Now it is not actually certain that these dogs were understood originally to be refraining from growling, as Levinas and his rabbinic sources assume. Most English translations do read something like "no dog will growl," and versions as old as the Septuagint and Targum understand the passage to refer to canine noisemaking. The passage refers literally in Hebrew, however, to actions made with the tongue. Some scholars suggest that these actions may be a kind of licking rather than growling or barking, perhaps implying the lapping of the blood of the dead.[50] Such an interpretation would be consistent with the multiple passages that do clearly refer to dogs eating dead humans or drinking their blood, though the language in such passages differs from the language used in Exodus 11. However, a similar expression in Joshua 10:21 (which represents humans rather than dogs moving their tongues) involves speech. Thus, despite ambiguities, there are grounds for concluding that Exodus 11 refers to growling or barking. Within some later Jewish traditions, in fact, these dogs were understood to be magical watchdogs belonging to the Egyptians, who would normally bark to alert the Egyptians but who are here silenced by Moses.[51] And the appearance of these dogs on a night when mass death is taking place might be another example of a recurring cross-cultural representation of canines that, in the words of Susan McHugh, "positions the dog at the gateway of life and death."[52]

So far as the question of the animal is concerned, however, the point to underscore is the way in which actions taken, or rather not taken, by these dogs cut across the boundary between animal and human. For the text is explicit about the fact that the dogs will not move their tongues against either human Israelites or their animals (11:7). The firstborn of all those animals associated with the Israelites shall live. By contrast, Moses specifies two verses earlier that every firstborn Egyptian will die, including their firstborn animals (11:5). Thus, there are humans and animals who die among the Egyptians, and humans and animals who live among the Israelites. God's actions for life and death here transgress the division between humans and animals and are taken instead on the basis of a distinction between Egypt and Israel. And whatever they are or are not doing with their tongues, the dogs of Exodus, like God, recognize and act on the basis of this alternative distinction.

What, then, might we conclude from this reading of the dogs of Exodus? A growing body of contemporary literature suggests, for a range of ethical, ecological, ethological, and philosophical reasons, that traditional Western ways of drawing lines between human and animal need to be rethought. In truth, the instability of this distinction has been apparent since Darwin.[53] But over against Darwin, it is only too easy to assume that the Bible works with a single, stable division between human and animal. Yet it is not clear that biblical views about animals are stable or unified. Although biblical texts do make distinctions between humans and animals, they also blur those distinctions, as I have suggested. Moreover, biblical texts undermine the existence of any single category, "the animal," by pluralizing it, sometimes in unexpected ways (e.g., associating some humans with donkeys, associating other humans with animals that can be sacrificed, associating some animals with the poor, differentiating domestic animals from wild animals, dividing animals among ethnic groups of humans, and distinguishing the clean from the unclean). Written, as it was, prior to modern humanism, biblical literature fails to provide us with a clear picture of a unified human subject that can be distinguished easily from "the animal," as such. There may not exist a single "biblical view" of humans and animals at all. What we have in the Bible are, rather, to recall the words of Derrida, "many fractures, heterogeneities, differential structures." And close attention to the dogs of Exodus, and the passages in which they appear, offers us one way to begin exploring some of those differential structures.

But let us return, finally, to the fact that these dogs appear in a biblical book that, as Levinas notes, is often associated with human freedom. Today any association between Exodus and freedom is perhaps more difficult to make uncritically than it was at the time Levinas wrote his article. After all, limitations to the use of Exodus as a model for human liberation have been much discussed in recent years.[54] However, the difficulties Levinas seems to have had making room for animals in his ethics may be indicative of difficulties that others experience as well. Advocates for human freedom and social justice are, unfortunately, sometimes skeptical of attempts to take seriously the question of the animal. Some of these skeptics recognize that animal rights and environmental activists are occasionally too cautious in their advocacy for human rights and welfare. But others simply adopt uncritically the anthropocentric assumption that matters of animal suffering and flourishing are too trivial to be taken seriously by advocates for justice.

However, attention to the dogs of Exodus and the passages associated with them brings to light the fact that, whatever its limitations as a resource for modern liberation, the book of Exodus at least does not simplistically cordon off concerns for human welfare from concerns about animal welfare. Such concerns are inextricably intertwined with one another. Animals and humans do die together as objects of sacrifice and slaughter. But animals and the poor are also juxtaposed as beneficiaries of prescribed agricultural practices, as we have seen. And in the Exodus narrative, the deliverance of the Israelites from Egypt itself involves animals. Those Israelite animals, against whom no dog moves its tongue, leave Egypt with the Israelite humans. Animals are already there in this paradigmatic story of liberation, already participating in the exodus of the Israelite slaves. Thus, attempts to work for their survival and welfare now may simply honor their presence among the Israelites then, as they walked together out of the house of bondage under the watchful eyes of the silent dogs of Exodus.

✒ Devouring the Human: Digestion of a Corporeal Soteriology

ERIKA MURPHY

Traditional wisdom holds that the category *human* comes with the privilege of an untouchable corporeality: We are, it is often quipped, at the top of the food chain. And yet the term *food chain* itself represents a kind of scientific misnomer: All organisms, including humans, return to the earth through the mouths and stomachs of insects, bacteria, and sometimes larger predators who find us a rather easy meal. Acknowledging that humans are a consumable product, I contend, is not just a point of ecological correctness: Recognizing our fleshy vulnerability may be vital to creating an opening for the divine. The philosopher Hélenè Cixous draws our attention to human corporeal vulnerability when she recounts being bitten as a child by the family dog, Fips. After Fips releases his grip from her ankle, she tells us, "I saw the meat we are. We came out of the mortal spasms broken lame and delirious. Unrecognizable."[1] Cixous's glimpse of the meaty human interior becomes a transformative moment that changes her both somatically and psychically. Strikingly, the bite draws this atheistic postmodern thinker into the world of the biblical: The experience with Fips echoes, for Cixous, the narratives of both Job and Jesus. What Cixous hints at but does not name is that this biblical material is not simply related to this somatic interiority but is actually about "the meat we are." As Stephen Moore reminds us, Jesus as he appears flogged before Pilate is "a slaughtered lamb . . . soon to be hung from a crude cross hewn from a butcher's block."[2] I suggest that seeing Christ as animal can offer us what Fips offered Cixous: the experience of a vulnerable corporeality that both reveals our limits and expands our capacity for connection to the transcendent. By recognizing that the "human" is also at every moment a consumable animal, we make room for the radical relationality that is necessary for transformation. It is in this way that a somatic reeducation—an opening of the body—can point us toward a soteriology of the flesh.

Cixous does not spare us any details in the painful description of her childhood relationship with the family dog: After her father suddenly dies, extreme neglect and suffering set in. Fips, along with the rest of the family, becomes a target for stone-throwing Arab neighbors who are unhappy with the "Jew-French" family in their midst. Fips remains chained outside, vulnerable to attack, his body increasingly swollen with ticks. When Cixous answers the door one morning, the catastrophic fold occurs: Without warning, Fips charges and latches on to her ankle. The washerwoman strikes Fips with a wet sheet until his jaw finally releases. Cixous recounts, "At the thirteenth stroke the muzzle cracked"; but she reflects, "When we were at last separated the one from the other, it was too late. The root had been reached. On the inside of my brain the very slight bleeding of a small lack of forgetting, a minuscule wound would not close its eyes."[3] The bite on the ankle resonates through her entire body, creating a wound with eyes of its own. As a new vision(ary), Cixous correlates this somatic trauma to a psychic transformation: As Fips reaches the root of the body, he also touches an ontological root. The exposure of "the meat that we are" indelibly entwines Cixous and the animal that bit her. As Hugh Pyper puts it, the story of Fips is "about the *bite* . . . the act of violence, severing and eating."[4] The bite, perhaps, could have begun and ended at the ankle. But Cixous allows the trauma to become completely consuming, and the human/animal boundary is blurred. As a result, Fips's violent demonstration of the human body as meat paves the way for a transformed capacity for compassion and connection to the other.

Indeed, the depth of Fips's instruction is so profound that the reverberations take on biblical proportions. "Job was that dog I am sure," Cixous tells us. "The scourges were sent to him, god was well hidden, the father dead, the house ruined and now the plagues and the ulcers."[5] Cixous also experiences Fips's sorrow-filled life and death as a Christ-like sacrifice: It is only through experiencing her lack of compassion toward Fips that Cixous eventually learns to love openly and infinitely. She loves Fips "not then," she tells us, "not there in the garden of war, not yet, but later."[6] The bite seems to sink in fully only as an adult when she is haunted by recurring dreams. After two years of strange nighttime narratives, Cixous is struck: "Suddenly, the resurrection. Of which I had never thought," she declares. "It happened one morning, and it had the features of a cat. . . . My cat came from my dog, which explains the singular power of my cat over my heart, an absolute power that makes of this young and childish beast my daily prophet."[7] Returning as resurrected animal, Fips and his sacrifice succeed in transforming Cixous's human limitations: She now claims an increased capacity for connection and more capacity to love. "As for me," Cixous declares, "I am ready to give my life for my cat, but it was necessary that Fips should first have given his life for me."[8] Although acknowledging Fips's martyrdom, Cixous does not explicitly address the sacrifice made by both sides; before Fips can sacrifice himself for her, Cixous herself must permit herself to be consumed. She allows the violence of the bite to penetrate in a way that dissolves her sense of human invulnerability and somatic wholeness. It is only after many years that the festering, eye-opening wound winds its way through her body and produces oneiric visions. After her sacrifice of self, the resurrection occurs.

If Fips indeed embodies Christ's sacrifice, this event may not simply reveal a connection between Cixous's experience and the biblical, but it may also reveal a crucial corporeal aspect of biblical revelation itself. Christ on the cross, while most often celebrated for his simultaneous humanity and divinity, is also a sacrificial animal, as Moore points out. The Lamb of God becomes the sacrificial lamb on the cross, his meaty interior exposed on the cross "hewn from a butcher's block." But although we receive clear testimony from Cixous that her somatic encounter with the animal leads to revelation, the biblical witness to Jesus' role as animal—and as fleshy meal—is much less clear. Although corporeality is obviously quite germane to incarnation, orthodox attitudes toward flesh have been fraught with ambiguity.[9] The Johannine text in particular offers an intriguing example of scripture's struggle between flesh, spirit, and soteriology. It is in John that Jesus warns, "Unless you eat the flesh of the Son of Man and drink his blood, you have no life in you" (John 6:53). And yet this admonition is soon followed by the declaration that "it is the spirit that gives life; the flesh is useless" (John 6:63). Is the flesh indeed useless, or does salvation depend on our ability to claim Christ as a meal? Biblical scholars such as Craig Keener find scripture's message quite clear. He tells us: "It is not the *literal* flesh (cf. 6:5) that brings life, but the Spirit." Therefore, Keener instructs, "Disciples must imbibe his Spirit, not his literal flesh (cf. 20:22); his life is present also in his words (6:68; cf. 15:7)."[10] And yet it seems we do a disservice to Jesus' message if we claim that "flesh" in this case simply falls into the category of figurative language while the "real" message—that we need to consume Jesus' words—is a subtext. In *Poststructuralism and the New Testament*, Stephen Moore addresses the figurative versus literal in a deconstructive reading of John: At the well with the Samaritan woman, Jesus holds up "living water" as superior to the literal water being drawn from the well. And yet when Jesus is crucified and the spear strikes his side, it is indeed literal, earthly water that flows from Jesus' body; water that can also be seen as, in Moore's words, "a further token of the promised living water or Spirit."[11] At this moment, water is both of the spirit and of the earth. As Moore explains, "It is a spiritual material and a literal figure. Literality and figurality intermingle in the flow from Jesus' side, each contaminating the other, which is to say that we cannot keep the literal clearly separate from the figurative in the end."[12] The truth that inhabits Jesus' body is one in which categories are disarmed and seemingly obvious oppositions overwhelm each other. Also striking is that Jesus' body seems to out-articulate Jesus himself. Moore observes that Jesus "speaks to the Samaritan woman and all his other dialogue partners as though he were a mixture composed of separable elements, as though the living water could be clearly distinguished from spring water . . . the spiritual from the material, and the heavenly from the earthly. What Jesus *says* is contradicted by what he *is*."[13] We can say this contradiction also plays out in Jesus' Johannine dialogue regarding flesh and spirit: Whatever Jesus may say about flesh versus spirit, his performance as slaughtered lamb speaks to an extreme engagement with both flesh and spirit that does not allow us to disentangle one from the other. On the cross as the lamb, the flesh of the animal overflows like either an eternal or earthly spring, surpassing our ability to articulate the deep paradox at its root. Flesh offers the gift of performance, which adds its own layers of wisdom to the body of the text.

And yet, in John, it is not enough to simply recognize Jesus' flesh as indelibly commingled with spirit. The Johannine text seems to demand that we consume this flesh-spirit cocktail by not simply drawing our attention to the idea of flesh, but by interweaving flesh, spirit, and food. As Virginia Burrus observes, John seems "strangely preoccupied with the matter of eating and drinking even in passages where 'flesh' is only implicitly invoked."[14] Jesus continually negotiates issues of drink and food, including his conversion of water into wine, his exchange with the Samaritan woman at the well that involves both a request for a drink and the offer of water that banishes thirst, and his offering of a breakfast of fish and bread to his disciples postresurrection.[15] Taking in the spirit is both literally and figuratively a material consumption, involving an absorption by and processing of the body. And although Jesus may indeed say that "the flesh is useless," we can refer to Moore's testimony that "what Jesus *says* is contradicted by what he *is*." Although in this case, we might suggest that Jesus' words are contradicted by what the text is: The body of John's text continually encourages us to devour the spirit in whatever form it takes. We find ourselves making a meal of the lamb, despite any intellectual debate over the meaning of the biblical text. And yet, I propose, as we sit down to eat, we must also allow ourselves to be consumed by the lamb. The slaughtered carcass must sink its teeth into our own flesh with the same shock that arrived with the bite on Cixous's ankle. Jesus as slaughtered lamb—and as potential meal—must provide an opening through which we experience our own somatic vulnerability. To look into the depths of corporeal interiority and see ourselves as animal is to make room for the other, to be actively open to the mutual indwelling for which Christ calls when he commands, "Abide in me as I abide in you" (John 15:4). And if we indeed abide by the thread of John's consumptive trope, we need to consume and be consumed absolutely in order to be transformed by the spirit.

John's text, we can say, seduces us into consumption, tempting our taste buds with food that promises to enlighten. As Moore points out, the text itself becomes a body urgently demanding that the Word be digested. The "book sent from God, whose name was John," Moore reminds us, speaks: "'Read me,' urges the book, 'that you may have life.' 'Eat me,' urges the Word, in the book; 'whoever eats me [*ho trōgōn me*] will live because of me (6:57). Eat me, drink me (cf. 6:53–56), ingest me, digest me!'"[16] Acquiescing to these demands to devour, however, are not without their risks. John's text may in fact have a similar taste to Revelation's little scroll: sweet to the mouth but bitter to the stomach. The text, too, has teeth, the ability to strip us down to the root. In "Extreme Fidelity," Cixous explores the moment of Eve's encounter with the apple, explaining that "what we are told is that knowledge might begin with the mouth, with the discovery of the taste of something: knowledge and taste go together."[17] And indeed, Cixous's biblical reading also gives us a new taste and a deeper epistemological experience of the text, one that becomes more complex and fraught with risk. Hugh Pyper notes that Cixous "reminds me as a gentile reader that the text, too, can bite—the text that renders me unclean, then clean, thereby renders me edible, open to being devoured by the text."[18] We taste the apple along with Eve, along with the text; and the text, at the same time, tastes us. As the flesh of the apple is pierced, the epistemological root is exposed, and disobedience brings death to Eden. However, the death of eternal life brings with it an appetite for depth, expansiveness, and potentiality. Is it possible that the sting of mortality is necessary for ontological transformation? Cixous indeed sees Eve's bite not as an unfortunate defiance but rather as a movement toward penetrating relationality: "The apple is visible and it can be held up to the mouth, it is full, it has an *inside*. And what Eve will discover in her relationship to simple reality, is the inside of the apple, and that this inside is good."[19] Eve becomes familiar with the interior of the other, losing her fear of exploring and exposing. And although "consuming" this biblical text may indeed evoke a bittersweet taste, it also allows us to recognize existential complexity. To know death is to also know our connection to the fleshy interior of the other: It is only through this vulnerability that we can enter the dangerously raw interiority of scripture and experience the potentiality of flesh unfolding.

The fact that death is tied to Eve and Adam's epistemological discovery points to a curious relationship between loss and insight. The moment when the skin is pierced—whether that of the apple or of Cixous's ankle—can be seen as a moment of simultaneous trauma and revelation. God sentences Eve to birth pains, condemns Adam to toil the earth, and assures them that they will return to the dust from which they were made. And yet Eve and Adam's new suffering is accompanied by an enlightened epistemological state in the ways of good and evil. Humanity has entered a space where life and death are intertwined and interdependently influence human epistemology and ontology. The theologian Shelly Rambo's work on trauma speaks to this often overlooked contingency between death and life as she explores the theological implications for moving too quickly past the effects of loss. Although Rambo's focus on traumatic events such as war and natural disaster does not allow a direct correlation with Eve's taste of fruit in the garden, Rambo's conclusions do inform the lingering aftereffects of loss. Trauma, Rambo avers, is often such a shock to the human psyche that it cannot be properly processed; the result is a sense of death that continually resides with us. Living in the midst of this loss places us in a liminal state where life and death are inseparable. Rambo characterizes this middle space as "the figurative site in which life and death are no longer bounded. Instead, the middle speaks to the perplexing space of survival." This middle space "is subject to elisions of time, body, and language and is therefore difficult to witness."[20] This concept of an existential middle can be applied to the event in Eden, which is fraught with a similar complexity and ambiguity: The death that enters the world because of Eve's curious taste buds places humanity into such a "perplexing space of survival" where life—the world of relationship, evolution, and transformation—is always entangled with loss. Often within the wake of trauma, we are left to experience what Rambo calls "death in life," a sense of death that is always present and folded into living.[21] Embracing the entwined reality of the death-in-life experience requires allowing the bite to take place—either our own or that of the other. Cixous's encounter with Fips and Eve's encounter with the apple are brave ventures into the fleshy interior that allow us to see the meat that we are instead of the invulnerable body that we wish to be. To encounter flesh is to risk being made unclean by making contact with unknown ontological depths.

Allowing ourselves to inhabit a liminal experience of death in life may also offer a unique experience of the spirit: As we fold ourselves into the intensity of flesh's vulnerability, the expansiveness of the spirit reveals itself in new ways. Cixous's revelation arrives only after she has experienced the extreme fragility of her body and its relationship to the other. We might say, then, that exploring the flesh in its full intensity—its potential for devouring as well as being devoured—allows a unique space for transcendence within the creaturely body. Perhaps the limits of the body are not necessarily in opposition to the infinity of the divine, but rather are part of a path to the spirit. The flesh/spirit relationship then becomes part of a constant experiential exchange that fosters the ontological change necessary for revelation. Although the presentation of spirit and flesh as an oppositional dichotomy is prevalent in traditional Christian scriptures such as John, we find alternative notions of the body from other Christian sources. In the *Gospel of Thomas* Jesus proclaims, "Whoever has come to know the world has discovered the body, and whoever has discovered the body, of that one the world is not worthy" (*Gospel of Thomas* 87). This mysterious proclamation suggests, among other things, that we do not quite know what the body *is*. What does it mean to discover the body instead of simply having one? The discovery, though, as we see from Cixous's encounter with Fips, does not arise from a place of corporeal intactness; realizing "the meat that we are" arrives through somatic exposure. The theologian Sharon Betcher suggests that preoccupation with bodily wholeness as presented in the traditional Christian context creates a harmful "eschatological idealism," a delusion that salvation and the wholesome body are linked. Persons with disabilities, she insists, "refuse to be resolved, saved, made whole," choosing instead "our histories of flesh."[22] The history of flesh may indeed prove key to our soteriological approach: If the body is always being discovered and revised, then refusing somatic resolution may offer a path toward revelation. The human body that recognizes itself as animal, that refuses to resolve, also retains its sense of creational process, history, and relationality. The body then becomes a paradoxical integration of both predictable material limits and perpetual novelty. This is, Derrida explains, Christ's own corporeal process. Derrida notes that "one also speaks of the invention of the body of Christ to designate an experience that consists in discovering, in an inaugural fashion, to be sure, but all the same a body that was already there, in some place or other, and that had to be found, discovered, *invented*. Even though it unveils the body of what was already there, this invention is an event."[23] Although Christ had a body like any other, the body of Christ as "invented" in a soteriological context produces an event of somatic novelty. Recognizing the Lamb of God as invention has interesting implications for our own somatic futures; the body of Christ, while in many ways unique unto itself, has the potential to guide a unique discovery of our own bodies. We too have "histories of flesh" that, when open, can guide us toward the transcendent. To imitate Christ is perhaps not just to follow Jesus' actions based on scriptural study, but also to aspire to the eventiveness of Christ's body as both human and animal. Seen from this perspective, we might find that the vulnerability of the flesh—the potential for openings, scars, and depressions—is not a flaw to be overcome, but rather that which makes possible our experience of the infinite.

And yet engaging the flesh in this way demands that our sense of the body become strangely both more precise in its sensitivity and less robust in its demand for corporeal organization. If we are to allow ourselves to be consumed, we must see and experience ourselves as structurally open, as human and as animal, as consumers and as food. Burrus points out that flesh in the Johannine text "is the only food that matters. . . . Flesh precedes, saturates, and exceeds the cosmos. . . . It is crucial to both the making and the unmaking of the body, constituting the womb as well as the ongoing source of nurturance for 'eternal life.'"[24] It is no secret that food affects our bodies; but this call for radical consumption seems to point to the fact that we need to experience the effect of this food, to be likewise totally consumed by what we eat. This is, as Burrus notes, partly an "unmaking" of the body: We must open ourselves not only to eat and experience, but to reconsider what food actually is. Divine nourishment may arrive as a seemingly indigestible and improper event. But if our bodies are unmade as well as made, we may sustain enough permeability to allow a radical exchange between self and other, humanity and divinity. John's consumptive trope suggests that the truth may lie in the tender area of somatic mystery that both holds and refuses structure, where our cosmic womb is woven from flesh that is cut through, but not apart, where eternal / maternal nurturance arrives along with the marks of impermanence and death.

Following the biblical theme of consumption may lead us to a perhaps counterintuitive connection between our unmaking and connectivity. The call to consume Christ is not simply a demand to dissolve oneself and become one with God, but to partake in a somatic experience that allows the deepest kind of relationality. The call to unmake ourselves in the process of consuming and being consumed is not a mandate for individual salvation, but a call to experience a kind of death that is necessary for authentic love. Jesus' famous commandment to "love one another as I have loved you," although widely embraced, still exists in the realm of the abstract (John 15:12). How do we practice this (r)evolutionary love that remains so elusive? If we explore the consumptive trope in John as the psychic and physical manifestation of this commandment, we may find that the act of love becomes more textured and multilayered. Jesus as the lamb who both consumes his flock and is in turn consumed offers a somatic vision of the radical openness required for authentic relationship. Cixous herself delves into this space of animalistic mystery where love and the open body meet. For Cixous, seeing ourselves as animal is not simply a matter of seeing another side of the human, but rather uncovering the root of human relationality. "The wolf," she tells us, "is the truth of love, its cruelty, its fangs, its claws, our aptitude for ferocity. Love is when you suddenly wake up as a cannibal, and not just any old cannibal, or else wake up destined for devourment."[25]

Love, for Cixous, requires the depth that comes with devouring, where an open self is a self actively engaged with both life and death. Recognizing ourselves as animal flesh is indeed key, it seems, as we see in Cixous's meditation on Rembrandt's *The Slaughtered Ox*, a portrait of a flayed ox hung upside down tied to a wooden pole. "Why do we adore *The Slaughtered Ox*?" Cixous asks. "Because," she replies for us, "without our knowing it or wanting it, it is our anonymous humanity."[26] The lifeless flesh of the flayed ox resonates with our sense of helplessness, the raw vulnerability of "our captivity."[27] As Pyper describes Cixous's reading, "The ox, luminous, cruciform, is the interior exposed. It is meat, but not yet meat; it is butchery, but also beauty, it is shocking and it is iconic." And yet Pyper also notes that Cixous both implies and denies the ox's wider biblical implications. She protests, "We are not Christ, never, Christ. . . . No, I will not speak of this."[28] Pyper remarks on this omission, interjecting, "Where Cixous won't go, Stephen Moore will," drawing out Moore's connection of the slaughtered body to the body of Christ.[29]

Indeed, Moore begins *God's Gym* with a confession that his father was a butcher, who was indeed even "a lover of lamb with mint sauce."[30] His childhood visual memories include "the filling of basins with blood" and "the crimson floor littered with hooves."[31] Unlike Cixous, Moore does not shy away from connecting the butchered animals' sacrifice to Christ's crucifixion. Sights of the butcher's knives and narratives of "the atrocious agony felt by our sensitive Saviour as the spikes were driven through his wrists and feet" easily blend in Moore's childhood imagination.[32] This connection allows us to see the *Slaughtered Ox* as a portrait of Christ's own somatic performance. The "anonymous humanity" that Cixous identifies with the ox is both ours and Christ's, the animal flesh becoming an anonymous but universal indicator of vulnerability. Cixous even reminds us that "as children we would pass trembling before the butcher's window. Later on we want to forget death. We cut the dead one up into pieces and we call it meat."[33] Moore, with childhood memories of butchery and church in the fore, is able to remember both death and Christ, bringing us to the space where Cixous will not quite go. But Cixous's cataphatic refusal to speak of the flayed ox as both humanity and Christ, in essence, creates the connection for her. The very nature of flesh's overflow that Cixous so adeptly establishes cannot simply touch the biblical without also being an innate part of its performance. And it seems that the drawing together of the animal, the human, and the divine at the moment of sacrifice on the cross leads us to the somatic space that Cixous wants us to inhabit: where vulnerability allows love in its fullest expression.

Although Cixous never directly ties love to the divine, we do not have to travel far to find hints of transcendence in Cixous's work. Fips as Christ figure is both the attacker and the persecuted teacher, the wolf and the lamb. The lesson is no ordinary one by Cixous's own admission: Her Fips-inspired transformation is indeed a revelation, teaching a love so profound that she is ready to give her life for it. But this love is ultimately accessible only through a sense of something in Fips that extends beyond ordinary ontology: "At the bottom of the bottom of all my ignorances, I must have had a prescience inaccessible to myself, that this my dog was something else, that he *was*, much more than I, and that I do not know what a dog is nor what being a dog is."[34] Although Cixous never claims Fips *is* Christ, his strong somatic presence and his grief-stricken bite do lead Cixous to approach the transcendent through the animal, to experience a kind of re-lationship that could come about only through the clash of animal bodies. As "the meat" revealed by Fips's bite and in the portrait of *The Slaughtered Ox*, we are not only subject to the same vulnerabilities that the flesh re-veals but also capable of the same revelations. The vulnerability of animal flesh, as the sacrificial lamb demonstrates, can potentially lead us to the transcendent love of the divine. To realize that our extreme vulnerability is linked to our potential for the transcendent is to come closer to the de-vouring "truth of love," that fully inhabits our ability, need, and desire to taste and be tasted, to embody both the "anonymous humanity" of the ox and the devouring nature of the wolf.

This corporeal openness of consumption, I suggest, is the openness of the divine: It is the act that Jesus performs on the cross as an animal carcass, not simply exposing corporeal vulnerability as an act of love but asking that this vulnerability become our food and nourishment. And al-though Keener may not be wrong in his assertion that the biblical text is not instructing us to consume flesh literally, he is not quite right, ei-ther: The way we have consumed scripture historically goes beyond the literal or figurative. The Eucharist is a strangely routine Christian meal, a performance of consumptive salvation. Fear of the animal, of the "meat we are," then, becomes fear of not only our vulnerability but also our capacity for the infinite. Cixous locates this fear in our fear of the animal other, warning us: "A dog is a threat. What is threatening about a dog is their terrible love. . . . Meeting a dog you suddenly see the abyss of love. Such limitless love doesn't fit our economy. We cannot cope with such an open, superhuman relation."[35] The dog, perhaps, reveals our limitations whether it actually bites us nor not. And yet we can also remind ourselves that, as Jacques Derrida avers, "What threatens is also what makes possible the expectation or the promise."[36] To lose ourselves in the animal—as the animal—threatens us with the possibility of corporeal and perhaps psychic rupture. But what we potentially gain is the promise of the divine: the radical fold of relationality that forms the crux of Christ's simultaneously mundane and revelatory body. The scriptural word of the lamb is always a bit bitter, hinting at the threat of somatic dissolution. But if we meet that threat instead of resisting it, we may find ourselves at the edge of transcendence, where we have the capacity to transform that which we call "human" into something more human/e. We may even become a creature that abides, shockingly, in the wisdom of the flesh, with the ability to have the integrity of a body willing to be unmade at any moment.

◆ The Microbes and Pneuma That Therefore I Am

DENISE KIMBER BUELL

How connected we are with everyone.

The space of everyone that has just been inside of everyone mixing inside of everyone with nitrogen and oxygen and water vapor and argon and carbon dioxide and suspended dust spores and bacteria mixing inside of everyone with sulfur and sulfuric acid and titanium and nickel and minute silicon particles from pulverized glass and concrete.
—JULIANA SPAHR, "Poem Written after September 11, 2001"

Juliana Spahr's poem mimics the pulsation of breathing. She begins small: "Everyone with lungs breathes the space in and out as everyone with lungs breathes the space between the hands in and out,"[1] progressively extending this pneumatic interaction to a room, building, neighborhood, city, region, nation, continents, islands, oceans, troposphere, stratosphere, and finally mesosphere. From the all-encompassing mesospheric interconnection, Spahr reverses direction back to the hands to conclude the poem with the excerpt of the epigraph above. Here, she introduces a tragic dimension of breathing—the blasted bits from the twin towers inhaled by survivors, rescuers, and city residents[2]—closing the poem with this line: "How lovely and how doomed this connection of everyone with lungs."

By invoking various agents in the air (elements, dust spores, bacteria, the toxic dust arising from the wreckage of the twin towers), Spahr thus complicates what might have appeared to be simply a positive image of the way breath forms us interrelationally. Breath does not respect the kinds of borders we have created to group and divide humans as well as to distinguish humans from nonhumans and the environment. Invisible particles in the air we breathe partly arise from but also exceed the effects of human actions. As Nancy Tuana put it, "The boundaries between our flesh and the flesh of the world we are of and in is [sic] porous. While that porosity is what allows us to flourish—as we breathe in oxygen we need to survive and metabolize the nutrients out of which our flesh emerges—this porosity often does not discriminate against that which can kill us."[3] For Spahr, the breath both connects those with lungs and is the medium that transports particles and life-forms that alter us; in turn, we mix them inside us and return new breath to the spaces between us for others to inhale.

Spahr's poem and the "viscous porosity" of being that Tuana articulates offer a way of thinking about the meaning and place of the human in the cosmos that is radically relational and radically vulnerable. To begin to forge a "creaturely theology" that can resist anthropocentrism,[4] I argue that we need a relational ontology that imagines all beings as complex systems interacting with and being produced in relationship with other complex systems.[5] Agencies that are not immediately or easily visible, such as pneuma and microbes, serve as effective examples for how we can shift our epistemological lenses toward such a relational ontology. I build especially on the work of some feminist scholars who ask us to understand that what we are and how we live (and could live) defy claims of both species-boundedness and definitions of agency as the exertion of an individual's will on distinct others. Radically, they call for rethinking being, including "humanness," as the result rather than precondition of interactions and intra-actions.[6] Stacy Alaimo, Karen Barad, Donna Haraway, Myra Hird, Vicki Kirby, Nancy Tuana, and Elizabeth Wilson recast agency to account for nonhuman forces, ranging from nonhuman animals to the environment (radon, silicone, hurricanes), to political institutions, capitalism, language, and the complex interrelations among these.[7] This work argues for the continuous process of materializing differences, asking us to reframe our understanding of subjectivity and agency, and thus also of how "we" as humans are not only the result of ongoing material encounters but also that, in our being human, we are not separable from the "environment" or other "animals," including "microbes."

I see two challenging implications arising from this shift in how we think about the human: First, it underscores the vulnerability of being human, and second, it raises questions about ethics and accountability. Pneuma and microbes both *are* us and may cross our porous flesh, for better or for worse. Spahr passingly mentions "bacteria" as one kind of content in the air we breathe and share with others through the space between us. Breath turns out to be its own kind of shifting, materially complex agency, chemical but not of any single, static composition. Bacteria can be part of the invisible breath we inhale or exhale; moreover, bacteria and other microbes are integral to and constitutive of what we consider our human bodies.[8] Indeed, in the case of microbes, we must consider being human also as a community of microorganisms. But these nearly invisible agencies may be dangerous or deadly to the human, just as other organic and inorganic compounds that cross corporeal boundaries through breathing, eating, or absorption may be dangerous. This profound relationality is not simply something to celebrate; it is also unsettling.

Furthermore, this relational way of thinking about being may seem to undermine calls to action or accountability. After all, if the human is rethought as a community of microorganisms, constantly coming-into-being from my intra-actions with visible and invisible agencies, does this let me off the hook for environmental disaster as well as abusive relations of power among humans or between those communities produced as human in relationship to those produced as nonhuman animals? Such an interactive and intra-active understanding of being and becoming destabilizes any claims to fixed boundaries between human and nonhuman, let alone any claims to human superiority over nonhumans. Nonetheless, it is still possible to speak about accountability and ethics.[9] What counts as "waste"? What kinds of waste we generate and where we put it, for example, are decisions "we" as "humans" make (as individuals but also as groups and institutions), whose effects clearly give the lie to neat distinctions between humans and other living beings as well as organic and inorganic. Humans and nonhumans alike are significantly affected by the disposition and decomposition (or off-gassing, or preservation) of what we call waste (itself a relational product, of course). Waste produces material differences among living beings (those who breathe, absorb, and become in relation to the chemicals, life-forms, and compounds in any garbage dump), differences that produce differences among humans (often linked to political, structural arrangements of power and manifested as biological or neurological effects) but also that connect microbes, insects, rodents, humans, and other creatures.

At the same time, we are not fully in control of defining and interacting with waste, insofar as worms, microbes, chemical compounds, and other agents also make and remake it and its implications. Thinking in terms of the webs of relation, impact, and transformations entailed in the generation, placement, and treatment of waste calls us to form ethical responses that do not make sharp cuts between political and biological (where Superfund sites or dumps are placed in relation to the physiological impact on the water, dirt, air, and human and nonhuman animals), let alone the boundaries between human and nonhuman (toxin-infused dirt in which plants are grown that human and nonhuman animals alike partake of).

Attention to bacteria, viruses, protists, and other microbes from the vantage point of relational ontologies can help formulate positions on agency and ethics to evaluate afresh ancient views and practices.[10] In turn, ancient views about largely invisible agencies (such as pneuma and divinities) let us consider the implications in the range of modern views about largely invisible agencies (including microbial ones). By evaluating how temporally disparate examples articulate relational ontologies, we may interrogate both the value and limits of relational notions of becoming and being for crafting nonanthropocentric "creaturely theologies" for the present and future.

Spahr's poem presumes what Stacy Alaimo calls "trans-corporeality," that breath connects us with other agencies in ways that alter us and by which we are also agents of change.[11] Nancy Tuana's elegant phrase "viscous porosity" similarly emphasizes interactions across permeable boundaries that may result in transformations, for good or ill:[12] "There is a viscous porosity of flesh—my flesh and the flesh of the world. . . . I refer to it as viscous, for there are membranes that effect the interactions. *These membranes are of various types—skin and flesh, prejudgments and symbolic imaginaries, habits and embodiments.* They serve as mediators of interaction."[13] In other words, we may understand ourselves to be intact beings, with "cells, the movement of cells and the division of cells and then the general beating circulation and hands, and body and feet and skin that surrounds hands, body, feet,"[14] but this shape, although real, results from dynamic interactions and remains dynamic. As Sara Ahmed puts it, "Encounters are prior to ontology, the concept of separate beings is produced through the encounter, rather than preceding it."[15] Even textual productions such as poems and gospels, and their afterlives, are material results of encounters. That is, language, even the logos, matters; these material-discursive intra-actions may produce or unsettle human/nonhuman distinctions.[16] These encounters are fleshy but also, crucially, symbolic—Spahr's poem, not simply the breath about which she writes, matters.

This relational ontology has the potential to disrupt an assertion of an ontological break between "human" and other life-forms, but it does not ensure a disruption of anthropocentrism.[17] For example, even as it situates the breathers in relation to microscopic particles and the immense mesosphere, Spahr's poem implicitly positions humans as the referents of the "everyone with lungs"; other breathing life-forms are absent. In biblical and ancient noncanonical writings we also find pneumatic interaction used to construe the human as an entity formed and transformed through relational interactions, though in different ways from those in Spahr's poem.[18] In the second creation account (Gen. 2:4b–3:24), pneuma (or *ruah*) appears to mark what is distinctive about the human relative to other breathing life-forms—the human is the creature animated by divine breath: "Then the Lord God formed man of dust from the ground, and breathed into his nostrils the breath of life; and man became a living being" (2:7, RSV).[19] That is, there may be many kinds of creatures with lungs, but only the creature Adam explicitly receives the divine exhalation, figured as a key ingredient that renders it alive and different from other creatures.[20] Pneuma is not simply air that is breathed, but a special kind of enlivening substance.

Microbes, as well as other organic and inorganic compounds that may invisibly make up the air we breathe, are provocatively comparable to pneuma in ancient texts where it appears as breath but is also distinguishable as a special material agency that may travel through the air or by other means (through the waters of baptism, the spoken word figured as flesh, the Eucharistic elements figured as flesh and blood). Ancient and modern texts abound with assertions of the power of invisible agencies that exceed, enable, and often threaten humans. In both ancient discussions (not just Christian ones) of and practices pertaining to daimones and divinities, on the one hand, and, on the other hand, modern discussions of and practices pertaining to microbes, invisible forces are invested with agency—they are imagined and engaged as being and acting from without and from within bodies—humans as well as other animals, plants, earth, and even things such as statues.

Indeed, the formation of Christian ideas and practices turned in no small part on claims to understand, speak for, and produce reliable technologies for relating to and with invisible agencies. These agencies were not conceived of as microbes but as an array of forces depicted in terms such as daimones, archons, astrological powers, elements, psyche, deities, speech (logos), and pneuma. Ancient texts likewise offer accounts of how humanness, animality, divinity, and other possible categories of being (including sexual difference and status) are not things we and others have but are things that get determined through and at the level of encounters. In their writings and practices, early Christians parsed the distinctions and relations among humans, divinities, animals, and other kinds of beings—living (e.g., trees) and inanimate (e.g., statues)—partly in terms of the character and results of interactions among invisible and visible agencies.[21] If this is the case, we can ask about encounters that produce and relate provisional beings rather than static "others."[22]

One challenge of comparing the relational ontologies of ancient texts and modern thinkers is that the ancient sources often appear to define pneumatic substance as the true self, in contrast to the sense- and passion-filled body or flesh to be managed and ruled. This hierarchy of pneuma over flesh can be expressed so as to try to produce humans whose porous relationship with their environments—including the fleshy body—is a problem to be managed by crafting, as much as possible, a human separated from that environment, a human defined as essentially spirit. Microbes, in contrast, would seem to keep us fully in the realm of the biological and material. Comparing microbes with pneuma asks us to consider pneuma in radically materialized, fleshy terms, on the one hand; on the other hand, rather than quibble over whether pneuma could be viewed as material in antiquity (it could, as the Stoics attest), my interest in juxtaposing microbes and pneuma rests more with their related roles in figuring being and agency relationally.

But I do not merely want to note that both microbes and pneuma play analogous roles as transcorporeal agencies. Nor do I want to argue that microbes are nearly invisible creatures we should love for themselves, subordinating "the human" to its microbial alter. Nor do I think we ought to privilege pneuma over any other agency. Rather, I want to take microbes and pneuma as material and symbolic occasions to rethink agency and being such that we cannot presume the boundedness of humans or any other kind of creature. As I noted above, this approach is both exhilarating and terrifying in that it underscores the radical vulnerability of all creatures, including human ones, in ways that require a response. After all, some microbes are deadly to the collective life-form we understand ourselves to be as human. The promises linked to pneuma in ancient texts might provide some unexpected resources and cautions for crafting an environmentally responsible and nonanthropocentric ethics and theology in an endangered, dangerous, messy, beautiful cosmos. Likewise, they offer additional ways to analyze articulations of power and difference among humans.

VISCOUS POROSITY OF PNEUMA IN EARLY CHRISTIAN WRITINGS

The kinds of worlds and ethics that might be forged in the light of relational ontologies remain to be negotiated. I am arguing that a robust creaturely theology needs a relational ontology, and specifically that we need to ask whether and in what ways ancient and current sources offer relational ontologies that do not simply reinscribe anthropocentric epistemologies and ethics or oppressive relations of power among humans. Spahr's poem is still anthropocentric; Genesis and most early Christian texts generally frame relational interactions in clear hierarchies either among humans or between humans and other beings (divinity is superior because it is the creator/source of pneuma in humans; humans in turn are depicted as superior to other creatures, and those humans who receive divine pneuma in baptism are depicted as superior to other humans). I am interested in relational ontologies that account for dynamic materialized differences without naturalizing hierarchies that are used to justify oppressive or exploitative arrangements of power.

To craft a theology and/or ontology whose ethical outcomes can wisely inherit and transform the resources of Christian theological tradition (whether for Christian ends or not), we need to discern and evaluate both contemporary and ancient forms of relational understandings. When I speak of inheriting, I am following Jacques Derrida's discussion of inheritance as a process of ethical responsibility of choosing from a legacy that is never unified or singular, but always heterogeneous: An inheritance is that which one must *"reaffirm by choosing. . . . One must* filter, sift, criticize, one must sort out the several different possibles that inhabit the same injunction."[23] That is, there is nothing fixed or unified about an inheritance, including Christian tradition and scriptures; these must be re-affirmed, criticized, or transformed in the present, ongoingly.

In many texts that we read retrospectively as formulations of early Christianity, divine pneuma recurs as a key element. Even if understood as part of what makes a human a human at all, as in readings of Genesis 2, pneuma is also depicted as something humans can or still need to acquire. In the writings of Paul and in the Fourth Gospel, for example, we find pneuma used to mark a distinctively superior kind of human, such that the human/other creatures divide is sometimes displaced by attention to differences among humans according to how humans interact with divine and demonic spiritual powers.

In his letter to the Galatians, Paul asserts that God has "sent the *pneuma* of his son into our hearts," vividly portraying the transformation that ac-ceptance of Paul's gospel materializes through baptism as one from "slaves to elemental powers" to adopted sons of God (Gal. 4:3, 5–6). According to this imagery, receiving divine pneuma alters the status and lineage of the recipients, thus distinguishing them categorically from other kinds of hu-mans.[24] For Paul, pneuma rather than, say, oxygen (and whatever life-forms or chemicals might bind with it), is the agential force humans need to make our embodied selves truly live, a point that he makes vividly also in his let-ter to the Romans.[25] This transformation is at once material and symbolic.[26]

Along similar lines, the early second-century C.E. *Apocryphon of John* pro-claims that "those on whom the *pneuma* of life will descend" will be saved (*Apocryphon of John*, Nag Hammadi Library, II 25.23–24), ideally by the re-cipient's aligning his or her life with its power but also by the pneuma's transformation of the recipient (26.10–19). This text contrasts the pneuma of life with the "counterfeit [or despicable] *pneuma*" created by the "rul-ers of this world."[27] The counterfeit pneuma is meant to prevent humans from realizing our true connection with and return to the realm of the true god (26.20–22; 26.36–27.11; 27.32–30.11).[28]

In the *Apocryphon of John*, the human is imagined as the composite prod-uct of relations with external agencies, notably divine and debased cosmic powers. Humans have three constituent elements: a soul (psyche), formed by the rulers of this world, based on a reflection projected from the perfect heavenly realm (see Gen. 1:26–27); a spirit (pneuma) (Gen. 2:7) that links us substantively to the perfect realm; and the stuff that forms the fleshy (*hylic*) body enclosing these other finer aspects (Gen. 2:7).[29] Genesis 2:7 provides a key reference point for explaining how the initial creation of humans entailed the infusion of pneumatic essence from the realm of the true God, of the same essence as that perfect spirit contemporary humans will receive, which will ultimately serve as the basis of their salvation.[30]

The Fourth Gospel likewise echoes and extends Genesis 2. In one of his resurrection appearances, "Jesus said to [some of his disciples], 'Peace be with you. As the Father has sent me, even so I send you.' And when he had said this, *he breathed on them*, and said to them, 'Receive the holy spirit [*pneuma*]. If you forgive the sins of any, they are forgiven'" (John 20:21–23). In this context, Jesus' special exhalation doesn't simply make the recipients alive, as God's spirit does for Adam, but also grants them powers the gospel attributes to Jesus himself as God's agent. Instead of all humans receiving this additional pneuma, however, now only certain individuals are so privileged, suggesting a hierarchy linked to reception of pneuma even among followers of Jesus.

Central to the Fourth Gospel's project is the interpretation of scripture to link pneuma with the figure of Jesus. The speech attributed to Jesus in which he interprets the Exodus experience, notably the divine provision of manna to the Israelites in the wilderness, serves as a way for the gospel to suture its opening identification of Jesus as the enfleshed form of God's preexistent logos, the instrument of creation, with Jesus as the one whose flesh and blood needs to be ingested to have real, eternal life: "Unless you eat the flesh of the son of man and drink his blood, you have no life in you; one who eats my flesh and drinks my blood has eternal life" (John 6:53). The passage stresses the transcorporeal and transformative effects of this ingestion: "Those who eat my flesh and drink my blood abide in me, and I in them" (6:56). The narrative presents the audience, even Jesus' disciples, as resistant to this teaching; he further explains to his disciples: "It is the spirit [*pneuma*] that gives life; the flesh is of no avail; the words [*rhēmata*] that I have spoken to you are spirit and life" (6:63). Here, pneuma travels as speech, but it is also ingestible substance that creates life, transtemporally bringing together the moment of creation and the moment of resurrection through transcorporeality.

These ancient examples demonstrate some kinds of relational ontologies that foreground pneuma. They presume that the human will inevitably be affected by transcorporeal interactions. In these examples, pneuma figures linguistically the kinds of relations advocated and is used to argue that such relations are made, or enacted, through corporeal action; readers need to know about and engage in material practices to effect changes, although the texts may nonetheless insist that "the flesh is of no avail." The individual does not have full control over his or her interactions with external agencies, but the texts instruct readers how to respond to this inevitability. They assume that humans are viscously porous and offer arguments about the kinds of membranes humans have and how one should negotiate the inevitable porousness by trying to produce specific kinds of membranes of symbolic imaginaries (see also, e.g., Justin Martyr, *First Apology* 14.1; Tatian, *Oration to the Greeks* 13–15; Irenaeus, *Against Heresies* 3.8.2; Clement of Alexandria, *Excerpts of Theodotos* 67.1–73.3).[31]

It should be clear by now that recuperating relationality risks reinscribing the kinds of gendered, racist, and anthropocentric relations identified as problematic in the so-called enlightenment notions of "rational man." Although one's material context matters hugely, including for the very organic composition of one's being, it does not transparently determine how one knows or frames the world. The viscous membranes of our prejudgments and symbolic imaginaries are not neatly separable from those of our habits and embodiments, as Tuana insists. In other words, the premodern Christian tradition offers us both more viscously porous understandings of being that we might want to inherit (even if transforming in the process) and a legacy of anthropocentrism that modern humanism inherited. Premodern anthropologies and theologies transmitted textually are vitally important for us to put into conversation with current work to produce relational ontologies so that we do not perpetuate anthropocentric ethics likely to be deadly to this planet and many life-forms, including humans.

MEDIATING MEMBRANES

Attuning ourselves to the discourses and practices of invisible agents helps us ask how the quite recent articulation of microbial invisible agencies may mediate our understanding and reception of ancient claims about invisible agencies and unsettle the notion of rupture between premodern and modern ways of conceptualizing the human.

To bring ancient and contemporary materials together, we need to revisit the narratives in play that have worked to create a rift. One still widespread story narrates a "disenchantment" whereby humans, at least the "enlightened" or "civilized" ones, came to realize that nonhuman agencies were illusory, a view that affirms a kind of authority to (at least some) humans for making truthful knowledge claims about the world and the relationships various humans and other beings have in and with it. This story offers a specific way to inherit earlier epistemological / ontological frameworks, including Christian ones that emphasize self-cultivation in a hierarchical progression, such as from animal / slave / female to human / free / male. This story masks the way in which even "modern" European and white U.S. American notions of the human, through most of the nineteenth century, did not view the body as

a clearly bounded entity, separate and distinct from its surroundings; rather, it was porous and permeable. The skin did not close off an individual, separating him or her from the larger world. The body flowed into the environment, and the environment seeped into an individual body—through the air one breathed, the food one ate, the water one drank. These interactions were not only unavoidable; they were critical to health as well as illness. . . . A given environment inevitably left its mark in a body's shape, color, and strength, while radical changes in a person's environment could effect wondrous cures or induce sudden illness.[32]

Linda Nash artfully links this viscously porous view of the body both with ancient Hippocratic humoral theory and with specific modern concerns about race and white settler colonization of the Pacific coast of North America: "Health was not the product of successfully closing off a body from external influences but of intelligently managing the relationship between an individual and his or her surroundings";[33] "the local environment was sometimes healthful and sometimes threatening—but it was always active, contingent, and relevant to the bodies that resided there."[34] Nash contrasts this place-specific way of thinking about both health and self with the "germ theory" that supplants it in the late nineteenth century as the dominant medical model in North America and Europe with the rise of microbial discourse.

In the latter part of the nineteenth century, some scientists and hygienists redefined social relations by insisting that "society is not made up of just [humans], for everywhere microbes intervene and act."[35] As Bruno La-tour stresses in his analysis of the movement surrounding Louis Pasteur in France, this redefinition extended to relations not just among humans but other living beings. "No one," Latour writes, "toward the end of the [nine-teenth] century, could do without contagion in connecting men, plants, and animals."[36] One of these nineteenth-century writers, Louis Capitan, put it this way: "Society can exist, live, and survive only thanks to the con-stant intervention of microbes, the great deliverers of death, but also dis-pensers of matter."[37] Here we see a late nineteenth-century example of how the social and natural are not imagined as separable domains, nor is one reducible to the other:

> [Capitan] does not base society on biology . . . ; he redefines soci-ety itself, a society in which the new agents intervene now and at all points. . . . Microbes connect us through diseases, but *they* also connect us, through our intestinal flora, to the very things we eat: "We can hardly doubt the importance of the role played in the econ-omy of the individual by those table companions that help it break down organic substances." "Interdependence," "assistance," "power," "help," "table companions"—I have not imposed these terms. . . . It is the actors that thus redefine their worlds and decide what now must be taken into account.[38]

But how did it come to be known that "microbes are the third party in all relations"? Through those who produced the specialized knowledge about microbes, the "revealer of microbes"—the "Pasteurians," as Latour dubs them—scientists such as Louis Pasteur himself, who did the laboratory ex-periments and wrote up their work: "In redefining the social link as being made up everywhere of microbes, Pasteurians and hygienists regained the power to be present everywhere. . . . They become the spokesmen for these new innumerable, invisible, and dangerous agents."[39] And of course their work was simultaneously material: They were also the ones who designed and implemented new regimes for public health as well as vaccines.

Thus, even when not invoking spirits and demons, modern folks have regularly viewed themselves as part of a larger and largely invisible world, in which nonhuman agents interact with humans ongoingly. New versions of portraying and shaping human existence in relation to nonhuman agencies emerge in this apparently disenchanted era, notably discourses about microbes but also about spirits, electricity, nation, and capital among others.[40] But the shift from a place-based theory to a germ-theory understanding of health is not so straightforward as the replacing of one kind of account of the external agencies that affect humans with another.

This is because we are doubly heirs to this Pasteurized world and to ancient theological frameworks that offer varied ways of imagining how we are or come to be "human" or something else. We are no strangers to thinking with the idea of nonhuman agencies. Nonetheless, how we think and live with them matters. The Pasteurians proposed a way of thinking and acting about microbes that did not simply enfranchise their specialized knowledge and techniques; it also offered an understanding of the human as inevitably vulnerable and porous but in addition, paradoxically, as an entity to be contained, stabilized, and separated.

As noted earlier, biblical and early Christian treatments of pneuma certainly presume that humans interact with and are transformed by nonhuman agencies; at the same time, they are rhetorically unfolded to work to stabilize the boundaries of the human in particular ways. Indeed, early Christian writings share with Pasteurians a claim to provide effective technologies for stabilizing or transforming the human to achieve the optimal relations with invisible agencies.

In modern texts and lab practices, microbes transform inanimate matter (producing oxygen and food from inorganic compounds), can move through the air, and act in and through any manner of living organisms, not unlike stories told about how daimones and divinities may also animate and act through inanimate matter such as statues or natural elements and flora. Also in both ancient and modern contexts, these invisible agencies are discursively figured as forces that may harm or help. In ancient contexts, some illnesses may be understood as the work of invading daimones, and much modern writing about microbes casts them as primarily agents of disease. Through prophylactic prayer and practice one might ward off or expel such harmful spirits, perhaps through a dream vision from a healing god such as Asklepios prescribing the proper treatment or, today, through antibiotics. Divine pneuma may help heal and protect; so too can we speak about so-called good microbes as probiotics or controlled doses of virulent microbes (i.e., vaccinations) as protection against accidental and possibly deadly exposure to the same microbes.[41]

In producing a creaturely theology we need to grapple with the extent to which early Christian writings and readings of them, like nineteenth-century germ theory, also attempt to reformulate the human as ideally separable from the world, with practices and imagery of sealing or warding off or isolating that deny or suppress the competing paradigms of environmental interaction present in humoral theory. Furthermore, these early Christian texts may mask countervailing early Christian practices discernible through evidence such as amulets, spells, and divination techniques.[42] A brief examination of the current legacies of microbe theory will allow consideration of how a selective (feminist materialist) inheritance concerning microbes may be brought together with a selective inheritance of early Christian resources to help craft an effective creaturely theology.

INHERITING MICROBE THEORY

We are bombarded with the message that microbes are the invisible enemy. In addition to lacking the visibility and positive concern sparked by "big-like-us" animals, bacteria bear the brunt of quite relentless negative marketing and media. It is hard to avoid antibacterial soap and other cleaning products in stores or advertisements these days; every public restroom admonishes us to wash our hands (mandating it for employees), and hand sanitizers are ubiquitous. Few of us want to linger in hospitals; now we can add fear of contracting a MRSA (multiresistant strep) infection. Biological weapons (think anthrax) and species-leaping microbes (think "swine" flu or "bird" flu) are the stuff of modern warfare, medical research, and mass media.

TV shows such as *How Clean Is Your House?* (BBC America) feature a scare-tactic "reveal" based on the results of lab cultures of various bacteria samples swabbed from kitchens, bathrooms, pillowcases, couches, and other items. A mixture of social commentary about the moral shame of lazy living, homey tips for natural cleaners (made from things such as lemons or vinegar), and high-tech laboratory testing—every episode of *How Clean Is Your House?* communicates the message that a dirty home is a dangerous home, teeming with invisible agents that threaten to make you, your children, and your pets sick—even kill you. More than this, the show suggests that by following the experts' advice about how to clean properly and regularly one can extirpate the deadly microbes, and that clean living is happier and better living.

This kind of message is consistent with the idea that microbial illness is "essentially punitive," a view promoted notoriously around HIV-infection (especially in the 1980s) as well as in the film *Contagion* (Warner Brothers, 2011), about an imaginary pandemic. A *New York Times* article about the film stresses how it relied on "real" scientists and that "numerous studies have linked the origins of viruses to ecological transgressions like climate change and the loss of natural habitats. . . . 'This is about the process of being alive and sharing the planet,' [Steven] Soderbergh [the director] said."[43] Whether in the home, the environment, or on the big screen, microbial boundary-breachings are portrayed as a problem—primarily as a threat to humans, even if human activity and choices are held up as the reasons why dangerous and deadly invisible microbes invade us in the first place.

This way of understanding microbes and their interactions with humans is not simply a matter of how humans are defined as distinct from, in opposition to, and as of greater worth than microbes. We need to bear in mind how intrahuman differentiation and oppressive policies have sometimes built directly on this logic, with certain humans being collectively defined as agents of disease (as has been the case for the ways that HIV infection has been twinned with homophobia, racism, and imperialism) and/or the kind of human who lives in infested living conditions and spreads unhealthy microbes. An example from recent headlines illustrates this latter point. The French Interior Ministry justified the destruction of Roma camps in 2010 and 2012, on the grounds of "the difficulties and local health risks posed by the unsanitary camps."[44] French officials have repeatedly denied any systematic targeting of Roma people as a group, but

a leaked memo, dated 5 August 2010 and signed by the chief of staff for interior minister Brice Hortefeux, reminds French officials of a "specific objective" set out by [former French president Nicolas] Sarkozy. "Three hundred camps or illegal settlements must be evacuated within three months; Roma camps are a priority," the memo reads. "It is down to the *préfect* [state representative] in each department to begin a systematic dismantling of the illegal camps, particularly those of the Roma."[45]

This example helps illustrate how differences among humans intersect with ideals of a bounded human self whose borders must be protected against infection from microbes or those metonymically depicted as vectors of disease.[46] Although outside of the scope of this essay, it would be worth extending this analysis to debates about immigration and citizenship in any contemporary context, including the United States.

These discourses and practices surrounding microbes and other invisible agencies simultaneously undertake what Latour calls the "work of purification" (seeking to make humans distinct from nonhumans as well as seeking to make the present distinct from the past) and the work of "hybridization" (those entanglements that are always already taking place, including processes and formations distinguished as "natural" and "cultural").[47]

There is also a friendly face to mainstream portrayals of microbes that nonetheless fits this larger paradigm. When marketed as "probiotics," as yogurts often are, microbes can be portrayed as instrumentally valuable for human health, as medicinal. Whether the enemy or a digestive aid, microbes are ascribed an agency but one that implies that they are other to humans and other animals, even when ingested. The ideal remains a self with clear, firm boundaries—a human who makes choices and takes actions to repel unwanted microbial invaders. Even when doing so entails the ingestion of microbial "probiotic" allies into our human bodies, the premise is that microbes are powerful agencies that exceed our intents and regularly permeate our flesh, usually for ill. The vigilance we are called to enact by manufacturers of cleaning products, for example, trades on the knowledge of our porosity while exhorting us to act as if humans are ideally separable from "environment." Paradoxically, antimicrobial marketing often requires a willed ignorance about the use of toxic chemicals, another site of viscous porosity linking us with the world in ways that alter us and all life-forms.[48]

I see these ways of thinking about and relating with microbes, such as by ingesting probiotic agents, as strikingly compatible with the ontologies and ethics that may arise from some ancient Christian uses of pneuma and ritual practices that are concerned, for example, with sealing the body from the incursions of harmful spirits. Human permeability is acknowledged but viewed as a problem to be managed by very specific kinds of practices and precautions.

In the *Apostolic Tradition*, attributed to Hippolytus of Rome, baptism is immediately preceded by anointing with the "oil of exorcism" to expel spirits (21.8–10); another anointing immediately follows baptism, this time with the "oil of thanksgiving" (21.19; 22.2–3).[49] The *Gospel of Philip*, preserved in the second codex of the Nag Hammadi writings, portrays the human as a being that either good or evil spirits will "seize" or "cleave to"; the ideal is for one to join with the "holy spirit," beginning in baptism: "For if they had the holy spirit, no unclean spirit would cleave to them" (66.2–4).[50] According to Clement of Alexandria's notebook about the teachings of Theodotos, he similarly taught that baptism confers a sealing that may either lock out or seal in unclean spirits forever: "It is fitting to go to baptism with joy, but, since unclean spirits often go down into the water with some [of those who are being baptized] and these [unclean] spirits that follow and gain the seal together with the candidate become impossible to cure for the future, fear is joined with joy, in order that only one who is pure may go down to the water" (*Excerpts of Theodotos* 83).[51]

Some early Christian texts also exhort the ingestion of "probiotic" agents, especially figured as the body and blood of Christ. We become what we consume, these texts suggest, in ways that are soteriologically significant. Let me return for a moment to the Fourth Gospel, which has Jesus affirm that

> unless you eat the flesh of the Son of Man and drink his blood, you have no life in you; those who eat my flesh and drink my blood have eternal life, and I will raise them up on the last day. . . . Those who eat my flesh and drink my blood abide in me, and I in them. As the living Father sent me, and I live because of the Father, so one who eats me will live because of me. This is the bread which came down from heaven. . . . It is the spirit that gives life, the flesh is of no avail; the words I have spoken to you are spirit and life. (John 6:53–54, 56–58, 63, RSV slightly modified)

This passage makes the ingestion of Jesus seem to have a radically probiotic effect: Only through ingesting this kind of flesh and blood can one truly live.

Writing from an ecocritical perspective, Stacy Alaimo observes, "Perhaps the most palpable trans-corporeal substance is food, since eating transforms plants and animals into human flesh."[52] But, as she cautions, "for the most part the model of incorporation emphasizes the outline of the human: food disappears into the human body, which remains solidly bounded."[53] Ingestion as assimilation runs the risk of retaining the notion of bounded self. This passage from the Fourth Gospel, however, foregrounds ontological relationality and even mutability: "Those who eat my flesh and drink my blood abide in me, and I in them." Here, the boundaries of the human self are not simply transgressed, but the very distinction between the human and the divine is transgressed.

Nonetheless, for all of this transformative and boundary-crossing imagery, ancient texts depict animal, human, and divine in a hierarchical fashion. We see this, for example, in the way that the *Gospel of Philip* interprets the Fourth Gospel. The *Gospel of Philip* portrays the Christian as formed from the consumption of spiritual flesh and blood that produces a new kind of being, defined first as human, in positive contrast especially to "animals." A number of passages indicate an understanding of Jesus as nourishment to be sharply distinguished from that previously ingested by humans and all other animals: "Before Christ came there was no bread in the world, just as Paradise, the place where Adam was, had many trees to nourish the animals but no wheat to sustain humans. Humans used to feed like the animals, but when Christ came, the perfect human, he brought bread from heaven in order that humans might be nourished with the food of humans" (*Gospel of Philip*, 55.6–14). This passage fascinates me because its interpretation of Genesis and the Fourth Gospel seems to offer an etiology for the differentiation of humans from other animals on the basis of what is consumed. It also relies on the idea of the source of production of the food as ontologically significant; nevertheless, although the text repeatedly distinguishes between human and other animals, between kinds of humans, and between human and more-than-human, these distinctions are not fixed and must be produced—they result from various interactions, notably figured by eating and procreating.[54]

Another important context for elaborating the significance of eating occurs in texts that pair the Eucharist with decomposition. Irenaeus, for example, sketches a vivid transcorporeal scene in which Jesus enters into and transforms humans through the Eucharist, an effect that continues even during the process of the physical body's decomposition in the earth after death. Irenaeus writes:

"We are members of His body, of His flesh, and of His bones"
(Eph. 5.30). [Paul] does not speak these words of some spiritual and
invisible man, for a spirit has not bones nor flesh (cf. Luke 24.39); but
[he refers to] that dispensation [by which the Lord became] an actual
man, consisting of flesh, and nerves, and bones,—that [flesh] which is
nourished by the cup which is His blood, and receives increase from
the bread which is His body. And just as a cutting from the vine planted
in the ground fructifies in its season, or as a corn of wheat falling into
the earth and becoming decomposed, rises with manifold increase . . .
so also our bodies, being nourished by [the Eucharist], and deposited
in the earth, and suffering decomposition there, shall rise at the ap-
pointed time. (*Against Heresies* 5.2.3, Ante-Nicene Fathers translation)

For Irenaeus, as Caroline Walker Bynum puts it, "The fact that we are
what we eat—that we become Christ by consuming Christ, but Christ can
never be consumed—guarantees that our consumption by . . . the gaping
maw of the grave is *not* destruction;"[55] "we know that our flesh is capable
of surviving digestion exactly because we are able to digest the flesh of
Christ. . . . Flesh, defined as that which changes, is capable of the change
to changelessness."[56] In other words, although Irenaeus acknowledges the
transcorporeal transformation of the body after death, he nonetheless insists on its continued ability to be restabilized through the presence of the
Eucharistic elements. Although it might seem that Irenaeus is embracing
our fleshy existence by affirming a material resurrection, note that it depends on the idea that Christians ingest a very special kind of immutable
flesh that defies the ordinary material process of decay and can transform
the flesh of those who ingest it to share this property. According to Irenaeus, instead of becoming part of the earth again, Christian bodies never
truly decompose but await transformation.[57]

Despite their different histories of reception, both the *Gospel of Philip*
and Irenaeus's writings advance a kind of relationality organized hierarchically. To become fully human or a saved human, one must be transformed
by and in relationship to agencies portrayed as superior. The ingestion or
reception of salvific agencies suggests a porousness to humans but nonetheless works to effect a separation between humans and other creatures.
In the next section, I consider how microbes might help us think about
not just the incorporation of other as self but the self as a composite sys-

tem that is located in a complex system. Microbes accomplish the work of pneuma/divine agencies, linking us with the material world yet allowing us to differentiate among forms of being without presupposing a static ranking (such as animal-human-divine); moreover, thinking in terms of microbes keeps us thinking in terms of being in this world and accountable to it, rather than envisioning an escape from it.

THE KINGDOM IS INSIDE YOU, AND IT IS OUTSIDE YOU: ANCIENT AND CURRENT ALTERNATIVES FOR CREATURELY THEOLOGY

The kingdom is spread out upon the earth and people do not see it.
—*Gospel of Thomas*, 113

I love the fact that human genomes can be found in only about 10 percent of all the cells that occupy the mundane space I call my body; the other 90 percent of the cells are filled with the genomes of bacteria, fungi, protists, and such, some of which play in a symphony necessary to my being alive at all, and some of which are just hitching a ride and doing the rest of me, of us, no harm. I am vastly outnumbered by my tiny companions; better put, I become an adult human being in company with these tiny messmates. To be one is always to become with many.
—DONNA HARAWAY, *When Species Meet*

As the preceding section illustrates, the bulk of the ancient Christian sources that speak about ingestion and digestion presume transcorporeal production of bodies but do so in such a way as to define the human as distinct from and superior to other kinds of animals. Nonetheless, we might discern space to inherit some of this material to sustain practices and visions of becoming that resist this framing. After considering some ways we might inherit "germ theory" differently than antibacterial soap commercials might have us do, I revisit the *Gospel of Philip* and Irenaeus before turning to sketch how the *Gospel of Thomas* might offer some productive, if still ambiguous possibilities for creaturely theology.

Microscopic life-forms are "typically excluded from the literature concerned with bonds between humans and other animals (even while they are . . . part of all such bonds)."[58] As we have seen, this exclusion is at least partly owing to the widespread view of microbes as enemies to "the human." But "the biosphere intimately depends" on microbes, which are the "last common universal ancestor" of living organisms.[59] Microbes are both a means by which membranes are crossed—the bacteria in our guts that break down the food we eat—and among the possible "strange and toxic bedfellows" that may bind themselves to water, air, or food and cross the membrane of our flesh to become us for good or ill.[60] Although we more commonly think about microbes as pathogens, Donna Haraway reminds us that the viscously porous container we think of as our human self is home to many "messmates," commensal microbes who either do us no harm or whose activity we need to maintain our immune systems and basic functioning.

For Haraway microbes are not the insidious and invisible archenemy; instead, they destabilize our sense of what it means to be human and to urge for transformed ethics and new ways of "worlding," both goals that seem quite compatible with what creaturely theology might become. She asks us to take microbes into account, redefining humans as the ongoing processual and dynamic result of exchanges that happen inside and outside "the mundane space I call my body."[61] When Paul writes of God putting the pneuma into the hearts (*kardia*) of the Galatians (Gal. 4:6), or God's spirit dwelling in those who have been baptized (Rom. 8:9, 11), or God's pneuma enabling him to discern spiritual truths (1 Cor. 2:12–13), he is not speaking of the microbial messmates Haraway has in mind; nonetheless, both Paul and Haraway emphasize the necessity and value of invisible forces for living, and both understand these internal relations to have consequences for social relations and ethics transcorporeally.

Myra Hird, who builds on the work of Haraway, asks us to think and live as human bodies always already interconnected with the world, especially through interactions with microbes. She asks us to consider both the symbiotic relations with bacteria that enable all animals to digest what we consume and bacteria that produce the compounds we—and all life-forms—need to survive:

All animals are, metabolically, *consumers* (heterotrophs must use ready-made organic compounds). Autotrophic bacteria, by contrast, do not "eat" (they "fix" or otherwise convert the elements on which all living organisms depend). These bacteria are *producers*, engaging in a different economy of eating and thus relating with the world. Other kinds of bacteria, such as those found in rumens, termite guts and human intestines, live symbiotically with animals and other organisms, enabling food digestion.[62]

Thinking about production and consumption together as modes of relationality that themselves are forms of encounter that produce contingent kinds of beings gives us a fresh way to encounter ancient texts that are also concerned with production and consumption and which do so, in part, through imagery and practices of ingestion, assimilation, and transformation. Autotrophic microbes create relations between inorganic matter with organic, for example, by making nutrients available to plants and animals, such that bacteria and fungi are a necessary hinge between kinds of matter, roles that are reserved for the singular divinity and its emissaries (Logos, Sophia) in most ancient Christian texts; heterotrophic microbes interact through symbiosis.

Hird's distinction between autotrophic and heterotrophic microbes can help us reconsider the examples of ingestion discussed in the preceding section. For the Fourth Gospel, the *Gospel of Philip*, and Irenaeus, consumption is central to their views about the necessary transformations that produce the perfected, true human. For these texts, the spirit is the living part—but Irenaeus seems to imagine the Christian as a being consisting of flesh that has been purified through the consumption of the flesh and blood of Jesus; what lives eternally is this Spirit, which can, after the flesh has died, inherit the rotting bits and "translate" them into the kingdom of heaven.

Spirit (pneuma) in the *Gospel of Philip* is doing some of the work that microbes do for Hird. Spirit is autotrophic and heterotrophic; it is autotrophic in that spirit produces the "true" food for (autotrophic) and heterotrophic in that spirit symbiotically enables the transformation of this food into a new, human, being. For Irenaeus, the Eucharistic elements are likewise heterotrophic in effect but interpreted not as spirit but as flesh and blood. Participants do not just digest Jesus; the encounter with this particular nourishment is probiotic in a radical sense for the consumer's flesh and blood.

Even more amazing to me than the intra-actions of autotrophic and heterotrophic microbes with other life-forms is a form of internalized autotrophic microbial function now in all living cells—the mitochondria:

> Perhaps the best example of the depth of the human / microbial inter-
> connection comes from the mitochondria, organelles ("tiny organs")
> in human, animal, and plant (and fungal and protozoal) cells that con-
> vert food to usable energy via oxygen-consuming chemical reactions.
> Mitochondria are an absolutely indispensable part of each and every
> one of our "human cells." . . . These critical components of every hu-
> man cell have a profoundly bacterial origin. . . . The ancestors of all
> eukaryotic life (animals, plants, etc.) had oxygen-using bacteria living
> inside them. Eventually, these bacteria lost their ability to live outside
> the host and became part of the host cells.[63]

Mitochondria thus epitomize an autotrophic function internalized in the
cells of eukaryotes. "The late Nobel laureate Dr. Joshua Lederberg referred
to mitochondria as 'the most successful of all microbes' and used them to
illustrate the concept of the 'superorganism'—a 'chimera' of host/para-
site/commensal genomes linked together."[64] To think about ourselves as
chimera, at the cellular level, may be unsettling. It is hard to get my mind
around thinking of myself as dynamically composite, genomically linked
to bacteria both of an ancestral sort who have become me (as mitochondria in human cells) or who are me while nonetheless also being discernible as distinct. But it also opens up new ways of engaging the meaning of
the "kingdom [being] inside you and . . . outside of you" (Gospel of Thomas,
3) when the "us" as well as the boundaries between "inside" and "outside"
are perceived through this materialist lens.

Can we shift our ontology to account for a composite, chimerical self, a
community shared with microbes that constitutes each localized body, but
also locate that self as a provisional materialized expression of the shared
stuff of the cosmos? This would require a radical reengagement with the
proposition of traditional creation accounts and incarnational theologies
that both humans and Jesus are constitutively composite kinds of beings.
Although this task exceeds the scope of this essay, as a starting point, I turn
to the Gospel of Thomas with the proposition that it may offer, with limits,
more promise for creaturely theology than either the Gospel of Philip or
Irenaeus.

The Gospel of Thomas is a text that explicitly resists easy interpretation,
which makes it tantalizing to attempt interpretation, even as the text permits multiple contested readings. Having been promised that we will not

taste death if we grasp its sayings, that we will be transformed by a successful encounter with the text, we discover a number of sayings that focus on transformative interactions. Although still hierarchical in arranging the dynamic relations among animals, humans, and Jesus,[65] and still favoring spirit over body (e.g., *Gospel of Thomas*, 29, 80), the *Gospel of Thomas* also insists that the kind of salvation it offers is already "spread out over the earth," not merely accessed by the reader as a separable human being (*Gospel of Thomas*, 113).

The *Gospel of Thomas* contains sayings conducive to the kind of relational ontology I am advocating. In the *Gospel of Thomas* the kingdom is both inside and outside of us (*Gospel of Thomas*, 3). In this image we might find a useful hinge between microbes and this text to compose a creaturely theology that acknowledges the relations between our flesh and the flesh of the world, including but not limited to other kinds of animals. In saying 77b, Jesus exhorts readers to see (possibly make?) the kingdom present throughout the world: "Split a piece of wood, and I am there. Lift up the stone, and you will find me there." Here, we might read Jesus as the product of prior intra-actions whose ongoing disposition is for a kind of flourishing for all be(com)ings. As Haraway wisely notes, "Eating one another and developing indigestion are only one kind of transformative merger practice; living critters form consortia in a baroque medley of inter- and intra-actions."[66]

The exhortation to "make the inside like the outside and the outside like the inside" (22) as part of Jesus' answer to the disciples' question about what it will take for them to enter the kingdom supports a position that insists on ethical accountability and action even when agency and being are understood relationally and contingently. The reader is called to transform her epistemology and ontology simultaneously in this gospel—changing one's way of knowing is also a fundamental change in being. There is an important caveat, however. In the *Gospel of Thomas*, the kingdom is contrasted with "the world," the latter being that which one ought to renounce (and not misrecognize as true reality or source of being) (*Gospel of Thomas*, 80, 110, and see also 50). My sense is that any creaturely theology for the present will need to wrestle with how to inherit this problematic aspect of the gospel; a critical heir might contravene the gospel's implications by emphasizing the need for a changed vision about the world and our place in it to favor the kind of ontologies articulated by Haraway and Hird.

I have proposed that a temporal juxtaposition between premodern sources and contemporary ones is needed to confront a sticky legacy. The analogy with microbes discloses, in part, that acknowledgment of transcorporeality and of invisible agencies such as pneuma and microbes can be used to craft and sustain anthropocentric ways of thinking and being, in which the goal is to enclose, contain, and protect the human over and against invisible invaders and to distance the human and its porosity from the lives and concerns of other species and the environment. Nonetheless, in both ancient and contemporary sources we can also catch glimpses of alternative encounters and alternatives ways of knowing and being that we can foster. As a species we may yet be doomed in our lovely inter- and intraconnections,[67] but Spahr's poignant conclusion urges me to lean into this risky, messy interconnectedness that I cannot avoid so long as I still breathe.

The Apophatic Animal: Toward a Negative Zootheological *Imago Dei*

JACOB J. ERICKSON

Wilderness, finally, that is this great, intricate tangle of a world: stiff rock and foaming wave; the eternal return of the same and constant transformation into things that have never been before; order in the path of the stars and the thronging of atoms. . . . Yet does not the world constantly overflow every conceivable law with enigmatic freedom?
—HANS URS VON BALTHASAR, *Heart of the World*

I got some wild, wild life.
—THE TALKING HEADS

Jacques Derrida mentions the phrase so quickly—so dismissively—in the introductory essay to *The Animal That Therefore I Am*, that one might be sorely tempted to just keep following the essay along its creaturely path. In registering his vulnerable relation to a now infamous cat, Derrida interjects that he is not, even while it "seems" so obviously the case, "dedicating a negative zootheology" to the beloved feline.[1] Although that may not be the case, I, for one, would like to know who in fact would have assumed Derrida was doing "negative zootheology" in the first place.

But the phrase itself somehow entices me to follow instead. Not only do we have a fragment of "divinanimality" in this text but also a gesture that the creatures we encounter (and the even more that we do not) in our planetary lives might possibly relate (regardless of Derrida's intentions) to the mystical tradition of unsaying certain, peculiar and confident, names of the divine. My intent here is to explore the possibility of a negative zootheology as a corrective to hegemonic theological anthropologies of human exceptionalism, particularly in the wake of violent interpretations of that doctrine of the *imago dei*, of human beings created in the image of God. Along the way, I gesture toward a negative zootheological conception of the *imago dei* and offer the naturecultural image of *wilderness* (in a revised key) as a theopoetic course corrective. I do so by exploring the *imago dei* as a wild immanence of the Spirit in created life, a deconstructive movement in the midst of creaturely relationality. Such a Spirit-image is neither stagnant nor a fixed essentiality; rather, it follows, migrates, moves, and unsettles the dust of our creatureliness in the divine wake of biodiversity. To unleash possibility, earthy life in the image of the Spirit is constantly "becoming undone," to borrow a thematic from philosophers as diverse as Judith Butler and Elizabeth Grosz.[2] In such a key, the *imago dei* might be theopoetically akin to what Max Oelschlaeger calls "the wilderness within the human soul and without, in that living profusion that envelops all creation."[3]

IMAGES, MENAGERIES, AND LIMITROPHIES

Of the doctrines and symbols of the Christian theological tradition, the human *imago dei* as read from the creation myths in Genesis has played a particularly destructive role in obliterating planetary life for the sake of human opportunism. As Larry Rasmussen observes, "*Imago dei* set us apart from the rest of nature as free agents who act upon it in responsibility before God. . . . But it was stewardship in the mode of mastery, control, and good management, all determined by an anthropocentrism of interests."[4] As a particular doctrinal reading of a poetic biblical mythos, this anthropocentrism of interests created a menagerie out of the ecological world for human pleasure and control.

Yet the *imago dei* itself is a slippery conceptual creature to track. For much of Christian theology as noted above, the *imago* is the unique crux of defining humanity, of distinguishing human beings from animals, human culture from the wild nature of the world. And, usually, those theologians working in the throes of modern theological anthropology articulate the image in terms of positive characteristics and contours; they presume the divine image is stable, fixed, unmoving, and irreducibly human.

In the midst of these theologies, multiple anthropocentric options emerge. In *The Divine Image*, Ian A. McFarland helpfully sketches a number of the popular theological paths. In one option the *"imago* has been understood in primarily cognitive terms as referring to a particular created capacity, whether that be reason, freedom, the capacity for self-transcendence, or even an intrinsic orientation to God."[5] Another of the destructive options is functional: The divine image is what humans *do* or *how* humans are (called stewards, mostly). Third is a relational option where "human beings image God insofar as their existence as persons in relation (paradigmatically as male and female) is a creaturely analogue to the relationships among the three persons of the Trinity."[6] And, finally, a perhaps more contemporary option that McFarland himself takes is to remove the *imago dei* from theological anthropology proper altogether.[7] The actual image of God is located in Christology, these theologies often suggest, and human beings are imprinted with the image of God insofar as they participate in Christ or figure as "the church."

In all of these schemas (though with different nuances, anthropological and Christological), a human *imago dei* attempts to transcend and master the ecological world. The being and role in creation of the human is isolated, extracted from the ecological webs of existence. In most of these theologies, humans live unrelated, unaffected, and never acted upon by other creatures; only proper human relationships (in mostly heterosexist formulations) could ever resemble the triune persons or relate to the human form of Christ. The *imago dei*, needless to say, is dominated by the demanding crowds of human faces.

In searching to leave these human crowds behind us (or to humble them), Jacques Derrida's observations of "the animal" in the philosophical-textual tradition may point toward a new possibility for conceiving an ecological *imago dei*. Indeed, the title essay of *The Animal That Therefore I Am* reads, in some ways, as a gloss of not only the sacrifice of animal Others in the philosophical tradition but also in certain theological readings of the human from the Priestly and Jahwist creation myths.[8] Derrida observes, "More precisely, God has created man in his likeness *so that* man will *subject, tame, dominate, train,* or *domesticate* the animals born before him and assert his authority over them."[9] This strange sort of midrash, then, reaches into one of the traditional exegetical cores of theological anthropology itself.

Derrida begins by engaging the concept of the animal as a way of anthropological, autobiographical self-knowledge. Coyly, he observes, "I often ask myself, just to see, *who I am*—and who I am (following) at the moment when, caught naked, in silence, by the gaze of an animal, for example, the eyes of a cat, I have trouble, yes, a bad time overcoming my embarrassment."[10] Derrida's naked exposure evokes the otherness and the agency of the animal gaze, and he begins to lose himself in that mysterious feline look.

The feline gaze in this text evokes what we might call a reconfigured ethical anthropology, playing with the ambiguous trope of "following." And "following" becomes the most important question in relation to what Derrida calls "this awful tale of Genesis."[11] As Derrida reads the narrative, God leaves the novelty of naming up to Adam as God's image, as if the peculiarities and lives of the created animals don't matter in the divine scheme of things, "whereby Ish would begin to see them and name them without allowing himself to be seen or named by them."[12] The naming of the animals occurs without mutuality or any regard for the animals themselves in their singularity.

Without regard for the animals and without any ethical accounting to them, the human delineates the value of the animal creature, a creature that oddly exceeds him. Derrida observes, "God lets Ish call the other living things all on his own, give them their names in his own name, these animals that are older and younger than him, these living things that came into the world before him but were named after him, on his initiative."[13] The animals that came before the man are treated as though they are under him. They surround him temporally and physically, saturating his imagination, and yet he claims a kind of transcendence over them.

This odd scene of naming exposes the location of the human, and the potential figural ambiguities of a human following animals. Derrida asserts, "In both cases, man is in both senses of the word *after* the animal. He follows him. This 'after,' which determines a sequence, a consequence, or a persecution, is not in time, nor is it temporal: it is the very genesis of time."[14] The human being comes after the animals in creation. That is, humans do not reign from time immemorial but exist in the midst of other animal creatures. It is the following, tracking, naming, and destruction of the animal that allows the human to come-to-be, categorically.

Derrida here observes that the concept of *the animal* does incredible violence to the vast biodiversity and differences within that category. Looking at this philosophical homogenization of the animal kingdom, he writes,

Confined within this catch-all concept, within the vast encampment of the animal, in this general singular, within the strict enclosure of this definite article ('the Animal' and not 'animals'), as in a virgin forest, a zoo, a hunting or fishing ground, a paddock or an abattoir, a space of domestication, are *all the living things* that man does not recognize as his fellows, his neighbors, or his brothers.[15]

Theologies of the human generally name animal others as a vast category—a categorical menagerie that neither recognizes the tremendous biodiversity of the planet nor the particular creatures we encounter on a daily basis.

In response to this philosophical violence, Derrida attempts to write philosophy under the gaze of the "animal," that awkwardly violent, general name we give to the "living other."[16] And here is where we might begin to see a wild apophaticism beginning to emerge. Derrida engages in a process that he calls *limitrophy* to begin to pull us deeper into a strange biodiversity of life. He writes, "Everything I'll say will consist, certainly not in effacing the limit, but in multiplying its figures, in complicating, thickening, delinearizing, folding, and dividing the line precisely by making it increase and multiply."[17] Derrida begins a practice of unsaying the hegemonic category of animal through a wild growth of inadequate names and creaturely singularities. One might say that this "unsaying" of the term animal is a theopoetic explosion of a kind of lush and abyssal wilderness serendipitously exposing creaturely limits and subtly blossoming them into further infinitesimal limits in the midst of creaturely life.

TOWARD A NEGATIVE ZOOTHEOLOGICAL *IMAGO DEI*: A THEOLOGY OF WILD IMMANENCE

As a strange practice, limitrophies burst open theological menageries of the "animal" by taking biological multiplicity into account. As Derrida observes, "As with every bottomless gaze, as with the eyes of the other, the gaze called 'animal' offers to my sight the abyssal limit of the human: the inhuman or the ahuman, the ends of man, that is to say, the border-crossing from which vantage man dares to announce himself to himself, thereby calling himself by the name that he believes he gives himself."[18] We can never fully account for this living multiplicity. The explosion of limits and creaturely peculiarities unsays the vast category of "animal" and then proceeds to unsay the names humans create. The limits constantly move, shift, and in so doing, might acknowledge a deeper sense of relationality than Derrida is willing to admit. In her writing on "companion species," the posthuman theorist Donna Haraway offers two important constructive critiques of Derrida's project. She suggests that although he considers the theoretical implications of a peculiar feline animal looking at him, Derrida never fully asks a question of reciprocity between the human and the animal. She writes, "Yet he did not seriously consider an alternative form of engagement either, one that risked knowing something more about cats and *how to look back*, perhaps even scientifically, biologically, and *therefore* also philosophically and intimately."[19] The relational response to the animal is never fully accounted for, and the human responding to the particularity of the animal never becomes fully embodied in Derrida's testimony or theory. He does not choose to respond to his cat directly.

Not only does Derrida not respond differently, but Haraway suggests that Derrida actually narrows the field of play for how to philosophically consider the animal by asking only the question of suffering and pity. Haraway speculates, "What if work and play, and not just pity, open up when the possibility of mutual response, without names, is taken seriously as an everyday practice available to philosophy and to science?"[20] Haraway's questioning of Derrida might lead us to think of this animal *imago* not just in terms of suffering, but in terms of a queer pleasure and movement.[21] Human-animal companions, in their particularity, address each other, take joy in each other, and respond to each other's sufferings. A joyful mutuality does not require, and may even counter, the scapegoating practice of naming that occurs without taking the singular creature into account.

What Derrida's text and these two criticisms expose is a deep, animating relationality between animal Others in their singularity and peculiar human beings in theirs. Philosophical and embodied animals and humans concresce and coconstitute each other. They interact, play, suffer, build, and work together in surprising ways.[22] They live out histories of heterogeneous interaction together—a history, I would add, deeply embedded in the history of Western colonialism in the Columbian exchange,[23] and ecoracism, ecopatriarchy, and ecoheternormativity in their multiple manifestations. But for Derrida to expose the abyss of these interactions is to profoundly expose, multiply, and deconstruct the limits between what we consider "human" and "animal." The limits between humanity and animality, he asserts, are deeper than any dual conception of the two in a "heterogeneous multiplicity of the living."[24]

Deep limitrophy and deep relationality to animal Others, an alternative deep ecology, this not-quite "negative zootheology" urges us to rethink human lives in the most fragile of places. My fragile hunch here is that our particular deconstructive relation with animal others, our mutual gazing, might be better understood in pneumatological terms. A creatively ethical "following" of animals might be urged along a theology of the Spirit's immanent and heterogeneous relationality among creatures. What might it mean to rethink this mysterious entanglement of human and animal as a "live wire" of Spirit? It might mean that tracking the Spirit in these relations to the "living other" is a tracking of a deeply ecological *imago dei*. To put it too simplistically, we might think of the image of God as a creaturely imaging of the divine wilderness of the Spirit. An image (singular human and animal) of God in these spaces is a wild plastic, indiscrete, migrating movement of a holy *anima*.

In another treatment of ecological *anima*, Sharon Betcher argued for a "grounding" of the Spirit, an ecofeminist pneumatology that takes seriously the flesh and materialisms of the world. She writes, "Rather than viewing Spirit in dialectical opposition to need, transience, temporality, limits, and dependence, an ecofeminist pneumatology would acknowledge such organic interdependence, biotic vulnerability, and even nature's tragic tears, without employing these as a divide between Spirit and body or Spirit and nature."[25] That is to say that Spirit is an immanently "living other" evoking the limits and oozing in the midst of the living and dying relations of animal creatures.[26] This grounding of the spirit is a grounding of the *imago dei* as well—in, with, and under all dimensions of life. All creatures are created in an image of Spirit-with them in the dusty flesh of the earth. This creation is a *mysterium convivium*, a mysterious conviviality of life together.

In this way, the Spirit becomes a matrix of convivial interaction between creatures, working in the suffering, play, and work of creatures together. Pneuma is elemental, animating together, rather than confined to human corners of a philosophical system. Even more, the Spirit inhabits the whole of life in life's concreteness, animating-with the peculiar animality of singular creatures, exploding in the heterogeneity of life. Seen through the lens of the planet's remarkable biodiversity, the Spirit evokes

multiple tongues that bark, chirp, leave tracks, and interact in subtle communicative diversity. The immanence of wild divinity disturbs megafauna,
schools of fish, and birds and calls them to regard each other's peculiarity,
whether that regard is in symbiosis or in voraciousness. And that includes
the human and the human's sensuous attentiveness to life and death.
As the wondrous Wangari Maathai once wrote, "Nature—and in particular, the wild—feeds our spirit, and a direct encounter with it is vital in
helping us appreciate it. For unless we see it, smell it, or touch it, we tend
to forget about it, and our souls wither."[27]

HORIZONTAL IMAGES OF THE DIVINE: *IMAGO DEI*
AS INCARNATION OF DIVINE WILDERNESS

To think of the Spirit's wild immanence in creative, animated life, we might
begin to think of Spirit as an incarnation of Divine Wilderness. Wilderness
is a remarkable theological metaphor: Biblical wilderness abounds; Jesus
is driven into the wilderness. Classical apophatic theologians and mystics
use the language of mysticism in creative ways to talk about the unspeakable mysteries of the divine. Meister Eckhart, for instance, deploys the
image of wilderness as the "far country," an image that even Karl Barth—
hardly mystically inclined—will deploy in the service of Christological
reflection.[28]

In his stunning little book *Heart of the World*, Hans Urs von Balthasar
meditates on the complex wilderness that is ordinary and divine love. He
is, of course, a mysteriously orthodox Catholic theologian meditating on
the Johannine passion narratives, and a long way from ecotheology. But the
last chapter of his theopoetic masterwork is aptly titled "Love—A Wilderness." There, he too, obliquely speaks of the *imago dei* as human dominion,
but von Balthasar also laments over the difficulty of his view of human
dominion in that *imago dei*: "The world is entrusted to man as a garden
for him to cultivate and bring to never-ending progress. And yet the world
is a careless chaos which ever anew spills over every enclosure, breaking
tips which have been overly sharpened, forcing rising curves to descend as
if by nature, making overripe forms return to the primal womb."[29] Von
Balthasar strangely, like Derrida, points toward the heterogeneous explosion of limits, the overly sharpened, and then the transgressals of limits.
Yet this worldly wilderness seems to bewilder him too much to stay in the
thick of it, to love its creatureliness.

Sadly, von Balthasar falls into a dualism of submitting worldly wilderness to divine wilderness. He doxologizes, "How I thank you, Lord, that you resolve the painful wilderness of the world only by dissolving it into the blessed wilderness of your love, and that everything conflicting and raging within us is melted together in the crucible of your creator's might."[30] But similar to what Betcher suggests, what if the wilderness of created flesh coincides with the wilderness of divine love in the Spirit, rather than resolving it? That loving wilderness would ever be an improvisational unsaying of the certainties of love and creatureliness, beckoning us to follow new limits, new wonders at the wildness of the world.

Earlier, von Balthasar questions and loves such mysteries: "Who can tame the jungle of [the Lord's] incomprehensibility? See how man's spirit and whole being lies, like the bowl of an impetuous fountain, under the downpour of so many mysteries. Let it gush!"[31] Von Balthasar's mysterious gushing, spread out in the Spirited wilderness of the world, is closer to a negative zootheological *imago dei* that I want to follow. The wild flow of Spirit is no "silent spring" but rather undoes our perspectives.

Following such a deconstructive movement of the Spirit is to follow the movements and agitations of Spirit in the flesh. Spirit opens up the depths of the larger incarnate transcorporealities of creaturely life. In *Bodily Natures: Science, Environment, and the Material Self*, Stacy Alaimo argues that we must recognize the capacious relationality in human and nonhuman bodies. She writes, "Imagining human corporeality as trans-corporeality, in which the human is always intermeshed with the more-than-human world, underlines the extent to which the substance of the human is ultimately inseparable from 'the environment.'"[32] The image of the divine that proliferates through all creatures—from particular specks of dust to quarks to a particular herd of elephants to this particular human—migrates in between bodies, in the midst of bodily exchanges and fluid territories.

HORIZONTAL IMAGES OF THE DIVINE:
IMAGO DEI AS MIGRATORY CREATIVITY

In another key, what I'm saying is that to follow the gushing movements of animated creatures in their relations is to follow the relating, wild immanence of the Spirit as well. This migratory creativity of life is often why cultural images of the Spirit turn to the dynamic movement of animal images—that of dove, eagle, or rabbit—for discerning, locating, following the Spirit is a notoriously difficult theological project. The perichoretic movement of Spirit-breath resists all forms of domestication as it moves, plays, bends, dives, and bursts. Cheaply echoing von Balthasar's favorite Johannine gospel, "The wind blows where it chooses, and you hear the sound of it, but you do not know where it comes from or where it goes. So it is with everyone who is born of the Spirit."[33] Everyone born of the Spirit might includes both "humans" and "animals" here, playing with the heterogeneity between them. The Spirit engenders intensities, affectivities, and imaginative possibilities in the midst of heterogeneous creatures.

We might play in that heterogeneity with a variety of theopoetic images. The ecofeminist theologian Anne Primavesi suggests that we envision creaturely relationality in the "biodiversity" of God. Indeed, in her book *Cultivating Unity within the Biodiversity of God*, Primavesi argues, "Both science and experience teach us that we are but one particular earthy life form that began to exist and continues to thrive only *together with* 'all things'—for both like them and together with them, we are involved in the process of *creating* our environments, societies, and relationships."[34] Such adherence to a convivial ecology is dependent on the risky undoings of relationality. Primavesi continues: "The creative energy this requires flows from a sensitivity to the interdependence and mutual vulnerability of the whole, and a refusal to attribute its products to any one constituent—or to God."[35] Any hegemonic focus that neglects the multiplicitous diversities of creaturely life must be reevaluated and must look deeply to the vulnerable pains and pleasures of life.

Although Primavesi brings our attention to the biodiversity possible in the wilderness of the divine, "biodiversity" itself is not an entirely unproblematic concept. In his beautiful work, *The Animal Side*, Jean-Christophe Bailly meditates: "It is one thing to invoke 'biodiversity' as an abstract right, using its abstract name; it is something else again to attend very closely to the multiplicity of exposures and states through which the animal world is revealed and concealed in the vast game of hide-and-seek played out in its native places."[36] Conceptually, the image of "biodiversity" could function to erase creaturely peculiarity, and Bailly likens this functioning to Derrida's articulations of the word *animal*. Bailly hesitates, "Biodiversity, no, that doesn't sound right, that doesn't sound like the infinite declension of the diverse through which animals declare themselves."[37] Although we might hope that biodiversity deployed ecologically or ecotheologically urges an attentiveness to difference required for ecological living, we might be required to look even deeper. As a corollary to the language of biodiversity, Bailly suggests "an infinity, then, of shapes and curves, an infinity of variations and practices."[38] Variations, oddities, eccentricities, practices, minutiae with cosmic and microcosmic implications—all shimmer in subtle games of hide-and-seek in the wilderness of the Spirit. These variations expose, as the old Lutheran doctrine argued, a mysterious *finitum capax infiniti*, the finite bearing the infinite, collectively.

The infinity of wilderness, then, as the *imago dei*, can emerge anywhere spatially or temporally. William Cronon, in his now classic essay, "The Trouble with Wilderness," argues that far from being a distant occurrence, "out there" or "in nature," the concept of "wilderness" opens up otherness in a multiplicity of contexts. He writes,

> Wilderness gets us into trouble only if we imagine that this experience of wonder and otherness is limited to the remote corners of the planet, or that it somehow depends on pristine landscapes we ourselves do not inhabit. Nothing could be more misleading. The tree in the garden is in reality no less other, no less worthy of our wonder and respect, than the tree in an ancient forest that has never known an ax or a saw—even though the tree in the forest reflects a more intricate web of ecological relationships.[39]

The divine wilderness of which I'm speaking does not rely on the popular naturecultural images of wildness as "set apart" or "in the wild." With its blooming wildness, wilderness occurs when the spirit undoes us by exposing the strange alterity of our everyday spaces. The succulents sitting on the desk before me now, as I write, elude my descriptive grasp in their strange beauty, the water pulsing through them, the subtle hints of oxygen they offer me. This diversity, seemingly "domestic," can be the occasion of a wilderness experience.

The movement of this mysterious, biodiverse Spirit within creaturely relations leaves a dynamic sense of the wilderness that is both a horizontal and abyssal *imago dei*. As Terra Rowe has argued, "In our touchability—our fleshiness, leafiness, or rockiness, we encounter the wild other who, as wild other, is beyond my control and thus dangerously free."[40] Indeed, the Spirit migrates through *this* created reality just as all animated creatures do, just as wild plants and creatures often begin to retake failed human constructions.[41] Migrations kick up dust as creatures discern their convivial paths—the paths are rarely clear, pristine, or easily discernible; rarely are they wholesome or straight. Discerning this Spirited image of God in creaturely relations is an attempt to trace infinite and queer migratory tracks, infinite and heterogeneous limits. The Spirit traces a wild immanence in the human, that *imago dei* in a dynamic encounter of animal creatures, a trace ever on the move, ungraspable, often erased, and always unsaying creatures in its wake.

This movement of Spirit, in exposing heterogeneities, I want to argue, actually engenders political agencies of transformation. In Spirit, creatures encounter the vulnerabilities and resiliencies of the infinite migratory relations that constitute us. To expose or be exposed to an other by the Spirit in our vulnerability is to ask questions about our responsibility toward those others, not as a fetishizing of their alterity, but as a cherishing of their ecological postures and friendship for us. To play hide-and-seek with these animal others is to discern responsibility in the deep ambiguities of those lives, in the deep ambiguities of our own lives.

To think of the *imago dei* as a lush and divine wilderness finally is to encounter our incarnate bodies as vibrant and moving thickets of divinity, vibrant ecologies of flesh immanent yet wildly eluding creaturely feel or comprehension. The wilderness of animal bodies is a "vibrant matter," to borrow a phrase from the political ecologist Jane Bennett. The creaturely bones, organs, neurons, and other companion creatures with our fragile bodies explode with an agency beyond our control. Parasites and microbial organisms mysteriously occupy our body with the fierce love of survival.[42] The Spirit's "living profusion" of animal bodies is ever-becoming apophatic, unsaying itself in unexpected ways, in unexpected porosities. Perhaps, then, when a certain border collie chases her tail, she encounters her body as a wild, mysterious, playful force. Or when my companion horse is startled by the sounds of his own hoofbeats, he encounters his walking a strange immanence. But I may have already said too much. And not enough. . . .

❧ The Divinanimality
of Lord Sequoia

TERRA S. ROWE

Dear Mrs. Carr:
Do behold the King in his glory, King Sequoia. Behold! Behold! Some time ago I
left all for Sequoia: have been and am at his feet fasting and praying for light, for
is he not the greatest light in the woods; in the world. . . . But I'm in the woods
woods, woods, and they are in me-ee-ee. The King tree and me have sworn eter-
nal love—sworn it without swearing and I've taken the sacrament with Douglas
Squirrel drank Sequoia wine, Sequoia blood, and with its rosy purple drops I
am writing this woody gospel letter. . . . I wish I was so drunk and Sequoical
that I could preach the green brown woods to all the juiceless world, descend-
ing from this divine wilderness like a John Baptist eating Douglas Squirrels and
wild honey or wild anything, crying, Repent for the Kingdom of Sequoia is at
hand. . . . Come Suck Sequoia and be saved. . . . You say, [Mrs. Carr], When are
You Coming down? Ask the Lord—Lord Sequoia.
—JOHN MUIR, undated personal letter to Jeanne Carr

In his characteristically ebullient and whimsical style John Muir describes
to his Wisconsin friend and supporter a profound conversion. His language
may be exuberant and lighthearted, but it is, to be sure, a fervent transformation to Lord Sequoia. Muir's reality has been transfigured—even to his
experience of time and space. Although the "juiceless" world would say
this letter was written in the latter half of the nineteenth century in what
has (through Muir's work) become Yosemite National Park, in his juicy
Sequoical world Muir writes from "Squirrelville" of "Sequoia County" in
"Nut Time."[1] Here the world, especially the other-than-human world, is

saturated with divinity. What's more, this world of juicy Sequoia blood is not exterior to Muir but flows into him and he into it.

With eucharistic imagery and biblical analogy Muir's poetic prose suggests an earthy, twiggy, leafy, divinarbor. Separated only by the Santa Cruz Mountains (and a century of time and thought) the biologist and feminist scholar Donna Haraway conjures another curious figure: the anima-arbor. Haraway introduces her readers to the figure of her friend Jim Clifford's dog in the introduction of *When Species Meet*. Jim Clifford's big green dog (we'll call him Clifford) is a figure literally growing at the limit of the chloroplastic, the animalistic, the technological, the cultural, and the natural. Jim encountered this fern-coated canine on a hike in Santa Cruz, took a picture with a digital camera, and sent it to Haraway as a jpg, which she has included in her text, thus allowing her readers to also encounter Clifford. Clifford's body is a contact zone for a plurality of "messmates": a burnt-out tree trunk, small mammals, mosses, ferns, pine needles, bacteria, and fungi, just to name a few.[2] Just as her human body is in major part constituted by organisms that do not share human genetic material, Haraway explains, so Clifford is constituted more as a meeting place of organisms and matter than as a substantial or decidable technocultural "human" or "natural" "plant" or "animal."[3]

Muir's and Haraway's arbors remind us of the stakes in critical animal discourse for the way we live with not just animals but the entire web of relations that make possible our lives, as well as our thought about what it means to be a thinking animal. These curious creatures represent life as a series of "contact zones" where the plant, animal, human, social, cultural, technological, and natural not only meet one another but are also continually constituted by and in these encounters.[4]

Haraway makes clear there is nothing divine about her anima-arbor. Muir's Lord Sequoia, however, raises important questions for Christian theology about the possibility of God's embodiment in creation. No place in Christian theology makes it quite so clear (save the creation story perhaps—which is so frequently referenced in ecotheology and critical animal theory discourses) that humans are divinely set apart from the rest of creation than the doctrine of the incarnation. The Nicene-Chalcedonian tradition reserves the distinctive meeting place of the divine and matter for the human. Christian incarnation is celebrated as God with us, God made flesh, Christ as "brother," as fellow "man." But Jacques Derrida's question, "What happens to the fraternity of brothers when an animal appears on the scene?"[5] should give this tradition pause for thought: If God became human exclusively, what does this mean for the human in relation to the animal? Conversely, what does it do to a Christian understanding of incarnation to throw animality into the mix of humanity and divinity? What if "purely human" is a distorting myth? What does it mean for Christian theology to accept the "humanity of God" while the "animality of God" remains repulsive? Or, as Muir might add, what about the "arboreality of God"? What would be the difference between these? Would it merely be the difference between the human, the animal, and the arboreal itself? Where are the lines between divine, animal, human, and arboreal? Perhaps it would be more proper to speak of a continuum, or blurring?

The intimacy and relationality traditionally implied between God and humanity in incarnation has played an important role in twentieth-century Christian liberation theology movements.[6] A pause for thought should not dismantle the significant work that an empathetic and relatable God has done and can do in systems and experiences of oppression and exploitation. It remains necessary, nonetheless, to continue to think of justice, responsibility, and interconnectedness in critical and material ways beyond the anthropocentric.

In many Christian ecotheologies incarnation is celebrated as a divine affirmation of materiality.[7] In order to combat the anthropocentrism of incarnation, ecotheologians have tended to sacrifice the particular materiality of incarnation in Jesus[8] or downplayed the particularity of incarnational Christology by emphasizing a continuing-creation incarnational pneumatology.[9] I am suggesting there is another way that preserves both the materiality and the particularity of divine embodiment in Christ while loosing Christ from an exclusive enmeshment with humanity.

Animated by Muir's Lord Sequoia, enticed by Derrida's and Haraway's boundary-breaking posthumanism and theologically guided by Laurel Schneider's divine multiplicity and Joseph Sittler's ecological self, this is a proposal of a Christ figure who/which does not shore up human identity against the other-than-human world. In Derrida's discussion of the limitrophic divinanimal we will see that the limit has been the place to establish the human subject. Instead, Derrida invites radical hospitality. Here we are reminded that the limit is also a border and, as such, a place of encounter where we may find ourselves outside of ourselves as given, graced, by a bottomless multitude of others—divine and otherwise. With a reinterpretation of Laurel Schneider's incarnation, void of all "numerical reckoning,"[10] we might move from an exclusive incarnation of a human to a figure of Christ multiplied across the species of creation. In this view Christ embodies and reveals grace, life, and communion in places least expected and God-forsaken: among the "excluded, foreclosed, disavowed, tamed, and sacrificed."[11]

ANTHROPOCENTRISM AND CHRISTOCENTRISM

Thematically ours is not an unfamiliar problem, Mary Daly might remind us, for modern Christian thought: If God became human, humans become God.[12] As early as the 1950s (before Lynn White's frequently cited essay) the Lutheran theologian Joseph Sittler suggested that ecology and the care of the earth were a concern of central importance for Christian theology. At a time when people had to go look up *ecology* in their dictionaries after his lectures Sittler argued that the Christian's lack of interest in environmental concerns could be traced to a restricted doctrine of grace and an overly personalized Christ. Sittler acknowledged the anthropocentrism of Protestant thought in particular. He also argued, however, that there was potential within the tradition to unsettle this tendency. Luther's maxim, "Man seeks himself in everything—even God,"[13] became Sittler's key to interpreting the Augustinian-Lutheran definition of sin (*incurvatus in se*) as a basic anthropocentric tendency that must be checked by an understanding of grace beyond human history. He acknowledged that a major roadblock to the development of an ecotheology from his tradition was its Christocentrism.[14] However, his solution was not to de-emphasize Christ, but to articulate a nature Christology, expanding the doctrine of grace and Christ's work beyond the human to all the cosmos. Sittler grounded his ecotheology not in the doctrine of creation, but in the doctrines of grace and incarnation. Grace, Christ, and the self must be rethought, he believed, in order to account for the reality of humanity embedded in an ecological system where "no thing exists apart from all things."[15]

Sittler challenged the separative individualism implicit in his theological and cultural tradition. Instead, he suggested an "ecological self." "We are constituted by our transactions with nature," he writes.[16] No self exists outside a web of relations. Instead of being a static substance, the self exists at an "intersection" of multiple organisms (as Haraway also reminds us) and influences. For Sittler, the ecological self implies a generalized condition of creation as given in grace. "I have no self by myself or for myself. I really have no identity that I can specify except the intersection point of a multitude of things that are not mine. They have been given to me."[17] For Sittler the ecological self is necessarily a graced self. Humanity exists only in and through communion with the other-than-human. Everything we have and are has been given by our creaturely neighbors and God who abides "in, with, and under" creation, saturating it with relational, dynamic, grace.[18]

Sittler's 1961 New Delhi speech to the World Council of Churches sparked debate about the nature and scope of God's grace.[19] In a room of attendees anticipating a lecture on ecumenical unity Sittler instead challenged his audience to think beyond ecumenism to unity with all of creation. He insisted that God's grace must not be limited to the realm of redemption—and if the doctrine of grace must be expanded, so must Christ. In *Essays on Nature and Grace*, written after the New Delhi speech, he expanded on his claim that the limited scope of grace and Christ could be traced to the Reformation where it became focused on the personal. When grace in the world became tied solely to the work of the incarnated Christ, the almost sole focus of Christ's work became the redemption of the individual person from sin. Sittler sought to reaffirm Christ's work beyond the human realm where, according to the Gospel of John, Christ was active and present in creation and, according to Paul, will be the key to the redemption of all creation. He rejected the reduction of Christology to soteriology for the individual human, insisting that, "a doctrine of redemption is meaningful only when it swings within the orbit of a larger doctrine of creation."[20] Paul Santmire, a contemporary Lutheran ecotheologian, suggests that Sittler's "radical and revolutionary" challenge to Western theology "is in fact a call for a kind of paradigm shift . . . away from an exclusively the-anthropological soteriology, to what can be called an inclusive or universal soteriology, which envisions the final salvation of all things as the telos of creation."[21] Sittler shifts Christ's relevance beyond an exclusively human realm toward a cosmic Christ. The cosmos has come into being through Christ, and thus redeeming grace cannot be limited to a particular time in human history. Grace is therefore "inherent in and given in, with, and under the creation."[22] This sacramental language clearly signals Sittler's desire to expand the means of grace beyond the walls of the church to all of creation.[23]

Sittler's work is a significant step for Christian ecotheology. His work combats anthropocentric Christology, and yet tensions remain. A description of Sittler's work by one of his commentators is revealing. Conrad Simonson writes that Sittler's "unique and lasting contribution . . . is his 'christology of nature'—a christology 'as large as the nature and destiny of man' and 'expanded to its cosmic dimensions.'"[24] Intended as a glowing endorsement, the statement also reveals a remnant human triumphalism. It reveals the potential danger of the cosmic Christ. Where Christ remains fettered to the human being in abstraction from its environment, the power and significance of the human being rises to cosmic dimensions with Christ rather than remaining among its web of creaturely relations. Sittler does not adequately neutralize this danger that undermines his ecotheology wherever the divine human is placed at the center of the cosmos.[25] With Sittler we can see the dangers of an overly personalized, intimate, brotherly Christ, even as he attempts to thwart this danger by emphasizing Christ's role in creation and its redemption. In a critical analysis of Sittler's constructive work one gets a sense of both the promise and precarious nature of the doctrine of incarnation and Christology for Christian ecotheology. Because of the implications of Christ for God and humanity and their relation to creation, I would submit that these doctrines lie at the heart of the matter for Christian theology in a world facing eco-crisis. So what happens to this "brotherhood" when the other-than-human arrives on the scene?

INTERRUPTED BY ONE "WHOLLY OTHER"

In the late twentieth and early twenty-first centuries the Jewish-Algerian-born, "rightly pass[ing] for an atheist," French philosopher Jacques Derrida challenged Western philosophy with the question of the animal.[26] Toward the end of his life he paid particular attention to the role of the animal in the history of Western philosophy and the founding of a concept of the human in general. Derrida highlighted the question of the animal in such a way as to insist on its unique significance for questions that have occupied philosophical and ethical thought all along:

The "question of animality" is not one question among others, of course. I have long considered it to be decisive (as one says), in itself and for its strategic value; and that's because, while it is difficult and enigmatic in itself, it also represents the limit upon which all the great questions are formed and determined, as well as all the concepts that attempt to delimit what is "proper to man," the essence and future of humanity, ethics, politics, law, "human rights," "crimes against humanity," "genocide," etc.[27]

In *The Animal That Therefore I Am* Derrida emphasizes the pivotal role Descartes has played in the conceptualization of the human being, law, ethics, and rights. Descartes broke from the tradition of Aristotle who argued that humans were "rational animals," which implied that humans were on some kind of a continuum of life alongside all other living beings.[28] Descartes put all of this into question by arguing that the only thing one could know to begin with was that "I think." If there is thought there must be a being behind this thought: "I think, therefore I am." In order to ground the modern human subject in certitude all else was put into question—including the place of the human alongside other creatures. Descartes drew a line between the human and all other life-forms. In this sense Descartes created the modern animal.[29] Humans could reflect on themselves; they were self-conscious, self-aware, and could thus respond ethically and morally to other humans. Furthermore, they could be responsible and could be held responsible by law for their behavior. The animal, it was clear to Descartes, could not. The human alone held the divine gift of self-consciousness. If the animal could not know itself, it could not respond, but only react. "This radical reconception of the nonhuman animal," Stephen Moore notes, "was subsequently termed the *bête-machine* ('beast-machine') doctrine for its equation of animals with clocks and other machines with automatic moving parts."[30]

Early on in *The Animal*, Derrida describes a peculiar and significant encounter. He sees his cat seeing him naked, and he feels ashamed. This ignites Derrida's thought: Why am I ashamed? Who or what sees me? "Before the cat that looks at me naked, would I be ashamed *like* a beast that no longer has the sense of its nudity? Or, on the contrary, *like* a man who retains the sense of his nudity?" The questions, sparked by the disruptive gaze of the animal, lead to a more familiar philosophical question: "Who am I, therefore?"[31] The repetition of the same—of reflection, self-consciousness, autobiography—does not spark thought about his "autobiography," "being," or "existence," as it were. Instead, the interruption of something completely and absolutely other presents an opening for thought. But this is no general or universalized other. Derrida remarks that his cat "comes to me as *this* irreplaceable living being that one day enters my space, into this place where it can encounter me, see me, even see me naked. Nothing can ever rob me of the certainty that what we have here is an existence that refuses to be conceptualized."[32] Whereas Descartes's certainty starts with doubt that excludes everything save self-consciousness, which remains the single foundational truth, Derrida's thought begins with the face-to-face encounter with the absolute other who refuses to be conceptualized. Descartes's thought begins with the self-same, the similar, familial, or familiar. This Derrida rejects, arguing—with the help of his little cat—that rather than a reflection of the same, the "point of view of the absolute other," the interruption of something completely different, opens the possibility for thought.[33]

The wholly other is an important Derridean insight throughout *The Animal That Therefore I Am*. Derrida's earlier work *The Gift of Death* provides an important perspective on this theme. Here Derrida does not broaden or blur but multiplies the wholly other. God, the traditional absolute other, is not known through homogeneity or any kind of sameness but remains unknown and fully heterogeneous to humanity. This surprisingly banal and traditional theological position is, however, not where Derrida leaves us. Derrida draws attention to Kierkegaard's ethical move in *Fear and Trembling*. Kierkegaard insists that in nearly sacrificing Isaac Abraham betrays the ethical for the religious. Kierkegaard refers here to Hegel's "ethics of the same" that insists that "the highest expression of the ethical is in terms of what binds us to our own and to our fellows."[34] Instead of opposing the ethical to the religious, Derrida radicalizes wholly otherness to transform both the ethical and religious:

> If God is the wholly other, the figure, or name of the wholly other, then every other (one) is every (bit) other. *Tout autre est tout autre.* . . . [This formula] implies that God, as wholly other, is to be found everywhere there is something of the wholly other. . . . What can be

said about Abraham's relation to God can be said about my relation without relation to *every other (one) as every (bit) other.*[35]

Derrida multiplies the characteristic that traditionally has been thought of as God's alone. Rather than imply some kind of sameness within God where humanity can have access to God or knowledge of God, Derrida radicalizes God's wholly otherness by multiplying it to every other. In other words, the "infinite alterity" of God is not reserved for God alone but can be recognized "in each, each one . . . indeed each living thing, human or not."[36]

If this infinite alterity, which traditionally has been associated with God alone, now describes every other, then one can no longer distinguish between ethical responsibility to the created other and religious duty to God. Here Derrida follows Emmanuel Levinas. The Jewish-Lithuanian-born French philosopher Levinas—and here in particular his ethic of the Other—was a significant influence on Derrida, which can be credited for much of the ethical or "religious turn" in continental philosophy today.[37] Levinas's ethics blur into religion, and religion becomes indistinguishable from ethics: Levinas's "ethics is already a religion."[38] But where Levinas expands the wholly otherness of God to all human others, Derrida wants a more radical understanding of the other to include the other-than-human.

AT THE LIMIT: DIVINANIMALITY AND
WHAT IS "PROPER" TO "MAN"

The special and exclusive relationship between God and human implied in the traditional Christian incarnation can be complicated by two interconnected insights in *The Animal*: "divinanimality" and "limitrophy." Here Derrida exposes and analyzes the way the human has been defined over and against the other-than-human. He approaches divinanimality in the third lecture of those published in *The Animal*. In dialogue with the French psychoanalyst and philosopher Jacques Lacan, Derrida works to reveal the structure of sacrifice and the constitutive relation of the other at the heart of Western subjectivity. Despite the Western philosophical view of the subject as sovereign and self-sufficient, in its very becoming subject it is "subject to its being-subject, its being-host or -hostage, that is to say, its being-subjected-to-the-other, to the Wholly Other or to every single other."[39]

Derrida's deconstruction of subjectivity reveals it as always de-centered and multiple. Just as in his early work he has followed the trace, since we always start with the trace of the trace with no true original starting place of immediate presence, so here he follows the trace of the other, who-ever this one may be.[40] Throughout *The Animal* Derrida demonstrates this by refusing to reference his being without also making reference to the fact that he isn't apart from those he follows. In *The Animal* Derrida con-stantly references Descartes's proposition: *cogito ergo sum*. He frequently asks, "Whom am I (following)?" or states, "I am (following)." He reminds us that the "I am" (being, consciousness, etc.) is always interrupted by an-other. It is always interrupted by those we follow or who follow (or hunt!) us. In this way he substitutes following for the "I am"—for "being."[41] The animal is there before him, beside him, and behind him: The animal, as he says, "surrounds me." He "is" with the animal.

Derrida contrasts this animal following with Lacan's subject. Despite Lacan's disruption of Cartesian subjectivity through his work on the un-conscious, Lacan follows Descartes, Derrida argues, by insisting that the animal does not have the capability (namely speech, response, deception) to be a subject. Derrida turns the tables, revealing the way in which the human subject is dependent on, and thus subject to, the animal. Lacan did not want to acknowledge this kind of dependence of the subject, but in typical Derridean fashion he shows that Lacan's thought depends on what it excludes. Lacan insists on the necessity of the Other for speech. "Speech begins," Derrida explains, describing Lacan's position, "only with the pas-sage from 'pretense' to the order of the signifier, and that the signifier re-quires another locus—the locus of the Other, the Other witness."[42] In spite of himself Lacan insists on the priority of the other. Lacan's subject is typi-cally independent and separative, but Derrida reveals its dependence on the other-than-human; but not just any other human will do. The human is too familiar, too "brotherly," too similar. This other must "break with the image and with the likeness of a fellow," Derrida argues. It must "be at least situated in a place of alterity that is radical enough to break with every identification of an image of self, with every fellow living creature, and so with every fraternity or human proximity, with all humanity. Must not this place of the Other be ahuman?"[43]

According to Derrida, in the philosophical tradition following Descartes the divine and the animal share the status of the ahuman as nonfellow.

Both have been excluded by Descartes (along with that limitrophic figure, the chimera) for the delineation of the thinking human subject.[44] Furthermore, both share—one could conclude from Heidegger—a lack of world and death.[45] The divine and the animal are united by their exclusion and lack, and thus they are deemed, by Derrida, "inseparable."[46] Only the divinanimal is other enough for the human to become a subject. In Western thought subjectivity has been necessary for conceptions of agency, responsibility, law, and politics. Therefore, this divinanimal must be the "excluded, foreclosed, disavowed, tamed, and sacrificed foundation of what it founds, namely, the symbolic order, the human order, law and justice."[47] The divinanimal is necessary for the founding of a sovereign subjectivity; therefore, the subject's dependence on anything other than itself must be erased.

At the very last Derrida reveals his strategy for thinking differently about human/animal relations. Derrida wants to thicken, multiply, and complicate the line between the human and animal. Even broader than that, he wants to pluralize what it means to be living, to radically reinterpret "what is living, naturally, but not in terms of the 'essence of living,' of the 'essence of the animal.'"[48] Instead of a limit, line, or border dualistically separating the human and the animal, Derrida emphasizes "what sprouts or grows at the limit, around the limit, by maintaining the limit, but also what *feeds the limit*, generates it, raises it, and complicates it." This is what Derrida calls "limitrophy," and it is, he announces, "my subject."[49] His interest in limitrophy is not in "effacing the limit, but in multiplying its figures, in complicating, thickening, delinearizing, folding, and dividing the line precisely by making it increase and multiply."[50] His concern is not for blurring or melding. The singular and particular remain key. The divinanimal is just such a limitrophic figure for thinking differently about human/animal/divine relations.

We have followed Derrida from an encounter with his cat to his limitrophic divinanimal. We have followed him, "surrounded by" the animal as he is. Here, also, we find Haraway at Derrida's own limit. Haraway describes herself not as a secular but a "worldly" thinker. Biologist, feminist, and neo-Marxist, she is fully committed to the mundane. In *When Species Meet* Haraway acknowledges the significant work done by Derrida. Referring specifically to Derrida's face-to-face with his cat, she credits him with understanding "that actual animals look back at actual human beings." He "knew he was in the presence of someone, not of a machine reacting."[51]

However, she also notes that Derrida "came right to the edge of respect, but was sidetracked by his textual canon of Western philosophy and literature."[52] In other words, Haraway insists animals are not only good to think with, they are to live with.[53] Derrida seems unsure how far one can go down this path toward being-with: "Being after, being alongside, being near would appear as different modes of being, indeed of being-with. With the animal." But then he adds that "in spite of appearances, it isn't certain that these modes of being come to modify a preestablished being, even less a primitive 'I am.'"[54] Haraway, however, insists that "those who are to be in the world are constituted in intra- and interaction. The partners do not precede the meeting; species of all kinds, living and not, are consequent on a subject- and object-shaping dance of encounters."[55]

Where Derrida makes significant steps toward thinking the human and its relations with other-than-humans, Haraway shifts the conversation toward the worldly encounter. Similarly, here we are after not only a new way to think the human, animal, and divine. We seek a new way of living, and for this we follow Christ, as ever, to the limit. Haraway reminds us that the limit is not only the place to shore up human subjectivity or to rethink human/animal relations. The limit is also the border that proves porous enough for the encounters that shape who and what we are in the world. The only way to act responsibly is to be responsive and to allow the other, even the other-than-human-other, to respond to us as well. We are tied together with a host of others—all "coshaping one another in layers of reciprocating complexity all the way down."[56] The source of responsibility is not a pure, self-conscious, detached, fortified, and unwavering self. Rather, "Response and respect are possible only in those knots"[57] between self and other, human and other-than human, divine and creature.

Fully human, fully divine—Chalceonian Christology holds the body of Christ perpetually at these limits. If Haraway's biology holds sway, the body of Jesus must have been even more complex. If fully human as well as fully divine, Jesus' body, like ours, must not have been purely human. "I love the fact," Haraway writes, "that human genomes can be found in only about 10 percent of all the cells that occupy the mundane space I call my body; the other 90 percent of the cells are filled with genomes of bacteria, fungi, protists, and such, some of which play in a symphony necessary to my being alive at all, and some of which are hitching a ride and doing the rest of me, of us, no harm."[58] She continues by arguing that given this biological reality, we must conclude that we become human only through and with these other-than-human creatures. "To be one is always to become with many," she contends.[59] Jesus, like us, must have been more than human. He must have been more than divine. Jesus as the Christ must be some kind of divinanimal.

WHAT SPROUTS AT THE LIMIT

At the heart of this exploration of incarnation is a question of limits: the limit between God and humanity, God and other-than-human creation, and the limitation or self-limitation of God. In traditional Christian thought God is embodied as human and only human. But perhaps we should distinguish between particularity and exclusivity. Perhaps particularity can be seen not only as a scandal but also as a way forward. Derrida insisted that the particularity or singularity of his cat resists the limits of conceptualization. In a similar way, Laurel Schneider insists on the singularity of embodied life as a way toward multiplicity.

In *Beyond Monotheism: A Theology of Multiplicity* the theologian Laurel Schneider insists on the singularity of Jesus precisely because it allows for his profusion. Schneider's objective is to introduce plurality into Christian theology and subvert the domination of the "logic of the One," which continually leads to dichotomous alternatives and violent, hierarchical oppositions. Schneider insists that the key to a Christian theology of multiplicity has been lying almost dormant within the Christian tradition: Incarnation is this key, but it must be disentangled from the hold the "logic of the One" has on it. Schneider redefines incarnation as "not just the event of a man named Jesus who is affirmed in the Nicene creed as 'true God from true God made man.'" Rather, incarnation is an "orientation toward reality," which attends to the fleshiness of reality and the "mutability of bodies."[60]

Schneider does not reject the Nicene/Chalcedonian orthodoxy of the humanity/divinity of Christ, but rather asserts that "'fully divine and fully human' is in fact a wonderful opening."[61] Unfortunately, she adds, this formula lost much of its power when the councils insisted that it was Jesus' "absolute divinity and not his embodiment that determines his singularity. He alone is divine and human; all others are only human."[62] Furthermore, rather than marking his singularity, his body is universalized. His body becomes what "determines his sameness with all of humankind, not his utter singularity."[63] Jesus' body becomes the body of "Everyman." His body can be exchanged for every other human body in order to atone for the sins of "Everyman." In Jesus God becomes universally human: one of "us," a "brother," a "fellow."

Rejecting this universalization, Schneider insists instead on Jesus' plurality according to the singularity of his flesh. "Jesus," she writes, "was a singular divine incarnation, not because he was the One God in a single Everyman coat, but because divinity unfolded in his limbs into utter complicity in the world—as divinity ever does. 'Jesus' is a multiplicity, not just because he is a story but because, as a man, he had a body and so he exceeded the narrow limits of oneness; he himself was legion."[64] In his singularity as human and divine Jesus multiplies the figure of Christ. Christ is at the limit—growing there, proliferating its borders.

Insisting on the singularity of Jesus' fleshiness and thereby also his more-than-oneness, the Christ may become unhinged from the exclusive necessity of human flesh. The multiplicity of Jesus refuses to exclude the incarnation of the Christ from a host of time and place singularities and suggests that Christ is a revelation of the way that the divine can and does materialize in the world. Singularity reveals not logocentric Oneness but an irreplaceability and a vulnerability inherent in material, mortal life.

For Schneider incarnation should not be limited to just Christ. Whereas Schneider wants to affirm a diversity of incarnations beyond Christ, I want to propose the reverse: Christ flourishing in, on "the face" of, in the "figure"[65] of every incarnation. Christ diversifies the borders, the limits between human and animal, God and human, God and the other-than-human, in each incarnation. I'm proposing that incarnation is singularly multiple and that Christ is active and present in each one so that the metamorphic, limitrophic, chimeral figure of Christ is a trace on each incarnation. As Christ is multiplied in matter, he/she/it is left as a trace on every wholly other that has been deemed necessary for a foundation and then discarded. In every instance of the other we see the figure of Christ as wholly other.[66]

The divinanimality of Christ must be repeated, constantly counterbalancing any figure of Christ's empathetic likeness to humans in their condition. Christ is at the limit of God and the world, thickening, complicating, folding, and making it increase and flourish. Christ does not efface the limit between creator and creation; in, with, and under mundane matter Christ as God's worldly body is replicated and recapitulated.

LORD SEQUOIA

We have encountered the divinanimal as a playful creature: bending, twisting, chasing, hunting, surprising, metamorphosing, responding, and calling forth our response/ability. The limitrophic divinanimal, like Muir's Lord Sequoia, grows in the fertile ground at the abyssal limit of the divine and other-than-divine. Muir has left all to follow Sequoia, and it in turn follows him, surrounds him. He is with Sequoia: "I am in the woods woods woods and they are in me-ee-ee!" He has communed with—drank the blood of— Sequoia as this limitrophic figure morphs again into his woodland gospel.

But from Derrida's analysis rather than Muir's poetics we learn that this divinanimal, Lord Sequoia, is also the sacrificed foundation of what it founds. Again, this figure of Christ is an exclusion or sacrifice outside the limits of human society—be it Golgotha or wilderness space—deemed necessary in order to found and secure a certain kind of human society, politics, morality, order, and law.[67] These divinanimals have been simultaneously necessary and excluded for the founding of "humanity" and a "humane society." Muir's woods, in order to remain woods and not be developed or consumed, have become the excluded, the foreclosed, disavowed, and tamed foundation of what is properly human society.

Muir furthermore tends to divinize wilderness space for its very lack of humanity. We cannot see the trace of the figure of Christ on the divinanimal without recognizing that their bodies reveal both tragedy and interconnection. Derrida's deconstruction of all dualisms remind us that wilderness space, the arboreal, or animal cannot be divinized in purity. What Muir tended to sanctify in purity from human society, we cannot. The sacredness of these spaces, objects, or entities is not their purity from humanity or even their innocence, for in them we see what has been rejected to delineate a conception of the human individual and social identity.

As a limitrophic figure, Christ is not only the sacrificed foundation of what it founds but also the revelation of a repressed interdependence— this, anyway, is what Muir and Haraway might answer back to Derrida. Christ remains perpetually at these limits, surprising us with divinity in the midst of seeming God-forsakenness, revealing our very selves as bottomless vessels of grace, since all that we call "ours" has been given to us. With Sittler we might also see the limit as a space for grace. A limit of the porous or communing (with Muir who has drunk Sequoia blood) might be a place where we find ourselves only outside of ourselves. It might be a place where we come to see ourselves as impurely riddled with a host of others. We reflect on these encounters and come to see ourselves as bottomlessly given—graced, by a multitude of divine and creaturely others. Divinanimality reveals not that it is purged of the trace of humanity, but that the embodiment of Jesus as Christ makes manifest divinity in the weakness and vulnerability of materiality. Amid the tragedy of rejection and sacrifice a recollection rises ever again as something Muir could intuitively feel and ebulliently rejoice over but could not yet theorize: that we only are as interconnected. To be we must have communed with Lord Sequoia or one of its many other incarnations. We are in the woods, woods, woods, and they are in us, us, us.

❧ Animal Calls

KATE RIGBY

In his lecture "The Animal That Therefore I Am (More to Follow)," Jacques Derrida makes the vital move of questioning the rigid boundary between humans and (other) animals, which, in the predominantly phallogocentric philosophical traditions of the West, has been intimately tied to the question of language:

> *Animal* is a word that men have given themselves the right to give. These humans have been found giving it to themselves, this word, but as if they have received it as an inheritance. They have given themselves the word in order to corral a large number of living beings within a single concept: "the Animal," they say. . . . Men would be first and foremost those living creatures who have given themselves the word that enables them to speak of the animal with a single voice and to designate it as the single being that remains without a response, without a word with which to respond.[1]

This passage is cited by Laura Hobgood-Oster in her book on animals in the Christian tradition, *Holy Dogs and Asses*, in which she traces some of the salient ways in which this philosophical silencing of other-than-human animals has been variously, and ambiguously, reinforced and resisted within Euro-Western religious thought and practice in the Christian tradition.[2] In this essay, I want to revisit the question of language as the first step along the path toward an ecotheologically informed practice of becoming-with more-than-human others, which, recalling Bruno Latour's political vision of a "parliament of things,"[3] opens up the possibility of conceiving a more inclusive "communion of creatures." In particular, I want to consider how cultivating the practice of attending to animal calls might help us overcome the perilous condition of human self-enclosure, which, in Val Plumwood's trenchant ecopolitical analysis, has come to characterize the dominant culture of Euro-Western modernity, severing its citizens from the semiosis of the more-than-human world, obscuring their ethical responsibility toward other-than-human creatures, and rendering them dangerously oblivious to their interdependence with those multifarious others whose existence, if it is acknowledged at all, is generally considered a mere background to exclusively human activities and interests.[4]

TUNING IN TO THE CALL: COMMUNICATION IN A MORE-THAN-HUMAN WORLD

There is a poem by one of Australia's preeminent twentieth-century writers, A. D. Hope, in which the speaker recalls from childhood the enchanting song of Tasmanian magpies, "Fluting at dawn through pure, clear rills of sound." But what they called to him, those "magpies of that earlier day," was a human word, and it was this that held him spellbound: "Ethiopia! They used to say. . . . Dulcimer of no Abyssinian maid / Was ever so doucely played. / Ethiōpia, Ethiopiā! / Echoes went round me of Mount Abora." By contrast, the magpie song of the Monaro plains of New South Wales, where the poet had come to reside (in the federal capital, Canberra) as an adult, is said to lack "the enchantment of that warbled name." Dismissing the possibility that this was primarily a matter of differences in magpie dialect, the speaker concludes by wondering ruefully whether the alteration lay rather in his own mode of apprehension:

> Can it perhaps be true
> That I have lost those languages I knew
> In boyhood, when each bird,
> Stone, cloud and every tree that grew
> Spoke and I had by heart all that I heard?

Yet with this loss, there is also the hint of a gain. Hearing in the Tasmanian magpies' song the syllables of an African place-name, the child was entranced by the birds' ability to summon in him visions of another world:

exotic, erotic, far distant, and deeply alluring; but for all that, a human world, bearing the distinct trace, moreover, of a colonial cultural imaginary. Lost in the fantasy of an idealized Abyssinia, the boy has not yet glimpsed the possibility of hearing in the magpies' vocalizations the trace of another other world, a material reality that was being disclosed to him in the here and now: that of the birds themselves. By contrast, the song of the Monaro magpies, disenchanted as it is, actually re-sounds more distinctly in the poet's verse: "The same pure grace-notes, the same exquisite trill, / The lilt, the liquid ease." In the verbal musicality of these lines, with their lilting rhythm and trilling alliteration and assonance, Hope shows his attention to the wordless musicality of the magpies' song: an attention premised on the surrendering of a naive anthropomorphism. No longer projecting human words into the birds' beaks, he is now able to apprehend something of the magpies' other-than-human manner of being and singing: "Monaro magpies bursting into song / Soar through new cadences, fresh jubilee; / But in an unknown tongue / Rejoice."[5] Yet this recognition of avian alterity is presented as primarily privative, leading to a sense of disconnection. Rather than evincing a curiosity about what the magpies might be communicating to one another—and possibly other others—with their caroling, beyond a generalized jubilation, the speaker turns his attention inward, lamenting the change in his own subjectivity that has broken the imagined communion with the more-than-human world that he enjoyed as a child.

The movement toward and then back away from the animal other that is traced in Hope's poem parallels to some degree that which Donna Haraway tracks in the Derrida lecture mentioned earlier. The philosopher's ponderings were prompted not by the call of a wild animal but by the gaze of his domestic companion, the little cat who so unsettled Derrida by beholding him in his human-animal nakedness. As Donna Haraway observes, Derrida "came right to the edge of respect, of the move to *respecere*, but he was sidetracked by his textual canon of Western philosophy and literature and by his linked worries about being naked in front of his cat," and thereby "failed a simple obligation of companion species: he did not become curious about what the cat might actually be doing, feeling, thinking, or perhaps making available to him in looking back that morning."[6] Haraway links this failure, which is perpetuated in *The Animal That Therefore I Am*,[7] to the philosopher's reluctance to engage with scientific studies of animal cognition and emotion—a reluctance that is perhaps not unrelated to Derrida's somewhat puzzling and uncharacteristically dogmatic insistence on the abyssal distinction between humans and (other) animals, as Matthew Calarco notes.[8] However that may be, I want to follow Haraway in departing from Derrida and making this further step toward respectful curiosity. However, I believe that this move should not be restricted to the companionable relationship with domestic animals that Haraway tends to privilege. At the very least, it should be extended, in my view, to those undomesticated creatures who have the capacity to become what Val Plumwood terms our "familiars," a familiar being in her definition, "a free-living animal in your local surroundings you can see sufficiently often to come to know individually" and with whom you "can form some kind of communicative bond, friendship, protective relationship, companionship, or acquaintance."[9]

Plumwood cultivated such a relationship with a succession of wombats, who helpfully kept her grass clipped in return for an evening treat of oats and carrots. For several years, "Victor" continued to graze the lawn beneath which she is buried, her body in death having been willingly offered up as food for those nonhuman others whose cause she had championed throughout her life's work as a pioneering ecophilosopher and environmental activist.[10] Fortunately, though, in view of the seemingly unstoppable growth of cities, you do not have to live in the bush, as she did, to find a familiar—or several. For urban Australians, one species that affords this possibility in abundance is none other than the magpie (of which there are hordes in Canberra) that Hope poeticized. To begin with, this is a creature who happily pays no heed to the biblical ordinance according to which God's countenancing of human predation following the Flood implied that "the fear and dread of [humankind] shall rest on every animal of the earth, and on every bird of the air, on everything that creeps on the ground, and on all the fish of the sea" (Gen. 9:2).[11] On the contrary, it is more likely to be the humans who live in fear and dread of magpies, at least in the spring, on account of the agonistic behavior of many a magpie father-to-be during nesting season. Despite their seasonal propensity for swooping, many Australians, myself included, nonetheless delight not only in their mellifluous yearlong song but also in their readiness to return your gaze and even take a polite interest in your whistled ditties, should you stop to pass the time of day with them. If food is on offer, they will confidently march right up to, and even through, your front door, and if encouraged to do so safely, they will quickly become regular visitors, raising their young to treat you as friends, and learning to trust that no swooping should be necessary to keep you in line in the spring.

One person who has set out to learn something of the magpie's "unknown tongue" is the ethologist Gisela Kaplan. Not unlike the primatologist Barbara Smuts, whose unconventional approach to studying baboons is described by Donna Haraway in *When Species Meet*, Kaplan has learned about magpies, not by keeping her distance, but by entering into relationship with them, discovering in the process that these highly social creatures are capable of the most tender expressions of affection, as well as a stern sense of propriety and a joyous propensity for play. Whereas Smuts managed to establish mutual respect with the baboons she was studying, however, Kaplan's relationship with those magpies that she hand-raised looks very much like love. Studying also several groups of wild magpies in various locations in New South Wales and drawing on earlier research findings, Kaplan has begun to illuminate the fascinating ways of this curious creature, which is one of the foremost songbirds of the world, and possibly among the most intelligent of species. Not that this would be news for Aboriginal Australians, who have long recognized their cleverness, and for some of whom, such as the Wodi-Wodi people of the Illawara region south of Sydney, the magpie is claimed as kin.[12]

The Australian magpie (*Gymnorhina tibicen*) lives on average up to around twenty-five years. Some join together in nomadic bands, but most tend to form family groups within a more or less defined territory, and they have elaborate diplomatic codes for settling boundary disputes. They communicate with one another and with some other species (including, potentially, humans) in a range of ways, including facial expression, plumage ruffling, bodily posture, flight trajectory, beak clacking, and, of course, vocalization. Audible over long distances, magpie songs and call types are in Kaplan's assessment so varied in function and structure that "it would be difficult to explain their existence and diversity other than as a highly developed communication system."[13] The jubilant caroling that Hope recalls in "Tasmanian Magpies" Kaplan relates to bonding and territoriality. Members of the same territorial group develop their own distinctive song, which changes over time and possibly includes individual variations. Regional dialects have also been observed, so Hope's first impression was right: The Monaro magpies probably do not share that song snippet, resembling "Ethiopia," that he heard among their Tasmanian cousins. Magpies call and respond to one another in sequential duets, as well as delighting in singing solo, warbling tunefully and meditatively, sometimes for up to an hour or more, in what Kaplan believes is a kind of leisure-time activity. Intriguingly, magpies also weave into their songs the sounds of other creatures commonly heard in their territory, such as cats, dogs, horses, humans, other birds, and potential predators, leading Kaplan to speculate that this might serve as a means of mapping the membership of their local community. Among the many messages that magpies convey vocally are ones relating to identity and locality ("Here I am, over here"), as well as affection, rivalry, victory, disapproval, hunger, anxiety, alarm, and warning. Magpies call directives to one another to come, to go, and to follow, and they also warn of particular threats (for example, from a cat, an owl, or an eagle) using distinctive calls, which also appear to be understood by other avian species with whom they share a territory. Heeding the warning call of the magpie is something that I too am learning to do, but the threat in this case is of a different order, as I explain below.

Kaplan's study of magpie communication provides but one example of the ways in which articulate human language is currently being resituated as but one, admittedly highly complex, flexible, and adaptive, mode of communication among a vast array of others, including of course those forms of communication—facial, gestural, tonal, haptic, kinetic, and chemical—that also inform human interchanges, albeit generally below the level of consciousness. Tuning in to the communicative calls of companion animals or animal familiars can extend our own communicative capacities, inducting us into the fascinating world of "creature language"[14] and potentially opening a pathway of reconnection with the more-than-human world in general. From a theological perspective, the biosemiotic reconceptualization of Earth as a polylogic semiosphere[15]—one that was preempted by Maurice Merleau-Ponty in his lectures on nature from the late 1950s[16]—enables an enhanced appreciation of creation as a communicative process comprising countless exchanges of more-than-human call-and-response, all gloriously lured into being by the primal call of divine love: a call to which each of us responds, as Jean-Louis Chrétien stresses, in the first place simply by existing, but which none of us can ever answer entirely adequately (because there is always more to the summons than any one of us can discern).[17] This does not necessarily imply the seamless identification of what theologians call "creation" with what scientists call "nature" in a renovated version of physico-theological deism.[18] Rather, it enjoins an endeavor to discern and nurture within the dynamically "intra-active"[19] becoming of the material-discursive world, the ceaseless coming-into-being of a creation that could be once more (as, in a sense, it always has been) "very good"—which is to say, not only suffused with signs, but also tilted toward justice and compassion. Within this understanding of creation-in-process, the "messianic age remains *always* yet to come in history: it is not a literal time-to-come, but an ideal that *resists* every realized eschatology."[20]

James Hatley, elaborating ecophilosophically on Levinas's ethical understanding of what is involved in responding with a "yes, here I am" (*hineini*, in Hebrew) to the Other who "faces" me with my ethical responsibility toward them, writes of the goodness of creation (at once primordial and yet to come) in these terms:

> In *hineini*, responsibility transcends the created world otherwise than as the hypostatization of yet another world, or as rendering abstract to the point of numbness the palpability and sensitivity of my own creatureliness. Transcendence here does not betray earthly creation but breaks it loose from its usual habits, its inveterate repetitions. Rather than signifying a continuum of sustained existence, creation is revealed to be a renewal that cannot be quelled, a call to responsiveness and responsibility that cannot be limited and anticipated.[21]

Nor can this responsiveness and responsibility be limited to others of our own kind. If the human vocation as *imago dei* (a deeply problematic, but perhaps not entirely irredeemable term) is to collaborate with what process theologians term the "divine mystery" in helping this anarchically good creation to keep on coming forth in the midst of our broken world, then surely this entails a readiness to answer to a particular kind of animal call: that of the suffering creature.

RESPONDING TO THE CALL: ETHICS IN A MORE-THAN-HUMAN WORLD

As Charles Pinches and Jay McDaniel have observed, the Christian scriptures do not offer much by way of "good news" for nonhumans, at least, not explicitly.[22] Animals do nonetheless figure significantly in some of the apocrypha and hagiographies of saints. Among the many such tales that give a voice to animals, as discussed by Hobgood-Oster, there is one in particular that stands out for me. Whereas in most of these stories, as in Hope's recollection of Tasmanian magpie song, animal voices are heard to speak human words, in the Coptic narrative of the beaten mule, the animal in question does not talk. But neither does he communicate in an "unknown tongue": at least, not to the one who hears his call. Let me retell the story, as it appears in English translation in Roderic Dunkerley's *Beyond the Gospels*:

> It happened that the Lord went forth from the city and walked with his disciples over the mountains. And they came to a mountain, and the road which led to it was steep. There they found a man with a sumpter-mule. But the animal had fallen for the burden was too heavy, and he beat it that it bled. And Jesus came to him and said, Man, why dost thou beat thine animal? Seest thou not that it suffers pains? But the man answered and said, What good is that to you? I can beat it as much as I please, since it is my property, and I bought it for a good sum of money. Ask those that are with thee, for they know me and know thereof. And some of the disciples said, Yea Lord, it is as he says. We have seen how he bought it. But the Lord said, Do you not notice how it bleeds, and hear you not how it laments and cries? But they answered and said, Nay Lord, we hear not how it laments and cries. And the Lord was sad and exclaimed, Woe to you, that ye hear not how it complains to the Creator in heaven, and cries for mercy. But three times woe to him of whom it complains and cries in its distress. And he came forth and touched the animal. And it arose and its wounds were healed. And Jesus said to the man, Now go on and beat it no more, that you also may find mercy.[23]

Unlike Immanuel Kant, the Jesus of this apocryphal tale clearly does not view the mistreatment of a domestic animal as interdicted solely on the grounds of the indirect harm that might accrue to its human owner. On the contrary, human moral accountability before God toward the animal, no less than toward the human other, evidently trumps the claims of private property. Moreover, awareness of this accountability is shown to arise from the apprehension of a language that, contra Descartes, is shared by human and nonhuman creatures: that of bodily suffering.[24] Rendered indifferent by their unconsidered anthropocentrism, however, the benighted disciples are deaf to the cries of the mule. What this suggests is that the ability to respond to the ethical call of other-than-human suffering is contingent on the recognition of a shared creatureliness. Moved by the mule's cries, Jesus extends to him a healing touch, while admonishing his owner to treat him more kindly, in order that he too might meet with a merciful response from his Creator.

Read intertextually with this apocryphal text, the biblical parable of the Good Samaritan (Luke 10:25–37) might also be seen to link ethical responsiveness toward the other, who might be not only a stranger but potentially also a strange (nonhuman) stranger,[25] to the recognition of our own creatureliness. For what distinguishes the Samaritan from the Priest and Levite who fail to aid the Jewish man left robbed, naked, and beaten half to death on the perilous road to Jericho is the literally visceral nature of his response. As the ecohermeneutical Lukan scholar Anne Elvey explains, he alone not only sees the injured man, as do the others, but also senses his suffering in his own innards. This crucial element is largely lost in translation: There is a world of difference between the bland English expression "moved to pity" (10:33) and the vivid earthiness of the Greek *splangchnizomai*, which literally means "to be moved in the guts."[26] Here the ethical call is discerned in the response that has already occurred in the flesh, prior to any conscious intention or verbal articulation; it is this corporeal capacity to be touched by the plight of another that stops the Samaritan in his tracks, interrupting his journey and disrupting the pursuit of whatever business had taken him on the road to Jericho. Apprehending the other's suffering in the depths of his own bodily being, the Samaritan shoulders his responsibility toward this half-dead stranger in an equally bodily way: "Prompted by an inner touch, the movement is directed toward an outer touch" in an act of "compassionate contact,"[27] which is effected with the assistance of a range of other earthly materials: oil and bandages to tend the man's wounds; another creature, "his own animal" (10:34), to bear him to the inn; and a fellow human, the innkeeper, along with the metal coins the Samaritan pays him to give the man lodging until he is recovered sufficiently to continue his journey.

In view of the antagonistic relationship that existed between Jews and Samaritans in Jesus' day, the corporeality of the Samaritan's response points to the recognition of a shared human creatureliness subtending, and potentially overriding, the social distinction of "friend" from "enemy"; it is this corporeal, creaturely "fellow-feeling"[28] that impels the extension of love of neighbor to those whom we would not normally consider as neighbors, including those whom we might even take to be enemies. Importantly, this narrative also shows that the other's call does not have to be mediated by articulate speech: The voice of this injured man, as Elvey notes, is visible in his suffering flesh.[29] Recalling the narrative of the mistreated mule, I would argue that the acceptance of our own creatureliness, and with it, the capacity to be corporeally moved to respond compassionately to the visible voice of those whose suffering cannot even be spoken, opens us up to experience fellow-feeling with other-than-human creatures as well, the gut-wrenching realization of whose suffering, whether beheld in the flesh or mediated by the testimony of others, summons us toward ethical action. For the ecological ethicist Mick Smith, whose concern extends to such "unloved others" as the little critters called mycorrhizal fungi who live in certain soils, this is not a question of the abstract rights, of which we might deem this or that category of creature worthy; rather, it is a matter of what he (in another ecophilosophical elaboration, and corrective, of Levinas, via Scheler and Heidegger) calls ethical "appearance":

> Ethics . . . is a particular mode of attending and responding to the beings that transcend, yet are nonetheless made manifest through, their [phenomenal] appearances. . . . In this sense, ecological ethics might be understood as an un-selfish "benevolence" initiated through "fellow-feeling" in "the event of the face of the Earth" (*physis*), and as the significant appearance of a community that can include "soils, plants and animals, or collectively, the land." And if we think about nature in this way, then it becomes obvious that only an arrogant anthropocentrism would assume that there is more hidden about the existence of another individual human being than about all of more-than-human nature in its myriad forms.[30]

This ecological ethic of more-than-human love of neighbor is modeled by the speaker of Mary Oliver's poem, "How Turtles Come to Spend the Winter in the Aquarium, Then Are Flown South and Released Back into the Sea." Moved by fellow-feeling for the large stranded turtle she found one morning, "at water's edge," the speaker nonetheless recognizes the abiding alterity of this strange stranger ("The eyes opened, I don't know what they thought"), as she carries him laboriously, her mouth open and heart roaring, over two miles of soft sand back to her car. Yet far from portraying herself as a martyr, the speaker also discloses, with gentle self-mockery, the profound pleasure of achieving this feat of animal rescue:

Jesus could walk over water.
I had to walk ankle-deep in the sand, and I did it.
My bones didn't quite snap.
Come in and see me smile.
I probably won't stop for hours.
Already, in the warmth, the turtle has raised its head,
                    is looking around.
Today, who would deny it, I am an important person.[31]

In another poem of animal rescue, "Sometimes I Am Victorious and Even Beautiful," in which the speaker furtively frees a river turtle from a trap, the sense of self-satisfaction is also evident; but so too is an unsentimental awareness of the potentially conflictual aspects of this act. As the trap is opened, the turtle:

. . . sees me
     and he thrashes

and I gaze into his pink throat and haul him higher
and he hisses, his eyes shine
and the tongue wags in the gaping, beak-shaped mouth
and I shake him from the trap, his thick head flashing,
     and he swims away

and I close the trap with the heels of my boots, and fling it
into the bullbriar wracked and useless,

and the pink sun rises and sees me, by the black water,
smiling,
     washing my hands.[32]

The turtle is recognized as a fellow creature, one with a face who returns the speaker's gaze, but his alterity also is marked, along with his evident failure to apprehend her benevolent intentions. Moreover, in the gap between her triumphant smile and her hand-washing, with its intertextual echo of Lady Macbeth, an unspoken question arises around the morality of destroying another person's property, and possibly interfering with his or her livelihood, in the defense of a wild animal.

Toward the end of Milan Kundera's novel *The Unbearable Lightness of Being*, the narrator reflects that "mankind's true moral test, its fundamental test (which lies deeply buried from view) consists of its attitude toward those who are at its mercy: animals. And in this respect, mankind has suffered a fundamental debacle, a debacle so fundamental that all others stem from it."[33] This quote haunts the internet in any number of animal advocacy sites, but nonetheless it's important to recognize that not all human cultures are equally culpable. It would be hubristic to assume that all non-human animals are, in fact, at our mercy (certain disease-bearing biota, for instance, are doing a disturbingly good job at evading human control). However, at a time when humanly induced changes to ecosystems the world over, many of them driven or exacerbated by global warming, are pushing ever more species into extinction, causing immeasurable suffering to countless individual creatures along the way, we must acknowledge that it is no longer only domesticated animals whose lives are in our hands. As Deborah Bird Rose, recalling the testimony of earlier intrahuman waves of enslavement and oppression, frames our historical hour:

> These are the days of violent extinctions, of global dimming and moving dust bowls, of habitat fragmentation, ice melt, and plundered lives. Animals are experiencing all this loss, and if we could better hear the waves of their agony, we would know this and be tormented. We would know that for the rest of our lives we will hear a growing chorus of increasingly diverse voices:
>   "For the wicked carried us away in captivity,
>   Required from us a song,
>   How can we sing King Alfa's song in a strange land?"[34]

Responding to the ethical call of endangered wild creatures, no less than that of ill-treated domesticated ones, clearly runs counter to the commercial interests of some fellow humans (such as those who profit from the fossil-fuel industry), and ending the agonies to which experimental animals are subjected could be seen to conflict with the worthy endeavor of enhancing human health and well-being (or, as is too often the case, the desire to profit from our boundless vanity). There is no easy resolution to such conflicts. Yet to avert our gaze from animal suffering, to insist that it is of no consequence, and to place the claims of private property above not only the well-being of individual animals but also the survival needs of entire species is to endorse a form of "human racism"[35] that is, in my view, both unethical and dysfunctional, for it is likely to imperil us all in the end.

HEEDING THE CALL: THE PROPHETIC IMAGINATION IN A MORE-THAN-HUMAN WORLD

At this point I want to return to the magpie's warning call, but in a rather different key. Several years ago, magpies, or maybe a particular magpie (let me call him or her Magpie) began haunting my dreams. I am not in the habit of recounting my dreams in an academic context, but I would like to share the first, and most powerful, of these Magpie dreams here, trusting that the transdisciplinarity of this collection is capacious enough to accommodate a personal narrative. So, here goes:

I am walking in a park at nightfall with somebody whom I take to be a visitor from overseas. Spotting a magpie high up at the top of a very tall gum tree, I point it out to my guest excitedly, foolishly attempting to parade my self-professed facility for interspecies communication by warbling up at it. The bird responds sure enough, but not in a manner that I had anticipated. Suddenly, I am up in the tree-top, face-to-face with Magpie's wide-opened beak, and half-deafened by the torrent of urgent caroling that is issuing from it. At this, I simply fall apart—literally—splitting in two, so that I am now staring into my own face, seeing my own mouth, open wide to scream. But my breath has been snatched away; I am unable to either move or make the slightest sound. As an onlooker, I have no idea what Magpie is conveying to me so fervently; but the horrified response of my other moiety, the immediate addressee of the call, suggests that it is so unspeakably horrible that I awake, heart-thumping, in alarm.

It would no doubt be possible to psychoanalyze this dream in terms of the dreamer's personal hang-ups. But for my purposes, the person to whom this dream was given is irrelevant. Indeed, I suspect that many people might be having this kind of dream today; one that might be interpreted transpersonally and mythopoetically, by considering its unconscious promptings not in the narrowly Freudian sense, but rather, with F. W. J. Schelling, as extending into the wider natural order, or more precisely, into what Robert S. Corrington terms the "underconscious" of the world (a term he takes from Schelling's most avid English reader around 1800, Samuel Taylor Coleridge).[36] For the biosemiotician Wendy Wheeler, as "whole creatures," humans, in concert and often in communication with other living beings, are constantly picking up signs of various kinds from the world around us, most of which get processed below the level of consciousness. Occasionally, this stream of unconscious semiosis surfaces in those intuitive insights commonly called "hunches" in a process that Charles Sanders Peirce termed "abduction."[37] Might dreams too sometimes enlighten in the modality of abduction? And might such abductive insights not present themselves to the dreaming mind as communications from a nonhuman other—as the warning call, for instance, of an animal familiar?

Animal oracles, frequently birds, certainly abound in many cultures. According to Marija Gimbutas, there is evidence of oracular bird cults in several parts of Neolithic Europe, for example, a survival of which might be glimpsed in the owl of Athena, "the Farseeing."[38] Within the Christian tradition, one of the ways that the Holy Spirit is symbolized is also in the form of a bird: the heavenly dove, which, in the deep green pneumatology of Mark I. Wallace, for example, is conceived panentheistically as figuring the inherence of the divine in the earthly.[39] Animals also appear quasi-prophetically as witnesses to divine revelation in the apocrypha, recognizing the Word made flesh in advance of humans (as do, for instance, the ox and ass by the manger in the *Gospel of Pseudo-Matthew*, echoing, perhaps, Balaam's ass's recognition of the angel of the Lord in Numbers 22:21–35). Hauntingly, the dog who is said to utter explicitly prophetic words in *The Acts of Peter*, as discussed in Hobgood-Oster's contribution to this volume, falls down dead after telling Simon and Peter of the counterposed fates that await them. In the case of my dream, by contrast, it was the human hearer who was mortified by the prophesying animal's utterance.

The vision unfolded by Magpie was evidently so horrendous that it was partially veiled from the dreamer, such that the warning call could be discerned only in the corporeal response of that part of her being that is evidently able to understand Magpie language (or at any rate, the kind of language that things manifesting as magpies might utter in human dreams). Although there was undoubtedly something apocalyptic about this unspeakable vision, I prefer to consider its revelatory force as more closely aligned with the voice of the ancient Hebrew prophets than that of the later Jewish and Christian apocalyptic writers. The apocalyptic shares with prophetic imagination the revelation that humans, for all their self-proclaimed apartness, belong ultimately to a more-than-human community of fate, but it differs in its construction of history as predetermined in its outcome, leaving human agents little option other than to prepare themselves for the millennial end that heralds a glorious new beginning.[40] By contrast, the prophetic voice insists on the ever-present possibility of a change in direction in the present, in the absence of which there is no promise of a redemptive *deus ex machina*. As Terry Eagleton laconically observes, "The role of the prophet is not to predict the future, but to remind the people that if they carry on as they are doing, the future will be exceedingly bleak."[41] The central trope of prophetic writing is that of turning and returning, on the part of both the people and their God, whose relationship is conceived as dialogical. The prophetic voice, moreover, although understood as uttering the speech of heaven, does not speak from a place of purity: The prophet is both implicated in and wounded by the wrongdoing that is shown to be driving his or her world headlong into catastrophe. "There is in the prophetic voice," writes Rose, citing Susan Handelman, "an 'ethical self-exposure' in which subjectivity lays bare its vulnerability, and opens itself consciously to others."[42] Prophetic speech is inspired by the imaginative capacity to see through and beyond those conventional attitudes, assumptions, and patterns of behavior that engender or support oppression and wrongdoing; and it is propelled by the hunger for justice, underpinned by compassion, that cannot tolerate complacency in the face of another's suffering. Breaching the fortress of "royal consciousness," as Walter Brueggeman terms it, the mind-set of mastery and privilege that renders us indifferent to the suffering of others and unmindful of our own vulnerability, the prophet speaks with the voice of grief—but also, implicitly or explicitly, of hope.[43] Prophetic speech incites lamentation in order to engender transformation, at the same time that it warns of what will ensue if the people fail to heed the call.

Whereas later apocalyptic visions, such as those of Daniel and John, as discussed in the contributions to this volume by Koosed and Seesengood and Moore, prefigure a redemption from which animals are largely, if not entirely, excluded, the earlier Hebrew prophets sometimes take the suffering of animals as crucial evidence of the human wrongdoing that they seek to disclose. If, as Brueggeman argues, the prophetic voice is called forth by the cry of the oppressed (paradigmatically, "the Israelites . . . cried out," as we read in Exodus 2:23), then it is important to recognize that this not an exclusively human cry in the Hebrew scriptures, where the dialogical relationship between people and God is triangulated by the figure of the land or earth (*erets*). In Jeremiah and Hosea, for example, it is the grieving earth itself that is said to bear the brunt, and thereby also to mark the measure, of human wrongdoing. In the drying up of the land and in the dying of their fellow creatures, on the land and in the sea, the people stand accused of breaking their covenant with God: "Therefore the land mourns, and all who live in it languish; together with the wild animals and the birds of the air, even the fish of the sea are perishing" (Hos. 4:3); "because of this the earth will mourn [dry up], and the heavens above become dark" (Jer. 4:28); "How long will the land [earth] mourn [dry up], / and the grass of every field wither? / For the wickedness of those who live in it / the animals and the birds are swept away. . . . They made it a desolation; / desolate it mourns to me. / The whole land is made desolate, / but no one lays it to heart" (Jer. 12:4 and 11).[44]

Considered intertextually (and, as Catherine Keller would recommend, "counter-apocalyptically") with such biblical passages, then, Magpie's urgent call might be read as a figure of the ecoprophetic imagination, disclosing the immense extent of humanly engendered animal suffering and species extinction and warning of the potentially dire consequences, should the sovereign species not change its ways in time. Magpies might not be among those creatures that are currently endangered, but I think that clever bird, with her far-carrying song, might be well placed to give utterance to Earth's cry: the cry, that is, of the many voiceless—or silenced—ones, human and otherwise, who are in the front line of environmental destruction.

From this ecoprophetic perspective it is precisely in the silencing of their voices as they disappear forever from Earth's increasingly desolate lands and waters that other-than-human animals call to us most powerfully in the present hour. As these other voices are lost, we face the nightmare, etched starkly by Judith Wright in her "Lament for Passenger Pigeons," not only of a growing solitude, but also of a collective solipsism:

> Trapped in the fouling nests of time and space,
> we turn the music on; but it is man,
> and it is man who leans a deafening ear.
>
> And it is man we eat and man we drink
> and man who thickens round us like a stain.
> Ice at the polar axis smells of me.

At the end of this poem, Wright offers the poetic word as a form of compensation for species extinction in the modality of "penitential witness":[45]

> What is the being and the end of man?
> Blank surfaces reverb a human voice
> Whose echo tells us that we choose to die:
>
> or else, against the blank of everything,
> to reinvent that passenger, that bird-
> siren-and-angel image we contain
> essential in a constellating word.
> To sing of Being, its escaping wing,
> to utter absence in a human chord
> and recreate the meaning as we sing.[46]

In this (distinctly Heideggerian) recourse to the "constellating word," however, Wright courts the risk of another kind of retreat into human self-enclosure (one that Wright herself nonetheless avoided, not only in her later verse, but also in her pioneering environmental and Aboriginal rights activism).[47] There is a place for poetic witness, especially, perhaps, in penitential mode, but I think that we can do more than that. As Rabbi Lawrence Troster has observed, "In our ignorance, our greed, and our egotism, we have silenced many of the voices of creation. It is these voices that cry out to us in the latest revelation not in the text but in the earth itself."[48] To respond to this cry, for Troster, and not just in texts, but through our compassionate contact with the earth and its diverse more-than-human denizens, would be to participate in the practice known in the Jewish tradition as *tikkun 'olam*, the "repair of the world." Tuning in to the communicative exchanges of the animals that continue to thrive in our midst and cultivating a sense of fellow-feeling with those who suffer unjustly at our hands, we could yet be called out of the perilous condition of solipsistic self-enclosure in time to enable renewed practices of multi-species co-becoming. For eco-Christians, this might be understood as a call to enter into an enlarged communion: a communion of all creatures. What that might actually entail, though, remains unclear. On this point, then, there is "more to follow."

❧ Little Bird in My Praying Hands: Rainer Maria Rilke and God's Animal Body

BEATRICE MAROVICH

That life might be especially difficult for that creaky old creature called God is not a new idea: *If God lived on earth, people would break his windows,* the old Yiddish proverb muses. But the German poet Rainer Maria Rilke illuminates another order of a god's vulnerability. In a little book of tales that's been translated into English as *Stories of God,* Rilke fabulates a god who is not only vulnerable to the cruel judgments of human beings but is also so divided against himself he nearly self-destructs. He almost lets himself die. He is an immortal who is vulnerable to the possibility of death—the conditional threat of creaturely (mortal) life. He is a creaturely immortal—a strange sort of god, with an animal body and (as you might expect) animal problems. In his creatureliness he also stages questions about how to live in a vulnerable, animal body and still love the world. This is a god who, perhaps, doesn't really have the ability to save this world so much as he can act as its salve.

You see, this all goes back to the creation story that Rilke tells in the first fable of this series—"The Tale of God's Hands." God is busy with the act of creation. Making what we've dubbed "inanimate" objects is pretty easy. But once he starts in on the animals, he's absorbed. "He bent over this work and only rarely raised His broad brows to cast a glance at the earth."[1] But there are all sorts of distractions. An angel flies above him, singing (*a bunch of heavenly lies,* as Rilke clarifies for us) and calling God, "Thou who seest everything."[2] Then one of these earth angels (a bird, that is) gets lost on its way home. God's getting frustrated. He can't figure out which woods he'd created the bird for, in the first place. Next, a little dog (a terrier, God's informed) is threatening to jump off the very edge of the flat earth. The world's already a mess, and so is God, in troubleshooting mode. So when he finally gets back to the creation of the little animal who looks most like him (the human, who else?), all he can hear is the sound of his own hands, nervously kneading and kneading away. The clay he's been working with is gone. "Then, all at once, He saw something tumbling through space, something dark falling at such an angle that it seemed to have come from quite near him."[3] The human's gone. And God calls up his hands, charging them with responsibility. They bicker between themselves about who's to blame. And then they both admit, together, that the human "was so impatient . . . he kept wanting to be alive already. Neither one of us could do anything about it. Definitely, we are both innocent." But God is seriously angry (completing the human was the special treat he'd been looking forward to). He pushes both hands away and condemns them: "I know you no longer: do what you will."[4]

Consequence: God begins to hate a part of himself. God's body becomes infected, made vulnerable, by his own self-hatred. He cannot forgive his hands. In a later tale, "The Stranger," God is on the verge of affecting forgiveness for his right hand, asking of it a favor. But before he can, that curmudgeon Saint Paul severs the hand, and an archangel hides it under its robes, stealing off to some unknown corner of the earth. God is wounded, "and the whole earth was red with God's blood, and it was impossible to see what was happening beneath it." God might be perilously close to death, but finally the shocked little hand comes crawling back: "It came pale and trembling and lay down in its place like a sick animal."[5] His own hand—part of his own body—seems to have become something of an animal in itself. This is a god who is subject to the same conditions of life as all other creaturely bodies—a vulnerable sort of god, whose animal body and animal parts can (like ours) be cut, severed, and bleed. This god doesn't command compassion and kinship among creatures through his absolute and omnipotent authority. Rather, this god seems to ally himself with (and appear within) the raw animality of creaturely bodies in order to (perhaps lovingly) dehumanize us, to animalize us through a kind of sympathetic resonance—to spill the tidy contents of a purely, uniquely, holy human life on earth into the very flesh of the world, and let it bleed.

RILKE, SOVEREIGNTY, AND CREATURELY LIFE

In the developing field of animal studies, Rilke has been making fitful appearances and is establishing something of an ambiguous "legacy." In his eighth "Duino Elegy" Rilke sketches the figure of what he calls "the open"—a space-time (within the world) that animal perception can explore and receive but human perception cannot. "With full gaze the animal (*die Kreatur*) sees the open," Rilke writes. But "our eyes, as if reversed, are like snares set around it," which "block the freedom of its going." We get in the way of The Open; we cannot perceive it; and thus we keep it from growing, from living. Even children, Rilke suggests, turn their heads around to look back at "the world of forms." Even children, in other words, are too abstracted from The Open to really see it.

The animal (*die Kreatur*), in contrast, is so attuned to The Open that it becomes—effectively—immortal. The animal is "free from death" as it "has its death always behind it and God before it, and when it walks it goes toward eternity, as springs flow."[6] The animal seems to be—in some sense—immortalized by its tight and umbilical connection to The Open, which is also a kind of connection to the divine. This is not to say that animals are already divine. But they are creatures with a privileged relation to the eternal, by virtue of the fact that they are able to perceive it, to resonate with it. Traditional Christian theologies ordered the creation hierarchically. Creatures with animal bodies were placed at the bottom, and spiritual creatures (animated, in some cases, by nothing but their rational and intellectual souls) were at the top. Humans, as fused entities (animal bodies with rational souls), were placed in the middle. The Italian philosopher Giorgio Agamben describes Rilke's figure of The Open as a kind of "reversal of the hierarchical relationship between man and animal."[7] Indeed, even beyond that, the world of forms (the world of substances that lack matter, the site that excludes animal bodies) seems to be displaced entirely by becoming something "backward" and is severed from its traditional close alliance with the divine.

Agamben was intrigued enough by Rilke's poetic propositions about The Open to name an entire book after this figure: *The Open: Man and Animal* (2002). And, indeed, Agamben ends this volume with a reflection on what it means that we can resist this hierarchical relation between the human and the animal. We can "render inoperative" what Agamben calls the abstract "anthropological machine," the one that biopolitically manages and governs the shape of both human and animal subjects (especially the line that claims to divide them). He wants to "show the central emptiness" of the boundary, or the "hiatus," that divides human from animal in order to develop something like a "Shabbat of both animal and man"[8]—the quasi-messianic hope that each might let the other be, in peace.

But Agamben is also intent on complicating Rilke's simple charge (that humans are incapable of perceiving The Open, that humans may be—in a crucial sense—less perceptive than other animals). And so Agamben also illuminates and develops—at great length—Martin Heidegger's critique of Rilke's Open. In his 1929/1930 lecture series—exploring the human's constituent worldedness—Heidegger accuses Rilke of "a monstrous anthropomorphization of . . . the animal and a corresponding animalization of man." He thus determines to reverse Rilke's own reversal. Ultimately, Heidegger argues, "Only man, indeed only the gaze of authentic thought, can see the open which names the unconcealedness of being. The animal, on the contrast, never sees this open."[9] Rilke's reversal, his dehumanization (or deprioritization of the human) becomes the very site of Heidegger's notorious charge that animals are "poor in world." Heidegger both upholds the classical structure of the creation and simultaneously attempts to render Rilke's reversal simplistic and naïve. Rilke's figure of The Open does not surface from Agamben's analysis untainted by all of these considerations. Indeed, The Open—as Agamben reads it—is not the sort of Open that we find in Rilke.

Eric Santner, in his *On Creaturely Life* (2006) examines the three-way conversation between Rilke, Heidegger, and Agamben at greater depth. Importantly, what Santner wants to argue is that this theoretical conversation (about the nature of the human, the nature of its connections, its relation to the world, or to The Open) corresponds to real and actual changes in our biopolitical lives—our biopolitical lives in a secular world. He is taking direction from the German legal theorist Carl Schmitt, who famously suggested that all Western political concepts (such as sovereignty) are actually secularized theological concepts.[10] The figure of creaturely life, for Santner, is not plugged into anything divine but instead the political form of sovereign power. Rilke's attempt to elevate animal life to "the status of a superhuman exception"[11] does not indicate, for Santner, that there is anything particularly "salvational," or holy, in animal life. Rather, in this fusion of the divine into the animal Santner sees the representation of something rather tragic and traumatic happening to human life. This move, Santner argues, makes human life begin to look quite creaturely in a most perverse manner. When the boundaries between the sovereign and the animal collapse, the result is (as Santner finds in Kafka), "a chronic state of agitation and disorientation,"[12] where there is (in the secular context into which the figure of The Open emerges) an "ongoing and passionate subjection not to a Creator God or even to a sovereign whose legitimacy is figured on the model of the Creator, but to an agency, a master's discourse, that has been attenuated and dispersed across a field of relays and points of contact that no longer cohere, even in fantasy, as a consistent 'other' of possible address."[13] The form of life that Santner names "creaturely" is the form of life that is subjected to this master's discourse—that twists in a kind of uncomfortable perversion, in its wake, or in its grasp. This is, crucially, a form of ontological vulnerability to which human life is subject: The creaturely names the ontological vulnerability of a human life.

What Santner ultimately calls for is the transition out of creaturely life. This form of creaturely life marks a kind of perversion that must both be confronted (faced, understood, diagnosed in a Freudian sense—as Santner is a Freudian theorist) and yet also resisted. It is a form of disorder. In his 2011 text *The Royal Remains* Santner goes so far as to suggest that projects in fields such as animal studies that seek out forms of kinship with the nonhuman are deluded in their basic approach. Efforts to posit creaturely life "as an opening or passage to our animal nature function as a kind of screen or defense against the anxiety provoked by the proximity of creaturely life," he argues.[14] What is crucial, in Santner's analysis, is that we look clearly at the vulnerability of our creaturely life—as it is exposed to the biopolitical mechanism that results from a collapse of animality into sovereign power. We must be able to face the anxieties that this confronts us with. Indeed, if we are not clear-headed about it, we will be stuck like an automaton in creaturely life.

The ontological vulnerability that Santner draws our attention to is crucial. Although I would suggest that the collapse of animality into a sovereignty, which from some angles is still divine, does not simply generate the ontological vulnerability of the human. Animality also faces a strange transition into a sphere of power where it is—as even a form of quasi sovereignty—liable to face new forms of attack, disgust, dissent, or simply resistance. The (possibly divine) sovereign also confronts its own vulnerability, as it examines its mortal animal body and its attendant limits. The ontological vulnerability, I think, is spread through the subjective spectrum. It is shared—a kind of mutuality in vulnerability, the underbelly or shadow of power sharing. The human and the animal both exist within this excluded space.

The particular shape of this conundrum and the kinds of stakes it raises become a bit clearer in the late work of Jacques Derrida—preoccupied with both questions of sovereignty and those of animality. Derrida, like Carl Schmitt, took God to be the paradigmatic figure of sovereign authority, conditioning all other political forms of sovereignty in what now seems the globalized imaginary. As Michael Naas writes, "The sovereignty of God is the exceptional case that defines the very essence and exceptionality of sovereignty."[15] God is, in a sense, the point of greatest intensity in the concept that describes and explains sovereignty. But despite God's exemplarity, Derrida recognized the complicated entanglement that the divine sovereign faced as both divinity and animality were "othered" by the figure of a democratic, politically sovereign human subject. It is for this reason that Derrida's analysis becomes useful in analyzing Rilke's thought—there is still in Rilke, a figure of the divine. The divinity of the god figure seems, in some strange form, to continue.[16] For Derrida, the animal and the divine stand outside the sovereign human's political subjectivity—exceptions that serve as the very foundation of what is excluded from this "symbolic order, the human order, law and justice."[17] Derrida names this excluded subjective space "divinanimality." It is within just such an excluded space, I want to suggest, that Rilke seems to find his figure of this animal god, this creaturely immortal—confronting his human audience with a whisper of something he fears they've forgotten.

This excluded space of the "divinanimal" is not unproblematic—for Derrida—in its claims to power. It is not the site of some sweet and vulnerable creature who merits nothing but our doting compassion. The fusion of animality and sovereignty feels a bit risky, a bit dangerous. This was especially true, perhaps, before the exclusively human subject became the primary site of sovereign power in political thought. Commenting on Rousseau's *The Social Contract* (1762), written at the dawn of the human's new political era, Derrida finds the human caught up in (engulfed by, we might even say) the exceptional space of the divinanimal. "There are gods and there are beasts, there is, there is only, the theo-zoological, and in the theo-anthropo-zoological, man is caught, evanescent, disappearing, at the very most a simple mediation, a hyphen between the sovereign and the beast, between God and cattle."[18] The human, here, would certainly appear to be the most ontologically vulnerable figure. In this political spectrum, what Derrida sees is that "the sovereign and the beast seem to have in common their being-outside-the-law. It is as though both of them were situated by definition at a distance from or above the law, in nonrespect for the absolute law, the absolute law that they make or that they are but that they do not have to respect."[19] They have a "troubling resemblance" that Derrida calls "*unheimlich.*" The end result is a kind of "onto-zoo-anthropo-theologico-political copulation."[20] In this orgiastic figure of political intimacies, the human seems indiscriminately folded in—liable to get lost. The possibility that this exceptional coupling of political sovereign and animality might be ruthless, fierce, dominating—that it might subject the human to any and all forms of vulnerability possible—seems high. This is, I suggest, something more like the ontological situation in Santner's work. The ontological vulnerability of the human—exposed to this beastly sovereignty—seems rather similar to what Santner calls "creaturely life."

What Derrida finds in the figure of Hobbes's Leviathan, however, marks what seems to me a kind of advance in ontological power for the human figure and the advent of what might also be seen as greater vulnerability in the figure of the divinanimal, the fusion of sovereignty and animality. The figure of the Leviathan, as Derrida describes it, is indeed an animalistic sovereign. But because there is also an artificial aspect to it, the Leviathan, which is the figure of the state, "is like an iron lung, an artificial respiration, an 'Artificiall *Soul.*' So the state is a sort of robot, an animal monster, which, in the figure of man, or of man in the figure of the animal monster, is stronger, etc. than natural man."[21] This figure is, indeed, terrifying. This sheer terror "inspires" obedience to the law. "The political subject is primarily subjected to fear."[22] The human is deeply, ontologically, vulnerable to its own fear of the sovereign.

Why, however, does this terrifying sovereign animal monstrosity, with its bizarre power configuration, not render the human ontologically vulnerable in the extreme? Why does it not render the human incapable of political action to (for example) confront aspects of this sovereign authority? Derrida points suggestively to the fact that, in Hobbes, this very fear that the political subject experiences is a part of human nature. And despite the fact that this animal monster sovereign is terrifying for the human subject, despite the fact that it constantly threatens the human with its dictates and laws, the human (in its own human nature) should understand that "sovereignty, laws, law, and therefore the state are nothing natural and are posited by contract and convention." What this means, in essence, is that "law, sovereignty, the institution of the state are historical and always provisional, let's say deconstructible, essentially fragile or finite or mortal, even if sovereignty is *posited as immortal.*"[23] Natural law, in other words, is grounded in and finds support in humanity. The sovereign is an artificial construct—immortal only in a fictional or fabular sense—a prosthetic apparatus of human nature. This is not to say that sovereignty should not be taken seriously or will not be terrifying. But it does indicate that there is something in the figure of the human with the ability to deconstruct (to, perhaps, even disable) the functions of sovereignty. The divinanimal, here, has a certain kind of power. But this power appears to be illusory; its power is a fragile myth to be deconstructed.

As I have suggested, this marks a new space of animalized sovereignty, of beastly sovereignty. This is, precisely, the realm of the divinanimal—the space of the exclusion of both the gods and animals, outside the political realm of the human. It is toward this space—this site of exclusion—that, I want to suggest, Rilke himself is gesturing. I might even go so far as to suggest that Rilke is playing in this space. When Rilke paints (with words) the figure of The Open, he gestures toward a space-time that excludes the purely human and includes both the animal and the divine. He does not suggest (as Hobbes intimates with the beastly sovereign that is the Leviathan) that this divinanimal space (The Open) has any political authority over us. Indeed, we might recall Rilke's charge that we humans turn our backs to The Open. Our life plays out in a kind of indifference to The Open.

The situation is, I think, differently dramatized in both *Stories of God* and *Book of Hours: Prayers to a Lowly God* (1900). These texts were written relatively close together, before the *Duino Elegies* (1922), and both display a similar sort of animalization, or creaturization, of God. Each focuses on the animality of God's own body. But each also seems to demonstrate something of the ontology that emerges suggestively in the figure of The Open—that the lives of both the animal and the divine unfold in a temporal register that humans are unable (or perhaps merely unwilling) to perceive. This register does not exert what might be called the terrifying force of political authority. Such force seems almost out of character for Rilke's god, whose contours are "thinglike," who is a creature, a mortal, just like us. Rather, the vulnerability of this divinanimal life seems to lure us—with the power of suggestion—to resonate with it.

LITTLE BIRD IN MY PRAYING HANDS

In his *Book of Hours: Prayers to a Lowly God* Rilke becomes a monk who writes out a very long song to the creaturely God he knows. This God, the monk reports, is thinglike. His hands hold onto God, he says, "so anxiously and uncouth," and he wishes that he could, with greater confidence, throw God, "like a ball / into any possible delight," where someone would inevitably "catch and brace your fall / with outstretched and lifted hands, / you thing of all things," who is also (strangely and simultaneously) "you all in all."[24] God is a tree, "though just one branch hardly looks like him."[25] God is the "strange yellow hand" that emerges "as if out of one's coat."[26] God is the soft little bird wriggling in the praying hands of a child—the reason this child knows beyond a doubt that this God is real—who disappears when the prayer is over. God is the little creature who has fallen out of his nest, "like a little bird with yellow claws / and eyes that cause pity in my chest. / (My hand is so big next to you)," the monk exclaims to this fallen God. And he professes a desire to give him water to drink. "I lift with my finger a drop from a spring; / that you lap it up is what I want to hear, / and I feel your heart beat and mine too / out of fear."[27] God has an animal body that takes on thinglike properties and does exactly the sort of things an animal body might do—with some variations on the theme, some interesting differences.

Rilke's monk charges that not only is God thinglike but God is also a thing that we create. We are "craftsmen" who "build you up, you tallest middle ship."[28] But this does not mean that this God is no longer great. Indeed, it is part of God's own desire (part of the divine's death drive) to be mortalized in the form of a poem or a song. God, says the monk, is "the gentle evening hour / which makes all poets similar; / you squeeze yourself into their mouths / and, feeling proud of what they found, / they decorate your brow."[29] Simply because he is a constructed object does not mean that he is not an integral or necessary one, cosmologically speaking—that he is not, in other words, real. We cannot, then, simply dismiss this God, with his animal body and thinglike properties because God continues (in his constructedness) to correspond to something real. In this sense, perhaps, God is similar to Isabelle Stengers's neutrino—the paradigmatic scientific object that is "both constructed" and also "defined as an ingredient in all weak nuclear interactions and, as such, is an integral part of our cosmological models." Or in other words, the neutrino "is as old as the period in which its existence was first demonstrated, that is, produced in our laboratories, and that it dates back to the origins of the universe."[30] Reality (actuality) and constructedness are not, here, mutually exclusive. Cannot the gods (at least within the *scientia theologica*—that drag queen of the sciences) not become scientific objects in just such a manner?

It is important to remember that objectification is not a reduction, nor does it mean that human beings would then have control over God. Rilke reminds us of this when his monk comforts God about the very same thing. "Don't worry God," he says, "They call 'mine' / everything that is patient. / They are like the wind brushing the branch / and saying: *my* tree. / They hardly see / the glow of all they touch / unaware that they couldn't even hold its outer edge / without burning up." In other words, the foolishness of humans causes them to face everything "and call it theirs although / everything withdraws when they approach."[31] It is not, in other words, the objectification of God that would provide a negative limit but, instead, the greediness of humans who are driven to privately propertize everything we come in contact with.

God's creatureliness cannot help but yank him into the temporal, or to magnetize other creatures into the nontemporal. Somehow, a confusion is affected over lines in the sand that were drawn to divide creatureliness and immortality. This thinglike God—with a creaturely, animal, autoimmune body—becomes a creaturely immortal. So, instead of control, the consequence of the actualization (or objectification) of God into the shapeshifting form of a creaturely immortal's animal body turns out not to be ownership, but greater intimacy.

It also turns out (in a move that might make feminist theologians uncomfortable) that Rilke sometimes indulges in patriarchalizing imagery, in order to bring God's animal body to life. The big Man-God reappears. "So strangely soft you cradle me," the monk says, "and listen to how my hands run through / your old and grizzled beard."[32] But there is a tenderness here that comes from Rilke's simultaneous recognition that the father is "a symbol of the past; / of years gone by, appearing in strange / outdated ways, and ancient dress / of wilted hands and faded hair? / And though acclaimed as a hero in his time, / he is the leaf that drops as we progress."[33] This kind of personalization (into the great big man in the sky) is, for Rilke, ultimately just one more actualization, or objectification, of God— one more opportunity to make the creaturely contours of this strange immortal more discernible.

The ultimate consequence is that God's creaturely vulnerability is exposed. And this creaturely vulnerability is not something that only corrupt and finite creatures have. It is not something that can be understood as a punishment—any more than being alive on this wild earth in the first place is a punishment. Vulnerability is not something that either radically mortal or creaturely immortal animal bodies can immunize themselves against. It is, instead, the very infection—one might even name it love—that connects us. It is what makes the divine, the human, the animal, the mineral, the vegetable, hang together. It is the very condition of the possibility of a life together. Gods too, Rilke suggests, are collapsed into this vulnerable space where life plays out. But this is also their very condition of possibility, or reality. God's animal body waits, in infinite possibility, all around, for tenderness too. In this sort of a world, the gods seem to have no agency to take us outside of it. But they seem to entice us into certain kinds of connections within it. This sort of god might not save us from the world, but might be a salve within it. This sort of creaturely immortal seems to suggest that the world can still be loved—and that there might just be some nearly immortal loves wandering around, within it.

Rilke's monk confesses to God that he disturbs him (my "neighbor") during the dark of a lonely night, "with heavy raps" because "I rarely hear you breathe." But the monk knows, he says, that God is in there. "I am listening," he promises. "Just give me a sign. / I am close by."[34] Is this an actual door he knocks on? Or does he only adopt the posture of knocking on the hard sensible wooden plank of a door? Does it make a difference? Perhaps what's important is that the creaturely opening of this monk's endless and patient concern is held ajar, by the strange stirrings of a creaturely immortal. "What will you do God, when I'm dead?" the monk asks as a lover asks another. "I am your cloak and career; / without me you end up losing making sense. / I fret about you, God."[35] And the little bird wriggles in the hand; another little bird falls out of the nest; another little bird is lost in the sky; the grizzled beard asks for fingers to run through it. All of these things come, somehow, to pass in their own strange space-time. And when a stranger appears at your door, it's suddenly difficult not to stand ready, already awash with that intimate concern.

The Logos of God and the End of Humanity: Giorgio Agamben and the Gospel of John on Animality as Light and Life

ERIC DARYL MEYER

The light came unto its own; but its own did not receive it.
—JOHN 1:11

The Gospel of John begins with a *Logos*, a Word sounding out the earliest origins of creation and measuring up even to God. After asserting that everything in existence resonates with echoes of the Logos, having come into being through it, John narrows his view and writes that this Logos is life (*zōē*), and that this life is the light of human beings (*anthrōpōn*). Human life (*zōē*) radiates as light from the Logos of God. But John's text is not all light and life. John quickly modulates into a minor key and writes of a darkness that refuses the light. The world of humanity, the *kosmos*, is the site of this darkness; humanity fails to recognize the Logos as its very life.

Despite John's ominous tone, logos actually does pretty well in the world of humanity. Whether logos is rendered as reason, speech, argument, thought, logic, or discourse, it is hardly a marginal and undervalued aspect of human existence. Logos frequently appears as the criterion to distinguish humans from other creatures. Humans are rational; animals are irrational. Humans communicate articulately; animals are mute and lack speech. Human subjects are formed in language; animals interact with the world directly without language's mediation. So contrary to John, logos has not historically lacked for recognition, prestige, and honor. Is John simply mistaken, or are there two radically different *logoi* in play here?

In fact, the remainder of John's gospel goes on to describe a deep antagonism between the Logos of God and the reason, speech, or discourse of humanity. Humanity's own logos stands in some form of opposition to the *zōē* with which the Logos illuminates human life. The luminous *zōē* of John's text cuts between Logos and logos. Humanity bends around an abyssal *zōē* which it can never understand but which nevertheless animates it. Humanity lives out of a light and a life which never quite seems to fall into words.

What I would like to offer, what I have already started to offer, is a re-reading of the prologue of John with an eye toward theological anthropology and "the question of the animal."[1] This is not an effort to retrieve the hidden splendor of John's "original meaning." Rather, inasmuch as John's prologue functions as a locus classicus for the doctrine of the incarnation, the text haunts every Christian who seeks to narrate what happens when God becomes flesh. The whole Christian theological tradition labors under the weight of John's first chapter without much regard for John's original intentions. This exploratory essay inverts a number of the assumptions underlying the traditional theological reading of the text in order to shift the burden and attempt to carry the text forward differently. In short, this essay reckons with the theological reception of John's prologue as it has informed Christian teaching at the intersection of the incarnation and theological anthropology. The goal is to sketch a counterreception or alternate reception that would refigure the place of animals and animality at this critical intersection.

John does not employ *logos* primarily as an anthropological category. Nevertheless, very early in Christian history *logos* became an indispensable anthropological term that determined the angle from which John's prologue was read.[2] For reasons historical and philosophical, John's Christian readers have overwhelmingly presumed that human logos and divine Logos are commensurate, if not contiguous. The presumption is that the Divine Word is specially aligned with human discourse; whatever the quantitative excess of divine Logos over human logos, a qualitative continuity remains.

My proposed rereading calls into question this continuity of logos, taking with utmost seriousness the fundamental difference in John's prologue—on the scale of light and dark—between the operations of human logos and the work of the Logos incarnate. Furthermore, rather than read John's *zōē* abstractly as a supplement added to humanity alone, John's "life" may be understood as the *zōē* of the *zōon* (the animal). That "life" that is the light of human beings might be understood as "bare life" or as "animality," as zoological rather than ethereal, in which case John traces a zoological division between the logos of humanity and the living, illuminating Logos-in-flesh.

The stakes emerge in this question: Should God's incarnation be understood as a celestial endorsement of the exceptional status of humanity over against all other creatures or as the deconstruction of humanity from within, a salvifically subversive maneuver undertaken for the sake of all God's beloved creatures? My essay labors to provide a plausible framework for the latter option.

The essay proceeds in three sections. First, I begin with several traditional readings that assume fundamental continuity between divine and human logos. Second, I lay out some theoretical distinctions from the work of Giorgio Agamben and Jacques Derrida that underlie my rereading of John's prologue. Finally, I sketch an understanding of the incarnation in which logos theology does not affirm humanity's high rank in a cosmic hierarchy, but portends a fundamental restructuring of human identity and a radically different ecological politics.

THE DIVINE-HUMAN COMMUNITY OF LOGOS IN ATHANASIUS OF ALEXANDRIA AND GREGORY OF NAZIANZUS

Theology is very strict on the following point: there are no werewolves, human beings cannot become animal.

—GILLES DELEUZE AND FÉLIX GUATTARI, *A Thousand Plateaus*

Though the traditional continuity assumed between divine and human logos is likely familiar to most theologically attuned readers, two examples will illustrate its pervasiveness. Athanasius's treatise *De incarnatione verbi dei* is not only a foundational text for trinitarian theology and teaching on the incarnation, it also explains God's rationale for becoming incarnate in terms of a familial bond between human logos and the divine Logos that sets humanity apart from other animals.

Out of what did not exist God has made all things [*ta panta*] through God's very own *Logos*, our Lord Jesus Christ. And God created human beings [*anthrōpous*], showing mercy to the human species [*to anthrōpōn genos*] among all the creatures on earth, having seen that they would not be sufficient to persist forever according to their own special discourse [*logos*], God showed kindness to them in particular (not generally as with all the non-discursive animals [*aloga zōa*]). God made them according to God's own image, sharing with them even the power of God's very own *Logos*, so that possessing some kind of shadow of the *Logos* and becoming discursive [*logikoi*], they might be empowered to persist in happiness, living [*zōntes*] the true and genuine life [*bion*] of the saints in paradise. . . . Since we set out at some point to speak of the becoming-human [*enanthrōpēseōs*] of the *Logos*, you may justly wonder why we are describing the origin of human beings. But indeed, this is not outside the purview of the narrative. For speaking about the manifestation of the Savior to us, it is necessary for us also to speak of the origin of human beings [*tēs tōn anthrōpōn archēs*] in order that you should know that our blame became the motive for his descent, and our deviation required the magnanimous love [*philanthrōpian*] of the *Logos*, that he might overtake us and be manifest, the Lord among human beings [*en anthrōpois*].[3]

Among all creatures, humanity uniquely reflects the Logos by being *logikos* (discursive, rational), possessing its own derivative and participatory logos. This unique connection is also the implied reason for the incarnation.

Gregory of Nazianzus traces a more subtle connection between divine and human logos, but Gregory's presumption of continuity is all the more pervasive, being integral to baptism, spirituality, and salvation in his teaching. Gregory frames his thirty-ninth oration, "On the Holy Lights," with John's prologue. The discourse was delivered on the feast of the Epiphany on the occasion of some significant baptisms in Constantinople, and his choice of John is notable because at the Epiphany one would rather expect to hear one of the synoptic texts on Jesus' baptism in the Jordan.[4] Within the first few sentences Gregory uses John's pervasive light metaphors to describe baptism as illumination, invoking Christ as "the true light [*phōs*] which illumines [*phōtizei*] every human being."[5] Gregory's appropriation of the Johannine vocabulary, however, also executes a subtle displacement within it. Within John's prologue, the effect of the light [*phōs*] of the divine Logos is animation [*zōē*]; the Logos radiates life. "What came about through this one [the *Logos*] was life [*zōē*] and that life was the light [*phōs*] of human beings [*anthrōpōn*]" (John 1:4).[6] Within Gregory's oration,

however, light becomes a metaphor for enlightenment rather than animation; the light of the Logos bears *knowledge*. "Let us light within ourselves
[*phōtisōmen*] the light of knowledge [*phōs gnōseōs*]!"[7] The Logos that illumines the world is contiguous with human thought and speech. In this
way greater proximity to God's radiance accentuates human uniqueness
in relation to other animals (measured for Gregory by the possession of a
mind [*nous*] and the exercise of logos), rather than multiplying the life (*zōē*)
shared with all other animals (*zōa*). Gregory buries the Johannine connection between *phōs* and *zōē* in order to undergird human uniqueness and
reinforce a continuity between human and divine logos.

Gregory's discourse on baptism enjoins a spirituality of purification
(*katharsis*) as an ongoing preparation for full illumination (*ellampsis*). Im-
purities within human life (which Gregory repeatedly describes with animal imagery) must be purged in order to render the human being more
receptive to the knowledge of God.[8] Gregory's own discourse (logos) leads
the way in purification:

> By discourse [*tō logō*] we have thoroughly purified [*anekathēramen*]
> this assembly hall. So come! Now let us do a bit of philosophizing
> about the holiday; let us celebrate together with those souls who love
> holidays and love God! And since the whole point of a holiday is the
> memory of God, let us remember.[9]

The process of this purification removes the obscurities that would prevent a full and complete knowledge of God through illumination:

> By fear they are rectified, purified [*kathairomenous*], and (so to speak)
> rarefied in order to rise up to the heights. For where fear is, there
> is heeding of commands. Where heeding of commands is, there is
> purification of flesh [*sarkos katharsis*]—that cloud eclipsing the soul,
> not allowing it to see the beam of divine light in purity [*katharōs*]. But
> where purification [*katharsis*] is, there is illumination [*ellampsis*].[10]

Finally, Gregory encourages his hearers to seek for themselves the
purification that leads, through the light of the Logos, to greater knowledge of God:

The same *Logos* is *both* naturally fearsome for the unworthy *and* attainable out of benevolence [*philanthrōpian*] for those who are well prepared—that is, as many as have purged the impure [*akatharton*] and material spirit from their souls and swept clean and ordered their souls with knowledge [*epignōsei*]. . . . Let us light within ourselves [*phōtisōmen*] the light of knowledge [*phōs gnōseōs*]. At that time we should speak of God's wisdom, which has been hidden in a mystery and we should shine out to others. But until then, we should purify [*kathairōmetha*] and initiate ourselves in the *Logos* in order that we might do exceedingly good things for ourselves, working ourselves into godlikeness [*theoeideis*] and welcoming the coming *Logos*—not only that, but seizing and showing forth [the *Logos*] to others.[11]

The light of the divine Logos bears fruit within the human mind, transforming humanity through an ever-deepening knowledge.

Gregory is manifestly at home in the Johannine vocabulary as he expounds the theology and spirituality of baptism. Quite clearly, however, Gregory's particular inhabitation of John's terminology presumes an affinity or continuity between human and divine logos. Rather than bearing life (*zōē*) as in John, for Gregory the illumination of the Logos bears knowledge, a subtle shift that aligns the operation of the divine Logos with human logos. Whether intentional or not, Gregory's shift signals his presumption of a categorical difference between human beings and other animals on the basis of an intrinsic connection between humanity and God in logos.

LOGOS AND LIFE

Politics supposes livestock.

—JACQUES DERRIDA, *The Animal That Therefore I Am,*
summarizing Immanuel Kant

In addition to featuring prominently in John's prologue, *zōē* is also the "protagonist" of Giorgio Agamben's 1995 text *Homo Sacer.*[12] Agamben quotes a famous distinction in Aristotle's *Metaphysics* between bare, prepolitical, undirected life (*zēn*) and life that is politically ordered toward higher goods such as justice and friendship (*eu zēn*).[13] In a maneuver that has led to some confusion, Agamben maintains Aristotle's basic conceptual distinction but replaces Aristotle's specific terms (*zēn* / *eu zēn*), arguing that the tensive relationship between *zōē* (bare life) and *bios* (a way of life, a politically ordered life) represents the "fundamental categorical pair of Western politics."[14] The goal of political life (*bios*) in the city is to provide a setting where the bare life (*zōē*) of eating, sleeping, breathing, and procreation may be arranged for deeper flourishing. Bare life (*zōē*) is dissolute, concerned only with basic material urges; it must be ordered, organized into *bios* in order to attain the "good life" with its higher goods—justice, friendship, and true happiness.

For Agamben, it is not the case that one finds *zōē* out in the world in order to organize it and found a city. Agamben inverts the commonsense political myth of origins, arguing that the production of the category *zōē* is the fundamental task of political life. So *bios* is not so much an improvement on a *zōē* that was already there, but an operation that is suspended over *zōē* as a rhetorically necessary category. Western politics operates as a superstructure that claims to be making life better than "bare life," *zōē*, but actually consolidates power precisely by perpetuating the distinction between *zōē* and *bios*. "The fundamental activity of sovereign power is the production of bare life as originary political element and as threshold of articulation between nature and culture, *zōē* and *bios*."[15] Suspending *bios* over *zōē* generates an interminable, indistinct threat: If one is excluded from the city, from the law, from the protection of the political arrangement, one "returns" to a state of bare life. Political life (*bios*) produces bare life (*zōē*), then, in two ways: First, bare life functions as a mythical Ur-concept that marks political life as better than the brute life that preceded it, even if no concrete memory of such a life exists. Second, political life produces bare life by exclusion, occasionally denuding someone of the protection of the law and exposing him or her to whatever death or misfortune might befall him or her. Political life actualizes bare life by baring lives and exposing them to harm, an operation that also reinforces the legitimating effect of the founding myth.

The fundamental political relation, then, is the ban in which someone faces exile from the subjecthood, subjection, and subjectivity offered by the protection of the law—whether the ban operates as a threat or is actually enacted.[16] Conceptually, *zōē* is both excluded from the city (because city life is not uncivilized brute life) and incorporated into the city as the "raw stuff" that is felicitously arranged. This productive "zone of indistinction"—where zoē is both excluded from the city and presumed as its foundation—represents a constitutive ambiguity that holds the city together.

Agamben moves on to show how the conceptual distinction between zoē and bios operates both in the twentieth century's totalitarian regimes and its market-driven democracies: millions upon millions were reduced to "bare life" as they were stripped of citizenship before being sent to death camps;[17] the liberal discourse of "human rights" invokes an inviolable, minimum standard of human decency, a "bare life" to which the invisible hand of global capitalism reduces millions more.[18] My purpose, however, does not require that we follow Agamben's argument in that direction. Instead, I want to consider the preceding analysis from *Homo Sacer* in relation to Agamben's other texts, and specifically *The Open*.

Pressing questions have been raised about *Homo Sacer*. How can Agamben locate the origin of Western politics in a distinction between bare life and political life and yet fail to analyze the ways that this distinction is conceptually bound up with human relations to animals?[19] It is hard not to regard the ban of animals from human societies as a more original political relation than Agamben's originary intrahuman ban—and a model for it. The person exiled from the city must contend with the animals who have already been excluded, be devoured by them or live like them. "Bare life" is first of all the life of animals; it is animality. To equate bare life and animality is not at all to retreat from Agamben's assertion that zoē is produced by the political discourse of the city rather than "discovered" and modulated. The notion of a disordered natural world devoid of higher goods in which bare animal life barely survives amid chaos is as much a construct when applied to the lives of trout, elk, wolves, hyenas, and sloths as it is when applied to human beings stripped of citizenship. The work of Jacques Derrida in *The Animal That Therefore I Am* and *The Beast and the Sovereign* might helpfully supplement Agamben's thought here, inasmuch as Derrida analyzes the political uses of the abstract catchall category *animal*—which supposedly captures and tames the difference between earthworms and elephants in one breath.[20]

One need not turn to Derrida, however, for the necessary supplement. Although Agamben never makes the connection explicit, *The Open*—a text published seven years later—both frames and completes the argument of

Homo Sacer.[21] The tight parallel in the structure and content of the arguments justifies reading the two texts together. I would like to add several terms to the "fundamental categorical pair of Western politics" in order to link *Homo Sacer* and *The Open*. On the one hand, we may align *humanity* with *bios* and the project of political life; on the other, we may align *human beings* with *zōē* and "bare life." A human being is a bare living animal, a creature conceptually embedded in humanity, a discursive superstructure that promulgates and celebrates the norms, boundaries, and expectations of civilized subjectivity. Human beings, almost without exception, participate in humanity from birth simply because it is inseparable from language acquisition, enculturation, and identity formation. To borrow language from Louis Althusser, humanity is an ideological regime in which all human beings are subjectivized, interpellated, a regime that all human beings support. We hail each other and make demands on each other in ways that continually reinscribe the logos of humanity in the patterns of life that we animals perform.[22] In keeping with Agamben's analysis, sovereign power retains the capacity to strip a human being of his or her place in humanity so that someone is perceived formally as human but treated morally and politically "like an animal." Most of Agamben's own examples of *homines sacri* have been "dehumanized" in this way.

The Open argues that humanity is not a stable entity with a readily discoverable nature, but is instead the ongoing operation of what Agamben calls an "anthropological machine."[23] Just like the political function of the distinction between *zōē* and *bios* in *Homo Sacer*, the operation of the anthropological machine establishes a "zone of indistinction" between human and animal, in which animality is both included as the "raw stuff" of humanity, and excluded inasmuch as humanity is supposed to rise above the "brutes."[24] The machine safeguards the conceptual integrity of the category *humanity* by discerning and disavowing an inner animality. Distinguishing an "animal part" within (mute desire, passion, irrationality, bodily functions, etc.) from a kernel of true humanity (rationality, language, self-awareness, openness to a transcendent horizon, etc.) stabilizes the identity of humanity by recognizing animals as categorically other:

> It is possible to oppose man to other living things, and at the same
> time to organize the complex—and not always edifying—economy
> of relations between men and animals, only because something like

an animal life has been separated within man, only because his distance and proximity to the animal have been measured and recognized first of all in the closest and most intimate place. . . . What is
man, if he is always the place—and at the same time, the result—of
ceaseless divisions and caesurae? It is more urgent to work on these
divisions, to ask in what way—within man—has man been separated
from non-man, and the animal from the human, than it is to take
positions on the great issues, on so-called human rights and values.
And perhaps even the most luminous sphere of our relations with the
divine depends, in some way, on that darker one which separates us
from the animal.[25]

Agamben's analysis in *The Open* repeats the analytical maneuvers of *Homo
Sacer* but does so with regard to the conceptual difference between humanity and animality. *Humanity* is produced as a pure category by means of the
discernment of a second category, *animality*, which lies at the foundation
of human life (the human is a kind of animal) but must be disavowed in
order to live an authentically human life.

There are three mutually involved distinctions within Agamben's cor-
pus, then, which should be aligned as coterminous. First, the distinction
in *Homo Sacer* between bare life and the "good life" of citizenship; second,
from *The Open*, the distinction between the animality of nonhuman creatures and the humanity of human beings; and third, an inner distinction
between the animality of the human being and the kernel of true humanity. In both the mechanisms of politics and the anthropological machine a
logos of humanity safeguards its exceptional status by positing something
"lower" from which authentic humanity rises. In each case, this logos sup-
presses and excludes *zōē* as a wildness or disorder that threatens to consume the fragile arrangements of humanity.

Read through the perspective of *The Open*, several of the problems most
frequently noted in *Homo Sacer* diminish considerably. Most important, this
framing reduces the pressure on Agamben's somewhat tenuous attempt
to locate the origin of Western politics in a distinction between *bios* and
zōē, as found in Aristotle's text. In the twelfth session of "The Beast and
the Sovereign," Derrida is highly critical of Agamben's claim to "discover"
Foucauldian biopolitics in a germinal form within Aristotle's *Metaphysics*.[26]
Rooting the tension between *bios* and *zōē* "further back" (as it were) in the

production of humanity over against animality takes the weight off Aristotle as an origin point for Western biopolitics. Framing *Homo Sacer* with *The Open* would also significantly align Agamben's analysis of sovereignty with Derrida's—inasmuch as an adequate understanding of sovereignty for both thinkers would require an analysis of the relation of animality to politics. If authentic humanity (*bios*) is defined by efforts to modulate and control animality (*zōē*) both internally and externally, then not only is it the case that "all politics is biopolitics," as Agamben claims, but biopolitics is conceptually and historically coterminous with hominization.[27]

Derrida claims that the distinction between *zōē* and *bios* is too clumsy a tool to execute the analysis that Agamben undertakes, yet Agamben's and Derrida's analyses are, perhaps, closer than Derrida acknowledges.[28] Derrida describes an operation similar to Agamben's anthropological machine that produces and inculcates the concept "humanity" in relation to "animality" in his text *The Animal That Therefore I Am*, drawing attention to the stabilizing function of the term *animal* in relation to human identity and subjectivity as it provides a (falsely) homogenous point of contrast. His neologism *animot* is meant to displace and expose the word (*mot*) which audially masks the plurality of actual animals (*animaux*) summed up with the single term *animal*. The larger argumentative arc of *The Beast and the Sovereign* resists any thinking about politics as control over animality (human animality or the animals of nature) by some sovereignty conceptually separable from animality. Human beings, he argues, are political precisely *in* their animality, and not as a means of rising above it. To summarize (all too briefly), for Derrida the foundations of human thought and language— what we might again call the logos of humanity—rest on the supposition of a break between human life and the lives of animals, a break repeatedly enacted in disavowals of animals and animality.[29] Derrida recognizes that for human beings there is no way out of the logos of humanity. Nevertheless, he deconstructs its conceptual integrity from within and seeks the threshold of a different mode of speech and thought (a different mode of subjectivity) in "following an animal," being identified in and by the gaze of an animal—even fleetingly—rather than through the human logos.

Despite their differences, Derrida and Agamben converge in thinking about the relation of animality to human politics. Both Derrida and Agamben explore (and to some degree assume) the rhetorical and conceptual distinction between humans and animals—precisely in order to destabilize it from within. Both thinkers describe the constitution of humanity (as we understand and live into it) as an operation of human logos on *zōē*, a discourse that carves out a space of privilege and uniqueness by positing *zōē* as something to be managed and studied, something ultimately pliable under humanity's sovereign discretion.[30] Agamben's anthropological machine strategically maps a "zone of indistinction" where humanity is both animal and not-animal; humanity lives out "bare life" and makes life something categorically other than bare. Similarly, for Derrida, human subjectivity is founded on a self-recognition denied to animals in one way or another. Taking Descartes, Kant, Levinas, Lacan, and Heidegger at their word, that human subjectivity is something other-than-animal, Derrida perceives the logos of humanity as neither a living creature nor something inert and innocent. Humanity speaks its logos from the realm of the undead.[31]

THE LOGOS OF GOD AND THE END OF HUMANITY: DIVINANIMALITY

It is not just that animals, like nature according to Heraclitus, "love to hide"; it is also that they have to hide, and that since the dawn of time, over and above their own conflicts, they have identified man not only as a predator but also as a strange, unpredictable, lawless being.

—JEAN-CHRISTOPHE BAILLY, *The Animal Side*

Characteristically, Derrida avoids speculative leaps and political commitments; nevertheless, *The Animal That Therefore I Am* does trace out a positive movement. Repeatedly Derrida exempts himself from those who naïvely refer to *the animal* as a coherent category.[32] His tentative silence at "the bordercrossing" between humanity and animality enables him to encounter a discomfiting solidarity in the eyes of fellow animals and opens up within himself what he calls "the abyssal limit of the human: the inhuman or the ahuman, the ends of man."[33] Derrida abandons the anthropological function of the category *animal* in exchange for a finer-grained attention to difference.[34] Agamben does not exude any more political optimism than Derrida, but he nevertheless invokes the "jamming of the anthropological machine" as a messianic opening. To find the point of inoperativity and cease distinguishing between animality and humanity (which is not to deny the many distinctions among creatures) would "show the central emptiness, the hiatus that—within man—separates man and animal, and [would] risk ourselves in this emptiness: the suspension of the suspension, Shabbat of both animal and man."[35] The remainder of this essay takes the positive momentum of these suggestions in a theological direction.

Gregory and Athanasius certainly represent the overwhelming norm within the Christian tradition in their investment not only in anthropocentrism but also in anthropological exceptionalism. That is, humanity is not only God's most treasured creature, but humanity is a qualitatively different kind of creature than all the others. Traditionally, the incarnation has been employed as a linchpin of anthropological exceptionalism, validating the assumption that God redeems humanity because of something like a familial obligation.[36] Everyone acknowledges that no necessity compels God to act redemptively, but the work of the divine Logos is nevertheless imagined to honor a continuity between human and divine logos, like caring for like. I would like to resist the tradition's anthropological exceptionalism by exploring an understanding of the incarnation rooted in a basic discontinuity between human and divine logos, in which the work of the logos is evidenced more in zōē than in human thought and speech.

It will be helpful to locate the divine Logos within each of the three aligned distinctions from Agamben's texts. First, with regard to the distinction between bare life and political life, it is commonplace to recognize Jesus as the figure of the outcast, the scapegoat, the refugee, whose life cannot be assimilated to the order of his society. Jesus is not far from the figure of the *homo sacer*, exposed to death outside the city (not murdered) for the sake of the political order. In this regard, Jesus the Logos clearly stands on the side of zōē rather than citizenship. Second, with regard to the human-animal distinction, the Logos obviously bears human flesh, but his alignment with humanity rather than animality is less secure than it might first appear. The Logos seems to impart life (zōē) at the particular places to which humanity relegates animals. God's Logos appears as the flesh-meal around which humanity unites, the sacrificial lamb slaughtered for ritual purity, the scapegoat cast out by the fury of human sin, and the symbolic lion whose ferocity lends courage to the disheartened. One might ask whether the Logos of God appears in the place of the animal to endorse eating, slaughter, and experimentation, or to loose the knots holding these cultural structures together? Third, where is the Logos situated with regard to the interior distinction between humanity proper and human animality? Does the incarnation of the Logos as a human being underwrite or undermine the workings of the anthropological machine? Does the Logos further the conceptual transcendence of humanity over animality by participating in it, or does the Logos subvert that transcendence as a false pretension? I suggest that the Logos—as the very *zōē* of human beings—is aligned with human animality against humanity's proprietary logos as it disavows animality through the anthropological machine. The becoming-flesh of the Logos is not the endorsement of the present structure of human subjectivity and self-understanding, but an effort to knock loose the gears of the destructive machine that produces it. The Logos, then, from the closest proximity to humanity's own logos, opposes it for the sake of *zōē*.

If these three placements are correct, then John's description of humanity's inability to recognize and receive the light of the divine Logos should be connected to humanity's self-constructed alienation from animality. In all three divisions, an autonomous, self-reflective, self-constituting human logos maneuvers to transcend and disavow a *zōē* that nevertheless remains internal to it. In contrast to the traditional interpretation that supposes continuity between divine and human logos, however, God now appears on the side of *zōē* rather than as the transcendent anchor of human uniqueness.

God is present as the incarnate *zōē*-Logos of creation, but the human form of the Logos does not validate humanity's ideological projects, but presents God's most personal judgment upon them. In Barthian terms, the Logos of God sounds out a thundering *"Nein!"* to humanity precisely by taking on human flesh.[37] In order to redeem the groaning creation, God became a human being so that human beings might become *zōē*, become-animal with God.[38] The incarnation is the inspired dismantling of humanity from within, a divine deconstruction-in-flesh, the advent of the messiah as the divinanimal *zōē* that humanity's self-conception is bent on excluding.

If the Logos is indeed the *zōē* of creation, and if the logos of human subjectivity systematically differentiates itself from this *zōē*, then the redemption of the Logos cannot but entail a fundamental personal transformation.[39] The messianic horizon of redemption into the *zōē* of the Logos unshackles human beings from the interpellation and subjectivization of humanity, not as the effect of a "dehumanizing" sovereign power, but as the suspension or cessation of the human logos's self-differentiation from *zōē*. Nor is such a radical conversion foreign to Christian rhetoric and spirituality. Jesus enjoins his followers to bear crosses and "deny themselves"— though this "self" denied is rarely understood as the self that differentiates humanity from animality.

On this understanding, the Logos of God is no longer the Master Signifier, the keystone that anchors the logos of self-reflective human thought and speech in a stable economy of meaning. Instead, relative to the logos of humanity, the Logos of God is negatively transcendent. God's Logos is the charged silence over which humanity finds itself interminably babbling. The logos of humanity can find no entryway into the Logos of God; it tries to speak its way over a communicative abyss rather than being immersed in the silence of divinanimality. The unsettling eyes of animals— whose gazes have so little regard for human discourse—are unsettling not because they lack meaning but because they convey an excess of meaning that cannot be borne in language; they are icons of the mystery of the *zōē* of God. The living silence of the divinanimal Logos offers (or threatens) to swallow whole the logos of humanity—and no one can guess what kind of new *zōē* might emerge from this end.

The *zōē aiōnios* (eternal life) of the Logos is not an abstract quality added to one isolated creature (the human) upon the extraction of that creature from the whole network of living relations in the world.[40] Rather the *zōē aiōnios* is the embedding-into-created-immanence of an alienated creature—what Colossians calls the reconciliation of all things (*ta panta* [Col. 1:15–19]). The redemption of the Logos cannot be attained or preserved within any wilderness or romantic ecological utopia. Instead, it must be anticipated expectantly as a messianic kingdom "not of this world" that breaks out transformatively within the relations among living creatures, rather than as the conflagration that wipes clean the face of the earth. Rather than *zōē aiōnios* being the distilled, extracted, and rarefied body of one resurrected (but hardly animal) species, the *zōē* of the divine Logos may be understood as the rhizomatic multiplication of life in diversity. It is still possible to cling to the parochial logos whose mechanized superiority over every other creature cannot be questioned, but on this rereading of John, the question of life and death looms in the haunted silences where the logos of humanity pauses, ever so briefly, for breath.

❧ Anzaldúa's Animal Abyss: *Mestizaje* and the Late Ancient Imagination

AN YOUNTAE AND PETER ANTHONY MENA

What does Gloria Anzaldúa, the Chicana lesbian poet, thinker, and borderland theorist, have to do with posthuman animality studies?[1] And what could she offer to a collection of essays that ventures to triangulate reflections on the human and the animal with reflections on the divine? Cursory glances through recent publications in posthuman animality studies reveal nothing to indicate a marriage between Chicana/o or borderland thought and the proliferation of discourses centered on the animal. Yet as will become clear, we find in Anzaldúa important methodological tools for rethinking the dualistic terms of oppression, particularly in this case, of the human/animal binary. In her transgressive reading cultural symbols and identities converge in her unique political vision, in which a hybrid *mestizaje* becomes interwoven with a cosmic, intercorporeal spirituality. As we shall see, the animal occupies an important place in her thought.

In the spirit of transdisciplinarity this reflection is written by two thinkers within discrete yet overlapping disciplinary locations: one historical and literary (Mena), the other philosophical and theological (An). The division of the reflection into two parts will make clear our disciplinary differences, no less than our divergent approaches to Anzaldúa. Still, the shared trajectory of our individual readings will highlight the peculiar contribution that Gloria Anzaldúa's work can make to the discourses of posthumanism and animality studies.

In the first section Mena situates Anzaldúa within postcolonial studies. Her concepts of hybridity and ambiguity provide the multiple and open spaces in which identity formation can and does take place. Identity read in this way transcends its dualistic nature and thus dissolves the speciated divide between animal and human. Likewise, the animal, as Anzaldúa presents it, opens the possibility for the multiplicity and ambiguity of hybrid identities. A temporal slippage is necessary in order to read for similar hybridity and ambiguity in late antiquity. The unlikely resonances between Anzaldúa and fifth-century Christianity prove to be a productive site for thinking through the animal as constitutive of identity. More specifically, by reading a hagiographical text penned by Jerome, the fourth/fifth-century patristic writer and thinker, the transcendence Anzaldúa gestures toward can be gleaned. As will be demonstrated below, in this particular hagiography, the human/nonhuman binary is dissolved.

In the second section An homes in even more explicitly on the thought of Anzaldúa. A decolonial dialectical reading of Anzaldúa further elaborates the postcolonial framework of hybridity and ambiguity in order to account for political consequence and agency—both seemingly precluded by much postcolonial theory. Instead, a dialectical reading of Anzaldúa, hinging on her animal images, exposes her *mestiza* consciousness as the result of her arduous struggle and her search for selfhood.

Our two readings of Anzaldúa, although divergent in approach and exposition, lead to similar ends. On the one hand, we explore certain rich ways in which the intersections of politics, spirituality, and identity converge on her concept of the animal, particularly in the context of racial/colonial/sexual oppression. Consequently, the animal might signal a tactics of survival, toward what Anzaldúa calls the *mestiza* consciousness. Our reading might even suggest that Anzaldúa's animal *is* the "new consciousness" she calls for—a consciousness, or an animal, imbued with the potential for awareness of the self, of the divine, and of decolonial freedom. On the other hand, we aim to show the fertile ground Anzaldúa can provide scholars of posthuman animality studies. If posthumanism aims to end "violence against the social other of *whatever* species—or gender, or race, or class, or sexual difference," as Cary Wolfe has claimed[2]—then we must take seriously the ways in which the current discourses, with their reliance on poststructuralist philosophy, are limited by their Euro-American context, creating a gap between what posthumanism's proponents aim to accomplish and its actual liberating potential. What follows is our attempt to bridge this gap. Gloria Anzaldúa is our bridge.

MESTIZAJE AND THE ANIMALITY OF DESERT ASCETICISM

For Gloria Anzaldúa, *mestizaje* is a term that names—through its refusal to name—the distinct, particular, and multiple identities forged in the arid spaces of the U.S.–Mexican borderlands.[3] This *mestizaje*, characterized by its whiteness, blackness, brownness, humanity, animality, queerness, is at once all of these things; yet still there remains a failure to render *mestizaje* with complete clarity. The *mestiza* identity is multiple and abundant for Anzaldúa. "Identity is a river—a process. Contained within the river is its identity, and it needs to flow, to change to stay a river—if it stopped it would be a contained body of water such as a lake or a pond"[4] and thus no longer a river. The excess and excessiveness of *mestizaje* pushes at the limits of race, gender, sexuality, and humanity. And still, *mestizaje* is contained in and by its very formation. Thus the U.S.–Mexican borderlands figure prominently in the forging of this distinctly *new mestizaje*. Yet Anzaldúa understands the openness of her concept of borderlands:

> The actual physical borderland that I'm dealing with in this book [that is, her *Borderlands/LaFrontera*] is the Texas-U.S. Southwest/Mexican border. The psychological borderlands, the sexual borderlands and the spiritual borderlands, are not particular to the Southwest. In fact, the Borderlands are physically present wherever two or more cultures edge each other, where people of different races occupy the same territory, where under, lower, middle and upper classes touch, where the space between two individuals shrinks with intimacy.[5]

Borderlands are the intimate spaces of production where tensions, differences, and identities are made and negotiated. In her foundational work, *Borderlands/LaFrontera: The New Mestiza*, Anzaldúa traces the genealogy of *mestizaje*. She writes, "The *mestizos* who were genetically equipped to survive small pox, measles, and typhus . . . founded a new hybrid race and inherited Central and South America. *En 1521 nació una nueva raza, el mestizo, el mexicano* (people of mixed Indian and Spanish blood), a race that had never existed before. Chicanos, Mexican-Americans, are the offspring of those first matings."[6]

Anzaldúa is quick to point out that *mestizaje* is not simply a biological creation but a socially and politically constructed identity violently produced in the "third country" that is the U.S.–Mexican borderlands. Thus she traces the movement of white people from the northern parts of the United States into Texas and the subsequent Battle of the Alamo—and the later capture of Santa Anna—in which "*tejanos* (native Texans of Mexican descent) . . . lost their land and, overnight, became foreigners."[7] It is, however, the signing of the Treaty of Guadalupe-Hidalgo on February 2, 1848, which—as Sonia Saldívar-Hull puts it—"created a new U.S. minority: American citizens of Mexican descent."[8]

Anzaldúa traces this history in her "*autohistoria*" fashion. Weaving in and out of personal autobiographical narrative, she demonstrates a nonlinear history that narrates both the birth of *mestizaje* and the life of Anzaldúa. The "animality of *mestizaje*" as discussed by Anzaldúa opens up space for what she calls a "new consciousness," a "*mestiza consciousness*." Animality and *mestizaje* are constitutive of each other. For Anzaldúa they are not one and the same, yet neither can be understood independently of the other. She writes, "Forty years it's taken me to enter into the Serpent, to acknowledge that I have a body, that I am a body and to assimilate the animal body, the animal soul."[9] She recounts a childhood memory of a near-deadly interaction with a venomous rattlesnake. After being bitten, she uses a pocketknife to cut open the site of the snakebite. As the blood spills from the wound, she sucks out the venom and spits it onto the ground. She says, "That night I watched the window sill, watched the moon dry the blood on the tail, dreamed rattler fangs filled my mouth, scales covered my body. In the morning I saw through snake eyes, felt snake blood course through my body. The serpent, *mi tono*, my animal counterpart. I was immune to its venom. Forever immune."[10]

Anzaldúa's awakening and "entering into the serpent" is an experience of self-awareness. It is the beginning of her forty-year journey in which she learns her body, learns her power—her *tono*—and erodes the precarious boundary between animal and human subjectivities. The transgressed boundary is, again, one that links animality and *mestizaje*. Moreover, Anzaldúa is very much aware of the historical embeddedness of this pairing. She seems to employ what postcolonial theorist Neel Ahuja calls the "animal mask." He writes:

> In our supposedly postracial moment, an ironic stance provisionally embracing animality is actually a common strategy for disentangling

race and species in this context. I call this strategy, which appropriates the rhetoric of animalization to reveal its ongoing racial, neocolonial, or ecological legacies, the *animal mask*. By ironically appropriating an animal guise, the performer unveils a historical logic of animalization inherent in processes of racial subjection. The performance of the *animal mask* does not necessarily entail identification with nonhuman species, but it always points to the historical conjunctions of social difference and species discourse."[11]

Anzaldúa's scaled body and snake eyes certainly point to "the historical conjunctions of social difference and species discourse"; however, her appropriation of the rhetoric of animalization does not seem predominantly ironic. Anzaldúa's animal mask is, in fact, less a mask and more an embodiment of the animal. This embodiment is key to her concept of hybrid subjectivity, which expresses a new and different knowledge gained only via the processes of racial subjection and only within the space of the borderlands.[12]

The embodiment of the animal becomes most explicit with Anzaldúa's notions of language. The title of her chapter on language, "How to Tame a Wild Tongue," is indicative of this embodiment and its strong implications for identity formation. She tells us, "Wild tongues can't be tamed, they can only be cut out."[13] The violence of assimilation is not lost on Anzaldúa, and neither is the persistence of the wild, animal, *mestiza* tongue, which can be changed only by being severed from the rest of the body— resulting in, not a new form of communication, but rather, silence. And still this wild tongue that does persist, can do so only by constantly revealing itself—the wild *mestiza* self. Every word, every utterance, is a signification of the multiple, hybrid self forged in the space of the U.S.–Mexican borderlands. Furthermore, every word, every utterance, is a signification of the escape from a violent silencing. And so Anzaldúa urges us that the *mestiza* must be heard. And everyone else must listen. *"Oyé como ladra: el lenguaje de la frontera"* / "Hear Her Bark: The Language of the Borderlands," the title of a section in her chapter on language, is both an invocation and an indication. Hear her bark. The language of the borderlands is wild and perhaps—to some—incomprehensible. Still, it must be heard. Precisely because of its persistence, it must be heard. This language is tied to the *mestiza* life. Not only because language is a part of life—but because this language is an exact representation of the people to whom it belongs. "Chicano Spanish is a border tongue which developed naturally. Change, *evolución, enriquecimiento de palabras nuevas por invención o adopción* have created variants of Chicano Spanish, *un nuevo lenguaje. Un lenguaje que corresponde a un modo de vivir.* Chicano Spanish is not incorrect, it is a living language. . . . We speak a patois, a forked tongue."[14] Language for Anzaldúa is a key signifier of the *mestiza* life. Chicano Spanish—as she calls it—has utility as a form of communication, but its "natural" formation mirrors that of its millions of users.

In her theory of *mestiza* consciousness, Anzaldúa dissolves the dualistic nature of identities and thus erodes the boundary between species. She says:

> The work of *mestiza* consciousness is to break down the subject-object duality that keeps her a prisoner and to show in the flesh and through the images of her work how duality is transcended. The answer to the problem between the white race and the colored, between males and females, lies in healing the split that originates in the very foundation of our lives, our culture, our languages, our thoughts. . . . Collective consciousness is the beginning of a long struggle, but one that could, in our best hopes, bring us to the end of rape, of violence, of war.[15]

One could add human/nonhuman to the list of dualities that *mestiza* consciousness transcends. As the line between human and nonhuman fades into obscurity, the *mestiza* identity comes into stark relief.

Mestiza consciousness can be perceived at work in the making of a distinctly desert ascetic identity in a Christian text from the late ancient Mediterranean, namely, Jerome's *Life of Paul*. Shifting our eyes toward the late ancient Egyptian desert will allow us to see the unlikely resonances between an ancient ascetic in his own desert borderland and Anzaldúa. Given the historicity of catholic sensibilities and their own cultural hybridizations, these resonances can offer some surprising clues for current postcolonial thinking. Jerome's hagiography of the desert ascetic Paul depicts striking images of landscapes replete with animals, monsters, and other hybrid creatures who play vital roles by moving the plot of the narrative forward and by embodying a new consciousness, *"la conciencia de la mestiza."* This is (admittedly) a vast leap between distant cultural contexts.

Nevertheless, by opening the possibility of reading this text as one that employs its own embodiment of the animal, the reader can see how that embodiment is a moment of revelation of the *mestiza* self and hence more than an animal mask to be discarded at the moment of revelation of a truly human, constituted self, thereby reinscribing the speciated divide. This hybrid *mestiza* self is being forged here and in other contemporaneous texts in the arid spaces on the fringes of fourth- and fifth-century imperial and ecclesial authority. Desert space is then—ultimately—a space made both distinct from, and intimate with, the polis.

My reading of this *Life of Paul* will have some affinities with Patricia Cox Miller's article, "Jerome's Centaur: A Hyper-Icon of the Desert," as well as with Virginia Burrus's article, "Wyschogrod's Hand: Saints, Animality, and the Labor of Love."[16] Both scholars have not only highlighted the animality and hybridity of the creaturely inhabitants of Jerome's desert, but each has also suggested that these creatures are themselves reflections of ascetic identity. I build on these prior readings as I explore Jerome's desert as an important spatial construction utilized in the production of identity—that is, of a "late-ancient *mestizaje*."[17]

Jerome pens his hagiography of the first desert saint in order to recount "that which has been passed over" by previous writers (*Life of Paul* 1).[18] He is familiar with Athanasius's *Life of Antony*, and attempts to surpass that originary hagiography by writing about a man older, wiser, saintlier, and, perhaps more importantly, deeper in the desert than Antony. After discussing his intentions, Jerome moves swiftly into two queer martyrdom accounts situated during the Decian and Valerian persecutions. As Virginia Burrus has shown us, the queerness of these martyrdom texts lies in part in the failure of either martyr to be martyred.[19] Jerome describes one would-be martyr as being made to suffer the continuous bites of flies by being left out in the sun after having honey drizzled all over his body. Our second would-be martyr is tied down and forced to bite his tongue off in order to withstand the unwanted sexual advances of a "harlot of great beauty" (*meretrix seciosa*) (3). Jerome brings us to what we would expect to be the brink of death but instead forestalls both deaths—leaving us with bound, honey-dipped, and bloodied bodies, but, alas, no martyrs. In a text that will go on to celebrate the one-hundred-thirteen-year-old life of a Christian saint, it is not too much to suggest that Jerome's living martyrs are important preludes—one might even say transitions—to his account of the first desert saint. In this way, Jerome sets up the question European colonialists must have also asked themselves: What happens when subjugated identities find a way to stick around?

Jerome moves quickly away from the martyrs by introducing his readers to the very young Paul. Recently orphaned and made heir to his parents' fortune, Paul is forced to go into hiding because of the ongoing persecutions. Jerome hints at the depths of Paul's withdrawal into the desert, telling us that he "began with easy stages, and repeated halts, to advance into the desert" until finally "at length he found a rocky mountain, at the foot of which, closed by a stone, was a cave of no great size" (5).

Readers are then fast-forwarded to the one-hundred-thirteen-year-old Paul, and the story switches focus to the other already well known desert saint, Antony. Antony learns of Paul's existence when during "the stillness of the night it was revealed to him that there was farther in the desert a much better man than he, and that he ought to go and visit him" (7). With no guidance, Antony embarks on a journey to find this "better man." After several aimless, grueling hours of sun-scorched travel, Antony—no young man himself at the age of ninety—reminds himself—and us—of his faith in God and his journey. He says, "I believe in my God: some time or other he will show me the fellow servant whom he promised me." Immediately following his prayerful proclamation, Antony

at once beholds a creature of mingled shape, half horse half man, called by the poets hippocentaur. At the sight of this he arms himself by making on his forehead the sign of salvation, and then exclaims, "Hello! Where in these parts is a servant of God living?" The monster after gnashing out some kind of barbarous utterance, in words broken rather than spoken through his bristling lips, at length finds a friendly mode of communication, and extending his right hand points out the way desired.

The centaur—half man, half horse—is the emblem of hybridity. Building on classicist Page duBois's work on centaurs, Patricia Cox Miller notes the important symbolism behind this iconic figure from antiquity:

[Centaurs] were connected by analogy with barbarians as the "other" through which properly civilized individuals knew themselves to be such. In other words, as figurations of wildness and animal appetite, centaurs were opposed to culture—and yet, it is important to emphasize, it was only through them that civilized society recognized itself as civilized. Centaurs were a strange mixture of the animal and the human, of bestiality and civilization; negatively, they figured not only a literal "other" but also an intimate other, the wildness within the human.[20]

This creature of the desert, this late-ancient *mestiza*, enters the narrative abruptly and almost violently with its monstrous (*monstruosorum*) appearance and "barbarous" (*barbarum*) speech. But fear and confusion give way to "friendly communication" and comprehension. The centaur's wild tongue and broken speech need not be tamed in order for Antony to gain the knowledge necessary to proceed with his journey.

And proceed he does. It is not long, however, before he reaches the next denizen of the Egyptian desert—a satyr, or "homunculus with a hooked snout, horned forehead, and extremities like goats' feet" (8). Antony again approaches the creature with fear and steadfast determination. And again fear is allayed. The homunculus reaches out to offer Antony dates as nourishment for his long journey. Antony asks the homunculus what he is and is told, "I am a mortal being and one of those inhabitants of the desert [*et unus ex accolis eremi*]." Antony also learns that he is a Christian, which brings tears to Antony's eyes and sends him into a diatribe against the polis. But before he launches into his anti-urban polemic, Jerome informs us of Antony's amazement at the fact that he could understand the homunculus: Antony "rejoiced over the Glory of Christ and the destruction of Satan, and marveling all the while that he could understand the Satyr's language [*simulque admirans, quod ejus posset intelligere sermonem*]." Burrus has noted the curiousness of this interaction. She queries, "Do Antony and the homunculus, then, speak with the same tongue? Are they 'brothers'? If the appearance of the stereotypically randy figure of the satyr in an ascetic text is itself sufficiently astonishing, the implications of this friendly exchange are almost unthinkable."[21] Astonishing and unthinkable indeed, but if we linger here just a bit more we can see that Burrus's suggestive question pushes us to see a transformation occurring within Jerome's text. As Antony journeys deeper into the desert space, which is "typically capable of engendering monsters [*monstruosorum animalium ferax*]" (7), as

Jerome puts it, he is also in the process of self-discovery. The homunculus is at once hybrid, monstrous, *mestizo*, and *brother* to Antony. The fecundity of the desert has given birth not only to these monstrous creatures, but likewise to the Christian ascetic, himself a monster of sorts.

Antony's next and last guide is a wolf whom he spots in the distance and sets off to follow. She will lead him to the dwelling of the man he seeks, but not before she leads him on a chase.

> He saw a she-wolf gasping with parching thirst and creeping to the foot of the mountain. He followed it with his eyes; and after the beast had disappeared in a cave he drew near. . . . With halting step and bated breath he entered, carefully feeling his way; he advanced little by little and repeatedly listened for the sound. At length through the fearful midnight darkness a light appeared in the distance. In his eager haste he struck his foot against a stone and roused the echoes; whereupon the blessed Paul closed the open door and made it fast with a bar. (9)

Following the wolf, Antony reaches the home of the man he has sought long and hard for—parched and panting, like she. Only he is shut out and barred from entrance. He begins to cry and scream: "'Who I am, when, and why I have come, you know. I know I am not worthy to look upon you, yet unless I see you I will not go away. You welcome beasts, why not a man? I asked and I have found. I knock that it may be opened to me. But if I do not succeed, I will die here on your threshold. You will surely bury me when I am dead.' Such was his constant cry, unmoved he stood." Antony sits outside the cave, howling with tears. *Oye como ladra!* Hear him bark! He refuses to not be heard. He demands to know why Paul would admit a beast and not a human (*Qui bestias recipit, hominem cur repellis?*). And then, when he becomes most vulnerable, when he is able to realize his true hybrid, *mestizo* self, when human language fails him, and he is reduced to animal howling, his journey comes to an end. Paul opens the door.

Jerome's desert is abundantly populated with animals familiar and new. Ravens and lions await us still, but for the sake of brevity, I have considered only the creatures Antony encounters on his journey to Paul (also his journey toward selfhood and the divine). Again, Miller has already suggested Jerome's use of the centaur as a symbol for ascetic identity. Furthermore, she sees his use of the desert imaginary as a rhetorical tool for the production of such hybrid identities. Thus, "If the centaur is seen as a picture of human identity that conveys an ascetic sensibility, it is the *prominence of the animal* that is most striking. . . . In [Jerome's] *Life of Saint Paul . . .* it is a 'wild man' with an accentuated animal nature that points the way to the founder of asceticism."[22] I would further suggest that all of the desert creatures play this symbolic function for Jerome. It is the prominence of the animal in his Egyptian desert, like that of the serpent in Anzaldúa's borderlands, that is not only most striking but also most revealing.

Like Anzaldúa's borderlands, Jerome imagines the Egyptian desert to be a space for the production of hybrid identities. As Gloria Anzaldúa enters the serpent to come to her own *mestiza* consciousness, Antony has come into the desert (or to really push the metaphor—into the centaur, into the homunculus, into the wolf) in order to meet the same ends. Both Jerome's Egyptian desert and Anzaldúa's borderlands give birth to *mestizaje*—late-ancient and modern alike. Jerome's unmartyred martyrs transition us to a new Christian identity—the desert ascetic. Rebecca Lyman has characterized the fourth century as

> a highly competitive age . . . [in which] new models of asceticism, episcopacy, and theological authority were in intense and often violent political and literary confrontation. Rather than assuming the consolidation of a dogmatic peace of the church, one must analyze a complex alchemy of ecclesiastical idealism, passionate, but highly negotiated belief, and shrewd political manipulation which underlay the theological disputes of imperial Christianity.[23]

Discourses of domination via imperial authority assist in the production of *mestizaje*, which is aware of the fallacy of human/nonhuman distinctions. In this way, the employment and appropriation of animal identity within a *mestiza* consciousness remains a tactic of survival. The animal embodiment found in *mestizaje*, then, functions as a means to a livable life.

ANIMAL ABYSS, *MESTIZAJE*, AND DECOLONIAL FREEDOM

In my reading, I explore the multiple layers of signification that the animal symbolizes in Anzaldúa's work, and the ways in which the animal is epitomized by her own *mestiza* identity. Accordingly, the animal is both the decentering point of rupture toward a new consciousness and the point of *retorno* (return); both negation (animal gaze/darkness/the unknown) and affirmation (energy/creativity/birth); both the mark of interstitial identity and the trace of creaturely life/energy. In order to account for this ambiguity, I will read Anzaldúa's work as the dialectical unfolding of freedom vis-à-vis the abyss.

Born out of the vision of post-Enlightenment liberalism, the modern/contemporary notion of freedom has been associated with the idea of sovereignty accompanied by the individualistic understanding of subjectivity, thus mobilizing the Western ideals of both political freedom (the Western model of democracy) and economic freedom (global capitalism). These ideals of freedom imply a solid notion of "ground," that is, an ontological horizon within which the lives of autonomous subjects unfold.

Some contemporary thinkers offer a different way of understanding the notion of freedom. For instance, Slavoj Žižek has turned groundlessness into the very ground for the conception of freedom by drawing on the works of Schelling and Hegel and reflecting on the "abysmal dimension" of freedom.[24]

In resonance with the continental reconception of freedom, I explore the decolonial vision of Anzaldúa's work, which invokes a complex scrutiny of the abysmal dimension of freedom. I argue that the animal as a symbol of ambiguity in Anzaldúa's work materializes the dialectical tension between freedom and abyss. Arguably, since the mid-'90s, Homi Bhabha's theoretical contribution has been one of the most significant influences for interpreting the questions of "ambiguity" and "ambivalence" in postcolonial literature.[25] However, despite the innovative nature of its theoretical advances, postcolonial criticism's political effectiveness and accountability have been a constant subject of scholarly debate. I hope to address the issue by suggesting a dialectical reading of ambiguity in Anzaldúa. It is not my goal, however, to suggest the replacement of one paradigm or theoretical tool by the other. Rather, I intend to demonstrate that the radically subversive, yet integral elements lurking in Anzaldúa's thinking are fully disclosed only when the two different reading strategies (postcolonial and dialectical) are supplemented by each other. Ultimately, my reading of Anzaldúa's decolonial vision suggests that we conceive freedom as a collective vision of a new consciousness grounded in the groundless depth of the unknown, the abysmal gaze of the absolute other, and the unspeakable trauma of the colonial/sexual/nonhuman other.

Just as the animal signifies not only the vibrant energy but also the abysmal groundlessness of creaturely life, thus dissembling the notion of the sovereign subject, I argue that freedom, which is another name for (the possibility of) the divine, displaces the human subject by revealing both the precarious ground(lessness) of our social existence and the inexhaustibility of our creaturely existence.

Born out of the landscape of poststructuralist discourse, posthumanism in the form of animality studies has been providing innovative methodological resources for both the deconstruction of the human/animal dualism and the advancement of a new constructivist ontology. Specifically, the animal stands as a theoretical signifier that defies the absolutist claim of the Cartesian ego, that is, the metaphysical abstraction of the self whereby the corporeal entanglement of the self with his or her environment is reduced to the notion of the sovereign subject. According to certain proponents of animality studies, animals materialize the ontology of multiplicity and becoming with their behavioral patterns that are fluid, physical, and parasitic. As Gilles Deleuze, Félix Guattari, and Rosi Braidotti argue, animals embody the transgression of humanism at skin level, with their modes of existence guided by sensorial perceptions and bodily needs that are multiple, open-ended, and different each time.[26] By rejecting the philosophical vision that views negativity and lack as the constitutive element of subjectivity, Braidotti claims that she actively yearns for "a more joyful and empowering concept of desire."[27] Thus, the animal, in Braidotti's nomadic vision, materializes the desire and the potential of the power lying beneath the surface of our existence. Although she accuses both Lacanian psychoanalysis and Hegelian dialectic of negating the material grounds or corporeality, she claims that her positive affirmation of life and corporeality leads her vision of intersubjectivity across the boundaries between species, toward the matrix of cosmic resonance.[28]

However, when approached from a deconstructivist angle, the animal indicates the bottomless gaze of the unknown, which unsettles the ontological ground of the self. As Jacques Derrida has suggested, the animal is the other, the abysmal limit of the human whose gaze interrogates the animality in the human. For Derrida, the animal is not the mere exterior of the human, but both the anterior and the interior, which incessantly beckons to the undetermined outside of the human.[29] The animal, as the unfathomable mark of otherness constituting the very ground of being, discloses the abysmal fissure of being.

If the same critical tension between the constructivist approach and the deconstructivist approach in continental philosophy underlies, to a certain extent, the discourse on animality, I argue that a similar tension unfolds in Anzaldúa's deployment of animal metaphors. Anzaldúa's groundbreaking work on *mestizaje* carries a complex layer of multiple significations. Through her unique writing style in which she brings in personal stories, poetry, ancient symbolism, and philosophical articulation, Anzaldúa aims at constructing a *mestiza* identity, what she calls a new consciousness, which is born out of the in-between space of ambivalence. All dualistic terms that underlie the oppressive ideologies dividing subject/object, man/woman, straight/queer, human/nonhuman, and spiritual/political are collapsed within the space of *mestizaje*. With its pluralistic mode of operation, the *mestiza* celebrates the multiple, the hybrid, and the liminal as a form of embodied wholeness.

Nevertheless, there is a dipolar structure in Anzaldúa's writing, particularly in her use of animal metaphors. Behind her affirmation of *mestizaje* as a liberatory politics of self-writing lies the existential fear of facing the abysmal groundlessness that comes with the departure from her old self toward a new consciousness. Anzaldúa may here be contrasted instructively with Braidotti. What Braidotti fails to catch in her radical nomadic vision is the colonial difference underlying the ground that twenty-first-century nomadic subjects are inhabiting. Her privileged vision causes her to universalize her sense of a solid ontological ground and surface for a joyful becoming, instead of, in her own words, "wallow[ing] in a prolonged and at times ecstatic glorification of loss, mourning and melancholia."[30] For Anzaldúa, on the contrary, the freeing experience of gaining a new identity is not granted as a costless rupture. Rather, freedom emerges out of the unutterable memory of suffering and death. In consequence, Anzaldúa may offer us a different way of thinking about the animal from that which generally structures the continental discourse of posthumanism.

As someone who has been living alongside the edges of colonial/sexist/economic/heterosexist oppression, Anzaldúa finds that departing from this intense experience is not an easy step. Rather, she needs to face, name, and walk through her own wound before entering into the new consciousness so that she can integrate that wound into her new *mestiza* identity. At the same time, she is aware, after the experience of constant rejection, that what is awaiting her in this journey might be the terrifying experience of the unknown instead of the alluring promise of a freeing future. In other words, the complex location of Anzaldúa's decolonial struggle renders abysmal the very womb that gives birth to freedom.

A close reading of Anzaldúa helps us see that the animal in her work epitomizes the dipolar tension between freedom and abyss. A central metaphor of animality that Anzaldúa deploys is the image of the serpent. The serpent, the *Coatl* in the Olmec tradition, symbolizes the organic cosmology represented by Earth, life, creative energy, and spiritual integrity. She calls *mestiza*'s politics of becoming and survival a "serpent movement." The only way of surviving the crossroads of multiple oppressions or the interstitial space of liminality is through the serpent movement in which the Indian, the Mexican, and the Anglo are integrated into one.[31] In this way, the animal provides the material ground for an ontology of multiplicity through which the *mestiza* fearlessly reinterprets history, shapes new myths, and "transform[s] herself into a tree, a coyote, into another person."[32]

At the same time, however, the snake points to the fear ingrained in her psyche arising from the monstrous reality that she and her community inhabit though having internalized the imposed violence without being able to name it. As Žižek has reflected, coming face to face with the "abyss of free will" lying beneath the ground of matter, the kernel of one's existence, is traumatic.[33] In the same way, coming to terms with the reality of one's oppression, facing the truth lying beneath the constructed reality, is horrifying.

My argument is that the breakthrough within the trap of ambivalence happens not through a sudden, radical rupture or leap. Rather, transformation in Anzaldúa's work entails a ceaseless struggle through the two poles, via affirmation and a subsequent negation, followed by the negation of the negation. In other words, I suggest that by reading Anzaldúa's work through Hegelian dialectic, we might perhaps gain a fresh perspective on the ambiguities or contradictory tensions constituting the basic fabric of her work. For instance, the serpent, in Anzaldúa, brings about horror and fear in her. It thus took her forty years to "enter into the Serpent."

However, once she steps into the depth of groundlessness, her old self is negated, thus giving birth to a new consciousness so that she can acknowledge that she *has* a body, that she *is* a body, "to assimilate the animal body, the animal soul."[34] The serpent, symbol of prehuman creativity and the basis of all life, is more than an empowering ground for a futural becoming in Anzaldúa. Just as she tells us that she glimpsed "the otherworld serpent after four bouts with death,"[35] the serpent is the symbol of absolute alterity, which endlessly deconstructs her self-sovereignty by opening the chasm of her ontological ground.

Arguably, previous readings of Anzaldúa have relied mostly on the theoretical tools of postcolonial studies. They tend to read the ambivalence or ambiguity in Anzaldúa as a space that opens the possibility for a third meaning. In this context, ambiguity denotes the disavowal of the modern or colonial binary, which reduces the multifaceted dimension of polysemy embedded in the complexity of colonized culture. It follows that ambiguity is not a lack of clarity, but a strategy of disavowal, which paves the way for empowering new forms of subjectivities and new systems of meanings. However, the intensification of interest in postcolonial ambiguity without a scrupulous examination of its political consequences made its political angle rather ambiguous. Consequently, a similar question to Robert Young's regarding Homi Bhabha's notion of ambivalence can be posed here. For Bhabha, ambivalence is the innate structure that conditions both the colonial discourse and the dynamics between the colonial discourse and the colonial subjects: It represents the slippage produced in both the intention of the colonizer and the reception of it from the side of the colonized. Young's question regarding this process of slippage is whether such a misreading and misrecognition take place in the awareness of either, both, or neither of the two parties.[36] If ambivalence goes unnoticed by both parties (and Bhabha himself vacillates between the possibilities that it might or might not), then the questions of political effectiveness and agency remain unresolved. In the same way, the notion of ambiguity as frequently advocated by postcolonial critics tends to presuppose ambiguity as inherently destabilizing and disruptive of modern/colonial logic.

Therefore, following the voices of warning against the danger of romanticizing/overestimating the political effects of postcolonial theory, I ask: How is political agency generated or mobilized by postcolonial criticism?

What are the concrete political consequences that it brings about? How are the logic of colonialism and the ever-expanding logic of neocolonialism (global capital) confronted by postcolonial theory?[37] Postcolonial renderings of ambiguity and ambivalence leave these questions unanswered, so I suggest that the key terms of subversion/resistance deployed by Anzaldúa, such as *mestiza, borderland*, and *animal*, embody the very process of her critical engagement toward a new consciousness. If the notion of ambiguity rests on an assumption of an inherent power of subversiveness, thus seeding the danger of political passivity and the risk of creating a static term of resistance, my reading of Anzaldúa via dialectical negativity hopefully fleshes out how the animal embodies Anzaldúa's arduous struggle in the dialectical journey. Žižek has commented on Kierkegaard's distinction between "Socratic reminiscence" and "Christian repetition." Anzaldúa shows that Truth is not something that inherently dwells in oneself, as is the case with Socratic reminiscence. Rather, Anzaldúa makes the case for understanding Truth as an event, as Žižek has put it, as something almost violently rupturing from the Outside "through a traumatic encounter that shatters the very foundations" of her being.[38]

Against a Western liberal conception of freedom, Žižek has offered a fresh perspective on the notion of freedom through his account of materialist ontology. By adopting both Marxist-Hegelian dialectics and Schelling's notion of the ground (*Grund*), he argues that what lies at the ultimate base of reality is *matter*. Encountering the base of reality is horrifying, because the *Grund*, as he reads in Schelling, is not a unified ontological ground, but a "perturbed juxtaposition of conflicting elements lacking overall symmetrical measure, proportion, or ratio."[39] This is why, as Adrian Johnston claims, Žižek emphasizes that Schelling's "*Grund* is *Ungrund*, an abyssal groundlessness."[40] At this point, the question of freedom arises, as, for Schelling, the beginning point of autonomous subjectivity is rooted in the negation of the abysmal ground, that is, the abysmal freedom which seeks to avoid the void of groundlessness. Therefore, argues Žižek, the true horror of the Real is not the existence of materiality beneath the Symbolic, but "the truly terrifying abyss of freedom."[41]

If freedom is that which arises from the bottomless darkness beneath the surface of reality, it follows that freedom does not refer to the mere capacity to do whatever the autonomous subject wills. Instead, freedom signals the precarious groundlessness from which the self is undone, and in which loss and abyss opened up by the absolute alterity of the other haunt the horizon of freedom. As Judith Butler reminds us, the disavowed sites from which freedom emerges will always "reemerge as the haunted grounds of its own possibility: Specters, ghosts, traces—we are never quite free of them, and we can not think freedom without them."[42] Freedom, therefore, is always haunted by the abyss from which it emerges.

The ontological groundlessness of the colonial subject brings important challenges to some of the naïve conceptions of freedom attested by certain accounts of nomadic/cosmopolitan discourse. Exemplified by Braidotti, such discourses tend to flatten the power-asymmetry lying beneath the colonial difference by presupposing the notion of a solid ontological ground for the nomadic subjects on which they unfold their transgressive movements of endless becoming. With Anzaldúa, we see that for a colonized subject, the abyss is caused not only by the absolute alterity or the terrifying freedom lying beneath the surface of reality, as is the case with Žižek. Rather, the ontological surface of the colonial being is haunted by the omnipresent threat of death, which she faces in her everyday life. As Nelson Maldonado-Torres has remarked, drawing on Frantz Fanon, for the racialized subjects, death is a constitutive feature of their reality that is always already beside them.[43] This is what Maldonado-Torres, along with Walter Mignolo, calls the "coloniality of Being," and it is this horizon of death, marked by colonial/sexual difference, out of which Anzaldúa's postanthropomorphic vision emerges.

Therefore, Anzaldúa confesses that she "tremble(s) before the animal, the alien, the sub- or suprahuman,"[44] as her horizon of becoming is haunted by the reality of death. It is through this dislocated sense of the present, marked by the fear arising from both the haunting past and the unknown future, that the gaze of the absolute other breaks in, revealing that she has "something in common with the wind and the trees and the rock."[45] Via the gaze of the abyss, Anzaldúa's *mestizaje* undergoes a fundamental transformation so that it is finally brought into a dialectical synthesis.[46] The new *mestiza* consciousness born out of the journey through the abysmal darkness finally glimpses a new sense of freedom by becoming an agent of transformation. It is not, however, a dualistic sense of transformation in which one transforms and the other is transformed. As her pre-Columbian notion of *nahuatl* implies, the freeing power emerging from the abyss of the colonial trauma leads her to a de-essentialized ontology of becoming toward an intercosmic resonance in which she is "able to change herself and others into turkey, coyote, tree or human."[47]

As Žižek has noted, the dialectic movement in Hegel reveals that the one, or the subject, has contradiction as its internal condition.[48] In other words, it reveals the failure of subjectivity. This is the point where the crack of ontological ground opens up, for it is only in the negation, in the object that the subject can find itself.[49] And this is why Hegel claims in *Phenomenology of Spirit* that the spirit proceeds by "way of despair" that crushes and fragments the subject. The dialectical journey toward Absolute Knowledge in Hegel is strongly marked by the loss of the self, as Alexandre Kojève, one of the most influential interpreters of Hegel in twentieth-century France, wrote: "The man who contemplates is absorbed by what he contemplates; the knowing subject loses himself in the object that is known."[50] This gloomy vision is, according to Katrin Pahl, however, "largely covered over by the teleological narrative" of progress in the *Phenomenology of Spirit*.[51]

The dialectical journey of subject formation in Hegel starts with a consciousness that posits itself on a clearly defined world. On its way, however, it loses itself by being forced to abandon the certainty of its knowledge until it achieves, through the complete experience of itself, "the awareness of what it really is in itself," that is, "a crushed and consumed subject."[52] Anzaldúa's journey toward the new *mestiza* consciousness embodies, as my reading has hopefully demonstrated, this process of dialectical negativity. As she enters into the journey toward the new *mestizaje*, the certainty of being a self falls apart in the face of negativity. The animal, at this juncture, invites us to the abysmal space in which we are watched by the unfathomable gaze of the unknown, the absolute other, the *Diosa*—the "divine within" of Anzaldúa who takes control over her. With her unblinking serpentine eyes, adds Anzaldúa, she is "looking, always looking,"[53] thereby revealing her precarious existence before the gaze of the other.

Nevertheless, in the face of the bone-shattering negativity, her journey toward a transformed selfhood starts anew every time it is crushed. Perhaps this is the liberating power of freedom that we glimpse with Anzaldúa along the dialectical journey: that our groundlessness is the very soil from which our unending desire to build a ground originates; that between the haunting memory of death and the current reality of continuing suffering, our collective ontological vision is led by the restless power that seeks to negate the negative. It is in this incarnation of the fractured self in a new, transformed self that the liberating power of Anzaldúa's decolonial freedom finds its expression.

Although bearing a significant resonance with the continental discourse of freedom, abyss, and dialectic, Anzaldúa's sociopolitical context brings an important connection that is missing in continental philosophy: that for many nomadic subjects inhabiting the traumatic borderland of oppression, groundlessness points not only to the site of mystic encounter with the Real, but the hindered horizon of their social-political existence. Similarly, if posthumanism and animality studies arose as an extension of the critical discourse of gender, race, and sexuality, both their scope and their range of proponents have been limited, mainly, to the Euro-American context, with a heavy reliance on poststructuralism. Perhaps, Anzaldúa's work will help expand the horizon of animality studies by strengthening the link between questions of the human-animal and questions of race / class / gender / sex. Similarly, the liberating or subversive power harbored in Anzaldúa's postcolonial "ambiguity" might gain a stronger political meaning when complemented in dialectical terms.

The animal, in this sense, embodies the very corporeal struggle in Anzaldúa's decolonial politics. The echoes of "cosmic resonance," as Braidotti blithely put it,[54] resound on the groundless soil on which all the groaning bodies of the Earth stand in intersubjective entanglement amid the shared experience of suffering. Before the abysmal crack in which the precarious ground of our social existence is exposed, the animal opens our vision toward the intersubjective, toward the freeing encounter with the animal and divine within.

At the edge of our vulnerable life, the animal reminds us of the creaturely inexhaustibility within us. It signals its divine presence within us: the presence of the absolute other that splits open the rock of opposition and brings all the lost pieces of Anzaldúa's self back again, thus keeping her complete. It is in this *mestizaje* understood in dialectical terms, in its animal abyss, that Anzaldúa's bold confession turns our gaze toward the horizon of decolonial freedom: "Something pulsates in my body, a luminous thin thing grows thicker every day. Its presence never leaves me. I am never alone. That which abides: my vigilance, my thousand sleepless serpent eyes blinking in the night, forever open. And I am not afraid."[55]

෴

"At some point, on our way to a new consciousness, we will have to leave the opposite bank, the split between the two mortal combatants somehow so that we are on both shores at once and, at once, see through serpent and eagle eyes," claims Anzaldúa in proposing her vision of *mestizaje*.[56] Reading with Anzaldúa, we hope to have pointed to the possibility of extending the scope of posthuman animality studies to a broader political and theological context. The particular sociohistorical location of Anzaldúa's struggle (desert, or borderland) postulates a strong refusal of the divorce of the animal from the politics of survival. The animal, in other words, is not a metaphysical discourse but a corporeal reality rooted in the very ground of material life. It represents the coalescence of the spiritual and the political, the creaturely and the divine, or the finite and the infinite.

In the context of the desert (borderlands), both ancient and modern, the animal is the embodiment of hybrid identity through which both authors, Jerome and Anzaldúa, reclaim the fecund multiplicity or ambiguity of their creaturely lives. Following Bhabha's definition of hybridity, we observe that the animal displaces the demand of power by turning the gaze of the discriminated, the reflection of its (mis)appropriated image, "back upon the eye of power."[57] With its unsettling presence, the grotesque figure of the animal disassembles any sense of the sovereign self. However, the animal also denotes the process through which the self and its new consciousness comes to life via the life-and-death struggle. Read through the Hegelian-Žižekian perspective, the animal in Anzaldúa materializes the groundless ground of our vulnerable existence, which, paradoxically, is the very power that drives our will toward transformation and self-creation.

It is here, at the very brink of human finitude and vulnerability, where the sensitivities of human spirituality open up toward the creaturely, cosmic matrix of the divine. The animal embodies this very process of self-discovery through which both Anzaldúa and Antony come to realize their limits and discover how those limits are indicative of a greater sense of potency at the same time.

⌁ Daniel's Animal Apocalypse

JENNIFER L. KOOSED AND
ROBERT PAUL SEESENGOOD

Most will start at the beginning—with words, naked or otherwise, created and creating, a primordial shower, the blink of a cat.[1] Most will start at the beginning. We begin at the end—finitude, death, the cessation of time and history. We will be "starting from death," because that is the necessary condition of all that follows. As Jacques Derrida writes on his very last page, "That is why death is also such an important demarcation line; it is starting from mortality and from the possibility of being dead that one can let things be such as they are, in my absence, in a way, and my presence is there only to reveal what the thing would be in my absence."[2] We begin with apocalypse because the genre reveals the heart of our issues with animals and our issues with God: Our inability to imagine our own death, to really enter into the space Derrida invites. In the apocalypse, animals die; the planet is destroyed; time ceases—but we, the humans (at least the "good" ones) are transformed into immortals who leave our "animal nature" behind, escaping death and destruction altogether.

ENTERING DANIEL'S ZOO

The book of Daniel opens (Dan. 1–6) with six stories that recount the various adventures of Daniel and his three friends, all (textually if not actually) orphans, transported to a faraway kingdom and a surreal "prep school" where they train for royal service as diviners.[3] The book concludes with a series of five terrifying visions (7:1–28; 8:1–27; 9:1–27; 10:1–21 and 11:1–12:13) where a monstrous figure with magical powers, emerging from some foreign dimension, arises intent on destroying the entire world and is battled by "the anointed one" (9:26).[4] Nestled in the rear of the Ketuvim, itself at the end of the Bible, the book of Daniel is a collection of visions and an anthology of stories that have remained popular among children through-out millennia. As with most popular children's stories, animals appear throughout Daniel's polyglot text. Daniel refuses to eat animals (1:8–17); there is an attempt to feed him to the animals (6:10–24); the king turns into an animal (4:28–37); and animals run amok in the final visions (7–12). The Greek version of Daniel, with its three additional chapters, returns to the animal; Daniel first uses an explosive pitch-laden brisket to slay a monstrous, fire-breathing dragon, before he (alas, again) survives a den of hungry lions (15:23–40). All the stories and visions of Daniel explore tensions of living under foreign (and hostile) government; all arise from tensions and expectations found in the early Maccabean period.[5]

But the power of the book is not bound to its historical context, and the animal stories explore tensions not just of living under foreign domina-tion but those of simply living. Beasts—real, cooked, psychological, regal, divine, mythical, and monstrous—wriggle, graze, claw, and growl their way through every chapter of Daniel. From the beginning, the relation-ship between animal, man (and this text is, indeed, very much a "man's world"; women do not appear in the canonical Daniel), and God are entan-gled. Daniel declares that he will have a different relationship to animals (or, really, to God) when he decides not to eat meat rather than violate kosher regulations; he is rewarded for his faithfulness when the lions de-cline to eat him in turn. This human-animal mutuality mediated by God shifts to a clear hierarchy when the Babylonian king challenges God's sov-ereignty. God punishes Nebuchadnezzar by turning him into an animal, thus reestablishing and reinforcing the hierarchical chain of being: God-man-animal. Finally, as the court tales transform into apocalyptic visions, animals morph into fantastical beasts to be battled, and then they cease to be altogether: There are no animals at the end of time. As Daniel envi-sions the end, he disavows the animal as he defies human mortality. Yet the animal cannot be denied. In Daniel, sovereigns become beasts; monstrous beasts establish divinity; and the borders of God, human, and animal are repeatedly blurred. The animal keeps erupting at various levels of text and context; no category remains fixed or pure; not even the language of the text remains stable as the story arbitrarily changes from Hebrew to Aramaic then back again, added to, in time, by a stuttering Greek. In the book of Daniel, the human, the divine, and the bestial, like language and eschatology, do not have fixed spaces. Instead of saving the human and destroying the animal, the very mutability of the categories in the apocalypse reveals the shared mortality of human and animal.

ENCOUNTERS IN SIGNIFICANT (ANIMAL) OTHERNESS

We focus on four encounters Daniel has with animals, two in the court tales and two in the apocalyptic visions. All of the encounters entail transformations from human to animal either enacted or denied; all of the encounters reveal, in some sense, what Derrida calls *divinanimality*. Derrida asks:

> Must not this place of the Other be ahuman? If this is indeed the case, then the ahuman or at least the figure of some—in a word—*divinanimality*, even if it were to be felt through the human, would be the quasi-transcendental referent, the excluded, foreclosed, disavowed, tamed, and sacrificed foundation of what it founds, namely, the symbolic order, the human order, law and justice. . . . That is one of the reasons why it is so difficult to utter a discourse of mastery or of transcendence with regard to the animal and simultaneously to claim to do it in the name of God, in the name of the name of the Father, or in the name of the Law.[6]

At the level of the symbol, both the divine and the animal are our excluded Other out of which we all emerge. In paroxysms of fear and grief, Daniel attempts to master the animal as he grasps at the transcendence of God.

Our first animal encounter is found in Daniel 4:1–37 (Hebrew: 3:31–4:34), a first-person account of how God visited the king Nebuchadnezzar with an ominous dream about a magnificent tree chopped down at the root. Daniel interprets the dream: Nebuchadnezzar is the tree. He was given his throne by God, but he has become arrogant and neglectful of his kingdom. God will cast Nebuchadnezzar out from civilized society, where he will live in the wild and feed on grass. The sovereign will become a beast. Nebuchadnezzar does indeed go mad and roam the wilderness where his hair grows long "like a goat" and his nails become "like [those of] an eagle."[7] Nebuchadnezzar's account shifts from first person to third in verse 28, the beginning of the narration of Nebuchadnezzar's actual transformation into an animal. The text returns to first person in verse 34, as Nebuchadnezzar, at "the end of the days," turns in repentance to God. Becoming a beast, the king quite literally loses his voice. Reason and language are lost in the transformation from human to animal. Danna Nolan Fewell notes the "inherent irony" in this: "Nebuchadnezzar may think himself sovereign of the world, but he is not even sovereign of his own story. This powerful king who has conquered the world needs a little help recounting his experience."[8] The text mocks monarchy and asserts God as ultimate sovereign.[9]

Our next animal encounter is the story of Daniel in the lions' den (6:1–28). Jealous and bent on destroying him, the other presidents and satraps of the kingdom devise a law Daniel would be sure to violate. For thirty days, no one in the kingdom would be allowed to pray to anyone, divine or human, except for King Darius. Daniel, of course, adheres to his own religious practices and prays only to God. Even though the king does not want to destroy Daniel, once written, the law is immutable, and he has no choice but to consign Daniel to the lions' den. The king has the power to transform a person into an animal; if the animals were to eat Daniel, his body would literally become theirs. Daniel stands naked, at least in terms of his vulnerability, before a collection of very dangerous cats. Yet this is also a story of royal manipulation and the ultimate power of the rule of law; the king's law rules the king like God's law rules Daniel. The power to write laws actually strips the king of his power as the "discourse of mastery" becomes "discourse, the master." Daniel's power is also the power of words—his words of prayer break the words of law and call the ultimate Lawgiver and Sovereign to his aid.

The lions are housed in a *gob*, literally a "pit" covered atop by a stone.[10] These are not lions kept for the hunt or as royal symbols; they are lions kept in pits for the sole purpose of torture. Louis Hartman and Alexander Di Lella observe that "there is no ancient evidence for the keeping of lions in underground pits, apart from the present story. . . . Perhaps one might compare, for a later period, the hypogeum of the Roman Colosseum, where animals were kept before being brought up into the arena."[11] Darius "seals" the mouth of the pit (6:17), dooming Daniel. Fewell notes that Darius fasts through the night that Daniel is entombed with the hungry lions; worried Daniel is being eaten, the king does not eat. Of course, we later learn, neither do the lions.[12] Daniel is not harmed, the text says, because "God stopped the mouths" of the lions (6:22), delivering Daniel. The story avers that the king does not really have mastery over Daniel and the lions, or even over his own rule; God controls all.

Both stories assess the power of human tyrants and use animals as metaphors. In each story, a tyrant succumbs to hubris and must learn a terrible lesson; as a result, he recognizes the true sovereign, God. Both tyrants are equated with beasts in the story. Nebuchadnezzar, mad with power, is turned into a powerless grazing beast. Nebuchadnezzar's power comes from his embodiment of civilization itself. In his madness, a punishment for his arrogant rule, he is driven into the "lonely places" of the wilderness. Instead of becoming a majestic carnivore, he becomes a hairy, vegetarian cow. At his transformation, he becomes unable to even speak his own narrative. Darius's unthinking celebration of his own authority puts the life of his most loyal servant and friend at risk. Darius is like his lions, frequent symbols of royal authority. He, like them, would harm Daniel. Darius does not eat all night, devoted to prayer and worry, his mouth metaphorically "stopped by God." The lions do not eat all night, their mouths actually stopped by God.

In both stories, the limits on the tyrant's power are also symbolized by animals. In the first, the tyrant's own will and autonomy betray him. (Who can restrain a king, even when he is mad?) In the second, the tyrant's unencumbered will and unchecked arrogance are defeated by a servant turned martyr. The two stories combine to argue that no one, not even a king, can mandate worship or can rule without restraint. True worship is a response to true power, and all (human) authority has limits. Kings are, at best, a simulacrum and must remain mindful of the real power, God. Though sometimes they are beautiful, useful, or even deadly, ultimately tyrants are beasts that can be captured, harnessed, or domesticated by God. Tyrants seem terrible and unrestrained, so much the height of civilization that they become unchecked and, therefore, feral. Yet through God's greater power, they are really unthinking grazing cattle or captive predators. In Derrida's *The Beast and the Sovereign*, "the Beast" or the "bestial" is defined as that lawless, unrestrained force, set in contradistinction to the cultivated and the civilized. Yet the apex of the hierarchy of the civil, the sovereign, is likewise unrestrained and, by definition as the one who creates and enforces law, above law and restriction. Both beasts and kings are outside of the strictures of law; both beasts and kings are wild. In Daniel, this is true on two levels. First, mortal kings become excessive in their pride of place, above law, arbitrary. They become beasts—in one case actually, in several metaphorically. God "puts these beasts in their place," consigning them to madness, defeating their ambitions, curbing their excesses, and ultimately "domesticating" and taming them. Yet in doing so, God Godself becomes the most dominant being, above the strictures of civility and regulation, the ultimate "beastly sovereign."[13]

In discussing the differences between the first and second halves of Daniel, John J. Collins draws particular attention to the ways in which Gentile kings are portrayed. In the first half, they have the potential of acting in ways that God approves; in other words, they can treat their Jewish subjects well. In the second half, such potential is gone—Gentile kings are demonic monsters.[14] Yet the focus on the animal actually demonstrates more continuity between the two sections than conventional scholarship allows. The distinction between the beast and the sovereign is unstable in both parts of Daniel, and in both parts of Daniel, the distinction is maintained by God.

Turning to Daniel's second half, his apocalyptic visions, animals again appear twice. In Daniel's first vision, purportedly occurring in the first year of Belshazzar (553 B.C.E.), he sees four beasts rising from the sea (7:1–28).[15] The first beast is a winged lion, the second a talking bear, the third is a multiheaded, winged leopard. The fourth is so horrendous he cannot be described beyond his iron teeth. Among his ten horns is one with eyes that speaks "great things." The fourth beast is confronted by the "Ancient of Days" who rides a fire-spewing throne and is surrounded by "thousands of thousands" of his followers. The horn continues speaking until the dead beast is dismembered and burned. The other three beasts persist until "one like the Son of Man" comes and destroys them. The strange vision is interpreted for Daniel: It, like Nebuchadnezzar's dream in chapter 2, is a prediction of the rise of the Greeks. In 7, it is extended by the "prediction" of the coming rule of the Seleucids, the terrible reign of Antiochus, and the eventual victory of faithful Jews.

The hybrid animals are deeply symbolic. Lions, bears, and leopards are symbols of kingship and power, particularly of Assyrian, Babylonian, and Medo-Persian kings. Winged beasts are very common in Mesopotamian and ancient Near Eastern art; they are all beings associated with divine "court" scenes, and they are expressions of the "cosmic" reality and power

of kings. Horns are symbols of kingly power and virility. As John Goldingay notes,

> Animals feature throughout the OT in metaphor, simile, and allegory,
> to portray God, Israel, leaders or nobles, and other nations. . . . The
> lion and the horn are common metaphors for violent and aggressive
> strength, exercised by Yahweh, by Israel, or by their enemies: Dan 7
> sees the gentile predators attacking God's flock in the light of psalms
> that lament such attacks, and sees the promise of final deliverance
> from them that features in psalms and prophets as about to be ful-
> filled. The portrayal of the nations as hybrids, which transgress na-
> ture's laws and threaten nature's harmony, and as predators who are
> as such unclean, has part of its background in the Torah's categoriza-
> tion of the animal world and its concern with preserving distinctions
> between species.[16]

In addition, he observes that Daniel 7 "has clear links outside the actual
OT with *1 Enoch*. The animal allegory in chaps. 85–90 also features predators symbolizing rulers or kingdoms, an animal transformed into a man,
animals with horns of extraordinary size, a throne set up for God to sit in
judgment as books are opened before him, and animals being destroyed by
fire."[17] The symbols, rather obviously drawn and common in context, can
hardly be attempts to render the text so opaque that it avoids the censure
of the authorities (Montgomery), nor does it inscribe "great mysteries" of
scripture (Goldingay). The text is explicit in its symbolism: Human kings
and empires are not just symbolized by the animal; they are bestial and
savage. The dream is explicitly interpreted: These kings are at war with
God and destined to lose. In the cosmic array of Daniel, tyrants become
beasts; God becomes human; and God, the human, destroys the tyrants,
the beasts.

The overwhelming interest of scholarship in chapter 7 is Daniel's "one
like the Son of Man." Most of the interest in this figure arises from well
beyond the enclosure of Daniel. In many ways, he is more interesting because the figure recurs in later Jewish and proto-Christian literature. In
the context of Daniel, however, the phrase is relatively clear and straightforward. "One like the son of man" simply means "one who looks human," in contrast with the hyperanimal hybrid beasts Daniel first sees.[18]

In a move similar to one in part 1 of Daniel, the visions argue that what appear to be glorious and powerful human tyrants are actually mutilated and grotesque beasts. Though they may seem the height of civilization, they are so unfettered in their power and lust that they are feral and bestial. God is not bestial but, instead, appears in human form: first as a very old man upon a throne, second as a mortal soldier. God, Daniel would argue, is not a beast. God is "like a son of man"; God is human.

The second vision of Daniel is the last appearance of the animal (8:1–27). A two-horned, powerful ram appears (the Medo-Persians). He is defeated by a strangely horned goat (Alexander I of Macedon). The goat's horn fragments into four parts, with one dominant (surely Antiochus IV). Again, the "little horn" grows and becomes a tyrant that blasphemes God and enacts the "transgression of desolation" at the sanctuary (matching the outrages ascribed to Antiochus in 1 Macc. 1:54–61; 2 Macc. 4:11–6:11).[19] A man[20] comes and stands before Daniel and explains the vision, promising that the little horn will be "broken without hand" by the Prince of Princes (i.e., "highest prince"). Daniel is told to seal the vision, and he does not say how or when the little horn will be defeated (nor exactly whom the little horn represents). Even so, he seems to have already let the cat out of the bag. In comparison with the earlier vision, the succession of king(dom)s in Daniel 8 is much more focused on Antiochus IV and his immediate successors.[21]

Unlike the previous vision, in this case the animals are domesticated.[22] They are also animals subject to being sacrificed and suitable for food under kosher regulations. The chapter revolves around sacrifices so improper they defile the sanctuary (8:11–14).[23] Daniel 1 was concerned with consumption of meat, always already an issue of proper slaughter/sacrifice; those concerns are implied here, as well. Beasts cannot designate appropriate sacrifice. Tyrants, in their arrogance, become beasts and can only offer desecration, not sanctification.

In *The Animal That Therefore I Am*, Derrida struggles to remain focused on the animal not as the Animal, not as a figure or sign or symbol, but as a living being, present, irreducible, alive.[24] He follows the Animal through the canon of Western philosophy, periodically pausing to draw his reader back to the real animals who inhabit the world.[25] As Derrida demonstrates, philosophers have sought to define the human and the animal as essentially and permanently different, even mitigating the fact of finitude by claiming that animals do not die in the same way people do—they cease living, but they do not die. From Descartes to Kant, Heidegger to Levinas, the animal can be put to death without anyone "killing" or "murdering" it.[26] Daniel is replete with the Animal as symbol. Such figuration is part of the strategy of the apocalypse to construct a great divide between humans and animals, one that allows humanity to be divided into the good and the evil, where the evil is consigned to the category *animal* and slaughtered accordingly.[27]

Any turn in our attention toward the "real" beneath the symbolic animal in Daniel's visions invites a turn in attention toward the "real" community of humans behind the text of Daniel, itself—those who have composed, collected, and revered this book. Daniel is a document articulating the grief, anger, and hope of people under colonial oppression, and it remains a text of foundational significance to a host of subsequent communities of oppressed believers. Postcolonial theory argues that the moment of colonization is simultaneously a moment of constructive and destructive hybridization. Though this essay has not placed postcolonial readings or concerns at its fore, the mechanics of the postcolonial are present beneath many of our arguments. As a mode of reading, postcolonialism, through the always already notions of hybridity, mimicry, and mockery, disrupts interstitial spaces between colonized and colonizer, between ethics and pragmatics, between success and failure, between survival and dissolution. Daniel does the same in its hybridization of monarch and beast, in its complex polyglot, polymorphous zoology that disrupts the interstitial space(s) between God, human, and animal. But what of the communities behind Daniel, those anonymous colonized Jews resisting the forces of Greek cultural and ideological as well as political and economic imperialism? If we engage such questions of class and ethnicity in and behind Daniel, whose text is this? Who is othering animals? Who decides who deserves to be killed? How does Daniel's animalogic affect real, not metaphoric, humans?

Daniel is an apocalyptic protest and expression of rage against the injustice of the empire. But apocalypse often fails. The unveiling leaves much that is hidden; eschatology is often little more than (re)creation. Daniel does not dismantle empire and the politics of injustice. In Judaism, the community that wrote Daniel was (probably) not the community that took up arms and rid itself of the Greek colonial presence. The communities that read Daniel now are primarily Christian evangelical and pentecostal, premillennial dispensationalists. Daniel is read as part of their "end-time prophecies," so Daniel is roped into their agenda of, among other things, the annihilation of Judaism (in conjunction with the annihilation of all Jews who do not convert to Christianity). This text may have begun life as a Jewish act of resistance against people who wanted to destroy Judaism and did not care how many Jewish bodies had to be tortured and destroyed in order to do so, but now this text has been appropriated by people with the exact same agenda to destroy Judaism, even as Daniel has, essentially, vanished from the contemporary Jewish imagination. Daniel is not read in the standard cycle of readings used by Judaism. It does not substantially affect the language of Jewish liturgy. Daniel, a text originating in a moment of yearned-for Jewish liturgical, cultural, and political freedom is, in our modern era, no longer a text read by many Jews; instead, it is a text that has become absolutely central for dispensationalist theologies of Christian supersession and (at least eschatological) Jewish erasure.

Naming the other as animal is, indeed, a method of colonial dehumanization of the subaltern, a technique nearly ubiquitous in colonial history. Colonization has overwritten many indigenous communities who self-identified with the animal, turning this self-designation into a weapon in the rhetoric of exclusion.[28] In many ways, Daniel as a text is appropriating the rhetorical weapons of hegemonic control to construct a literature of resistance and defiance. But Daniel also cultivates a relationship with the animal (animal as familiar?)—he does not eat meat and he survives the lions' den. Daniel eats only vegetables as part of his relationship to God, kin to animals. In Daniel, some humans self-identify in positive ways with the animal.

Yet in the history of colonization, the colonized are, again and again, identified as lesser beings, as animal, a distortion of this self-identification. The two sections of Daniel contrast positive animals and positive relationships with animals, in the first section, with negative animals, where animals become beasts, in the second. In this move, Daniel uses the rhetorical tools of the colonizer as a means of constructing a counterassault against the colonizer. Like other aspects of its apocalyptic nature, this move is both successful and unsuccessful at once. Daniel does construct a space for critique of colonial control. It does manage to offer a vision of victory. It does rebuke and condemn exploitation and oppression, and it does manage to mete out a (rhetorical) vision of justice. Yet it fails, even in this triumph. To achieve its end Daniel co-opts the logic and language of the very system it opposes. Daniel mimics the rhetoric of the oppressor mockingly to articulate a counter epistemological and ontological claim. Yet in its own hybridization, in the uncritical adoption of the ideology of the "killable" animal, it becomes what it opposes. It seems to offer little hope of a space for ethical coexistence between the human and the animal, the colonized and colonizer, God and creation. Daniel leaves us with little hope for more than perpetual tension and struggle; this is largely a result of its fundamental logic of conflict, a logic most articulate when speaking about beasts and defining the animal as "killable." Whether referring to actual animals or people symbolized as animals, the logic of the apocalypse relies on the killability of the animal. The hope inscribed in the book of Daniel is that we are more like the divine than the animal, that we can enter into the infinity of divinity, escaping the death of animality. The significance of living escapes the flesh of animality.

ANIMAL APOCALYPSE

Every eschatology is also another beginning, which is one reason why apocalypses like Daniel are fecund with images of creation. And so as we end we are drawn back to our own origins. In his book *The Open*, Giorgio Agamben notes that some eschatological understandings seem to imply that human and animal alike will be transformed and reconciled as in Isaiah 11:6,[29] whereas others clearly see the eschaton as humanity's final escape from both animals and our own animal nature.[30] Consequently, Agamben declares,

> The messianic end of history of the completion of the divine *oikonomia* of salvation defines a critical threshold, at which the difference between animal and human, which is so decisive for our culture, threatens to vanish. That is to say, the relation between man and animal marks the boundary of an essential domain, in which historical inquiry must necessarily confront that fringe of ultrahistory which cannot be reached without making recourse to first philosophy. It is as if determining the border between human and animal were not just one question among many discussed by philosophers and theologians, scientists and politicians, but rather a fundamental metaphysico-political operation in which alone something like "man" can

be decided upon and produced. If animal life and human life could be superimposed perfectly, then neither man nor animal—and, perhaps, not even the divine—would any longer be thinkable. For this reason, the arrival at posthistory necessarily entails the reactualization of the prehistoric threshold at which that border had been defined. Paradise calls Eden back into question.[31]

In the beginning, the eschaton's sea monsters were simply snakes. In Genesis 3, the snake "ruins" humanity's chance for immortality and thus begins human alienation from animals and plants through the new need for clothing (made by God from animal skins, presumably the first animals to be killed in the post-Edenic world) and the rigors of life outside of the garden where the earth itself thwarts human need. Such a situation is also evident in the Epic of Gilgamesh. The plant that grants immortality is finally in Gilgamesh's possession when it is eaten by a snake—another ruined quest for immortality.

Immortality is again held out as a hope in Daniel. On the brink of the end of time, God manifests as "the Ancient of Days" and summons "one like the son of man" and "Gabriel" in order to suppress human tyrants, symbolized as beasts. As W. Sibley Towner notes: "An animal allegory must be considered a polemical device, and its effect is evaluative as well as figurative."[32] In Daniel, kings are not the most civil of the civilized. At the apex of the social ladder, they lack restraint and are feral animals that will either be tamed by God or captured and slain. God becomes human to subdue the savage humans who are really, cosmically, apocalyptic animals. Ironically, the immortal and powerful God is the truest "human" because divinity is humanity utterly stripped of animality; only God is capable of being both apocalyptically sovereign and human at the same time. Animals will be slain in Daniel's eschaton, and there will be no more wildness. Anyone faithful to God must resist the rule of feral kings. They should refuse even to eat meat, slaughtered without regard to God's control, and so prevent, in any way, allowing themselves to become animal. The risk is real; the boundaries between the human and the animal are movable. In Daniel, the continuum between animal, human, and God is in constant, apocalyptic flux charged throughout with the language of hierarchy.

The risk is also real for those of us living outside of Daniel's apocalypse. The inability to face mortality and acknowledge the shared mortality between ourselves and our animal companions is a failure of ethics. The fundamental divide between the Animal and the Human on which apocalypse is predicated, even as it simultaneously undermines it, works to reassure "the Human of his excellence by the very ontological impoverishment of a lifeworld that cannot be its own end or know its own condition. . . . In this gap lies the logic of sacrifice, within which there is no responsibility toward the living world other than the human."[33] In an apocalypse such a condition is acute—no one else matters because they will all die anyway. Donna Haraway suggests that the commandment "'Thou shalt not kill' should be rewritten: Thou shalt not consign whole classes of living beings into the category of the killable."[34] The apocalypse demonstrates the danger to both animals and humans in this classificatory system. In Daniel, certain human beings are labeled animals because that automatically makes them killable.

Haraway, like Derrida, beckons us to look at death, to face the reality of death, of killing, of being killed. The snake snatches immortality away from Adam and Eve and Gilgamesh; our end is embedded in our beginning. In this myth of alienation from the animal, we are forced to face our own mortality, indeed our own animality—we are pushed out of and into the animal at the same moment. For Adam and Eve, this movement frees them from dependence, naïveté, and stasis. Their first act outside of the garden is to have a baby—they are no longer just creatures but also creators. All of human history and culture, then, unfurls before them. Gilgamesh returns to Uruk and embraces his role as king. He builds Uruk's walls and inaugurates a time of great peace and prosperity, even instituting a reign marked by social justice. When he no longer worries about immortality (either figuratively by making a name for himself or literally by escaping death), then he focuses on the business of caring about the world and living well now.

We need to put apocalypse aside. The word *animal*, human and nonhuman alike, includes an almost infinite variety, "an immense multiplicity of other living things that cannot in any way be homogenized, except by means of violence and willful ignorance."[35] Maintaining the figure of the Animal perpetuates the subjugation of animals and always also carries within it the danger of the apocalyptic logic of consigning certain humans into the category *animal*. Maintaining the figure of the Animal obscures its multiplicity and also obscures the myriad ways in which we are all enmeshed, the ways in which we are all dependent on one another. As Haraway continues, "Individuated critters matter; they are mortal and fleshly knotting, not ultimate units of being. Kinds matter; they are also mortal and fleshly knotting not typological units of beings. Individuals and kinds at whatever scale of time and space are not autopoietic wholes; they are sticky dynamic openings and closures in finite, mortal, world-making, ontological play."[36] It is past time (we are running out of time) to turn away from apocalypse and face the reality of our shared, global, finitude.

⟿ Ecotherology

STEPHEN D. MOORE

Midway through the first of the thirteen weekly course lectures from the year 2001–2 that make up the first volume of *The Beast and the Sovereign*, Jacques Derrida alludes to "all the beasts from John's Revelation, . . . the reading of which would merit more than one seminar."[1] Whether all or any of these beasts receive even one seminar of the fourteen thousand pages of unpublished seminars that Derrida left behind at his death in 2004, I am not in a position to know.[2] Taking a back-row seat in Derrida's weekly seminar, I attempt in this essay to read *The Beast and the Sovereign*,[3] together with *The Animal That Therefore I Am*,[4] as incisive, if unintended, commentary on Revelation's theological bestiary—its theotherology, if you will. In effect, I read the Beast of *The Beast and the Sovereign* as the Beast of the book of Revelation. Midway through the essay, however, I slip out of the seminar, leaving Derrida to his characteristic preoccupations, in order to extend my analysis into the area of sex and gender in Revelation where it bleeds into the area of animality. My focus in this section of the essay is on Revelation's notorious wild woman astride her wild beast ("I saw a woman sitting on a scarlet beast" [17:3]).[5] My focus is even more on that other, far queerer instance of interspecies intimacy, the radiant bride who is married to a sheep ("the marriage of the Lamb has come, and his bride has made herself ready" [19:7]). In the final section of the essay, I fall in behind the joyful throng of those who "follow the Lamb wherever he goes" (Rev. 14:4), and trail them into the continent-sized shopping mall that, as we shall see, is the centerpiece of Revelation's climactic vision. As will become particularly apparent in this final section, the aim of the essay is to relate what Revelation has to say about nonhuman animals—and about creatures that are neither human, animal, nor divine—to the plight of nonhuman animals in our apocalyptically theriocidal world.

APOCALYPTIC ANIMETAPHORS

I will explain the mysterious symbol of . . . the Beast to you.
   —REVELATION 17:7

To begin to address the theme of animality in Revelation is to run immediately into a problem. On the one hand (hoof, paw, claw . . . ?), Revelation is an animal book extraordinaire, a bizarre bestiary, more thickly populated with nonhuman animals than any other early Christian text. On the other hand, there are almost no nonhuman animals as such represented anywhere in Revelation,[6] only metaphorical animals, chimerical animals, and metaphorical-chimerical animals, beginning with the many-eyed, multihorned Lamb, "standing as if it had been slaughtered" (5:6), and extending to the many-eyed, multiwinged "living creatures," ensconced in the heavenly throne room (4:6b–8); the human-faced, lion-toothed, scorpion-tailed, human-torturing locusts that swarm out of the bottomless abyss (9:1–10); the lion-headed, fire-breathing, serpent-tailed horses sent forth "to kill a third of humankind" (9:13–19); the many-headed, multihorned, great red dragon whose tail "[sweeps] down a third of the stars of heaven and [throws] them to the earth" (12:3–4); the many-headed, multihorned, species-blurring beast that rises out of the sea (13:1–2); and the lamb-horned, dragon-voiced beast that rises out of the earth (13:11). The animals that do not automatically fit into the metaphorical or chimerical categories, meanwhile, are, more often than not, philosophical conundrums. For instance, can the Greek word *hippos* ("horse") meaningfully be said to signify a bona fide nonhuman animal if it is being ridden by Conquest, War, Famine, or Death? (6:1–8).

Revelation stands loosely, then, within the fable tradition. "The fictional use of animals for didactic purposes reaches back to . . . Aesop's animal fables," notes Colleen Glenney Boggs. "The fable tradition, however, . . . is not interested in animals as such."[7] As Graham Huggan and Helen Tiffin phrase it, "The animal *as animal* becomes invisible."[8] Metaphorical animals—*animetaphors*[9]—are as thick on the ground in much of Revelation as in Aesop. How best to relate to them? I propose to take my lead from the fact that Revelation presents us with an anthropomorphism of the animal that is qualitatively indistinguishable from its anthropomorphism of the divine. And just as I have found it fruitful elsewhere to read Revelation's God as human—more precisely, to ask what kind of divine-human relations are encoded in this human, all too human deity[10]—so I am attempting here to read Revelation's metaphorical, all too metaphorical animals as animals in the interests of deciphering the human-animal relations encrypted in them. In other words, and taking my cue from Rosi Braidotti, I am attempting a "neoliteral" reading of Revelation's animetaphors.[11]

OF GOD AND OTHER BEASTS

Yet I have been the Lord your God
ever since the land of Egypt. . . .
It was I who fed you in the wilderness. . . .
When I fed them, they were satisfied; . . .
therefore they forgot me.
So I will become like a lion to them,
like a leopard I will lurk beside the way.
I will fall upon them like a bear robbed of her cubs,
and will tear open the covering of their hearts;
there I will devour them like a lion,
as a wild animal would mangle them.
    —HOSEA 13:4–8

What better place to begin a consideration of Revelation's bestiary than with the Beast, its best-known figure and most infamous animal? The most popular candidate at present for the Beast's secret identity appears to be Barack Obama,[12] a disturbing reality that merits an essay of its own.[13] The small tribe of critical biblical scholars takes a more pedantic view. For us, almost without exception, the Beast is a figure for ancient imperial Rome and/or its emperor(s). This unexceptional interpretation, however, immediately takes us to the heart of *The Beast and the Sovereign*.

A recurrent preoccupation of Derrida's in *The Beast and the Sovereign* is the rhetorical trope whereby "the essence of the political and, in particular, of the state and sovereignty has often been represented in the formless form of animal monstrosity."[14] As it happens, Revelation's Beast qualifies eminently as a monster: "And the Beast that I saw was like a leopard, its feet were like a bear's, and its mouth was like a lion's mouth" (13:2; cf. Dan. 7:2–6).[15] Of the chimera of classical antiquity, Derrida remarks: "Its monstrousness derived precisely from the multiplicity of animals . . . in it (head and chest of a lion, entrails of a goat, tail of a dragon)."[16] A monster, then, is that which does not respect the "proper" divisions between animal species—which divisions, however, the collective, catchall noun *animal* itself disregards, "in spite of the infinite space that separates the lizard from the dog, the protozoon from the dolphin, the shark from the lamb, the parrot from the chimpanzee, the camel from the eagle, the squirrel from the tiger, the elephant from the cat, the ant from the silkworm, or the hedgehog from the echidna."[17] As such, the animal is always a monster. Or, if you prefer, a Beast.

Bestiality has always been a convenient figure for political despotism. Derrida unpacks the logic of the metaphor. The absolute sovereign possesses the power not only to make the law but also to break the law, to suspend its operations at will. But this godlike power also has a beastly aspect. "This arbitrary suspension or rupture of right . . . runs the risk of making the sovereign look like the most brutal beast who respects nothing, scorns the law. . . . Sovereign and beast seem to have in common their being outside-the-law."[18] Is this, at base, why Rome is—must be—a Beast in Revelation? Because for the Christian-Jewish author of Revelation, Rome, as a blasphemous aberration (13:1, 5–6; 17:3), operates outside the law of God? But why, then, is divine power in Revelation also accorded an animal face, that of a Lamb? (see especially 5:6–14). Is it because the divine sovereign, too, and his messianic agent, are also outside and above the law, even (or especially) the law of God, including the divine command, "Thou shalt not kill"? (Exod. 20:13; Deut. 5:17). Mountains of corpses, both human and animal, loom over the landscapes of Revelation as the direct result of actions initiated by God or the Lamb.[19] For all who do not acknowledge their sovereignty, God and the Lamb are monstrous agents of terror, beastly objects of horror. "Fall on us," these terrified rebels cry out to the mountains, "and hide us from the face of the one seated on the throne and from the wrath of the Lamb; for the mighty day of their wrath has come and who can stand before it?" (6:16).

"Beast, criminal, and sovereign have a troubling resemblance," muses Derrida. "There is between [them] a sort of obscure and fascinating complicity, or even a worrying mutual attraction, . . . an . . . uncanny reciprocal haunting. . . . [They] resemble each other while seeming to be situated at . . . each other's antipodes."[20] This unsettling family resemblance finds telling expression in the description of Revelation's second Beast, the one that rises out of the earth, as having "two horns *like a lamb*," Revelation's master metaphor for Jesus, even while speaking *"like a dragon"* (13:11), Revelation's master metaphor for Satan (see 12:9; 20:2). In Revelation we discern "the face of the beast under the features of the sovereign" and vice versa—not least the divine sovereign—"the one inhabiting or housing the other," the one serving as "the intimate host of the other."[21]

All of this is to say that Revelation, compulsively if surreptitiously hybrid,[22] constantly undercuts its own insistent dualisms. For Revelation's God is a beastly figure in other ways as well. "The one seated on the throne" (Revelation's preferred term for its deity [4:2, 9–10; 5:1, 7, 13; 6:16; 7:10, 15; 19:4; 21:5]) is notably unresponsive, almost entirely aphasic, speaking only in 1:8 and 21:5–8.[23] As Derrida remarks of such divine monarchs, "The sovereign's sovereign, God himself, like the beast, does not respond. . . . And that is indeed the most profound definition of absolute sovereignty."[24] That the visible face of this sovereign in Revelation is an animal face, an ovine face, is no accident. And although this Lamb is not entirely incapable of response, in general it exhibits the imperial nonresponsiveness of the figure on the throne, even outdoing that figure in aphasic inexpressiveness. The Lamb is not assigned a single word in John's talking animal book (contrast 4:7–8; 5:13–14; 6:1, 3, 5, 7; 8:13; 19:4).[25] The Lamb is mute, precisely as humans have almost always imagined animals to be. The Lamb is as dumb as a beast—or as *the* Beast, which likewise has no speaking role in Revelation.

The Lamb and the Beast face each other mutely on the same side of the chasm long imagined to separate the human from the animal. In effect, this presumed aphasia is the abyss out of which the Beast has crawled ("the Beast that ascends from the abyss [*ek tēs abyssou*]" [11:7; see also 17:8]), but to which it is still tethered, perhaps by the "mighty chain" mentioned in 20:1 ("Then I saw an angel descending from heaven, holding in his hand the key of the abyss and a mighty chain [*kai halysin megalēn*]"). But the Lamb also seems to be tethered by it and so also perches precariously on the lip of the abyss. In other words, the Lamb and the Beast may each be figures of fable, human entities draped in animal skin, but their animality does not sit lightly on either of them. Especially in relation to the shibboleth of speech, they behave as animals have almost always been imagined to behave. They are animetaphors that know how to pass as animals—up to a point, at least. The Beast does not altogether succeed in passing its savagery off as animal savagery or predatory ferocity, as we are about to see.

Derrida remarks in a different context how the animal has traditionally been imagined "in the most contradictory and incompatible generic terms [espèces]: absolute (because natural) goodness, absolute innocence, prior to good and evil, the animal without fault or defect (that would be its superiority as inferiority), but also the animal as absolute evil, cruelty, murderous savagery."[26] Both versions of the animal pad their way through Revelation, the domestic animal and the wild animal—the Lamb ostensibly without fault or defect, which makes it the perfect sacrificial victim (5:6, 12; 7:14; 12:11; 13:8), and the Beast ostensibly the embodiment of absolute evil (11:7; 13:5, 14–15), its cruelty indicating that it is a figure for human savagery, for "cruelty implies humanity."[27]

THE SHEEP'S WIFE

Come, I will show you the Bride, the wife of the Lamb.
　　—REVELATION 21:9

Revelation's *thērion*, its "beast," is also a "wild animal." Not only does the Greek admit both meanings, but "wild animal" is what *thērion* most often meant according to most Greek lexicons (and what it means in Revelation 6:8: "They were accorded authority over a fourth of the earth, to kill by sword, famine, and plague, and by the wild animals [*tōn thēriōn*] of the earth"). Human savagery, however, is represented in Revelation not only by the figure of a wild animal but also by the figure of a wild woman, a sexualized woman utterly out of (male) control—"Babylon the great, mother of whores and of earth's abominations" (17:5).[28] Entire nations are drunk with lust for "the great whore" (14:8; 17:2; 18:3, 9; 19:2), but she herself is drunk on violence—"And I saw the woman drunk on the blood of the saints and the blood of Jesus' witnesses" (17:6; cf. 19:2)—a feral feast of blood that is subsequently and hyperbolically extended to "all who have been slaughtered on earth" (18:24). One cannot easily say where the ravenous woman ends and the ravening Beast begins, and not only because both are figures for imperial Rome: The woman's ferocious appetite for blood makes her akin to a predatory animal.

Just as the wicked woman and the wild animal are intimately inter-twined in Revelation, the woman's thighs wrapped around the Beast ("I saw a woman sitting astride a scarlet beast" [17:3]), so too are the virtuous woman and the domesticated animal intimately intertwined. But now we fully set foot—or hoof—on what Susan McHugh has termed the "queer spectrum of interspecies intimacies."[29] As it happens, McHugh is in the midst of a chapter titled "Breeding Narratives of Intimacy: Shaggy Dogs, Shagging Sheep." "Come, I will show you the Bride [nymphē], the wife of the Lamb," John is told (21:9), having earlier learned that "the marriage of the Lamb has come, and his Bride has made herself ready" (19:7). The apocalyptic bestiary is not innocent of bestiality—not that the sheep's marriage is a salacious tale, I hasten to add. If our sheep is involved in any shagging, it occurs discreetly behind the narrative curtain. What we are faced with, nonetheless (at least in our neoliteral construal of it), is what McHugh would term a "nonstandard intimacy" conducted across species lines.[30]

But who or what is "the Bride, the wife of the Lamb"? "I will show you the Bride," the angelic interpreter informs John, but what he sees instead is "the holy city Jerusalem" descending from heaven (21:9–10; cf. 21:2). The good empire, "the empire [basileia] of our Lord and his Messiah" (11:15), is here condensed as a good city, and that good city is figured in turn as a good wife. But the imagistic condensation and displacement does not end there, with the good wife cuddled up with her blood-drenched sheep. The imagery took a detour on its way from the city to the bridechamber. The detailed description given of the city (21:11–21) shows it to be nothing other than an elaborate multifaceted symbol for the redeemed people of God.[31] The upshot of John's intricately layered symbolism is that all the subjects in his ideal empire are represented by (indeed, reduced to) the figure of an ideal wife. In John's good empire, all other subjects are subsumed in that one subject. The Bride is the redeemed people of God. In consequence, no other relationship exists within the eschatological empire of empires than the submissive relationship of an obedient, worshipful wife to her husband and lord—a master who, however, happens also to be a domestic animal.[32]

The figure of the Lamb is fraught with paradox in Revelation.[33] The Lamb is a nonhegemonic symbol for a hegemonic entity, a docile (indeed, domesticated) trope for domination. But so too is the Bride. This is an all but wordless wife, who, as such, mimics the animal muteness of her four-legged bridegroom. Whereas the wild woman, "the Whore," is accorded only one line in Revelation (18:7), the domestic woman, "the Bride," is accorded only one word (albeit an enticing one): "And the Spirit and the Bride say, 'Come' [*erchou*]!" (22:17).[34] Yet as city, metropolis, and megalopolis, this domestic goddess will lord it over the kings of the earth who must bring tribute (in)to her (21:24, 26; cf. Isa. 60:1–16). And just as it is the destiny of the wicked city, Babylon / Rome, represented by the wicked woman, to be delivered back to undomesticated nature and become "a dwelling place of demons, a haunt of every foul and hateful bird, a haunt of every foul and hateful beast" (18:2), so is it the destiny of the virtuous city, "the new Jerusalem" (21:2), represented by the virtuous woman, to be the repository of domesticated nature, nature adapted to human needs. "Through the middle of the street of the city" will run "the river of the water of life," a river whose water is a life-giving gift for human beings (22:1–2; cf. 7:17; 21:6; 22:17; Gen. 2:10; Ezek. 47:1–11). On either side of the river, "the tree of life" will flourish, a tree whose leaves are for healing human beings (Rev. 22:2; cf. 2:7; 22:14, 19; Gen. 2:9; 3:22, 24; Ezek. 47:12; 4 Ezra 8:52). And at / as the source of the river and hence of the tree will stand the ultimate domestic animal—an always already slaughtered Lamb whose blood confers absolute benefit on human beings, which is to say, eternal life (Rev. 22:1; cf. 1:5b; 5:9; 7:14; 12:11). Already one wonders how good this good city is for thinking with ecologically, or ecotheologically, or, especially, ecotherologically. And we have yet to take the measure of the city's biggest drawback: its sheer, stupendous size.

THE SHEEP IN THE SHOPPING MALL

[They] follow the Lamb wherever he goes.
—REVELATION 14:4

Ecotheological and ecojustice engagement with Revelation has tended to have recourse to the blueprint of the New Jerusalem to extract positive ecological visions from the blighted landscapes of this disaster-ridden book. Such reflection has typically gravitated not to the heavenly city itself so much as its river (*potamos*), which, somewhat peculiarly, courses down the center of the city's main street (*en mesō tēs plateias autēs*)—less a river, then, than a stream or channel?—and to the tree (*xylon zōēs*) that straddles the stream, or, alternatively, lines its banks, if *xylon* is to be read as a collective noun (Rev. 22:1–2).[35] The obvious problem, however, is stated remarkably seldom in such reflection.

The metaphors on which we have been musing (stream, tree, animal) are themselves situated within another metaphoric structure (city) so surreally outsized as to look unsettlingly like a cartoon rendition of what we are so busily turning our planet into anyway, as though too impatient to await the promised arrival of the heavenly megalopolis. "The city lies foursquare," writes John, "its length the same as its width" (Rev. 21:16). John's angelic interpreter measures the city with his "measuring rod of gold" and discovers it to be exceedingly large (just how large we will see below).[36] The New Jerusalem is indeed a symbolic structure, as noted earlier. But size does matter here, as consultation of other ancient descriptions of the eschatological Jerusalem suggests. In the Dead Sea Scrolls (4Q554) its dimensions are 140 by 100 stadia (that is, 18.67 by 13.33 miles), "larger than any ancient city";[37] in the *Sibylline Oracles* (5.250–52) its wall will reach to Joppa on the Mediterranean coast, 30 miles distant; while in *Song of Songs Rabbah* (7.5.3) its walls will extend all the way to the gates of Damascus, 135 miles distant, prompting even as serious a scholar as David Aune to quip about "eschatological urban sprawl."[38] Presumably, the eschatological Jerusalem is outsized because in ancient thought colossal size could function as a metaphor for divine transcendence.[39] And Revelation's New Jerusalem is biggest of all, Brobdingnagian in its dimensions. "He measured the city with his rod, twelve thousand stadia; its length and width and height are equal" (Rev. 21:16). That amounts to "1,416–1,566 miles in each direction," depending on whether the city's 12,000 stadia cubed are Attic stadia, Olympic stadia, or Roman stadia.[40] The New Jerusalem is a sovereign city, not just in the sense that it is seat to a divine sovereign, but also in the sense that it partakes of the excess intrinsic to sovereignty. As Derrida observes, "What is essential and proper to sovereignty is . . . not grandeur or height as geometrically measurable, sensible, or intelligible, but excess, hyperbole . . . : higher than height, grander than grandeur, etc. It is the *more*, the *more than* that counts, . . . the absolute supplement that exceeds any comparative toward an absolute superlative."[41]

Revelation's vision of Edenic restoration, then, is more than a mere diversion of the river that watered the original garden (Gen. 2:10) and more than a mere transplantation of the tree of life that was the centerpiece of that garden (2:9). River and tree are now situated in a sovereign city whose literal dimensions (limiting ourselves to length and breadth alone) would encompass more than half the continental United States. The problem for ecotheology (and even more for ecotherology) is that the proportions are horribly wrong—but uncannily right if a dystopian vision is needed of where contemporary urban hyperdevelopment, and not just in the United States, is headed—if climate change does not put all our megalopolises under water before they have managed to link hands, or rather suburbs, and cover entire continents with housing developments and office developments, industrial parks and business parks, gas stations and fast food restaurants, strip malls and parking lots.

And Eden will have to adapt accordingly. The environmental historian Carolyn Merchant has argued compellingly that the high-end shopping mall may be read as emblematic of the re-creation of Eden through the anthropocentering of nature:

> The modern version of the Garden of Eden is the enclosed shopping mall. Surrounded by a desert of parking lots, malls comprise gardens of shops covered by glass domes, accessed by spiral staircases and escalators reaching upward toward heaven. . . . The "river that went out of Eden to water the garden" [Gen. 2:10] is reclaimed in meandering tree-lined streams and ponds filled with bright orange goldfish. . . . Within manicured spaces of trees, flowers, and fountains we can shop for nature at the Nature Company, purchase "natural" clothing at Esprit, sample organic foods and "rainforest crunch" in kitchen gardens . . . and play virtual reality games in which SimEve is reinvented in cyberspace. The spaces and commodities of the shopping mall epitomize consumer capitalism's vision of the recovery from the Fall of Adam and Eve.[42]

John's "measuring rod of gold" (21:15) may also be applied to the shopping mall, for size also matters to the shopping mall, most of all when it is a megamall. Merchant describes the surreal dimensions of a megamall: "Canada's West Edmonton Mall, the first of a generation of megamalls, is eight city blocks long by four blocks wide and covers 5.2 million square feet. It sports an indoor surfing beach with adjustable wave heights."[43] For millions, as she notes, "Malls are places of light, hope, and promise—transitions to new worlds. People are reinvented and redeemed by the mall. Said one ecstatic visitor, 'This place is heaven.'"[44] And heaven keeps getting bigger. By 2012, the West Edmonton Mall, once the largest mall in the world, had dropped to tenth place in the international megamall rankings. At the time of writing, the nine largest malls on the planet are all located in Asia, the most immense of all being the "New South China Mall, Living City" in Dongguan—which, paradoxically, is also a "dead mall,"[45] having been 99 percent vacant since its 2005 opening. It was the subject of a brief but notable documentary titled *Utopia, Part 3: The World's Largest Shopping Mall*.[46]

How should we classify the New Jerusalem—as a "living city," a "utopia," or a "dead mall"? Or simply as a megamall, whether living or dead? Is Revelation's heavenly city not all too readily—all too eerily—evocative of this most iconic of postmodern urban spaces, complete with its central fountain, single stream, and token tree? And as such, is it not singularly ill-designed to serve as a prophetic counterexample to the contemporary paving over of the planet and the attendant obliteration of plant and animal species? One animal does survive in the heavenly city, however, and to that singular creature we turn once again.

Derrida writes apocalyptically of an ongoing sacrificial war against the animal, and specifically of an Abrahamic war: "I think that Cartesianism belongs . . . to the Judeo-Christiano-Islamic tradition of a war against the animal, of a sacrificial war that is as old as Genesis."[47] Revelation's Lamb is ambiguously positioned in relation to this ancient war. As slaughtered sacrifice, the Lamb is a victim of the war and has the war wounds to prove it ("Then I saw . . . a Lamb standing as if it had been slaughtered" [5:6]). But the Lamb is also a prime perpetrator of the war. The Lamb's incremental opening of the "scroll . . . sealed with seven seals" (5:1; cf. 5:7) precipitates a chain of catastrophic events, many of which entail ecocidal devastation on a planetary scale (6:12–14; 8:7–12; 16:3–4, 8a, 10a, 12, 18, 20–21). Not only are "those [humans] who destroy the earth" destroyed (11:18),[48] but the earth itself is destroyed in the process, along with the nonhuman animals who depend on it for sustenance—yet another knotty contradiction in which the fraught figure of the Lamb is enmeshed.

Derrida warns that our sacrificial war against the animal—now characterized by exploitation and annihilation of the animal on an unprecedented scale—threatens to "end in a world without animals, without any animal worthy of the name living for something other than to become a means for [the human],"[49] whether as source of meat, source of dairy products, source of clothing, domestic pet, model for children's toys or cartoon characters, hunter's trophy, hunter's aide, zoo specimen, or experimental life-form. Is this the world with which Revelation presents us in the end, and as the end? What becomes of animals—animals other than the anomalous animal that is the Lamb—in Revelation's blueprint for the outsized urban enclosure that will form the center of the "new heaven and . . . new earth"? (21:1).

Explictly named in Revelation's climactic vision are "the dogs" (*hoi kynes* [22:15])—metaphoric canines, assumedly, even if not certainly.[50] They are metonymically associated with human iniquity ("dogs and sorcerers and fornicators and murderers and idolaters, and everyone who loves and practices falsehood"), and, most likely, they are metaphoric for a further form of activity that the author deems subhuman (homoeroticism is a common guess).[51] As a result, the dogs are banned from the heavenly city: "Outside [*exō*] are the dogs."

But if John casts the first stone at these dogs, the scholarly commentators on Revelation rush in with armfuls of rocks. Every slur leveled at dogs in the ancient world is scented out, tracked down, dug up, and uncritically brought to the pile. The boundaries between human "dogs" and nonhuman canines are thoroughly blurred in the process. Dogs are "despicable" and "despised" creatures, we learn,[52] because they behave like degenerate humans: They are "concerned only about their physical well-being";[53] are "unclean because of their habits"—they are, indeed, possessed of "disgusting habits";[54] are "sexually immoral,"[55] "impure and malicious,"[56] "cowards, unfaithful . . . , abominable,"[57] and much else of this ilk. Humans who practice such depravities are loathsome because they behave like dogs. Dogs are loathsome because they behave like depraved humans. Conspicuously absent from the constricting circle of this encaging logic, exiled from it as from the heavenly city itself, are dogs that simply behave like dogs.

The heavenly city is a little empty without the dogs. This continent-sized, lightly landscaped megamall contains but one named animal, sole companion to the single stream and the lone tree. That animal is, of course, the Lamb (21:22–23; 22:1, 3). How does it stack up against the dogs? Might this solitary animal be regarded as an "animal worthy of the name living for something other than to become a means for [the human]," to reinvoke

Derrida's poignant formulation?[58] It might and might not. It is represented as having died for human beings and at the hand of human beings to confer eternal life on human beings (5:6–10; 7:13–14, 17; 12:11; 13:8; 14:1, 4; 21:27), and to that extent emblematizes anthropocentric animality. And yet this solitary, seven-horned, seven-eyed sheep might also be said, against all the odds, to be an animal worthy of the name to the extent that it lives—lives eternally—for something other than as a means for the human. It does not exist to serve human animals because human animals now exist to serve it: "The throne of God and of the Lamb will be in it [the heavenly city], and his slaves [*hoi douloi autou*] will worship him" (22:3).[59] Revelation's heavenly megalopolis is far from being an ecological paradise, but its token animal is also far from being the final victim, the last animal standing, of the ecocidal drama that enabled the establishment of the heavenly city in the first place—the incremental demolition and progressive leveling of "the first heaven and the first earth" (21:1; see esp. 8:6–12; 16:1–12). In a final bizarre twist of this hypersurreal animal tale, the only animal worthy of the name ("Thou art worthy" [5:9; cf. 5:12]) has become other than a means to human ends because, in the end, all humans have become its property.

The hierarchical relationship of human beings and domestic animals is thus radically inverted in Revelation. But is it deconstructed? Hardly. The heavenly city remains a domestic enclosure constructed, like any enclosure, through the systemic exclusion of its others—in this case, undomesticated animality, wild animality, animality altogether unbeholden to the human. The "dogs" are excluded, as we saw. They trouble the human/ domestic animal opposition, because as ancient Mediterranean dogs, perched precariously on the jagged edges of human society, they are neither fully domesticated nor fully wild. Still more unequivocally outside the domestic enclosure that is the heavenly city is the *thērion*, the Beast or Wild Beast. Earlier, this Wild Beast was "thrown alive into the lake of fire that burns with sulfur" (19:20), probably not its optimal habitat; yet there it will survive "forever and ever," although only to be "tormented day and night" (20:10). Indeed, the consignment of the Wild Beast to unending destruction was one of the prime preconditions for the emergence of the heavenly city.

Is Revelation's heavenly city founded, then, like all our terrestrial cities, on the perpetual sacrifice of any and every "animal worthy of the name, living for something other than to become a means for the human"? Yes and no, yet again, because the Beast of Revelation is, at base, a figure for human despotism, for Roman imperialism. Even the Beast that must be burned eternally so that the domestic bliss of the Bride and the Lamb can ensue is not as wild, as untethered to the human, as ecotherology might wish it to be. All of which is to say that Revelation does, after all, "end in a world without animals," without "any animal worthy of the name," whether inside or outside the city. And to that extent at least, Revelation may, after all, be an unveiling of "what is" and "what must soon take place" (1:1, 19; 4:1; 22:6)—an apocalyptic uncovering of the already present future of our catastrophically theriocidal cultures.

And yet. . . . Revelation's multihorned, multieyed, multifaceted sheep is sufficiently complex, elusive, and exasperating to merit a final "and yet." The sheer ecotheological significance of this singular if sinister animal should not be lost sight of amid the paradoxes, contradictions, and disappointments that encircle it. Jesus of Nazareth enters Revelation as a Son of Man (1:12–13), transforms into a Lamb (5:6), and trots through the main body of the text in that theriomorphic guise and hence on all fours, only assuming anthropomorphic form again sporadically in 14:14–16 and 19:11–21. But when the shape-shifting eventually ends and the heavenly city arrives and God's Messiah is enthroned with God in the city center as eternal object of incessant worship, it is not as anthropomorph but as theriomorph that he comes into final focus (21:22–23; 22:3; see also 19:7, 9; 21:9, 14). Indeed, it is only in animal guise that Jesus is worshiped anywhere in Revelation (see also 5:8–14; cf. 7:9–12, 15–17). Revelation evinces a high Christology, as has often been remarked.[60] What has not been remarked is that Revelation's Christology is highest when it is an animal Christology. The ultimate Christological image in Revelation, then—and the image most deeply stamped with the mark of divinity to the extent that it is the one explicitly marked for worship[61]—is the image of a quadrupedal Christ. In an age of mass extinction this surely qualifies as an ecotheological image with legs, despite the contradictions that repeatedly trip it up.

❧ And Say the Animal Really Responded: Speaking Animals in the History of Christianity

LAURA HOBGOOD-OSTER

One day when he was hunting, [Placidus] came upon a herd of deer, among which one stag stood out by his size and beauty. . . . Placidus gave his full effort to pursuing the stag. . . . The deer . . . finally stopped at the top of a high peak. . . . Christ then spoke to Placidus through the stag's mouth. . . . "O Placidus, why are you pursuing me? For your sake I have appeared to you in this animal. I am the Christ, whom you worship without knowing it. Your alms have risen before me, and for this purpose I have come, that through this deer which you hunted, I myself might hunt you."
—JACOBUS DE VORAGINE, *The Golden Legend: Readings on the Saints*

In her thoughtful critique of Jacques Derrida's lecture series on the question of the animal, Donna Haraway points out something that was "oddly missing." Although Derrida understood that his cat was "a real cat, truly, believe me, a little cat. It isn't the figure of a cat" and that he was in the "presence of someone, not of a machine reacting," he still, in the long run, missed his own point. As Haraway explains, there is a weakness in Derrida's philosophical ponderings on this real cat:

> He came right to the edge of respect, of the move to *respecere*, but he was sidetracked by his textual canon of Western philosophy and literature and by his own linked worries about being naked in front of his cat. . . . Somehow in all this worrying and longing, the cat was never heard from again in the long essay dedicated to the crime against animals perpetrated by the great Singularities separating the

Animal and the Human in the canon Derrida so passionately read and reread so that it could never be read the same way again.[1]

Although deeply interested in animals and determined to challenge the generations of philosophers who had dismissed them, Derrida's interest did not ever really take him to the actual cat or to the heart of the important question he himself posed: "And Say the Animal Responded?"

The above quoted encounter between a soon-to-be saint, Placidus, and a stag, recounted in legend as well as in myriad images for over a thousand years of Christian history, introduces an unexpected, maybe even shocking, voice to the Christian chorus. Visual portrayals of this encounter between human-animal-divine show a human hunter, his horse and dogs kneeling reverently in front of a large stag. The massive deer has a cross with the "image of Jesus Christ" shining "more brightly than the sun" in the middle of his antlers. Then the mouth of the stag opens and the words he speaks are in the voice of the divine. Divine-animal-human voices all come together in one moment of hybridity, or as Derrida might call it, of "divinanimality."[2]

The complex nature of speaking, of response, and of the Word/words are central theological themes in Christianity, just as they are central philosophical constructs in the history of Western philosophy. "In the beginning was the Word [logos], and the Word was with God, and the Word was God" (John 1:1). The concept of logos is undeniably much broader than the idea of speech; it is the idea of divine agency in the world. The concretization of the concept in the power of human speech is quite pronounced in Christianity. Thus some might even claim that human speaking, hearing, and reading, in this more humanocentric form of the tradition, become a central theological idea undergirding the Christian belief system. God speaks to and through prophets; revelation relies on the insights of the written word in the form of canonical scripture. The written word in the form of the canonical biblical text carries a sacred quality and, for some Christians, is the literal unfolding of God's truth.

Certainly the religiously based elevation of the human above all other animals, thus making us dominant and even ontologically superior, is not unique to Christianity. Such is the case in varying degrees for most, if not all, human religious traditions. But one of the most evident and powerful ways that Christianity, supported by the sustained arguments of Western philosophical systems, positions human as superior and unique is through the Word and words, through language. As stated by a group of contemporary philosophers, including the widely recognized linguist Noam Chomsky:

> If a martian graced our planet, it would be struck by one remarkable similarity among Earth's living creatures and a key difference. . . . If our martian naturalist were meticulous, it might note that the faculty mediating human communication appears remarkably different from that of other living creatures. . . . One of the oldest problems among theorists is the "shared versus unique" distinction. Most current commentators agree that, although bees dance, birds sing, and chimpanzees grunt, these systems of communication differ qualitatively from human language.[3]

Interestingly, even the martian becomes "it" in this passage, questioning the supposed potential of subjectivity for any other-than-human being, even celestial ones. Resolutely determined to maintain a qualitative difference between human language and the communication systems of all other animals, philosophers and theologians continue to emphasize the differences and superiorities of human speech.

So what does it mean if (when) animals do speak? This question is ignored, deemed irrelevant, or simply disregarded in most Christian theologies, even in many of those theologies that address other animals. I contend that remembering the sometimes forgotten tales of speaking animals can provide a much-needed corrective to a tradition that has become a stronghold for anthropocentrism and human dominance. By entering the conversation, these speaking and even responding animals break the verbal exclusivity and privilege of humans in the tradition. In so doing, other animals and the divine are directly connected without the human intermediary in play. They provide a much-needed critique of the position of the animal in relationship to the word and to language. Speaking animals break the boundaries by definitively responding.

WORDS IN CHRISTIANITY

The Word of God preached now means . . . man's language about God, in which and through which God speaks about Himself.

—KARL BARTH, *Church Dogmatics*

In his major theological treatise, *Church Dogmatics*, Karl Barth amplifies the elevation of words, language, and Christian preaching in particular, as a marker of orthodox Christianity. He is one of many Christian theologians who reinforce the uniqueness of language as a distinctively human path to truth and understanding. So, as the mid-twentieth-century homiletician-theologian David Buttrick claims:

> Whatever our Christian stance, we are children of Saint Paul, of Chrysostom, of Augustine, perhaps of Luther. So when Saint Paul states flat out that "faith comes from hearing" (Rom. 10:17), should we correct him by suggesting that faith comes from visual aids . . . ?
> Do not Christians insist that God "spoke" and the world was; that God tossed the Word like a burning coal to scald the lips of the prophets; that the Word became flesh and spoke good news; that the church is built on the testimony of apostles, martyrs, and saints?[4]

In this tradition, "the Word" is a foundational theological concept, a tradition (including the canon and the history of ideas) and an ongoing action of preaching and response. The three modes are intricately connected with one another, of course. As already quoted, according to the canonical Gospel of John, "the Word" was in the beginning and was with God. For the evangelist who wrote John, Jesus Christ, who the writer claims is both the only begotten Son of God and is God, was equated directly with the complicated theological concept of "the Word" (more accurately translated as the Logos, but the Word has stuck in English, French, and German in particular).[5]

Throughout the history of Christianity words, in their written form as texts and in their spoken form in liturgy, articulate the basis of religious belief and practice. Creeds, carefully framed statements of belief with very particular words vetted, debated, and selected, served to institutionalize and regularize the tradition. Final binding, ecumenical forms of the creed took shape in the fourth century C.E. at the councils of Nicaea and Constantinople. With this creed in place, one could determine who was orthodox and who was heretical. Words decided that sometimes deadly fate. Christians died over the words they chose. Early Christians, such as Arius, and medieval Christians, such as Marguerite Porete, were proclaimed anathema, cut off, because the words they used to describe their theological positions or mystical experiences fell outside the normative and accepted definitions. No longer allowed to speak or to hear, they were excommunicated, excluded from sharing their own words or hearing the words of others in the Church.

Why are words so powerful in Christianity? Although many religious traditions focus on a central text or group of texts, the efficacy of words is an even more central component of Christianity because of its connection with the theological idea of the Logos embodied in Christ.[6] When most Christians gather for worship, with a few notable exceptions, reading scripture and hearing the homily or the sermon is central.[7] A passage from the accepted canon of sacred texts is usually read and then analyzed or explained by a selected person, often a member of the clergy. Layers and layers of words make up the belief and ritual system of Christianity. Martin Luther, often considered the father of the Reformation in the early sixteenth century, made this claim explicitly, using the preaching of "the gospel" as the referent here: "For the gospel—even more than the bread and baptism—is the unique, most certain, and noblest sign of the church, since it is through the gospel alone that the church is conceived, formed, nourished, born, trained, fed, clothed, adorned, strengthened, armed, and preserved."[8] John Calvin followed in Luther's footsteps, at least in terms of his elevation of preaching: "The Word of God is not distinguished from the word of the prophet. God does not wish to be heard but by the voice of his ministers. Christ acts by them in such a manner that he wishes their mouth to be reckoned as his mouth, and their lips as his lips."[9]

Following Luther and the Reformation, words occupied an increasingly significant place in Christian worship. In *The New England Soul*, his classic study of American Puritanism during the colonial period, Harry Stout claims that "the only regular medium of public communication" in New England was the sermon. With this power of the word in their hands, the founders of New England

> set out to create a unique and self-perpetuating "people of the Word," and by extending the sermon to all significant aspects of life—social and political as well as religious—they achieved exactly that. . . . The average weekly churchgoer in New England (and there were far more churchgoers than church members) listened to something like seven

thousand sermons in a lifetime, totaling somewhere around fifteen thousand hours of concentrated listening.[10]

The two periods of "Great Awakening" in early U.S. history (mid-eighteenth and early nineteenth centuries)—Awakenings that also were experienced in Great Britain—involved traveling preachers who would reportedly convert huge crowds by their exhortations. Preaching of the word became a central context for human social gathering and communal construction. Eventually, many Christians (particularly Protestants) stopped practicing other sacraments that had been central for centuries, such as the Eucharist, when they gathered, or they practiced these sacraments with less frequency. Instead, they focused on the sermon and the Word as heard and interpreted as the primary means for worship and as the way to understand the divine.

Into the twentieth century the significance of the word remained central to Christian theology. At times it was even overtly linked to the differentiation of humans from other animals:

> We live in language. Words are not merely stuff to thicken bulky dictionaries. . . . We are *Homo loquens*. We *do* with language. As human beings we could not *be* without words. The reason we find a book such as *Dr. Doolittle* amusing is that it portrays talking animals. While animals do seem to signal, and gorillas may be programmed with basic vocabulary, animals rarely write poems, make puns, deliver speeches, or shout out orders in the stock market. We are *human*, precisely because we are *Homo loquens*. . . . No wonder the Bible is big on words: God created with a Word, and we have faith by hearing.[11]

Christian theologians openly embraced the connections among preaching, language, words, the divine, and human exceptionality.

Do words necessarily exclude all other animals from Christianity? Is that the purpose of words, to grasp onto a supposedly unique human attribute? Adam did "speak" the names of the other animals in Genesis 2, giving him significant power over them. Then what does it mean when a stag, in a way that might be a bit shocking to some, speaks? What to do with these amazing narratives of speaking animals?

Before delving into those stories, though, it might be helpful to think, briefly, about why this inclusion of animals in Christian discourse might rattle some foundations. In addition to its focus on language, why is this tradition perceived as so anthropocentric? Lynn White, in a seminal and now oft-quoted essay published in the late 1960s, "The Historical Roots of Our Ecologic Crisis," linked Christianity directly to the root causes of global environmental demise.[12] The same argument could be posited for the demise of the significance of animals in the Christian tradition and the cultures that tradition influences. Christian orthodoxy seems to claim that humans are a unique creation, the only species that is a mirror of the divine. Animals, indeed the entire earth, are merely a stage on which the drama of human salvation is enacted. Some expressions of Christianity claim that God becomes human in order to save humanity and humanity alone; otherwise, God might have incarnated in some other way. True to White's hypothesis, this ideological foundation certainly does suggest that Christianity has the philosophical basis to justify its role as a major contributor to the demise of the planet, particularly in the forms that assume that only humans are connected to God and worthy of salvation.

In too many ways, then, the religious narrative of Christianity does seem to exclude other animals. But such a narrow reading of the tradition is mistaken or at least incomplete. Although this humanocentric Christianity is often considered orthodox, it is not a perspective that takes into account various other possibilities emphasized by Christian thinkers and practitioners throughout history. A focus on the Word amplifies one particular aspect of Christianity, one that seems to include only humans. The form of communication that the "Word" implies, at least on a popular level, is less than inclusive of the rest of creation.

Thus it is worthwhile, indeed urgent, to reconsider some of the sacred stories that have been ignored or buried—stories that include speaking animals and, sometimes, mute humans. Other-than-humans understand at times when the humans do not. There is a reason why Jesus lived with the wild animals; there is a divine presence and wisdom in the wilderness. Saints follow his pattern, and from the stories of Jesus and the saints we see animals who break into the closed human circle of the word.

THE VOICES OF ASSES, LIONS, AND DOGS

Then the LORD *opened the mouth of the donkey, and it said to Balaam, "What have I done to you, that you have struck me these three times?" Balaam said to the donkey, "Because you have made a fool of me! I wish I had a sword in my hand! I would kill you right now!" But the donkey said to Balaam, "Am I not your donkey, which you have ridden all your life to this day? Have I been in the habit of treating you this way?" And he said, "No."*

NUMBERS 22:28–30

Asses deserve to have their day in Jewish and Christian scripture. Over the two thousand or so years when these two traditions were born and developed in the Mediterranean world, donkeys served as beasts of burden, modes of transportation, and plowers of fields. They contributed immensely to the well-being of the growing human population. So when Balaam, a "seer," sets off on a journey to visit a king, he was lucky that his wise ass was carrying him. God was not very happy with Balaam since the king, Moab, hired Balaam to curse the Israelites. So God sent along an angel to block the pathway in order to thwart the seer's task. When they rounded a corner, the ass saw the armed angel ready to attack. So he did what any wise animal would do, he tried to steer clear. Still, his unseeing, eyes-wide-shut master tried to push forward, even beating the ass to get him to move along. As a last resort the ass plopped down and refused to budge, though he was taking a beating. Balaam grew angry and "struck the donkey with his staff." Finally, realizing that the only form of communication his master understood was language, the ass spoke. He pleaded with Balaam, asking why he was striking him. At this point, the Lord "opened the eyes of Balaam, and he saw the angel of the Lord standing in the road, with his drawn sword in his hand." Although humans do not understand, angels and animals do, so the angel points directly at Balaam, criticizing him and saying, "Why have you struck your donkey these three times. . . . The donkey saw me, and turned away from me these three times. If it had not turned away from me, surely just now I would have killed you and let it live."

Words finally worked, though the intricate dance of understanding was already taking place between the angel and the ass. But for the human, alternative forms of communication were ignored, so the animal responded with a voice that the human could understand. It's finally up to the ass to make sure Balaam gets it and survives this encounter with an angel.[13]

Balaam's (unnamed) ass sets the groundwork for speaking animals who followed him. *The Acts of Peter*, from the Christian apocrypha, recounts one of the most amazing speaking animal stories in the Christian tradition. This story of a preaching dog who responds to the call of the apostle to convert a heretic questions all boundaries placed on animals and their ability to respond. Peter had traveled to Rome to confront Simon Magus, one of the most well-known and influential of the early Christian heretics. On arriving at the house where Simon is hiding, Peter sees a large dog chained by the entrance. This dog is probably a large mastiff, the standard Roman guard dog. Since the doorkeeper has turned Peter away, he asks the dog to carry a message in for the heretic. The scene that follows goes beyond expectations, even those of Peter:

> And the dog ran away at once and went into the midst of the people who were with Simon, and lifting his front legs he said with a very loud voice, "Simon, Peter who stands at the door, bids you to come outside in public; for he says 'On your account have I come to Rome, you wicked man and destroyer of simple souls. You most wicked and shameless man. . . . A dumb animal, which received a human voice, has been sent to you to convict you and to prove that you are a cheat and deceiver. . . . You shall therefore be accursed, enemy and destroyer of the way of Christ's truth. He shall punish your iniquities, which you have done, with imperishable fire and you shall be in outer darkness.'"

The dog, who had done much more than instructed, ran back to Peter, "reported what had happened with Simon" and continued to elaborate. At this point the dog becomes not only a preacher, but a prophet:

> Peter, you shall have a hard fight with Simon, the enemy of Christ, and with his adherents, but many whom he deceived shall convert to the faith. For this you shall receive a reward for your work from God.[14]

The dog then fell at the apostle's feet and died. Crowds, astonished at the talking dog, also fall at Peter's feet. Interestingly at this point in the story, maybe in order to make the people forget the amazing preaching dog and refocus on his apostolic power, Peter resurrects a smoked fish, effectively changing the subject.

So what to make of this? On hearing the story of the preaching dog in the early Christian apocryphal text *The Acts of Peter*, most people are either amazed or skeptical or both. The dog receives a "human voice" thus marking the type of communication, but he goes beyond the instructions. The dog literally finds his voice and speaks the truth; he becomes an actor in this drama, not a mere puppet. Just as Balaam's ass became an actor in the world, so does the dog. The dog gave his life for the action, but nonetheless spoke the truth, not only to the heretic, but even to the apostle. It would be difficult to argue that the dog, after his preaching, still landed outside the realm of salvation.

Another amazing talking animal is recounted in the apocryphal *Acts of Paul*, a popular early Christian text. In one version of this text the reader is introduced to a lion whose "height was twelve cubits and his size that of a horse." Paul encountered the massive feline while walking toward a mountain one day. Interestingly, the text reports that the two immediately "saluted each other as though they knew each other." Equally compelling, it is the lion who speaks first, "Well met, Paul, servant of God and apostle of the Lord Jesus Christ! I have one thing which I ask thee to do unto me." Paul, seemingly unshaken by this encounter (why? was it expected?), replied, "Speak; I will hear." That amazing response from Paul, an early Christian figure who is problematic for feminist theologians and for ecofeminist historians (such as myself), speaks volumes.[15] Paul does not hesitate to enter a conversation with a lion and invites him to speak; Paul is also, amazingly, willing to listen! The lion asks to be instructed in "the great things" of Christianity and for the next seven days, no short time, Paul gives him instruction. We can only assume this was in the form of words.[16]

Both of these encounters—between Paul and the lion, between Peter and the dog—allowed for response. Haraway states that Derrida, with his cat, "failed a simple obligation of companion species; he did not become curious about what the cat might actually be doing, feeling, thinking or perhaps making available to him in looking back at him that morning."[17] Peter and Paul were more curious; they did not miss the invitation. And, it must be added, neither did the dog or the lion. The lion even initiated the invitation by speaking first.

Later, Paul and the lion encounter each other again. Paul has been captured by the Romans and put in an arena to be killed in a story that parallels the story of Daniel in the lions' den in the Hebrew scriptures. The crowd calls for the lion to be let loose on Paul in order to tear the apostle to pieces. When the lion looked at Paul,

Paul said, "Lion, was it you whom I baptized?" And the lion in answer said to Paul, "Yes." Paul spoke to it again and said, "And how were you captured?" The lion said with its own voice, "Just as you were, Paul." After Hieronymus sent many beasts so that Paul might be slain, and archers that the lion too might be killed, a violent and exceedingly heavy hail-storm fell from heaven, although the sky was clear: many died and all the rest took to flight. But it did not touch Paul or the lion. . . . And Paul took leave of the lion, which spoke no more, and went out of the stadium and down to the harbor and embarked on the ship. . . . So he embarked too like one of the fugitives, but the lion went away into the mountains as was natural for it.[18]

There are several striking aspects to this passage. First, the lion speaks with his own voice, not a human voice necessarily. The lion is granted words. At the end of the account, the lion goes away to be a lion again and speaks no more. What does this mean? It appears that the value of the lion as a lion was vital; he goes back to the mountains rather than remain among the humans. He was counted worthy as a lion and spoke with a lion's voice.

This returns me to Haraway's critique of Derrida. Although she acknowledges that Derrida "correctly criticized two kinds of representations, one set from those who observe real animals and write about them but never meet their gaze, and the other set from those who engage animals only as literary and mythological figures," she reminds Derrida that he also refused that intersecting gaze. His lack of curiosity about his own real cat kept him from examining the types of communication possible with animals' own responses as animals. She continues:

Why did Derrida not ask, even in principle, if a Gregory Bateson or Jane Goodall or Marc Bekoff or Barbara Smuts or many others have met the gaze of living, diverse animals and in response undone and redone themselves and their sciences? . . . Why did Derrida leave unexamined the practices of communication outside the writing technologies he did know how to talk about? . . . Actually to respond to the cat's response to his presence would have required his joining that flawed but rich philosophical canon to the risky project of asking what this cat on this morning cared about, what these bodily postures and visual entanglements might mean and might invite.[19]

Engaging real animals where they are and as they communicate opens new doors and invites new ways of thinking about words.

RETHINKING THE WORDS OF ANIMALS

Animals first entered the imagination as messengers and promises.
—JOHN BERGER, *About Looking*

John Berger, an extraordinary art historian with a keen interest in the role of animals in human culture, makes this claim about animals as messengers and promises in his classic essay "Why Look at Animals?"[20] It speaks to the place of animals in relationship to humans—animals are not just leather and horn and meat, they are messengers. But animals are still more than that symbolic category, just as they are more than their physical parts. They are more than messengers and promises to humans. Animals are independent, vibrant beings with their own languages and lives.

It seems that Derrida knew this when he looked at his cat. It is what troubled him so at the encounter. But the philosopher was then unable to make the full turn from the human to the real animal. He was stuck in the cycle of pondering the human condition and retreated from his own turn to curiosity about the animal and her response. Can speaking and responding animals in the stories of the Christian tradition facilitate such a turn?

Such a turn can only come about if the animals who spoke, and who speak, are recognized as real subjects, maybe even as ambassadors for the rest of the animals who share the planet. They speak because it is the only mode of communication that most humans are willing to hear. As soon as the message gets across—to Balaam, Simon, Peter, Paul, humans as a whole—the animal lets out a sigh of relief and becomes who she or he really is again, a real lion or donkey or dog. These animals enter the all-too-human world and in so doing they open up the tradition to reconsider the position of animals in the Christian story.

So, to return to the question at hand, "Say the animal really responded?" If, as Haraway proposes, humans are together with other animals "in situated histories, situated naturecultures, in which all of the actors become who they are *in the dance of relating*," then Christianity and the Western philosophical systems that are part of its own history suffer from an imaginary, but deeply ingrained, wall. This wall assumes that humans are so Other and that human language is so unique a quality that language is our salvation. Do Christians really only have faith by language and by hearing? What an impoverished life and faith that would be and, unfortunately, is. Animals really respond; humans just cover our eyes and plug our ears in order to claim that they are mute. The speaking animals in the history of the Christian tradition invite those who have ears to hear to enter the conversation with them in order that all species might have life together, "holding in esteem, and regard, open to those who look back reciprocally. Always tripping, this kind of truth has a multispecies future. *Respecere*."[21]

❧ So Many Faces: God, Humans, and Animals

JAY McDANIEL AND J. AARON SIMMONS

In this essay we give a brief summary of the promise offered by and the problems faced by continental philosophy and process philosophy for addressing animal ontology and animal welfare, and then we turn to a constructive proposal that draws on these two traditions. First, we look at two key obstacles that can be understood as challenges to continental philosophy's ability to address animal welfare. Then, after considering some possible implications of process thought, we identify six key ideas that, in our view, can serve as springboards for sensitivity to animal alterity and the development of a life-centered ethic built on respect for animals. In the concluding section, we suggest one further step in moving toward a greater respect for animals, namely, a way in which "listening to animals" can be understood as a form of prayer.

As a final prefatory note, we want to point out that this essay is meant as an exploratory dialogue between two scholars working in process thought (McDaniel) and continental philosophy (Simmons). Accordingly, there are many points where productive disagreement continues, but it is our hope that such disagreement can be understood to occur within mutually constructive attempts to learn from each other.

ANIMAL PHILOSOPHY IN A CONTINENTAL CONTEXT

In the context of a nearly ubiquitous concern for alterity, continental philosophy might be viewed as a sustained attempt to overcome the problematic dimensions of humanism that underlie so much of modernist philosophy. It would seem, then, that continental philosophy would be a productive place to look for productive analyses of how better to understand and relate not only to human others but (perhaps especially) also to nonhuman others.

To be sure, there are portals of insight in the works of such thinkers as Friedrich Nietzsche, Martin Heidegger, Georges Bataille, Emmanuel Levinas, Michel Foucault, Gilles Deleuze and Félix Guattari, Jacques Derrida, Luc Ferry, Hélène Cixous, and Luce Irigaray—all of whom are critically considered in a book titled *Animal Philosophy*.[1] Moreover, there has been a growing interest in what is sometimes referred to as the "animal question" in continental literature since the 1990s.[2]

Nevertheless, in the eyes of some, continental philosophy has largely failed to offer new ways forward for human relations to nonhuman animals, particularly in regard to their ethical treatment. For example, in the preface to *Animal Philosophy*, Peter Singer reflects on the incredible increase of philosophical attention to the treatment of animals and then asks the following probing question:

> How much of this philosophical impetus that gave rise to a practical challenge to the way we think about nonhuman animals came from writers in the philosophical traditions of Continental Europe, from such thinkers as Heidegger, Foucault, Levinas, and Deleuze, or those who take the work of these thinkers as setting a framework for their own thoughts?[3]

To this question, Singer says that "the answer is, as far as I can judge, none." Singer's assessment, if true, is a strong indictment of continental ethics. His claim is that continental philosophy is not where one should turn in order to find significant scholarship on human-animal relations that would facilitate the ethical treatment of animals.

Although one should take issue with some dimensions of Singer's claim,[4] it is important to weigh and consider Singer's charge as an important reminder of the excesses toward which continental ethics might slide and the problematic perceptions of continental ethics that seem to show up in the literature regarding a variety of applied moral and political issues. Has continental philosophy largely been concerned about the *Other* only insofar as that Other was sufficiently like us (humans), such that this Otherism, as it were, ultimately serves to reinforce a potentially problematic humanism? For example, is Emmanuel Levinas's thoroughgoing attempt to go beyond merely "relative alterity" (otherness that is merely a modification of sameness) in the attempt to locate "absolute alterity" (otherness not defined with reference to "us") best understood as amounting to a human concern for only other humans?[5] If so, one might rightly press Levinasians about whether animals even have "faces" and if so whether they continue to stand as a merely relative alterity that exposes the potentially humanist orbit of Levinasian ethics.[6]

In this direction, the central problem would be that Levinas can seem to leave in place the sort of speciesism worried about by such prominent philosophers as Peter Singer, Tom Regan, and Holmes Rolston III. For example, even in his provocative essay about the dog "Bobby," who greeted Levinas and his fellow prisoners of war as they would be marched from the prison camp out to work each day, Levinas can certainly seem not to see the dog as interrupting the primacy of the human face as the locus of the ethical relation but instead as merely of secondary moral worth.[7] Diane Perpich nicely gives voice to this worry about Levinasian ethics as follows:

> Readers have persistently noted the absence of animal others in Levinas's philosophy. They have worried about the humanism and anthropocentrism of his ethics. They have suggested that what concern for the environment is conveyed by his works is at most an interest in stewardship of the natural world for the sake of human ends rather than a direct ethical concern with nature or ecosystems. In effect, it seems to many that Levinas, that quintessential thinker of alterity and ethics, was relatively uninterested in the alterity of animals and of the possibility of ethical claims coming from the natural environment.[8]

Though Perpich goes on to suggest that Levinasian philosophy can productively respond, at least in part, to such criticisms, it is still important to realize that such worries continue to abound in the literature. For ease of reference, let's term this objection to Levinas the *secondary status objection*.

Importantly, the secondary status objection ought not to be seen as a case limited to Levinas's specific philosophical account. Indeed, some important voices in continental philosophy have pressed similar points regarding the possible problematic tendencies within continental ethics when it comes to considering adequately the status of animals. David Wood, for example, claims that "coming to terms with the nonhuman animal, or indeed, knowing when to leave one's terms aside, is perhaps the reef on which the originality of both Heidegger's and Levinas' thinking founders."[9] Similarly, Jacques Derrida's own extended meditation on animality, specifically as displayed in the gaze of a cat, in *The Animal That Therefore I Am* does not go as far as to explicitly recommend a specific revision of human behavior such that the future looks better for cats around the world.[10] Instead, what one finds in Derrida's text is a deconstructive problematization of the ease with which human categories operate as both descriptive and also, more importantly, as normative.[11]

Although such philosophical work is productively suggestive on a number of fronts, one might wonder, along with Singer, Perpich, and Wood, whether even such an important essay as Derrida's ends up being primarily a creative exploration of alternative ways of continuing to be human rather than a fundamental challenge to the humanism that pervades historical notions of animality. Consider, for example, Wood's critique of Derrida's comment at the 1993 Cerisy Conference: "I am a vegetarian in my soul."[12] For Wood, and one would imagine for Singer and others like Tom Regan, Cass Sunstein, and Martha Nussbaum, this is likely to be perceived as insufficient. In a time of continued animal exploitation and abuse, "soul vegetarianism," as it were, doesn't appear to go far enough toward promoting what Regan means by "animal welfare." Indeed, continued debate abounds about the prescriptive implications of Derrida's deconstructive account in "Eating Well," the famous interview in which he discusses vegetarianism.[13]

In Derrida's case, the potential problem is not so much one of animals having only secondary moral standing—indeed, he is critical of Levinas and especially Heidegger on just this point—but rather it is a worry about his stopping short. It can appear that Derrida problematizes but does not prescribe. Although he brilliantly and beautifully analyzes the problems that animals present to human thought and action, it seems that he does not clearly indicate a prescriptive way forward for that thought and action. Further, while he importantly considers the depth and limits of animality, he spends less time addressing the practical responses to such depth in the context of the applied specifics that Singer and others are attempting to address. Hence, it might be suggested that for all the rhetorical, and even spiritual, weight of the notion of soul vegetarianism, it is difficult to move from it to a normative call for vegetarianism as a moral obligation and the elimination of factory farms as an ethicopolitical necessity, for example.[14] Let's term this objection to Derrida the *inadequate activism objection*.

Although we are using Levinas and Derrida to illuminate these two objections, we take these worries to be general concerns that the continental tradition's considerations of animals must be able to address. For example, Martin Heidegger's (in)famous claim that animals are "poor in world" (*Weltarm*) is a version of the secondary status objection, and Georges Bataille's conception of "the poetic fallacy of animality" displays a modification of the inadequate activism objection.[15]

In the light of these objections, it might be tempting just to abandon continental thought on this issue and turn to the Anglo-American approaches to animal philosophy praised by Singer as contributing to the betterment of animals since about 1970. In some cases, this would not be a bad idea. If one wants to get into the specifics of the legal aspects attending to animal rights, say, going to Sunstein and Nussbaum is probably a better bet than going to Deleuze and Irigaray. However, this may or may not be that much of a problem. Not all philosophers need to address every philosophical issue—just because Sunstein and Deleuze are doing different things does not make one necessarily better than the other; it all depends on what you are trying to do. Different philosophical traditions should not be seen as necessarily mutually exclusive when it comes to animal philosophy but instead as various resources on which one can draw when it is helpful to do so depending on the problem that one is trying to address.

That said, we want to affirm the importance of going beyond merely Anglo-American philosophical resources for thinking about animality. In particular, we think that continental philosophy and process thought offer resources that have not been adequately appreciated and appropriated. For example, when it comes to meta-ethical questions underlying debates about intrinsic value and anthropocentrism, Levinas, Derrida, and Heidegger might be sensible places to look for arguments with which one ought to contend (regardless of what value theory one affirms).[16] In the same vein, activism does not occur in a conceptual and linguistic vacuum. Thus Derrida's account of the otherness of the face of the cat and Bataille's conception of the human/animal distinction as a matter of poetic depth rather than algorithmic distance might help resituate the way in which we think about animals as itself being a step toward our rethinking how we treat them. In short, when it comes to animal philosophy, broadly understood, continental philosophy should be seen as a potential archive on which future scholarship can productively draw in the attempt to work out new ways forward, rather than as a repository of answers to contemporary questions. We propose, then, that the promise of continental philosophy can be glimpsed when we view it as an indirect resource for animal welfare, but its limits begin to show when we try to understand it as a direct contributor to mainstream debates about such issues. This is not a problem but is instead an opportunity for continued work in continental philosophy that attempts to make more direct contributions than has largely been the case in the past. Peter Singer, himself, nicely articulates this view when he writes:

> Just as it is possible to argue that the premises of Anglo-American thinkers who oppose racism and sexism carry logical implications that also challenge the way we treat nonhuman animals, so too the ideas of thinkers in continental traditions may point beyond the conclusions that they themselves have reached.[17]

Before moving on, we want to conclude this section by briefly mentioning a few places where we think philosophers have begun to point beyond such conclusions in quite productive ways.

Ecophenomenology

The essays included in the volume *Eco-Phenomenology: Back to the Earth Itself* provide a range of ways in which phenomenology can be made relevant to environmental thinking.[18] In brief, the promise of ecophenomenology is that it recognizes the importance of experiential adequacy in environmental philosophy, which can and should be centrally applied to animal philosophy.

Environmental Appropriations of Deconstruction

The idea that deconstruction is a resource for environmental philosophy has been most decidedly proposed by such thinkers as David Wood[19] and John Llewelyn.[20] In agreement with Wood we believe that deconstruction stands as a constant challenge to complacency but might need to be pushed further than where Derrida himself goes in his important essays on relations to nonhumans. In agreement with Llewelyn, we think that it is likely that the religious dimensions in Derrida will serve as fecund loci for further thought in environmental philosophy. Additionally, in 2012 William Edelglass, James Hatley, and Christian Diehm edited a book on Levinas and environmental thought that is especially promising as a model for what an applied continental environmental philosophy might look like.[21]

Comparative Continental Ethics

By "comparative," here, we mean two things. On the one hand, we are thinking of those scholars who have begun to put continental philosophy into dialogue with alternative cultural traditions. For example, the work of William Edelglass on Levinas and Asian philosophy stands as a shining model of how such engagements can be transformative in both directions (especially given Edelglass's own impressive appreciation of environmental philosophy). Also, although not directly concerned with animals, the collection titled *Deconstruction and the Ethical in Asian Thought*, edited by Youru Wang,[22] includes essays that explore the porous boundaries between these traditions that need to be more fully engaged. On the other hand, we are thinking of those scholars who attempt to work constructively between the continental and Anglo-American traditions by drawing on both in the effort to open new spaces for thinking and action.[23] Such comparative work is beginning to make Peter Singer's distinction between the helpful Anglo-American philosophy and the not-so-helpful continental philosophy difficult consistently to maintain.

In all of these areas, we find reasons to be hopeful for the future of continental contributions, both to environmental philosophy and also to animal welfare.

᠅

Although more examples could be offered, these three areas illustrate that continental philosophy offers fecund resources for the future of philosophical engagements with nonhuman others. However, it would be a mistake to think that continental philosophy is the only place to turn when looking for alternative conceptual archives for animal philosophy. First and importantly, there is cognitive science, which we will consider below. Additionally and as already indicated, Asian philosophy is also becoming a prominent resource in the contemporary debates. We will be employing some ideas from Chinese thought in our own constructive endeavor. Finally, the tradition of process philosophy, especially as exemplified in the work of Alfred North Whitehead, stands as a valuable archive on which to draw. Let us concede at the outset that Whitehead and process thinkers have been variously charged with versions of the secondary status and inadequate activism objections and yet have been famously, and frequently, cited as a crucial wellspring from which such influential environmental thinkers as John Cobb[24] and Clare Palmer[25] have drawn. For Levinas and Derrida, these two objections should not be seen as devastating refutations, but pressing worries that should animate our engagements with their thought.[26] The same is true for a Whiteheadian process approach to animal philosophy.

There is an important deconstructive strand to process thinking insofar as it seeks to deconstruct habitual binaries of human thought, to criticize assumptions concerning a one-to-one correspondence of language and something called "reality," to criticize substantialist understandings of self and world, and to criticize notions that any philosophical perspective—including process philosophy—derives from an ahistorical perspective, on the basis of which finality of statement can be achieved.[27] Process thinkers, like their continental counterparts, are suspicious of easy claims to certainty; and process thinkers, like continental philosophers, are critical of attempts to disambiguate the world by pretending that the world, or language about the world, can and should always be clear and distinct. As Whitehead suggests, it is often the case that the most important things are those that remain vague.

Deconstruction can be most promisingly appropriated for ethical and political existence when it is understood to be a continuing call for going beyond where we had been previously. Its strength is located not in its definitive answers to questions about animal rights or anthropocentrism but in its challenge to the dominance of humanism as a conceptual framework. Deconstruction and process philosophy are both best understood as invitations to continued inquiry, but that inquiry, itself, can and should invite us to inhabit the world differently in relation to our animal neighbors.

A WHITEHEADIAN CONTRIBUTION

Process philosophy consists of thinkers who seek to solve conceptual problems by appeal to Whitehead's cosmology and to others who self-consciously "think in a Whiteheadian mode" by extending in novel ways the spirit of his thinking to topics he did not address. In this respect process philosophy bears important resemblance to analogous trajectories in the continental tradition, as cited above. Our aim in this section is to think in a Whiteheadian mode about possible process resources for animal philosophy. When Whitehead-influenced thinkers consider animals, two questions function as guiding aims: (1) How might Whitehead's philosophy help deconstruct modern humanisms which relegate animals to secondary ontological status and which disregard practical matters of animal welfare? And (2) how can Whitehead's philosophy help reconstruct understandings of animals which help awaken humans to their beauty and intrinsic value, thereby inspiring a sense of awe and respect and encouraging their respectful treatment?

Three points must be made at the outset. First, as with Levinas, Whitehead did not take animality, as such, as a primary interest. Nonetheless, he was interested in animal life, including animal subjectivity, and we think that his thought contains many resources for developing an animal-sensitive, postanthropocentric philosophy. Second, most process thinkers influenced by Whitehead—with a few important exceptions—have not devoted attention to resources within Whitehead that help overcome humanisms and encourage respect for animals. They have seen humans as dwelling within the wider web of life, but, with the exception of human individuals, they have been more interested in the web itself than in the individual nodes. Third, those Whiteheadian thinkers who have taken animals as special subjects of interest have typically not been part of the dominant conversations in philosophy on these subjects. There are at least five thinkers in the process tradition who have developed ethics for animal welfare and who, along the way, have in particular wrestled with the question of vegetarianism: John Cobb, Charles Birch, Dan Dombrowski, Charles Hartshorne, and Jay McDaniel. A 2011 article by Jan Deckers on their work argues that if they are consistent with their own Whiteheadian worldviews, they will recognize that "minimal moral veganism is therefore *required* from those who adopt a Whiteheadian worldview (or a worldview inspired by Whitehead's views)."[28] Accordingly, the development of a Whiteheadian ethic may be more a matter of being consistent with elements of Whitehead's thought that have heretofore been neglected. Birch and Cobb (1981) are especially important in this regard, since, on Whiteheadian grounds, they explicitly adopt and encourage the guidelines developed by the Humane Society of the United States, which deal not only with the eating of animals but also with the treatment of pets, animals as subjects to experimentation, and animals in the wild. Similar to the need for continental attempts to dig deeper into their own philosophical traditions for untapped resources for addressing legitimate problems with some continental approaches to non-humans, there is also need for Whiteheadian thinkers to admit limitations in Whiteheadian thought and then build on possible spaces where such limitations might be overcome.

How to do this?[29] Even as continental and process philosophers engage in important dialogue about animal philosophy—as occurs in the present volume, for example—we all must recognize that since there is already a great deal of constructive work being done by philosophers and psychologists on animal consciousness,[30] we should be wary of restricting the conversation too narrowly to continental and process texts and thinkers. One of the leading questions being addressed in contemporary cognitive science, for example, concerns whether animals do or do not grasp an appearance/reality distinction, which is a cardinal sign for what we call "consciousness." Words such as *seems* and *looks* and *appears* are taken to be verbal markers for consciousness. Accordingly, drawing on the literature in cognitive science and philosophy of mind, we might ask: Do animals have subjective states that correlate with these words, even as they do not have a language we recognize for expressing them? Donald Davidson argues that animals do not have the kinds of psychological states required for consciousness: beliefs, desires, and, most important, thoughts.[31] In response, Robert Lurz suggests that Davidson wrongly presupposes that facts about our language should tell us about whether animals have thoughts, beliefs, and desires.[32] By contrast, claims Lurz, the question of consciousness in animals can be addressed through experiments in the cognitive sciences. Experiments, not speculation, can help us determine the answer to the question. Lurz recognizes, however, that experiments are never undertaken in the absence of theories in terms of which the experiments are conceived. Thus he is interested in theorizing, too, and perhaps this is the place where process thinkers and continental philosophers can both productively enter into discussions with cognitive science regarding animality.

Whiteheadians and Levinasians, in particular, will likely appreciate two aspects of Lurz's project: (1) that conscious psychological states do not require language and (2) that experiments inevitably presuppose theories, which guide the interpretation of data.[33] What Whitehead's philosophy and Levinas's philosophy might offer, then, are specific theories that can be used in the design and implementation of experiments concerning animal consciousness.

SIX IDEAS FOR A GUIDING THEORY

Let's look specifically at possible aspects of a theoretical framework that draws on both Whitehead and Levinas. We think that such a model might consist of at least six core ideas—some ideas are more Whiteheadian and some are more Levinasian, but we think that together they offer a promising theoretical lens for future study.

1. *Animals are concrescing subjects.* They are subjects in the sense that, moment by moment, they have feelings and beliefs that belong to them and not to others; they make decisions on their own, guided by their own subjective aims; they have spatiotemporal-emotional perspectives of their own. These five elements—feelings, beliefs, decisions, aims, and perspective—coalesce into a single reality in the ongoing life of the animal: his or her lived subjectivity. Animals are concrescing subjects in the sense that, as they enjoy or suffer their feelings, and as they make their decisions, they are responding to the many influences they receive from their pasts and the surrounding world. Moment by moment, they are constituted, not only by their subjective feelings and beliefs and decisions but also by their own past experiences, by the chemistry within their bodies, and by other actualities in the world. These past experiences and bodily occurrences, as well as the other actualities in their surroundings, are part of the many that become one in their experience. Thus animals are living examples of the many becoming one. Their subjectivity is the activity of the many becoming one. It is not a thing or an entity but rather a process. As Levinas might say, the relation precedes the terms of the relation. How the many become one is who an animal is in the moment at hand. The animal's alterity, then, is not simply who he or she is, but also how he or she is. Every individual animal has his or her own way of being-in-the-world. Every individual animal has his or her individualized dao (道). Or, again, in Levinasian terms, each animal presents itself from itself and on its own terms. As Derrida might say, "Every other [animal] is absolutely other."[34]

2. *Understanding animals requires imagination as well as observation.* When cognitive scientists undertake experiments with animals, and when philos-

ophers and theologians reflect on animals, they are trying to understand the dao (道)—the subjective way—of the individual animal. Typically, they are also interested in how this way might illustrate the general way of being in the world of the kind or species of which the individual animal is an example. Such understanding requires more than observation, visual or otherwise. It also involves imagination or perspective-taking, in which a person tries to imagine himself or herself inside the life of the animal from the animal's point of view, and also empathy—that is, a sharing in the feelings of the animals. Understanding animals is not simply a science but also an art. It is rightly restrained by humility: that is, by a recognition that animal subjectivity may be quite different from what humans might imagine. Thus it must strike a balance between two potential fallacies: a *pathetic fallacy*, which projects onto the animal forms of human subjectivity that are not in the animal at all, and a *prosaic fallacy*, which so emphasizes the alterity of the animal—the strangeness of the animal's dao (道)—that the animal ends up being reduced to a bare singularity, devoid of life or consciousness.

3. Animals, like humans, can experience the world consciously or transconsciously. The consciousness that human beings and other animals enjoy and suffer is but the tip of the experiential iceberg. Drawing on Levinas's phenomenology of desire and need, we might say that consciousness is but one type of subjectivity, amid which a concrescing subject clearly perceives an item or items in his or her world, sensitive to the contrast between the fact that it is appearing, and the fact that it might not have appeared at all. Most experience—nonhuman animal as well as human—is nonconscious: that is, lacking in the quality of clear and distinct awareness but nevertheless powerful, important, dim, vague, rich, and complex. New phenomenological discussions of nonintentional intuition are possible resources here.[35] The richness of experience, whether conscious or nonconscious, is an aesthetic richness, in that it involves two qualities found in music: harmony and intensity. Animals and their human counterparts are continually seeking harmony and intensity, or some combination thereof. In a word, they are seeking beauty. Not so much the beauty of a painting or another work of art, but the beauty of enjoying the world harmoniously or intensely, or both. The satisfaction of hunger, the pursuit and enjoyment of sex, and the pleasures of sleep are all forms of beauty. Psychological states are themselves states-in-process, always indebted to a past and conditioned by given situations, and always in search of beauty.

4. *All animals are different from one another and from their pasts.* It is one thing to say that a given species of animal enjoys a certain kind of consciousness and still another to say that they enjoy the same kind of consciousness. Animals are different in many ways. First, every instance of animal subjectivity has its own unique qualities, none of which is reducible to the abstractions by which humans might try to understand them. To forget this is to fall into the fallacy of misplaced concreteness, amid which we forget that concrescing subjects are never contained within the conceptual headings under which we might try to subsume them. Animals are different, then, in that they differ from one another, even when members of the same species or kind, and, of course, from human beings. Second, every instance of animal subjectivity is different from preceding instances in the life of that animal, even though habitual patterns of feeling, belief, decision, and aim are repeated. Every moment is a new moment, and animals are the moments of their lives. Just as no human person steps into the same river twice, because the river is changing and he or she is, too, so no nonhuman animal steps into the same river twice, because he or she, too, is changing over time. To respect difference in animals is to respect who they are in the moments of their lives and also how they are changing over time. Developmental psychology applies to animals, too. In the language of Levinas and Derrida, we might say that this developmental reality is always constituted by the relation to others.

5. *Animals are beckoned by, and carriers of, a holy spirit.* Let the word *divine* refer to a spirit of goodness and beauty at work in the world, present throughout the planet, to which individual creatures and communities of creatures can respond in their respective ways, and by which they are called into the forms of beauty available to them. Here we use the word *spirit* to refer to what Whitehead calls the initial phase of the subjective aim of an emerging occasion of experience: that is, to the guiding lure, derived from God, for the ideal satisfaction relative to the conditions at hand. This spirit is akin to the breathing, or *ruah*, of which the Bible speaks, and it may or may not be conjoined with images of a divine concrescing subject to whom it belongs. As animals are drawn to find that satisfaction available to them in the various circumstances of their lives, they, too, are beckoned

by this spirit into whatever beauty is possible for them, just as humans are beckoned. Perhaps this is a concrete way of appropriating Derrida's notion of "hauntology" for animal philosophy.

6. *Animals deserve and demand ethical respect.* As concrescing subjects, individual animals are indeed subjects of ethical regard and not simply subjects of ontological rhapsody. They seek to live with satisfaction relative to the situation at hand; their very seeking imposes an ethical obligation on human beings, who are animals, too. It is true that, in order to live, human beings must kill animals or at least kill other living beings who seek satisfaction in their lives, even if primarily at a cellular level: plants and bacteria, for example. The lines are not sharp between these different forms of life, so guidelines are needed for ethical decision making. It is best to recognize that different kinds of subjectivity deserve and demand respect and that, even as it might be desirable, not all animals can be treated with equal respect. If, as Whitehead says, life is robbery, we must rob as lightly and gently as possible. As inspired by the ahimsa traditions of South and East Asia, and partly inspired by themes of compassion within the Abrahamic faiths, a responsible animal ethic must be based on two principles: a respect for the individual well-being of animals on their own terms and for their own sake, and a recognition of the instrumental value of animals and all forms of life for the weblike systems of which they are a part, as exemplified, for example, in predator-prey relations. From a Whiteheadian point of view, there is beauty or value in the lives of the individual animals and in the communities of which they are a part. Sometimes, as in predator-prey relations, the well-being of a community requires the sacrifice of an individual, even as there is tragedy in the sacrifice. When human beings enter the picture, guidelines are needed—as Levinas explains, we move from ethics to politics when relationships are plural. In general, the greater an individual animal's capacity for suffering in the present and then suffering from the memory of that suffering in the future, the greater the responsibility to do no harm to that animal.[36]

TOWARD A RELATIONAL SENSIBILITY

Let us assume that process thought and continental philosophy both indeed offer alternative conceptual archives for animal philosophy. Recall David Wood's words: "Coming to terms with the non-human animal, or indeed, knowing when to leave one's terms aside, is perhaps the reef on which the originality of both Heidegger's and Levinas' thinking founders." How can these terms be set aside, and how would one have such knowledge? Perhaps one way is to articulate a theological sensibility that draws on a way of thinking about divinity to help foster a "coming to terms" with the nonhuman animal. Here, in the light of the suggestion that comparative continental ethics is an important way forward, continental philosophy and process thought both might do well to draw on the idea of "sensibility," not as developed in Kant's dichotomy between reason and sensibility, but perhaps as proposed in some strands of Chinese thought. We will conclude, then, with something of a suggestive hypothesis. What follows is not meant to be a definitive proposal, but a thought worth considering by both continental philosophers and process thinkers. We offer potential points of contact between these two philosophical traditions that might emerge in the context of a framework inspired by a Chinese conception of relational sensibility.[37]

Historically there has never been a sharp separation of thinking and feeling in Chinese culture. The very characters which are translated by the English word *intelligence* are illustrative. The characters are 聰明. The first character is 聰 (cōng) and is composed of four parts. 耳 means ear; 眼 means eye; 口 means mouth and 心 means heart. The second character is composed of two parts: 日 means the sun, and 月 means the moon. In this character, sun and moon mean something like light. When we have the sun or the moon, something is illuminated so that we can see clearly. Think of the English-language phrase "to shed light on something." It is as if the sun and moon were shining on something, so that we can see clearly. Where, then, can light be found? 聰明 tells us that our lives are illuminated—that we find truths to live by—when we use our ears to listen, our eyes to see and observe, our mouth to talk or communicate, and our hearts to feel. "Intelligence" does not come from logical thinking and rational inference alone; it comes from the whole person as he or she is engaged with the world with his or her senses, listening, seeing, speaking with others, and, of course, feeling.

The idea that intelligence is an activity of the whole person is consonant with Whiteheadian thinking as well as continental philosophy. Recall Whitehead's idea of *concrescence*, which is the idea that at every moment of our lives we are experiencing the world through various kinds of prehensions: intellectual, emotional, recollective, anticipatory, and sensory. These prehensions are acts of taking into account other things: the feelings of others, memories, future possibilities, and material objects in the world. Similarly, Heidegger's conception of "being-in-the-world," Levinas's careful analysis of desire and need, Michel Henry's sophisticated consideration of affectation, and Judith Butler's proposal regarding performed identity are all ways in which an expansive relationality might be understood to undergird a conception of intelligence as a possibility only in the context of a world with others.[38]

Who, then, are the others whose feelings we might feel? One might worry, here, that the very idea that we can feel the feelings of others at all much less animals can be dangerous for continental thinkers who are interested in absolute alterity. The idea can be understood to presuppose a kind of intimacy that can be dishonest and disrespectful: (1) dishonest, so it seems, because we have no clear knowledge of what other animals are perceiving and thinking, given the fact that we are inevitably locked within our human perspectives; and (2) disrespectful, perhaps, because in presuming that we do know something about them, we subsume them into our worlds and fail to allow them to present themselves, on their own terms (as Levinas would say, *kath auto*).[39] Whitehead's idea of concrescence calls both of these arguments into question. His philosophy entails the view that humans are not entirely locked within our human ways of perceiving and thinking because in fact we feel the feelings of other more-than-human actualities all the time: namely, the feelings—the energetic resonances—that dwell within our own bodies. In feeling the feelings of the cellular activities within our bodies, the cellular realities form part of our own identities. We are embodied, and in our embodiment we are more than human even as we are also human. Being human is only part of our identity. It is perhaps in this regard that Wood is right to wonder about the Heideggerian "terms," which at least in his early thought focus so decidedly on the analytic of Dasein.

Moreover, with his idea of hybrid prehensions Whitehead's philosophy is open to the possibility that we can have mind-to-mind connections with other animals, as pet owners are likely to understand.[40] To paraphrase the Buddhist writer Thich Nhat Hanh, we humans are internally composed of nonhuman elements. The very category of *human* is problematic if, in employing it in our discourse, we presuppose that we and others are strictly or exhaustively human.

The Whiteheadian perspective goes a step further. It suggests that we can feel the feelings of the divine reality. This does not mean that we directly prehend the consciousness of a separate being named "God" and then report what we have prehended. Rather, it means that we enter into what might be called the divine sensibility, sharing in a love in heaven that floods into a love on earth. As entered into by human beings, this sensibility will be to imagine the world from the point of view of other animals, trustful that those points of view are part of—and known by—divinity. Picture a horse trainer or a wildlife biologist who specializes in the habits of grackles. As she imagines the world from a horse's perspective, or a grackle's perspective, she is entering into the divine sensibility. She can be said to be, in her own way, "putting on the mind of God." Though this is certainly a Whiteheadian approach, it is possible to see points of resonance with continental philosophy as well. For example, Derrida's rethinking of God in *The Gift of Death* can be importantly appropriated as not disconnected to his other works thinking through "the animal question."[41] Indeed, perhaps as Nietzsche understood so well, thinking about the human is always already to think both about the animal and God such that we begin to see, again, that "Every other [animal] is absolutely other."[42]

Extending these possible points of contact, we should say that, of course, as implied by the weight and depth of the "tout autre," taking on the "mind of God" would not be something that one can do completely or infallibly. One can always be corrected by further information from the horses and grackles, as well as one's neighbor next door. But in constantly attempting to do so, one potentially learns something about the divine reality itself, for the divine reality includes more—as Levinas and Derrida would say, infinitely more—than the human experiences that are part of it. In Whitehead's language, God is "a fellow sufferer who understands" each living being on its own terms and for its own sake. In a more deconstructive vocabulary, the trace of God "appears" in the face of the Other. When made concrete, we can say that the horse trainer, the wildlife biologist, the religious practitioner, and the philosopher or theologian are all seeking to participate in divine consciousness insofar as they seek to understand the others with whom they share the world, and to some extent they are doing so. As Levinas so rightly points out, the fact that the Other "overflows comprehension" does not mean that the Other is incomprehensible.[43] The very act of thus participating requires a kind of faith: a faith that there is more to life than human points of view can ever fully understand. This more-ness, or excess, as gathered into the unity of the divine life, is part of the divine transcendence; and it can be said to include animal points of view.

To be sure, this way of understanding divinity is likely to push against the bounds of some classical and supernaturalistic accounts of theism. It is, to use the language of process thought, likely to be described as panen-theistic. On such a Whiteheadian model, the fundamental idea is that the word *God* names a concrescing subject—everywhere at once—in whom the many of the universe become one, again and again, forever. This sub-ject is not entirely separate from the universe, but not entirely identical with it either. This subject is a reality who hears the prayers of human beings and who also hears the prayers of other living beings, whose very lives are prayers for satisfaction, relative to the situation at hand.[44] These prayers may well be at odds with one another. As the fox chases the rabbit, the fox prays for a satisfaction of hunger, and the rabbit prays for a satis-faction of safety. Both can be heard as legitimate prayers. Both are heard by the adventure of the universe as one. The panentheistic sensibility lies in human attempts to hear those prayers, too, humbly recognizing that human terms—whatever they might be—are limited and by no means in-clusive of the experiences that are part of the divine life. In addition to this panentheistic account, however, it is at least plausible that an alternative, and perhaps even more straightforwardly, though not "classical," theistic account could also countenance the basic idea that the relation to God is something always undertaken and lived out in relation to others, as pro-posed by many in both the process and the continental perspectives.[45]

For both continental and process thinkers, it is reasonable to suggest that in beholding the face of the cat, we see the face of God, too. So many faces. As many as there are creatures. In the beginning are the differences, and they delight God.

❧ A Spiritual Democracy of All God's Creatures: Ecotheology and the Animals of Lynn White Jr.

MATTHEW T. RILEY

As the inadvertent founder, it would seem, of the Theology of Ecology, I confess amusement at the speed with which the Churches have abandoned the old scion of Man's Dominion over Nature for the equally Biblical position of Man's Trusteeship of Nature. Since the Churches remain, despite some competition, the chief forges for hammering out values, this is important. I feel that before too long, however, they will find themselves going on to the third legitimately Biblical position, that Man is part of a democracy of all God's creatures, organic and inorganic, each praising his Maker according to the law of its being.
—WHITE, "A Remark from Lynn Townsend White, Jr."

This quote reveals a Lynn Townsend White, jr.,[1] that few know. Since its original publication in 1967, White's "The Historical Roots of Our Ecologic Crisis"[2] has been a source of continuous debate and controversy in the field of religion and ecology. Hundreds of books and articles, many of them by ecotheologians, have been written as a direct response to it.[3] Whether familiar with White's article or not, many have absorbed his now highly debated and frequently misunderstood thesis that "Christianity bears a huge burden of guilt" for the ecological crisis.[4] The field of ecotheology, especially in its earliest stages, largely shaped itself as a response to the accusations leveled at Christianity by White.[5] These include, but are not limited to, the ecological culpability of a biblically inspired attitude of dominion over nature, the environmental impact of anthropocentrism, and the degree to which Christianity has laid the foundations for the development of science and technology.

In response to this reductionistic view of White as merely a critic of Christianity, I wish to propose a different approach for understanding his work. As others, such as the theological ethicist Willis Jenkins and the historian Elspeth Whitney have already noted, the scholarship that has emerged from the controversy surrounding White's thesis has fixated almost exclusively on his environmental critiques of Christianity and the dominion-stewardship debate. I share Jenkins's and Whitney's concern that these tightly bounded interpretations of White have obfuscated the nuance and depth of his thesis and, by extension, limited the development of alternative ways of understanding the relationship between religion and ecology.[6] The narrow focus of most responses to White is primarily due, I believe, to the tendency of those who utilize White's ideas to not read beyond his "Historical Roots" article.[7]

In this essay, I suggest that a fairer assessment and a more accurate understanding of White is possible only when "Historical Roots" is read in the context of White's larger body of work. What I hope to demonstrate in the brief glimpse into his texts offered in this chapter is that White's intellectual engagement with animals was complex and frequent and offers an intriguing invitation to read his work on ecology as part of a larger theologically oriented project. In order to accomplish this task I include evidence from a wide sampling of his early publications and his numerous historical texts on technology, but I focus particularly on his publications on religion and ecology, such as "Historical Roots," "Continuing the Conversation," "Christian Impact on Ecology," "A Remark from Lynn White, Jr.," "Snake Nests and Icons," "Christians and Nature," "Commentary on St. Francis of Assisi," and "The Future of Compassion." What emerges when texts such as these are read together, rather than focusing on "Historical Roots" as a stand-alone piece, is not the work of an iconoclast, but the attempts of a scholar working across disciplines to apply his ideas constructively to an issue that he cares deeply about: the worsening ecological crisis and the potential of his own faith, Christianity, to help solve the dilemma. At the core of White's thought is an impassioned, albeit largely overlooked, theological interest in human relationships with other creatures.[8]

My goal, then, is twofold: First, throughout this chapter I draw attention to White's attitudes toward creatures by highlighting the presence and the ontological complexity of animals in White's texts and the prominent place that they inhabit in his constructive theological claims. Second, and more important, I show that reading beyond "Historical Roots" to understand the content and depth of his larger body of work reveals White's central and radical theological postulate that all creatures—whether animal, human, or something altogether different—are part of a "spiritual democracy of all God's creatures."[9] White is best understood, I argue, not just as a critic of Christianity but also as a prophetic Christian voice.

A NATURALLY THEOLOGICAL MIND

Before White's attitudes toward animals can be examined, it is first necessary to rethink how White is understood as a scholar. Although widely recognized for his thesis in "Historical Roots," it is essential to note that White spent the better part of his fifty-year publishing career as an influential historian of medieval European technology.[10] Reading beyond "Historical Roots," however, reveals both a complicated thinker and an engagement with a wide array of topics and scholarly methodologies that extends far beyond the academic scope of a historian of medieval technology. In short, White's writings, much like White himself, defy easy categorization. By reading from a broad selection of White's texts, several tractable themes can be identified and traced through the decades of his long career.

Distinctly layered among the strata of White's historical publications runs a continuous and forward-looking interest in religion and religious values. From his 1938 dissertation on medieval Sicilian monasteries to his final published works in the mid-1980s, White strove to understand the role of religion in shaping history.[11] Most, but not all, of these historical studies were attempts to make sense of the role that religious ideas and values played in shaping the use and development of technology. Technology, in his estimation, was a morally ambiguous phenomenon. In a wide range of texts, such as his 1961 "What Accelerated Technological Progress in the Western Middle Ages?,"[12] White praised the relationship between humanistic religious values and technological progress. The moral endorsement of technology by Christianity, he argued, was historically a liberating force in society that freed humans from mindless toil and drudgery. The shift in religious values away from animism and toward a more humanistic set of medieval Christian values allowed humans to replace human labor with animal and machine power. He spoke of teams of oxen, when yoked to new plow technology, for instance, as "a new power-engine" that freed people from meaningless labor.[13] Yet later that same decade White would begin focusing on the hidden ecological costs of this historical change in values. This shifting of the religious moral landscape and its impact on technological development was, for White, a conundrum that he continued to struggle with through his career as a historian as well as in his later writing on ecology.[14] These sediments and complexities in his thought, however, remain largely unearthed by White's ecotheological legatees.

Furthermore, it is essential to note that even when he was writing as a historian, White's interest in religion was more than academic. Throughout his life, White was an active and vocal Presbyterian,[15] and more important, he was explicit about the role his faith played in his work as a scholar. In an article written in 1961, "The Social Responsibility of Scholarship,"[16] to name one of the many instances where White couched his work in Christian terms, he described the work of a historian as an ongoing act of social responsibility that was rooted in religious purpose. "The professional historian," maintained White, "believes that his particular discipline has a peculiarly important spiritual function."[17] Scholarship was, in his words, "a profound emotional commitment, a 'calling,' a vocation in the religious sense."[18] So pervasive was White's own Christianity within his work that he was prone to describing his scholarly papers as his "sermons."[19]

That White's Christian beliefs were a defining personal characteristic that shaped his entire body of work was well known to his fellow historians. According to his friend and colleague Bert S. Hall, White's "deep [religious] convictions informed his writings in many ways."[20] Continuing, Hall states, "White regarded himself as both a defender of an old faith and as a pioneer. His old faith was a twofold belief in Christianity and humane letters; his role as a pioneer was to place technology into intimate connection with both."[21] This sense of religious purpose, along with White's willingness to formulate his academic arguments from a religious standpoint, remains clear throughout a significant portion of his published work. It also serves to undergird the prophetic Christian voice employed in his later works on religion and ecology.

White's religious commitments also provided the moral basis for his lifelong dedication to a broad range of social justice issues, about which he tirelessly wrote. Although evident throughout his expansive body of work, a few of his earliest publications from the 1940s and 1950s provide striking examples of the evolution of his thought. Shortly into his promising career as a young historian, the social upheaval brought on by World War II challenged some of the humanistic values that White held dear. During this time, he published several speeches and articles denouncing racism and extolling the virtues of democracy.[22] Additionally, he advocated for women's rights to better secondary education in texts such as his book *Educating Our Daughters: A Challenge to the Colleges.*[23] Undergirding these seemingly disparate subjects is White's belief in the inherent worth of each individual, an aversion to aggression, and an affinity for egalitarianism. His dedication to these democratic and humanistic ideals flowed from his Christian faith and shaped his scholarship for the duration of his career. His belief in the inherent worth and autonomy of the individual human, as well as his commitment to democracy, eventually evolved and expanded to include nonhumans, as evidenced in his later writing on ecology and religion in the last twenty years of his life. This concern for social justice issues stemmed from White's vantage point as a Christian. He felt that racism and aggression, for instance, grew out of a deep spiritual void and a sense of profound loneliness. Christianity, he believed, offered the spiritual, emotional, and moral solutions to these larger issues.[24]

Thus the tendency within ecotheological circles to downplay White's religious convictions runs counter to White's view of his work as religiously inspired. "Sometimes I claim to be the founder of the theology of ecology," he stated with his customary balance of acumen and self-deprecating wit in an audio interview, "but no one takes me seriously."[25] Indeed, although most scholars do not go so far as to label him as anti-Christian, few, if any, recognize that he was arguing from a religiously informed standpoint. It is not uncommon, for instance, for scholars to categorize White as a "secular" scholar.[26] This type of erasure via omission, I argue, is counterproductive to fairly assessing the nuances and deeply animal-friendly themes in White's thought.

Although it would be a stretch to label White a theologian, a title that he avoided, he does attempt to be more than a historian of medieval technology. Looking back on his writings in an autobiographical piece titled "History and Horseshoe Nails" published in 1970, White reflected on his tendencies to think theologically in his work as a historian. In addition to being raised as "the son of a liberal Calvinist professor of Christian ethics," White also explained that he was a graduate of Union Theological Seminary, where he studied theology "at the feet of the most passionate neo-

Augustinian of our times, Reinhold Niebuhr."[27] Taken together, claimed White, these experiences led him to favor theological explanations of historical change. "I have," he wrote, "a *mens naturaliter theologica*."[28]

His "naturally theological mind," as it were, shaped not just his writings as a historian but also his work on religion and the environment. What becomes clear if White's work is read in toto, rather than focusing on his "Historical Roots" article alone, is that White is no outsider to Christianity, nor can his scholarship be viewed as that of a secular historian. White was, more often than not, writing from a Christian standpoint, and he was interpreting Christian beliefs and texts to make theologically normative claims. Acknowledging this, in tandem with paying attention to his attitudes toward animals, should change the way White is understood by scholars.

WHITE'S CREATURES

Employing his theological approach to interpreting history, and in timely concurrence with the budding environmental movement in the late 1960s, White applied his keen historian's eye to the ecological crisis. It is in these writings on religion and ecology, I suggest, that paying close attention to White's attitudes toward animals most clearly reveals a different portrait of White than most are acquainted with. Perhaps the best way to attempt a recovery of White's prophetic theological voice, and to make sense of the peculiar presence of animals in his texts, is to seek out instances where White describes the impact of creatures on his own theological understanding of the relationship between humans and their environment. Six years after publishing his now infamous thesis, White penned a book chapter called "Continuing the Conversation" in which he expanded on his argument in "Historical Roots" and answered some of the complaints of his critics. In that text, White described the pivotal moment where he first began to perceive the connection between religious ideas and ecological attitudes. Here, to underscore the pivotal role that animals played in his thought, is the same anecdote, paraphrased, that White used to begin that article:

"The roots of my personal theology of ecology," wrote White, "go back to a time before I had heard the word *ecology*."[29] The year was 1926 and a young Lynn Townsend White, jr., had traveled to Ceylon. There he witnessed the efforts of colonial officials to cut roads through the dense, green jungles of the island's interior in order to expedite the shipping of tea. In the midst of these developing roadways, White observed conspicuous cones of earth that the local, non-British workers had left standing in the otherwise level paths through the thick vegetation. When he asked what the cones were, he was told that they were snakes' nests and that the laborers had left them undisturbed out of respect for the animals that lived there. "They were spared not because the workmen were afraid of snakes," White remarked, "but because of a feeling by the workers that the snake had a right to its house so long as it wanted to stay there."[30] He reported that this was because the local laborers were Buddhists, and their religious beliefs and values invited them to see animals much differently than their overseers saw them. "Many of the officials seemed to be Scots," he observed, "and it occurred to me that if the men with the shovels in their hands likewise had been Presbyterians the snakes would have fared less well."[31]

This chance encounter with snakes, White went on to explain, led him to his first insights regarding the relationship between religious ideas and ecological attitudes and actions.[32] In other words, it was, as just noted, the "roots" from which his "personal theology of ecology" grew. Recognizing that an encounter with an animal was a seminal moment in the formation of his thought, in and of itself, does not necessarily challenge scholars to reread his work with an eye toward animals. However, this inclusion of snakes is not an isolated incident. A close reading of White's texts reveals a surprising abundance of creatures scattered through his entire body of work. His writings on religion and ecology, in particular, seem to have animals leaping out from nearly every page. There are sacred cows, rejoicing birds, a repenting wolf, industrious ants, plow-pulling oxen, whales, squirrels, pigs, fish, wild animals, domesticated animals, spontaneously generating toads, abalone-eating sea otters, caribou, pets, religionless dinosaurs, and even swarms of not so "theologically minded" grasshoppers.[33] Even his "Historical Roots" article teems with life. On the first page alone, in order to support his argument that the relationship between living things and their environment is far more complex than most realize, White discussed more than a half-dozen species of animals, including environment-altering coral polyps, the "monster mammals of the Pleistocene," dwindling flocks of sparrows, manure-producing horses, overhunted and extinct European aurochs, the myxomatosis virus, rabbits, and, of course, humans.[34] Yet despite this superabundance of creatures, scholars have been largely abstemious in mentioning them in their analyses of White's thesis.

SAINT FRANCIS AND THE SPIRITUAL AUTONOMY OF CREATURES

Returning once again to White's theological approach to understanding history, the question remains as to what connection, if any, exists between the ubiquitous presence of animals in his texts and his constructive theological claims. White's thesis, in its simplest form, is essentially a postulate that the contemporary ecological crisis, historically understood, has its roots in Latinized medieval Christianity.[35] Whereas others have devoted considerable attention to White's discussion—or lack thereof—of the biblical mandate to have dominion over the Earth in the Genesis text, an important scholarly conversation that has emerged out of his rich and complex thesis,[36] I wish to highlight an equally significant aspect of his multifaceted argument: the erasure of the subjectivity and the spirituality of nonhuman creatures. Although clearly included for a variety of reasons, White brought in many of the animals in his writings on ecology to make the case that Christianity has lost—and needs to recover—its appreciation for other creatures as autonomous spiritual beings.

An important feature of Latinized medieval Christianity that led to the ecological crisis, White thought, was the triumph of Christianity over paganism. He posited that Christianity's attempts to eradicate paganism and its accompanying animistic view of the world laid down the ethical, psychological, religious, and social foundations that would later allow thinkers, such as Descartes, to proclaim animals to be nothing more than mere machines. This replacement of an animistic understanding of nature with a materialistic one, in turn, allowed all of nature—including animals—to be viewed as objects that could be exploited for human ends. "This indifference to the possibility of autonomy in other creatures," White wrote in "Continuing the Conversation," "has much facilitated our style of technology and thus has been a major force in polluting our globe."[37]

White continued to pursue this line of thought in a variety of texts. In both "Historical Roots" and in "Continuing the Conversation," White maintained that this indifference to the autonomy of other creatures and the extirpation of animistic understanding of nature from Christian theology and Western thought constituted a key theological hurdle to overcome. If the eradication of animistic understandings of nature led to an indifference to (and exploitation of) nature, then recovering such a view might be of help in reversing or slowing the ecological crisis. "The religious problem," he enigmatically wrote in "Continuing the Conversation," "is to find a viable equivalent to animism."[38] But he offered little explanation in his two most well known publications regarding what he meant by this. Fortunately, his other texts that have thus far existed outside the purview of most ecotheologians do contain more clues.

Church and Society staff member David Gill interviewed White during his visit to the World Council of Churches headquarters in Geneva. The transcript of the interview was published in 1972 as "Snake Nests and Icons: Some Observations on Theology and Ecology." In this conversation, White further articulated his thoughts on animism, the erasure of the autonomy and spirituality of other creatures, and the religious implications of this view:

> Perhaps the most shocking way in which we can phrase the quest for a theology of ecology at the present time is as follows: what is a viable, modern, *Christian equivalent* of animism? The question shouldn't be asked publicly in that way, because to ask it thus would be to alienate a good many people unnecessarily. I am not wanting a revival of animism! I am searching for ways to regain perception of the spirituality of all creatures and to demote modern man from absolute monarchy over nature.[39]

The religious problem, then, was not simply to stop thinking in terms of dominion. It was also a search for a way to recognize other creatures as spiritually autonomous beings.

The solution, White thought, might lie in the "recessive genes" of the Christian tradition.[40] One such recessive gene could be found in the thought of the "greatest spiritual revolutionary in Western history," Saint Francis of Assisi.[41] "We must rethink and refeel our nature and destiny," White wrote in his conclusion to "Historical Roots." "The profoundly religious, but heretical, sense of the primitive Franciscans for the spiritual autonomy of all parts of nature may point a direction."[42] He continued to expound on this theme and to praise Saint Francis's creature-friendly, ecological vision in most of his publications where ecology was a focus, such as "Continuing the Conversation," "A Commentary on St. Francis of Assisi," and

"The Future of Compassion." Saint Francis's attitude toward nature is so necessary, claimed White, because he "tried to substitute the idea of the equality of all creatures, including man, for the idea of man's limitless rule of creation."[43] Thus not only was White engaged in a historical analysis of the religious ideas and values that led to our present ecological crisis, but he was also exploring theological solutions.

BEYOND DOMINION AND STEWARDSHIP—A SPIRITUAL DEMOCRACY OF ALL GOD'S CREATURES

White's focus on Saint Francis and his repeated assertion that Christians need to recover their appreciation for the autonomy and spirituality of other creatures reveal much about White's personal theological outlook and his attitude toward his respondents. On the one hand, although it is an undeniably important theological task, and one that has proved incredibly fruitful in the development of contemporary ecotheology, White was critical of the widespread focus of scholars and religious leaders on the dominion-stewardship debate that grew out of the responses to his 1967 thesis. He framed this criticism in contrast to the more radical democratic model found in stories of Saint Francis.

The alacrity and consistency with which White made this critique of the ecotheological response to "Historical Roots" leaves little doubt as to where he stood on the issue. On May 12, 1967, just two months after publishing "Historical Roots," White was already giving voice to this concern in *Science*, the same journal that had published his original article. There, under the title "Christian Impact on Ecology," White and several other scholars published short responses to his thesis. The first author in this collection of short responses, Ernest Feenstra, wrote a rather positive review of White's thesis and suggested that, in light of White's argument, Christians ought to see themselves as stewards of God's nature. White, however, did not agree. Stewardship, or the idea that Christians are the caretakers rather than the rulers of God's creation, was viewed by White as being more like "enlightened despotism" when compared to Saint Francis's model.[44] White indicated that replacing the idea of humanity's dominion over nature with a stewardship model, or "Trusteeship" as he habitually called it, would be an inadequate response to the looming environmental crisis. Although only a few short sentences in length, White was clear, in his very first published response to his thesis, that attempts to reform Christianity must be more radical than a position of stewardship.

Eleven years later, White continued to espouse this position. In "The Future of Compassion," an essay exploring Christian values published in *The Ecumenical Review* in 1978, he wrote:

> Religious thinkers have been precipitously abandoning the doctrine of Man's Dominion over Nature for that of Man's Trusteeship of Nature. This is rational, because no other visible creature seems to be as capable of analysing complex situations and calculating the options as is *homo sapiens*. Yet it is precisely for this rational reason that this choice will only deepen disaster: it overlooks the fact of sin, which is compounded of inertia, of a nice talent for discovering moral reasons for committing evil deeds, and of self-love both individual and for our species as compared with other creatures. Mankind cannot be trusted to be trustee for the rest of nature. When we must decide whether to benefit lilies or sparrows or ourselves, we will recall that while our Heavenly Father is mindful of both lilies and sparrows, he cares even more deeply for us; so, in obedience to the divine preference, we shall opt for us.[45]

Put differently, White believed that replacing the notion of dominion with an ethic of stewardship would only exacerbate ecological problems because it continues to place humans above other creatures in a value hierarchy that allows nonhumans to be exploited. And, as White observes, a theology or ethic that claims to protect animals while maintaining the human-nature divide and allowing other creatures to be valued on prudential, anthropocentric grounds is nothing more than an "enlightened self-interest" that cannot stand the litmus test of theology, ecology, or ethics.[46]

On the other hand, White was not entirely critical of efforts to replace the biblical notion of dominion with a stewardship model. He viewed the move from dominion to stewardship as a necessary, albeit intermediate step, in the evolution of Christian attitudes toward nature and other creatures. Since an ethical position emphasizing stewardship is insufficient, White averred, a third theological step would be necessary. Drawing together his historical observation that the erasure of the autonomy and spirituality of other creatures has precipitated the ecological crisis along with his religious commitments to egalitarianism, democracy, and the inherent worth and dignity of each individual, he searched Christian history and Scripture for an alternative theological point of view. "Perhaps," wrote White as he reflected on the ecological crisis and his own belief that Christian history was punctuated by moments of divine revelation, "the Holy Ghost is whispering something to us."[47] Borrowing heavily from the "recessive genes" in Christianity, including stories about Saint Francis and Scriptural sources such as from Daniel 3:57–90 and the Psalms, White developed a theological position of his own:

> As the inadvertent founder, it would seem, of the Theology of Ecology, I confess amusement at the speed with which the Churches have abandoned the old scion of Man's Dominion over Nature for the equally Biblical position of Man's Trusteeship of Nature. Since the Churches remain, despite some competition, the chief forges for hammering out values, this is important. I feel that before too long, however, they will find themselves going on to the third legitimately Biblical position, that Man is part of a democracy of all God's creatures, organic and inorganic, each praising his Maker according to the law of its being.[48]

This third theological position appears with surprising frequency in White's texts. If "Historical Roots" is read alone, outside of the context of his larger body of work, then this notion of a "democracy of all God's creatures" appears to be but one small aspect of a multilayered and complex thesis. But when his larger body of work is read together, the importance and centrality of this third theological position in his thought is clear. In the overwhelming majority of his publications focused on ecology, White repeatedly emphasizes the theologically normative claim that Christians need to begin thinking of themselves as members of an expansive community of creatures.[49] This advocacy for a "democracy of all God's creatures," or as he sometimes calls it "a spiritual democracy of all God's creatures," is found in nearly all his published works on religion and ecology, including, but not limited to "Historical Roots," "Christian Impact on Ecology," "Snake Nests and Icons," "Continuing the Conversation," "A Remark from Lynn White, Jr.," "The Future of Compassion," and "Commentary on

St. Francis of Assisi." His perduring commitment to this notion when all of his texts are read together is too prevalent to ignore.

This understanding of White's thought as spread over multiple publications is substantiated by White's own views of his 1967 article. On a number of occasions, White suggested that his thesis, as it was published in *Science*, was incomplete. Originally written as a short speech that was given to the American Association for the Advancement of Science on the day after Christmas in 1966, White regretted that limitations on length forced him to limit the degree to which he developed his argument.[50] The sheer volume (and vociferousness) of the responses to his thesis prompted him to expand on his ideas and to reply to his critics in other publications such as "Continuing the Conversation." Although it would have certainly been convenient for scholars today if White had written a book on religion and ecology rather than a piecemeal collection of articles, speeches, short commentaries, and other published works in which he expanded and clarified his thesis, doing so might have been out of character for White. According to Hall, White described himself as "an 'article' man rather than a 'book' man,'"[51] a fact that is evidenced in his publishing record. For instance, even though White was arguably the most influential medieval historian of his day, he published only one monograph on the subject. His other two books on medieval technology are edited collections of his previously published essays. Thus since White felt more comfortable expressing his ideas in series of short publications and since he admitted that his 1967 thesis was underdeveloped, his "personal theology of ecology" can emerge only when all of his writings are read alongside one another.

CREATURES AS CO-WORSHIPPERS—INCLUSIVITY AND CHRISTIAN COMPASSION

The repeated emphasis on this democracy of creatures calls for more attention to be given to the animals in White's texts. As members of this "spiritual democracy," other animals are sometimes portrayed by White as co-worshippers of God. He maintained that creatures of all kinds were religious actors. Thus animals and other creatures were often understood, most notably in his writings on religion and ecology, to be more than mere symbols or examples to be cited in his historical arguments. Referring to the depictions of animals both in the Bible and in the stories of Saint Francis, he wrote that "the ant is no longer simply a homily for the lazy, flames a sign of the thrust of the soul towards union with God, now they are Brother Ant and Sister Fire, praising the Creator in their own ways as Brother Man does in his."[52] In his 1982 "Commentary on St. Francis of Assisi," to give another example, he wrote of the "little birds" who "flapped their wings and chirped rejoicing" in their "spiritual ecstasy."[53] Other creatures—and not just humans—as White pointed out in "Christians and Nature," "praise God in their own ways."[54] An important task for ecotheology, as noted earlier, was to recover an appreciation for the inherent "spirituality of all creatures."[55] This understanding of other creatures is important not just for its ecological implications, but also because it challenges the way that humans view themselves and the other creatures around them.

Within this spiritual democracy is a profound inclusivity. White's proposed opening up to the autonomy and spirituality of other creatures is not a spiritual demotion for humans in his eyes—far from it. Instead, humans and animals take their place in a great cosmic liturgy. Bestowed with a better understanding of their role in Creation, humans are able "to rejoice and to join the cosmic dance of the creatures,"[56] both in daily life and in worship. If anything, taking up a position in the democracy of creatures frees humans from their former loneliness. In a speech to the graduating class of the San Francisco Theological Seminary that was published in 1975 as "Christians and Nature," White passionately described what it means to view oneself as part of this community of co-worshippers:

> We are *not* alone. We human beings are here in exactly the same sense, and for the same purpose, that sea urchins, banana trees, icebergs, quartz crystals, asteroids, interstellar hydrogen clouds and astronomical black holes are here. Our purpose, and that of all our fellow creatures, is, as the Psalmist so often proclaims, to praise our Creator with all our being.[57]

Although few and far between, other scholars have noted this aspect of White's thought. Roderick Frazier Nash, one of the handful of scholars writing on the subject of ecotheology to work with texts beyond "Historical Roots" and "Continuing the Conversation," takes note of White's inclusive understanding of this spiritual community. "White's concept of a 'spiritual democracy,'" Nash observes, "stands out as one of the most radically inclusive ethical systems yet evolved. His sense of community literally knew no bounds."⁵⁸

This unbounded community imagined by White stretched the limits that are commonly thought to exist between humans, animals, and non-living entities. Throughout his writings on ecology, White used the term "creatures" loosely to indicate not just humans and animals, but also plants, viruses, and even nonliving objects and natural processes such as rocks and the cycles of nature.⁵⁹ He referred to nature, in its broadest sense, as "our fellow creature."⁶⁰ In the fellowship of creatures that he envisioned, all parts of nature are autonomous co-worshippers in a vast, cosmic spiritual democracy. White found biblical support, as well as inspiration in the stories of Saint Francis, for this position. Recalling the "jubilant exhortation to all created things to glorify their Maker" in Daniel 3:57–90, White pointed out that the biblical text "makes no distinctions between categories of creatures: the angels, the heavenly bodies, winds and rain, ice and snow, fire and heat, night and day, seas and rivers, mountains and hills, whales and birds and beasts, men and souls of the dead. All of these creatures," he wrote, "are urged to praise him and glorify him forever."⁶¹

Traces of this tendency to blur the boundaries of what he considered to be a creature can be found in White's earlier historical writings as well. On a number of occasions, he gave voice to his concern that dualistic thinking had gone too far in the categorization of "things." In his estimation, the Platonic-Cartesian dualisms of mind and matter, space and time, organic and inorganic, or animals and humans did not stand up in the face of science, biblical revelation, and individual experience.⁶² During an address given in Philadelphia to celebrate the 250th anniversary of the first American presbytery, a speech published in 1956 as "Presbyterians and the Intellectual Worship of God," a full decade before he wrote "Historical Roots," White framed his displeasure with dualistic conceptions of nature in terms of his own belief in the Incarnation of Christ as well as the discoveries of modern science. He asserted, "Just as the dogma of the Incarnation implies the flat denial of all Platonic-Cartesian dualisms of mind-body, time-eternity, spirit-matter, so scientific research has reached a point at which a materialistic interpretation of the universe is just as obsolete as a vitalistic interpretation."⁶³

During this same period, White wrote another article on the changing perceptions of technology in recent Western history called "Dynamo and

Virgin Reconsidered." There he also demonstrated a budding mistrust in the dualistic separation of humans, animals, and nonliving things in Western thought. In his words:

> We have been too easily impressed by the dualities of Descartes. . . . Closely observed, experience does not in fact fall into neat opposing categories—spirit and matter, religion and technology, man and cosmos, cathedral and powerhouse. Reality is more complex than this, and its parts more intricately interlocked. Man is a bit cosmic; the cosmos is a bit humane; and the free man may worship without despair.[64]

Thus the borders between humans, animals, technology, and the rest of nature were, for White, blurred. This applied particularly to the spiritual democracy of all God's creatures that he was attempting to articulate in his texts on ecology where he applied the term "creatures" in a broad, inclusive sense. "Francis was trying to set up a democracy of all creatures. And not simply living creatures," White wrote in 1982, "but also inorganic creatures like rocks and mountains. He taught that we are all brothers and sisters."[65] This blurring of boundaries is present, at least to some extent, in his depictions of individual animals as well.

Hidden among the biological animals in White's texts, one also finds a small population of boundary-blurring beings that defy perfunctory classification. Time and time again, for example, White marveled at the crystallizing of the tobacco mosaic virus by the Nobel Prize–winning scientist Wendell Stanley.[66] Although Stanley's experiments were later shown to be flawed, his work paved the way for others who would show that simple viruses could both be crystallized and broken into their constituent, nonliving RNA and protein parts and then reassembled again into living, functioning viruses. This smashing of "the artificial conceptual frontier between organic and inorganic matter"[67] gave White theological pause. Gone, he wrote, was the "recent and faulty distinction between the living and the non-living parts of God's creation."[68] So profound were the theological implications of this event for White that he referenced it in at least four of his texts dealing with religion and the environment.[69] This breaking down of the boundaries between a living being and nonliving matter confirmed, he believed, the need for Christians to rethink their attitudes toward nature. In particular, he was tuned in to the idea that the separation of humans, animals, and the nonliving parts of nature was inherently tied in with the present ecological crisis.

White used this complex understanding of nature to build upon and revise existing Christian ethics and to redraw the boundaires of moral considerability. To do so, he continued to push the ontological limits of creatureliness and the theological boundaries of Christian compassion in such texts as "Continuing the Conversation," where White wrote about animal welfare and animal rights as means of entering into a conversation regarding the ethical implications of the blurring of these boundaries. "During the past few generations, kindness to animals (as distinct from pets) has become a virtuous sentiment in Western culture," he observed. But, he countered, scientific evidence such as the crystallizing of the tobacco mosaic virus adds another layer of complexity to this inquiry. Building on this line of thought, he asked, "is it only to living creatures that we should be kind?"[70] Even though "more and more of us are inclined to think that we should have a decent respect for our living fellow creatures," he averred, limiting this question only to animals that we consider to be living does not get to the root of the theological issue. Since he felt strongly that all creatures—whether animal, human, mountain, or something altogether different—are God's creatures and spiritually autonomous co-worshippers, he argued that the question of animal rights does not dig deeply enough.[71] "The problem grows," he observed, if theologians ask: "'Do people have ethical obligations towards rocks?'"[72] In reply to his own question, he wrote:

> Today to almost all Americans, still saturated with ideas historically dominant in Christianity (although perhaps not necessarily so), the question makes no sense at all. If the time comes when to any considerable group of us such a question is no longer ridiculous, we may be on the verge of a change of value structures that will make possible measures to cope with the growing ecologic crisis.[73]

But in White's view the necessary foundations for such a value structure were already present in the recessive genes of his own faith, Christianity. The solution, he felt, was in the biblically supported idea of a spiritual democracy of all God's creatures. When viewed through this lens, he maintained, the question as to whether or not rocks had value did not seem ridiculous. A rock is one of God's creatures too. Not only that, rocks are co-worshippers alongside humans, animals, and other creatures.

Although White never offered an extended explanation of how this spiritual democracy of all God's creatures would function or how these values would play themselves out, his later writings on religion and ecology offer brief insights. The most salient example comes from "The Future of Compassion." In this article, White described Christianity as being in the "greatest crisis of its history of two millennia."[74] Christianity, he argued, has been so focused on human problems that it has excluded other creatures from the ethical community. "I have myself concluded," wrote White as he outlined the development of Christian compassion and ethics, "that Christian compassion must be based on an ascetic and self-restraining conviction of man's comradeship with the other creatures."[75] He pointed out, however, that this goes beyond Albert Schweitzer's "respect for life":

> Today, we have the creaturely companionship not only of the flowering tree that so enraptured Schweitzer, or the earthworm that he removed from the perils of the sidewalk: we can sense our comradeship with a glacier, a subatomic particle or a spiral nebula. Man must join the club of the creatures. They may help to save us from ourselves.[76]

White insisted, in short, that all of nature must be respected and included in the same manner, whether it is living, nonliving, or somewhere in between, as in the case of the tobacco mosaic virus.[77]

Thus the future of Christian compassion, as he saw it, must move beyond human-centered thinking as well as beyond utilitarian value systems. He grounded this view not on prudential concerns. but rather on a theological foundation. His view requires active respect and care for all creatures, not just living, biological ones.[78] In his words:

> From Christian compassion we must defend the continued existence of our fellow animal, plant, insect and marine species, as well as the integrity of landscapes, seascapes and airscapes that are periled by human activity, whether or not these in any way affect human existence. We must do this because of our belief that they are all creatures of

God, and not from expediency. We must extend compassion to rattle-snakes and not just to koala bears.[79]

Compassion, in this case, is an act that is both actively engaged in and rooted in nonanthropocentric theological values. "Compassion," he stated, "is showing reverence actively to another being."[80]

Building on this theme, he framed compassion for other creatures in terms of reciprocal courtesy. He argued that humans must respect the rights of all animals, and these animals must show the same "cosmic manners" to humans in return.[81] To add emphasis to his point, he referenced coyotes and locusts, two creatures that are regularly targeted by humans for extermination, to talk about what this courtesy entailed. Showing courtesy and compassion to other creatures does not mean extending rights to one creature at the expense of another. "But man too," stated White, "is a creature with rights that must be balanced—but not merely on an anthropocentric pivot—with those of his companion creatures."[82] Just as humans have a right to eat other living things and to build shelter for themselves, coyotes too have "a right to dig a den and to kill to eat."[83] Both humans and coyotes have the right to the resources they need to live, and they must not infringe on one another's right to flourish.

Having courtesy, in other words, means "not impinging on the ability of our companions to satisfy their needs."[84] Even locusts have a right to exist so long as they do not overwhelm other creatures in their environment. Although humans can defend their crops, White felt that humans go too far when they attempt to exterminate locusts en masse. Instead, he recommended that humans and locusts seek out a mutual accord. In short, humans have no right, whether through pollution, overpopulation, or deliberate destruction, to be discourteous to other creatures. According to White, the extension of compassion and courtesy to fellow creatures, and respecting their autonomy as co-worshippers of God, is necessary "so that we and other creatures may flourish together."[85] He called this compassion, "man's self-denying comradeship with the other creatures."[86]

RETHINKING WHITE'S LEGACY—WAYS FORWARD

By reading White with an attentive eye toward the ways in which he thought about animals throughout his larger body of work, it seems clear that White was more than the mere critic of Christianity that he is often caricaturized as. His work was more constructive, more complex, and more theologically concerned with creatures than scholars in the field of ecotheology usually credit him. Reclaiming White as a prophetic theological voice, especially one with distinctive ecological and animal-friendly insights, empowers scholars to move beyond White's thesis as it is traditionally understood. Opening up White's legacy in this manner, I argue, invites scholars to be less reactive to White's critiques of Christianity and to instead be more proactive in their exploration of alternative understandings of the relationship between religious ideas and environmental attitudes and action. Additionally, reading beyond "Historical Roots" and bringing White's unique theological voice to the forefront also introduces creative space for research on the relations of Christianity, ecology, and animals to flourish. Pioneers in the study of Christianity and animals such as Laura Hobgood-Oster and Paul Waldau have already noted the strong linkages between religious attitudes toward animals and religious attitudes toward the environment. Further exploration of White's theology can only strengthen this connection.

Perhaps most important, rethinking White's legacy brings a new framework to light for meaningful Christian engagement in human-animal, human-Earth, and human-God relationships. White acknowledged that he was not suggesting "that many contemporary Americans who are concerned about our ecologic crisis will be either able or willing to counsel with wolves or exhort birds" as Saint Francis did.[87] He insisted, however, that any theological answer to the environmental crisis needs to reconsider animal subjectivity. It needs to view all creatures as co-worshippers in a great spiritual democracy in order to create a viable, desirable, and necessary ecotheological vision for the future. Rather than viewing other creatures as lower in a hierarchy, Christians, White maintained, must be increasingly compassionate, courteous, democratic, and open to the spiritual autonomy of all creatures and all the messy overlap that exists between the living and nonliving parts of nature. For White this was not just an ecological problem; it was a theological, ethical, and ontological problem. If humanity is to stem the tide of the ecological crisis, White asserted, Christians must be like Saint Francis who "worshipped a God who was the God both of squirrels and of men."[88]

❧ Epilogue. Animals and Animality: Reflections on the Art of Jan Harrison

JAY McDANIEL

All life is animated. Each and every living being—from the smallest of microbes to the largest of mammals—carries a desire for satisfaction relative to the situation at hand. This desire is his or her "spirituality" and also his or her "animality." Spirituality and animality are not two.

Animality, then, is what links us with our closest biological and spiritual kin: the other-than-human animals. It links us with an Animality at the heart of the universe, whom some address as "God" and others as "the Soul of the Universe" and still others as "the Tilting toward Love." All of these realities, the animals and the Tilting, are flowing through time. This flow is not always harmonious. Sometimes it is fractured and abrupt, painful and violent. But always it is flowing, changing, moving. The cat (Figure 1) is not just looking at us. She is also flowing. And we are flowing as we look back into her eyes, too.

ANIMATED LIFE

Are we two realities, two instances of flow, so different from each other? We both have emotions, subjective aims, and attitudes about the world. We both struggle to survive with satisfaction relative to the situation at hand. We might like to think that life can be divided into a binary: "the human" and "the animal." But the actuality of being alive in the moment, whether in feline or human form, is more fundamental than "feline" or "human." At least this is how Alfred North Whitehead sees things. He thinks concrescing in the moment—experiencing and responding to a world—is the heart of existence. It is life.

Figure 1. Jan Harrison, *Big Cat—Mountain Lion with Foliage Fur*. 2011. Pastel, charcoal, and ink on rag paper. 45.25 × 34.25 inches. Seven-inch border of rag paper around image. Private collection.

The Korean postcolonial ecotheologian Jea Sophia Oh speaks of *Salim* (Life) as the place where the sacred is found in life. In her writings,[1] she invites us to recognize that Life is more fundamental than any *ism* we can imagine: religionism or atheism or modernism or postmodernism or humanism. Life can never be contained in our ideologies, and yet it is always concrete, as enfleshed in the lives of living beings like the cat. Like us.

To be alive in the moment, then, is to be a concrescing subject. As a subject each of us is a "you" and not simply an "it." There is a place—a psychological and bodily landscape—from which we perceive the world. And as concrescing subjects, we are an activity of experiencing our environments and, in the experiencing of those environments, making a complex world of the many realities we experience. Living cells make worlds, and so do microbes. Even the quantum events within the depths of atoms are, for Whitehead, moments of subjectivity rather than bare objects. They are acts of world-making. Wherever there is energy, there is subjectivity. Wherever there is subjectivity, there is world-making.

Of course, the worlds that we make are not reducible to our perceptions or projections. As the cat becomes part of our world, she remains herself, looking at us, albeit hybridized in her consciousness by our lives. And as we become part of her world, we remain ourselves, too, albeit hybridized in our consciousness by her life. Whitehead sees the universe as filled with entities that prehend other entities and make worlds for themselves: worlds that are partly composed of the other entities themselves. There are no isolated egos, Cartesian or feline. We might call this network of subjective mutuality *pan-prehensionality*. It might also be called *pan-psychism*. Whatever words are used, the point is simple. Everything is alive in one way or another. Even the Soul of the universe—the Tilting toward Love—is alive. The cat's body is the universe itself.

KNOWING WITH OTHER ANIMALS

Jan Harrison, the artist whose work we share in this essay, is especially attuned to the world-making subjectivity of our closest biological and spiritual kin: the other animals. She knows that their subjectivity cannot be separated from their bodies; thus she speaks of animals as body-souls. This makes good sense to those of us who are influenced by Whitehead's philosophy. Whitehead says that wherever living beings on our planet happen to be, they are always with their bodies, and their bodies provide a sense of location, a vantage point. This is part of what he means by the *withness of the body*. They—we—are not bodiless souls; we are embodied souls. Our bodies give us our vulnerability, our sense of location, our capacities for self-expression, and much of our wisdom. They are the most intimate part of our world.

Whitehead's philosophy also shows how we can know the subjectivity of other body-souls, even if they belong to different species. Consider this other cat (Figure 2). We can approach her from a third-person point of view, in which case she is one about whom we might claim some knowledge. This is the kind of knowledge a biologist might seek. But we can also approach her as a concrescing subject with whom we have rapport. This rapport is a kind of knowledge, too. But it is a knowing with rather than a knowing about. Jan Harrison is interested in knowing with other animals. She is interested in interspecies communication and, still more deeply, interspecies communion. As a Whiteheadian might put it, she is interested in how we can prehend the feelings of other animals empathically, in how we might feel their feelings through experience in the mode of causal efficacy.

Experience in the mode of causal efficacy is Whitehead's way of talking about experiences, conscious and unconscious, in which we receive feelings from others and are inwardly moved by the feelings we receive. In the reception the others become part of us, even as they are other than us. They become our bodies, too. This means that our own flesh is not reducible to our skin. It includes the feelings of others, too. This is what we know when we know with others. The colors Jan Harrison chooses are part of the withness of their bodies—and thus their feelings—in us.

RHYTHM AND SINGULARITY

To know with another animal we need to have a sense of the animal's modalities and rhythms. Consider the black cat who is looking at us now (Figure 3). She is experiencing us. There is a fire inside her eyes, revealing a kind of wildness. We contain within us a kind of wildness, too. As the cat looks at us, she is our teacher. If we ever lose our wildness, we become zombie-like.

But, of course, the cat is her own person, too. Some Western philosophers would speak of her as an irreducible singularity.[2] They use the word *singularity* to refer to the fact that she cannot be contained by our catego-

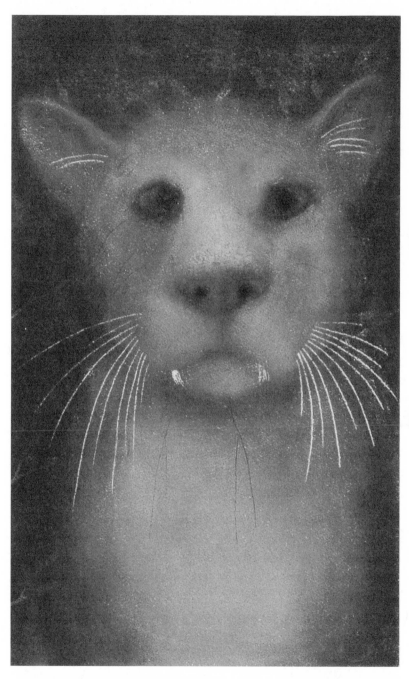

Figure 2. Jan Harrison, *The Corridor Series Cat #3—Blue Cat.* 2009. Pastel, charcoal, and ink on rag paper. 30.25 × 22.5 inches. Five-inch border of rag paper around image.

Figure 3. Jan Harrison, *Blackie #2*. 2011. Pastel, charcoal, and ink on rag paper. 10 × 7 inches. Private collection.

ries or, for that matter, by her own past memories or future possibilities. She is the unique individual who looks at us from her immediate vantage point in her here-and-now.

Whiteheadians appreciate singularity. Every concrescing subject is indeed unique and unsubstitutable. If we take away this black cat and replace her with another, thinking that she can be replaced, we have missed the point. Each living being is an *each* and not simply one among all. In the language of Buddhism, each living being is a Buddha, replaceable by no other Buddha.

But this uniqueness is not the unity of the number 1. In the cat as in us, singularity is a living and manifold reality that includes our felt relations to the many worlds around us and within us. In the case of the cat, we ourselves are part of her world. There is a transfer of energy and feeling between us and her. We are folded into her singularity and she into ours. Buddhists call this interbeing or, perhaps better, intersubjectivity. We might also call it mutual enfoldment. Things can be folded into one another and still be different.

But the very word *enfoldment* can be problematic, if it suggests a completed act. The cat's singularity is not static. It is an activity that takes time and makes time as it occurs: feline time. Feline time is one of many kinds of time. There is also atomic time and microbic time and plant time and divine time. What time is it? It depends on whom we are asking. Time, too, is a construct created out of the timing—the rhythms—of different creatures as they live their lives.

Whiteheadians might like to rename Heidegger's *Being and Time* as *Being and Rhythm*. It is arguable that in Caribbean and perhaps other cultures the idea of rhythm has priority over ground. We live and move and have our being in rhythm. There is a certain kind of groundlessness in rhythm, because it is always moving. The black cat's singularity is moving, too. As we move, she moves, even as she stays in the same location. She is not many or one, but rather the many becoming one. Her singularity is the becoming. Here Buddhist language helps: She is neither being nor not-being. She is pure becoming, moment by moment.

SEEKING SATISFACTION

Just as there are many times, so there are many worlds. Some are visible, but most are invisible. Microbes are part of the universe, but we cannot see them with our physical eyes. Dreams are also part of the universe, but they become visible only in dream time. Our physical eyes are wonderful but imperfect tools for taking into account the multiplicity of worlds to be perceived. Inside the body-souls of each animal there is a universe—no, a multiverse—of worlds. Part of wildness is the multiplicity itself. It cannot really be tamed, even when placed in a cage.

What animates all of this wildness? The Hebrew Bible calls the animating spirit of the world the divine Breathing. This Breathing is in the cat, too. Wherever there is the breath of life, there is the breath of the Breathing. Whitehead says that this Breathing is present in the cat as her own innermost lure to live with satisfaction relative to the situation at hand. This is the way it is with all flesh. We are always seeking satisfaction relative to the situation. The divine Breathing is present within each creature as the creature's desire for satisfaction. The Breathing is found in the desire to live and to live with satisfaction.

In human life the Breathing has an ethical side, which may have parallels in the moral lives of other animals. When we experience the Breathing, we feel called to live wisely, compassionately, and creatively. This is how we express our wildness. But the calling is also in other creatures, including the snow leopard (Figure 4). She, too, has a felt relation with the Lord of creation. She, too, has her way of walking in the love. Her calling is to be fully herself.

COMPANIONS IN FLESH

The dog (Figure 5) also has a calling. If we look carefully, we know that there are worlds inside him: worlds of consciousness, of feeling, of dreaming, of wisdom. He is making worlds, but he is also being made by worlds. As are we all.

With his capacity for loyalty and affection, this dog may well be at the leading edge of the loving arc of evolution—way ahead of most of us. Christians say that the love of God is revealed in Jesus. Surely love is revealed in the unconditional love of dogs too. Jesus may simply be a way of helping humans become more dog-like. One of the first messiahs may have been canine.

Still, through the dog's presence, including his eyes, we receive wisdom and energy for life. We can share moods and feelings. We can share vulnerability. We are kindred spirits in the way of all flesh.

Figure 4. Jan Harrison, *Big Cat—Snow Leopard #2*. 2011. Pastel, charcoal, and ink on rag paper. 45.25 × 34.25 inches. Seven-inch border of rag paper around image.

Figure 5. Jan Harrison, *The Corridor Series Study of a Dog #1*. 2009. Pastel, charcoal, and ink on rag paper. 20.75 × 17.5 inches. Private collection.

This flesh is more than our skin. It is our embodiment. It includes our surface membranes but also our psychological membranes: our feelings, our hopes, our desires, our aims. Every instance of flesh is unique, and yet every instance shares in every other instance.

Every creature is hybridized flesh. We are being hybridized by the presence of one another. We include one another within our worlds, even as we are also different from one another. All people who are claimed by dogs know this. They know that they could not be human without the dogs, that the dogs are part of, in Whitehead's words, the objective constitution of their momentary selves. To be embodied is to be incarnated by other beings. Our flesh does not simply belong to us. It belongs to the world that is enfleshed in us. Sometimes enfleshedness is profoundly painful. When the dog is harmed by others, his flesh is pain. And when people are harmed, their flesh is pain, too. Flesh is a source of pain and delight, tragedy and beauty. If there is life after death, it will be enfleshed, too, in some way. There is no life without flesh. The fear of death, then, is not really a fear of nonbeing. It is a fear of fractured relations, fractured flesh.

BELOVED COMMUNITY WITH ANIMALS INCLUDED

How far does flesh go down? From Whitehead's perspective, hybridity goes all the way down to microbes and molecules and atoms. Every actuality is an act of making a world out of the multiple influences that shape it. Whitehead calls this activity concrescence.

Fred in Figure 6, for example, is a concrescing subject. His concrescing includes his gazing at us, and through this gazing, we become incarnate in his life. We are part of his objective constitution and his subjectivity. As he gazes into our eyes, and as we gaze into his eyes, too, we are mutual becomings. We are becoming together, even if not in parallel fashion. He knows our odors and also our feelings. We are part of the withness of his own body.

Jan Harrison stands out as one who understands—and helps us see and feel—this intersubjectivity of mutual becoming. She helps us listen to animals with our eyes, our imaginations, and, with her Animal Tongues, with our ears.[3] Thus her art points us in the direction of a beloved community, because it helps us love and learn from our kindred spirits in the way of all flesh. If the beloved community is to be filled with love, it must include an affection for the Freds of our world, a sense that they, too, belong to the families from whom we gain sustenance. People today like to talk about sustainable futures. But sustainability is connected with the word *sustenance*. A sustainable future must be one where people play and dream and share in the way of all flesh. It must include the sustenance we receive from our animal kin. And it must include a sustenance—a respect

Figure 6. Jan Harrison, *The Corridor Series—Fred*. 2009. Pastel, charcoal, and ink on rag paper. 18.75 × 12.25 inches. Private collection.

and love—that we give them, too. Jan Harrison's artist's statement helps us understand all of this better. Hear her words:

A lifelong kinship and identification with animals has helped me to express what it is to be here as a flesh and blood being. Through a close relationship with animals, I feel as if their bodies are the same as my body. . . .

The myth in my art is intuitively known in my body, and not based on recorded mythology. We are animals . . . animals are within us. Animals are symbolic of the natural world. They possess knowledge and innocence, darkness and light. Their eyes invite us into their world.

A metamorphosis happens as I caress the surface, using pastels, wax, and clay, and working the surface with my hands. Simplifying the recent paintings and sculpture to portrait-like heads has revealed their essence as an intimate connection. In "The Corridor Series," animals exist in both ecological and psychological corridors. They are taking a stand, vanishing and returning. They are on the outside, inviting you to either join them, or to invite them into the viewing realm. "The Corridor Series" is both autobiographical and universal, having to do with personal feelings of various states of empowerment, and, expressing the similar states and plight of the animal nature.[4]

MYTHS KNOWN IN THE BODY

So much contemporary scholarship in the West is based on other texts, particularly written texts. We get the idea that myths come from the spoken word or the written word. But Jan Harrison makes us wonder if myths might not also come from our own bodies. Of course, these bodies are only part of our flesh. Whatever touches us is part of our flesh, and however we touch it is part of our flesh, too. Books are flesh. Images are flesh. Sounds are flesh. But it is possible that myths and stories can come from impulses within our own bodies, not unlike the way that feelings come from our own bodies. At least this is what Whiteheadians will suggest: the *withness of the body* as an ever-present reality in our lives. We experience it as a feeling of the feelings within our body.

If we can feel the feelings in our body, might we also feel the stories in our bodies? Indeed, don't our bodies already carry within them many stories: the stories carried in our genes, in the events of our lives as remembered in our brains and stomachs and muscles, both traumatic and beautiful? People who have suffered from physical abuse know that their bodies contain memories, which their minds might wish to suppress. Perhaps their bodies contain anticipations of the future, too. Anticipations that, with the support of life and community, with the support of clean air and healthy food, the mortal life can be lived fully, until death provides its end, at least to this phase of the journey.

Can a body-soul continue even after death? Might there be flesh after death, too? Might there be dimensions of existence in which body-souls continue in other kinds of bodies, perhaps even speaking back into this very plane of existence? Might we humans, and other animals as well, enjoy continuing journeys into that good night of death, until we discover some kind of completeness, some kind of full rapport, some kind of love, some kind of deep time, which is also a listening? And is it not possible that, in this deep time, the animals already dwell, at least partly, in their innocence, their vitality, their dreaming, their companionship, as flesh among flesh? Are they not emissaries of the Listening?

WISDOM FOR LISTENING

What is the wisdom we seek? Surely it is to listen in the deepest of senses. To listen with our eyes, our ears, our hands, our minds, our hopes, our fears, our dreams, our trust. In the listening perhaps we can hear a calling within our own bodies and within the bodies of others: a calling to live with respect and care for the community of life, to respect the wildness, to allow our own wildness to come forth in the arc of love. Perhaps we can even hear a deeper listening, a divine Concrescing, everywhere at once, who is engraced by the splendor of the world, and who shares in the world's sufferings, like a slaughtered sheep. And what would be the flesh of this Concrescing? The flesh of the divine Concrescing would be each creature and all creatures, on our earth and on any earth, in our galaxy and in any galaxy, however large or small. Microbes would be the flesh of the Concrescing. Quasars would be the flesh of the Concrescing. The owl would be the flesh of the Concrescing. And so would you and I.

And what would be its rhythms? Perhaps they would be the many rhythms of the multiverse itself: the timing of each pulsation, on its own terms, as indebted to the past and anticipating a future. The Concrescing of the universe would be like a really good drummer: polyrhythmic. In the beginning is not the word; it is the rhythm; and the rhythm is with God.

But of course we must speak, too. Perhaps this Concrescing beckons some among us to remember old languages—those of the other animals—who do not speak our tongues but who speak in so many other glorious ways, like the call of the magpie or the hooting of the owl. Jan Harrison enters into this kind of speaking, in ways that are sometimes funny, sometimes sad, sometimes delightful, sometimes mysterious, sometimes gorgeous, sometimes frightening, and always true. Not true to the canons of orthodoxy, but true to the canons of what one theologian, Catherine Keller, calls polydoxy.[5] Is there a glossolalia of, and from, the animals? Can the liberated tongue be a vessel through which the callings of our kindred spirits find blessing?

NOTES

FOREWORD | LAUREL KEARNS

1. Laurel Kearns and Catherine Keller, eds., *Ecospirit: Religions and Philosophies for the Earth*, Transdisciplinary Theological Colloquia (New York: Fordham University Press, 2007).

2. Jacques Derrida, *Animal That Therefore I Am*, ed. Marie-Louise Mallet, trans. David Wood, Perspectives in Continental Philosophy (New York: Fordham University Press, 2008).

3. Ibid., 90.

4. Donna Haraway, *When Species Meet*, Posthumanities (Minneapolis: University of Minnesota Press, 2008), 20.

5. Derrida, *Animal That Therefore I Am*, 32.

6. James Cone, "Whose Earth Is It Anyway?" in *Earth Habitat: Eco-Injustice and the Church's Response*, ed. Dieter Hessel and Larry Rasmussen (Minneapolis: Fortress Press, 2001), 23.

7. John Wesley, Sermon 23, "Upon Our Lord's Sermon on the Mount, III," in *Works of John Wesley* (London: Wesleyan Methodist Book Room, 1872), vol. 5, I.11.

8. Martin Luther, as quoted in Paul Santmire, *Nature Reborn: The Ecological and Cosmic Promise of Christian Theology* (Minneapolis: Fortress Press, 2000), 82.

9. Aldo Leopold, *A Sand County Almanac, and Sketches Here and There* (1948; New York: Oxford University Press, 1987), 129–32.

INTRODUCTION: FROM ANIMAL THEORY TO CREATURELY THEOLOGY | STEPHEN D. MOORE

1. Kari Weil, *Thinking Animals: Why Animal Studies Now?* (New York: Columbia University Press, 2012), 4. Further on the complex relations between animal

advocacy and advocacy for oppressed human groups, see Marianne DeKoven and Michael Lundblad, eds., *Species Matters: Humane Advocacy and Cultural Theory* (New York: Columbia University Press, 2012).

2. Marianne DeKoven, "Guest Column: Why Animals Now?" *PMLA* 124, no. 2 (2009): 368n3. See further Michael Lundblad, "From Animal to Animality Studies," *PMLA* 124, no. 2 (2009): 496–502). For the "zoocriticism" moniker, see Graham Huggan and Helen Tiffin, *Postcolonial Ecocriticism: Literature, Animals, Environment* (New York: Routledge, 2010), 18. Zoocriticism "is concerned not just with animal *representation* but also with animal *rights."*

3. See Dian Fossey, *Gorillas in the Mist* (Boston: Houghton Mifflin, 1983); Jane Goodall, *The Chimpanzees of Gombe: Patterns of Behavior* (Cambridge, Mass.: Belknap Press of Harvard University Press, 1986); Peter Singer, *Animal Liberation* (New York: Avon, 1975); Tom Regan, *The Case for Animal Rights* (Berkeley: University of California Press, 1983); J. M. Coetzee, *The Lives of Animals*, ed. Amy Gutmann (Princeton: Princeton University Press, 1999).

4. Lynn White Jr., "The Historical Roots of Our Ecologic Crisis," *Science* 155, no. 3767 (1967): 1203–7, reprinted in *The Ecocriticism Reader: Landmarks in Literary Ecology*, ed. Cheryll Glotfelty and Harold Fromm (Athens: University of Georgia Press, 1996), 3–14. Although White's native field was medieval history, his article is the opening selection in this anthology, which was the first full-length introduction to ecocriticism in the field of literary studies—testimony to White's cross-disciplinary reach.

5. Ibid., 9. Page references to White's article are from *The Ecocriticism Reader*.

6. Ibid., 13.

7. It is appropriate, then, that the last main essay in the volume, that of Matthew Riley, should engage explicitly with White's seminal article, while also radically reframing it.

8. Fossey, *Gorillas in the Mist*, 141.

9. Ibid., 141–42.

10. Jacques Derrida, "L'animal que donc je suis (à suivre)," in *L'animal autobiographique*, ed. Marie-Louise Mallet (Paris: Galilée, 1999), 251–303

11. Jacques Derrida, "The Animal That Therefore I Am (More to Follow)," trans. David Wills, *Critical Inquiry* 28, no. 2 (2002): 369–418.

12. Jacques Derrida, *The Animal That Therefore I Am*, ed. Marie-Louise Mallet; trans. David Wills, Perspectives in Continental Philosophy (New York: Fordham University Press, 2008).

13. Jacques Derrida, *The Beast and the Sovereign*, ed. Michel Lisse et al.; trans. Geoffrey Bennington, 2 vols., Seminars of Jacques Derrida (Chicago: University of Chicago Press, 2009–11), 1:1–2. Originally published as *Séminaire: La bête et*

le souverain, Volume I (2001–2002); Volume II (2002–2003), ed. Michel Lisse et al. (Paris: Galilée, 2008–10).

14. The quotation is from *The Animal That Therefore I Am*, 37–38, where Derrida provides a list of his texts in which mammals, birds, reptiles, fish, insects, and other "critters" range freely. The list, although lengthy, is cursory and incomplete. Generally speaking, however, it is mainly in relation to Heideggerian thought that Derrida engages in sustained fashion with "the question of the animal" prior to "The Animal That Therefore I Am." Two other Derridean engagements with animality are also worth noting: "'Eating Well'; or, The Calculation of the Subject," in *Who Comes after the Subject?* ed. Eduardo Cadava, Peter Connor, and Jean-Luc Nancy (New York: Routledge, 1991), 96–119; and "Violence against Animals," in *For What Tomorrow . . . : A Dialogue*, by Jacques Derrida and Elisabeth Roudinesco, trans. Jeff Fort, Cultural Memory in the Present (Stanford, Calif.: Stanford University Press, 2004), 62–76.

15. Cary Wolfe, "Human, All Too Human: 'Animal Studies' and the Humanities," *PMLA* 124, no. 2 (2009): 570. Wolfe's article is perhaps the best brief overview of animality studies to date. For book-length overviews (each rather differently focused), see Weil, *Thinking Animals*; Margo DeMello, *Animals and Society: An Introduction to Human-Animal Studies* (New York: Columbia University Press, 2012); and Dawne McCance, *Critical Animal Studies: An Introduction* (Albany: State University of New York Press, 2013). For the intersection of animality studies and postcolonial studies, see Huggan and Tiffin, *Postcolonial Ecocriticism*, which includes a biblically oriented chapter titled "Christianity, Cannibalism and Carnivory" (162–84). For the relationship of animality studies to posthumanism, see Cary Wolfe, *What Is Posthumanism?* Posthumanities (Minneapolis: University of Minnesota Press, 2009), 99–142.

16. The precise relationship of "theory" to poststructuralism is a contested issue, prompting Jonathan Culler to venture a more cautious (but perhaps overly expansive) definition of it as an umbrella term for "discourses that come to exercise influence outside their apparent disciplinary realm because they offer new and persuasive characterizations of problems or phenomena of general interest: language, consciousness, meaning, nature and culture . . . , and so on" (*The Literary in Theory*, Cultural Memory in the Present [Stanford, Calif.: Stanford University Press, 2007], 4.)

17. See Gilles Deleuze and Félix Guattari's *A Thousand Plateaus: Capitalism and Schizophrenia*, trans. Brian Massumi (1980; Minneapolis: University of Minnesota Press, 1987), 256–341.

18. See Julia Kristeva, *Powers of Horror: An Essay on Abjection*, trans. Leon S. Roudiez, European Perspectives (1980; New York: Columbia University Press,

1982); Kelly Oliver, *Animal Lessons: How They Teach Us to Be Human* (New York: Columbia University Press, 2009), 277–302.

19. See Emmanuel Levinas, "The Name of a Dog, or Natural Rights," in *Difficult Freedom: Essays on Judaism*, trans. Sean Hand (Baltimore: Johns Hopkins University Press, 1990), 151–53.

20. See Matthew Calarco and Peter Atterton, eds., *Animal Philosophy: Essential Readings in Continental Thought* (New York: Continuum, 2004), 31–36, 63–71, 193–201.

21. Even "animal theory," however capacious, is still a relatively bounded universe of discourse. When critical reflection on animality is loosed from "theory," it flies still farther afield—as far as Whitehead even, a crucial resource for Jay McDaniel and J. Aaron Simmons in their essay in the present volume. Oliver's *Animal Lessons*, more particularly, abandons itself to the disseminative trajectory, including chapters on Rousseau, Herder, Freud, Heidegger, Merleau-Ponty, and Beauvoir, as well as on acknowledged "theorists": Derrida, Lacan, Kristeva, and Agamben. For an important recent contribution to animal philosophy from the analytic rather than the continental side of the philosophical divide, see Stanley Cavell et al., *Philosophy and Animal Life* (New York: Columbia University Press, 2008).

22. Book-length engagements with Derrida's animal writings include Neil Badmington, ed., *DerridAnimals*, *Oxford Literary Review* 29, no. 1 (2007); Leonard Lawlor, *This Is Not Sufficient: An Essay on Animality and Human Nature in Derrida* (New York: Columbia University Press, 2007); Anne Emmanuelle Berger and Marta Segarra, eds., *Demenageries: Thinking (of) Animals after Derrida* (Amsterdam: Rodopi, 2011); and David Farrell Krell, *Derrida and Our Animal Others: Derrida's Final Seminar, the Beast and the Sovereign*, Studies in Continental Thought (Bloomington: Indiana University Press, 2013).

23. I am using the term *biopolitical* in its Foucauldian sense as entailing power over life and death. See further Cary Wolfe, *Before the Law: Humans and Other Animals in a Biopolitical Frame* (Chicago: University of Chicago Press, 2013).

24. Derrida, *Animal That Therefore I Am*, 88. All five philosophers also feature in Derrida's *The Beast and the Sovereign*, some more prominently than others. Heidegger is a major focus, especially in volume 2.

25. Derrida, *Animal That Therefore I Am*, 89.

26. Ibid., 90.

27. Ibid., 34.

28. Timothy Morton remarks, tongue-in-cheek: "Given the powerful affinity between them, it's as if Darwin had read Derrida" ("Guest Column: Queer Ecology," *PMLA* 125, no. 2 [2010]: 277).

29. Derrida, *Animal That Therefore I Am*, 29.

30. Ibid. Cf. Derrida, *Beast and the Sovereign*, 2:196: "The animal in general: that, then, is the first malaise."

31. Derrida, *Animal That Therefore I Am*, 47.

32. Ibid., 48.

33. Ibid., 75. For Derrida's most explicit engagement with Descartes on the question of the animal, see ibid., 69–87. There is nothing comparably sustained in *The Beast and the Sovereign*, despite recurrent invocations of Descartes.

34. More nuanced views of human-animal relations stemmed from the Platonic and Pythagorean traditions, and received extended expression in the works of such philosophers as Plutarch and Porphyry. For an overview of these ancient debates, see Ingvild Saelid Gilhus, *Animals, Gods and Humans: Changing Attitudes to Animals in Greek, Roman and Early Christian Ideas* (New York: Routledge, 2006), especially 37–63. For a detailed treatment of Descartes's ideas on animals in relation to those of Aristotle, Augustine, Aquinas, and other seminal philosophers and theologians, see Gary Steiner, *Anthropocentrism and Its Discontents: Animals and Their Moral Status in the History of Western Philosophy* (Pittsburgh: University of Pittsburgh Press, 2005), 132–52, together with 53–131.

35. For the doctrine, see René Descartes, *A Discourse on the Method*, trans. Ian Maclean, Oxford World's Classics (Oxford: Oxford University Press, 2006), 35–49, originally published in French in 1637; idem, *Philosophical Essays and Correspondence*, ed. Roger Ariew; trans. Roger Ariew et al. (Indianapolis: Hackett, 2000), 275–76, 292–96 (two letters from 1646 and 1649 respectively).

36. Giorgio Agamben, *The Open: Man and Animal*, trans. Kevin Attell (Stanford, Calif.: Stanford University Press, 2004), 23, originally published in Italian in 2002. Agamben is an important interlocutor for Eric Daryl Meyer in the present volume. Beatrice Marovich, Jennifer Koosed, and Robert Paul Seesengood also make strategic use of Agamben.

37. Donna J. Haraway, *When Species Meet*, Posthumanities (Minneapolis; University of Minnesota Press, 2007). Haraway is an important interlocutor for several of the contributors to the present volume, notably Denise Buell, Jacob Erickson, and Laura Hobgood-Oster.

38. Ibid., 3. The second guiding question is: "How is 'becoming with' a practice of becoming worldly?" (ibid.). The human-canine relation is a major focus of Haraway's recent work; see also her *The Companion Species Manifesto: Dogs, People, and Significant Otherness* (Chicago: Prickly Paradigm, 2003). Cary Wolfe, in his brief history of animal studies, assigns enormous significance to Haraway's *Primate Visions: Gender, Race, and Nature in the World of Modern Science* (New York: Routledge, 1990). Wolfe writes: "And the landmark publication of Donna

Haraway's *Primate Visions* opened the 1990s with a remarkable interdisciplinary synthesis that in effect defined a new, resolutely cultural studies era in what would come to be called animal studies" ("Human, All too Human," 565).

39. Haraway, *When Species Meet*, 3–4.

40. Ibid., 19–20, quoting Derrida, "The Animal That Therefore I Am (More to Follow)," 378–79.

41. Haraway, *When Species Meet*, 20.

42. Ibid., 21.

43. Ibid., 23, quoting Derrida, "The Animal That Therefore I Am (More to Follow)," 380. Derrida takes Levinas to task for his explicit hesitation, when challenged by a questioner at a symposium, to ascribe a "face" to the animal and hence the ethical obligation owed to the human. See Derrida, *Animal That Therefore I Am*, 105–18; idem, *Beast and the Sovereign*, 1:237–39.

44. Haraway, *When Species Meet*, 23.

45. Derrida, *Animal That Therefore I Am*, 18.

46. This primal scene ("this awful tale of Genesis") is analyzed at length by Derrida (ibid., 15–18; quotation from 18).

47. In Levinas's famous formulation, God is "the *he* [*sic*] in the depth of the you." Or again: "The Other is not the incarnation of God, but precisely by his face, in which he is disincarnate, is the manifestation of the height in which God is revealed." The first quotation is from "God and Philosophy," in *Emmanuel Levinas: Basic Philosophical Writings*, ed. Adriaan T. Peperzak et al., Studies in Continental Thought (Bloomington: Indiana University Press, 1996), 141, and the second is from *Totality and Infinity: An Essay on Exteriority*, trans. Alphonso Lingis (Dordrecht, The Netherlands: Kluwer, 1991), 79.

48. Levinas's centrality to much of Derrida's later work begins in earnest with *The Gift of Death*. See Jacques Derrida, *The Gift of Death*, trans. David Wills (Chicago: University of Chicago Press, 1995), especially 82–115, originally published in French in 1992.

49. "Yes, the wholly other, more other than any other, which *they* call an animal" (Derrida, *Animal That Therefore I Am*, 11).

50. Ibid., 6. One is put in mind of Derrida's (anxious) admission in his programmatic early essay, "Différance," that his deconstructive tactics "resemble those of negative theology, occasionally even to the point of being indistinguishable from negative theology" ("Différance" [1968], in *Margins of Philosophy*, trans. Alan Bass [Chicago: University of Chicago Press, 1982], 6).

51. Derrida, *Animal That Therefore I Am*, 132. Earlier he writes of "the ahuman combining god and animal according to all the theo-zoomorphic possibilities that properly constitute the myths, religions, idolatries, and even sacrificial prac-

tices within the monotheisms that claim to break with idolatry" (ibid., 131; see also Derrida, *Beast and the Sovereign*, 1:126–27).

52. Derrida, *Beast and the Sovereign*, 1:13.

53. Laurie Shannon, "The Eight Animals in Shakespeare; or, Before the Human," *PMLA* 124, no. 2 (2009): 476. Her title refers to the fact that the term "animal" occurs only eight times in Shakespeare's entire oeuvre, whereas the terms "beast" and "creature" occur hundreds of times. "As the *OED* confirms, *animal* hardly appears in English before the end of the sixteenth century" (ibid., 474). Shannon has since developed these ideas in more detail; see her *The Accommodated Animal: Cosmopolity in Shakespearean Locales* (Chicago: University of Chicago Press, 2013), especially 1–19.

54. Susan Crane, *Animal Encounters: Contacts and Concepts in Medieval Britain* (Philadelphia: University of Pennsylvania Press, 2013), 1–2, second emphasis added. Laura Hobgood-Oster's *Holy Dogs and Asses: Animals in the Christian Tradition* (Urbana: University of Illinois Press, 2008) is especially rich with medieval and earlier instances of human-animal blurring. Referring to certain of her central archival examples, she writes: "A baptized lion, a preaching dog, and a chorus of birds praising the Creator all bring into question the actuality of separating the human animal from all other animals" (6).

55. Crane, *Animal Encounters*, 2. Work on medieval views of human-animal relations began in earnest with Joyce E. Salisbury, *The Beast Within: Animals in the Middle Ages* (New York: Routledge, 1994). Not all medievalists would agree, however, that medieval culture at large was comfortable with soft human-animal distinctions. For a sharp contestation of that position, see Karl Steel, *How to Make a Human: Animals and Violence in the Middle Ages* (Columbus: Ohio State University Press, 2011).

56. Shannon, "The Eight Animals in Shakepeare," 476.

57. Ibid., 477.

58. Haraway, *When Species Meet*, 330n33.

59. This is the title of one of the essays gathered in *The Animal That Therefore I Am*.

60. Specifically theological work has included Jay B. McDaniel, *Of God and Pelicans: A Theology of Reverence for Life* (Louisville, Ky.: Westminster John Knox Press, 1989); a series of books by Andrew Linzey, beginning with *Animal Theology* (Champaign: University of Illinois Press, 1994); Andrew Linzey and Dorothy Yamamoto, eds., *Animals on the Agenda: Questions about Animals for Theology and Ethics* (London: SCM Press, 1998); Stephen H. Webb, *On God and Dogs: A Christian Theology of Compassion for Animals* (Oxford: Oxford University Press, 1998); Michael J. Murray, *Nature Red in Tooth and Claw: Theism and the Problem of Ani-*

mal Suffering (Oxford: Oxford University Press, 2008); Celia Deane-Drummond and David Clough, eds., *Creaturely Theology: God, Humans and Other Animals* (London: SCM Press, 2009); David L. Clough, *On Animals; Volume 1: Systematic Theology* (London: T&T Clark, 2012); and Daniel K. Miller, *Animal Ethics and Theology: The Lens of the Good Samaritan*, Routledge Studies in Religion 17 (New York: Routledge, 2012). Animal-centered work in biblical and early Christian studies has included certain of the essays in the five volumes of The Earth Bible series (Cleveland: Pilgrim Press, 2000–2002) and in Norman C. Habel and Peter Trudinger, eds., *Exploring Ecological Hermeneutics*, SBL Symposium 46 (Atlanta: Society of Biblical Literature, 2008), and most of the essays in Tripp York and Andy Alexis-Baker, eds., *A Faith Embracing All Creatures: Addressing Commonly Asked Questions about Christian Care for Animals*, The Peacable Kingdom 2 (Eugene, OR: Cascade Books, 2012), as well as Robert M. Grant, *Early Christians and Animals* (New York: Routledge, 1999); Janet E. Spittler, *Animals in the Apocryphal Acts of the Apostles: The Wild Kingdom of Early Christian Literature*, Wissenschaftliche Untersuchungen zum Neuen Testament 2. Reihe, 247 (Tübingen: Mohr Siebeck, 2008); and Richard Bauckham, *Living with Other Creatures: Green Exegesis and Theology* (Waco, Texas: Baylor University Press, 2011). See also Gilhus, *Animals, Gods and Humans*, 161–270; and Hobgood-Oster, *Holy Dogs and Asses*, 42–62. Also significant is the emerging subfield of new animism studies, exemplified by such work as Graham Harvey, *Animism: Respecting the Living World* (New York: Columbia University Press, 2006); David Abram, *Becoming Animal: An Earthly Cosmology* (New York: Vintage Books, 2010); and Mark I. Wallace, *Green Christianity: Five Ways to a Sustainable Future* (Minneapolis: Fortress Press, 2010).

61. See, however, Dave Aftandilian, "Animals and Religion," in *Grounding Religion: A Field Guide to the Study of Religion and Ecology*, ed. Whitney A. Bauman, Richard R. Bohannon II, and Kevin J. O'Brien (New York: Routledge, 2011), 113–29, together with the many articles on religion and animals in *Encyclopedia of Animal Rights and Animal Welfare*, ed. Marc Bekoff, 2nd ed. (Santa Barbara, Calif.: ABC-CLIO, 2010), vol. 2.

62. Paul Waldau and Kimberley Patton, eds., *A Communion of Subjects: Animals in Religion, Science, and Ethics* (New York: Columbia University Press, 2006).

63. Previous articles or essays in this mode have included several of the contributions to *Ecospirit: Religions and Philosophies for the Earth*, ed. Laurel Kearns and Catherine Keller, Transdisciplinary Theological Colloquia (New York: Fordham University Press, 2007), especially Glen A. Mazis, "Ecospirituality and the Blurred Boundaries of Humans, Animals, and Machines" (125–55); Luke Higgins, "Toward a Deleuze-Guattarian Micropneumatology of Spirit-Dust"

(252–63); and David Wood, "Specters of Derrida: On the Way to Econstruction" (264–89); Matthew Chrulew, "Feline Divinanimality: Derrida and the Discourse of Species in Genesis," *Bible and Critical Theory* 2, no. 2 (2008): http://www.relegere.org/index.php/bct/article/viewFile/87/73; Virginia Burrus, "Wyschogrod's Hand: Saints, Animality, and the Labor of Love," *Philosophy Today* (Winter 2011): 412–21; Stephen D. Moore, "Why There Are No Humans or Animals in the Gospel of Mark," in *Mark as Story: Retrospect and Prospect*, ed. Kelly R. Iverson and Christopher W. Skinner, Resources for Biblical Study (Atlanta: Society of Biblical Literature, 2011), 71–94; idem, "The Dog-Woman of Canaan, and Other Animal Tales in the Gospel of Matthew," in *Soundings in Cultural Criticism: Perspectives and Methods in Culture, Power, and Identity in the New Testament*, ed. Francisco Lozada Jr. and Greg Carey (Minneapolis: Fortress Press, 2013), 57–72; and especially Jennifer L. Koosed, ed., *The Bible and Posthumanism*, Semeia Studies 74 (Atlanta: Society of Biblical Literature, 2013), at least seven of whose essays engage centrally with animality. See also Glen A. Mazis, *Humans, Animals, Machines: Blurring Boundaries* (Albany: State University of New York Press, 2008), 251–57.

64. Deane-Drummond and Clough, eds., *Creaturely Theology*.

65. See Aaron S. Gross, "The Question of the Creature: Animals, Theology and Levinas's Dog," in *Creaturely Theology*, ed. Deane-Drummond and Clough, 121–37.

66. See especially Anat Pick, *Creaturely Poetics: Animality and Vulnerability in Literature and Film* (New York: Columbia University Press, 2011). Pick, whose book emerges out of the matrix of animality studies, writes: "The task at hand, I would . . . argue, is not only posthumanist and postanthropocentric, but also, and no less significantly, postsecular" (18).

67. Cf. Wolfe, "Human, All Too Human," 564.

ANIMALS, BEFORE ME, WITH WHOM I LIVE, BY WHOM I AM ADDRESSED: WRITING AFTER DERRIDA | GLEN A. MAZIS

1. Jean-Christophe Bailly, *The Animal Side*, trans. Catherine Porter (New York: Fordham University Press, 2011), 1.

2. Ibid., 2.

3. Ibid., 7.

4. Ibid., 8.

5. Jacques Derrida, *The Animal That Therefore I Am*, trans. David Wills (New York: Fordham University Press, 2008), 12.

6. Ibid., 13

7. Ibid., 14

8. Jacques Derrida, *The Beast and the Sovereign*, vol. 1, trans. Geoffrey Bennington (Chicago: University of Chicago Press, 2009), 293.

9. Ibid., 296.

10. Maurice Merleau-Ponty, *The Visible and the Invisible*, trans. Alphonso Lingis (Evanston, Ill.: Northwestern University Press, 1964), 134.

11. Ibid.

12. Ibid., 137–38: "It is Visibility sometimes wandering and sometimes reassembled."

13. Ibid., 113.

14. Bailly, *Animal Side*, 5.

15. Derrida, *Animal That Therefore I Am*, 17.

16. Ibid.

17. Ibid., 12.

18. Ibid., 11.

19. Bailly, *Animal Side*, 14.

20. Derrida, *Animal That Therefore I Am*, 18.

21. Ibid., 25.

22. Ibid., 23.

23. Ibid., 24.

24. Ibid., 101.

25. Ibid., 106.

26. Ibid., 101.

27. Ibid., 107.

28. Derrida, *Beast and the Sovereign*, 102–20.

29. Derrida, *Animal That Therefore I Am*, 103.

30. Ibid., 104.

31. Derrida, *Beast and the Sovereign*, 130.

32. Derrida, *Animal That Therefore I Am*, 159.

33. Ibid., 64.

34. Derrida, *Beast and the Sovereign*, 87–88.

35 Ibid., 60–61, 88–89.

36. Derrida, *Animal That Therefore I Am*, 64.

37. Derrida, *Beast and the Sovereign*, 96.

38. Ibid.

39. Robert Busch, *The Wolf Almanac: A Celebration of Wolves and Their World* (Guilford, Conn.: Lyons Press, 2007), 47.

40. Quoted in David L. Mech, *The Wolf: The Ecology and Behavior of an Endangered Species* (Minneapolis: University of Minnesota Press, 1970), 5.

41. Ibid., 292.

42. Ibid.

43. Farley Mowat, *Never Cry Wolf: The Amazing True Story of Life among Arctic Wolves* (New York: Little, Brown), 6.

44. Busch, *Wolf Almanac*, 110–11.

45. Mowat, *Never Cry Wolf*, vii.

46. Mech, *Wolf*, 148.

47. Busch, *Wolf Almanac*, 114.

48. I coined this term in my article "The World of Wolves: Lessons about the Sacredness of the Surround, Belonging, the Silent Dialogue of Interdependence and Death, and Speciocide," *Environmental Philosophy* 5, no. 2, guest ed. James Hatley (2008): 69–92.

49. Mech, *Wolf*, 145.

50. Ibid., 146.

51. Ibid., 94.

52. Derrida, *Animal That Therefore I Am* 131.

53. Ibid., 132.

54. Bailly, *Animal Side*, 5.

55. Derrida, *Animal That Therefore I Am*, 63.

56. Ibid., 27.

57. Ibid., 79.

58. Merleau-Ponty, *Visible and the Invisible*, 142.

59. Bailly, *Animal Side*, 15.

60. Ibid.

61. Derrida, *Animal That Therefore I Am*, 74.

62. Derrida, *Beast and the Sovereign*, 240.

63. Ibid., 238.

64. Ibid., 248.

65. Ibid., 243.

66. Bailly, *Animal Side*, 15.

THE DOGS OF EXODUS AND THE QUESTION OF THE ANIMAL | KEN STONE

1. Jacques Derrida, *The Animal That Therefore I Am*, ed. Marie-Louise Mallet, trans. David Wills (New York: Fordham University Press, 2008). The phrase "the question of the animal" is used throughout, beginning on page 8.

2. Cary Wolfe, *Animal Rites: American Culture, the Discourse of Species, and Posthumanist Theory* (Chicago: University of Chicago Press, 2003), 101.

3. Judith Butler, *Precarious Life: The Powers of Mourning and Violence* (London: Verso, 2004). Such themes are found throughout Butler's work, but in addi-

tion to *Precarious Life* see in particular her *Giving an Account of Oneself* (New York: Fordham University Press, 2005). Although Butler has had relatively little to say about the question of the animal, some of her arguments clearly have relevance for it. For an attempt to bring Butler's work to bear on animal ethics, see Chloë Taylor, "The Precarious Lives of Animals: Butler, Coetzee, and Animal Ethics," *Philosophy Today* 1, no. 52 (2008): 60–73. Cf. Kelly Oliver, *Animal Lessons: How They Teach Us to Be Human* (New York: Columbia University Press, 2009), 40–45.

4. In addition to *The Animal That Therefore I Am*, key texts in English include Derrida, "'Eating Well,' or the Calculation of the Subject," in *Points . . . : Interviews, 1974–1994*, ed. Elisabeth Weber, trans. Peggy Kamuf et al. (Stanford: Stanford University Press, 1995), 255–87; "Violence against Animals," in *For What Tomorrow . . . : A Dialogue*, by Jacques Derrida and Elisabeth Roudinesco, trans. Jeff Fort (Stanford: Stanford University Press, 2004), 62–76; *The Beast and the Sovereign: Volume I*, trans. Geoffrey Bennington (Chicago: University of Chicago Press, 2009); and *The Beast and the Sovereign: Volume II*, trans. Geoffrey Bennington (Chicago: University of Chicago Press, 2011). As Derrida himself points out, this theme appears already in less extended sections of several earlier works. For an excellent explication of this trajectory in Derrida's work by one of his translators, see Michael Naas, "Derrida's Flair (For the Animals to Follow . . .)," *Philosophy Today* 40, no. 2 (2010): 219–42.

5. Derrida, "Violence against Animals," 66.

6. Derrida, *Animal That Therefore I Am*, 30. For a thoughtful critique of Derrida for not going far enough in letting go of the distinction between humans and other animals, see Matthew Calarco, *Zoographies: The Question of the Animal from Heidegger to Derrida* (New York: Columbia University Press, 2008), especially 145–49.

7. Derrida, *Animal That Therefore I Am*, 29.

8. Ibid., 13.

9. Ibid., 55.

10. Ibid., 101.

11. See, for two useful examples, Edwin Firmage, "Zoology," in *The Anchor Bible Dictionary*, ed. David Noel Freedman et al. (New York: Doubleday, 1992), 6:1109–67, and Oded Borowski, *Every Living Thing: Daily Use of Animals in Ancient Israel* (Walnut Creek, Calif.: Altamira Press, 1998).

12. Emmanuel Levinas, "The Name of a Dog, or Natural Rights," in *Difficult Freedom: Essays on Judaism*, trans. Sean Hand (Baltimore: Johns Hopkins University Press, 1990), 151–53.

13. In order to engage more easily the discussions of Levinas and others, my English translations in this essay follow the New Revised Standard Version except in those places where I explicitly raise other possibilities for translation.

14. Levinas, "Name of a Dog," 151.

15. Though Levinas does not cite any specific sources for this tradition, it can be found among other places in the *Mekhilta* of Rabbi Ishmael, which, commenting on the meat that is thrown to dogs in Exodus 22, states: "This is to teach you that the Holy One, blessed be He, does not withhold the reward of any creature. It is said, 'But against any of the children of Israel shall not a dog whet his tongue' (Ex. 11.7). Said the Holy One, blessed be He: Give him his reward." Jacob Z. Lauterbach, *Mekhilta de-Rabbi Ishmael: A Critical Edition, Based on the Manuscripts and Early Editions, with an English Translation, Introduction, and Notes*, 2nd ed. (Philadelphia: Jewish Publication Society, 2004), 2:466.

16. Levinas, "Name of a Dog," 152.

17. Derrida, *Animal That Therefore I Am*, 114.

18. See, e.g., John Llewelyn, "Am I Obsessed by Bobby? Humanism of the Other Animal," in *Re-Reading Levinas*, ed. Robert Bernasconi and Simon Critchley (Bloomington: Indiana University Press, 1991), 234–45; John Llewelyn, *The Middle Voice of Ecological Conscience: A Chiasmic Reading of Responsibility in the Neighborhood of Levinas, Heidegger and Others* (New York: St. Martin's Press, 1991), 49–67; David Clark, "On Being 'The Last Kantian in Nazi Germany,'" in *Animal Acts: Configuring the Human in Western History*, ed. Jennifer Ham and Matthew Senior (New York: Routledge, 1997), 165–98; Wolfe, *Animal Rites*, 59–62; Peter Atterton, "Ethical Cynicism," in *Animal Philosophy: Ethics and Identity*, ed. Matthew Calarco and Peter Atterton (London: Continuum, 2004), 51–61; Alice A. Kuznia, *Melancholia's Dog: Reflections on Our Animal Kinship* (Chicago: University of Chicago Press, 2006), 32–35; Calarco, *Zoographies*, 55–77; Aaron S. Gross, "The Question of the Creature: Animals, Theology, and Levinas' Dog," in *Creaturely Theology: On God, Humans and Other Animals*, ed. Celia Deane-Drummond and David Clough (London: SCM Press, 2009), 121–37; Oliver, *Animal Lessons*, 41–42; Bob Plant, "Welcoming Dogs: Levinas and 'The Animal' Question," *Philosophy and Social Criticism* 37, no. 1 (2011): 49–71; Deborah Bird Rose, *Wild Dog Dreaming: Love and Extinction* (Charlottesville: University of Virginia Press, 2011), 29–41.

19. Clark, "On Being 'The Last Kantian in Nazi Germany,'" 166.

20. Llewelyn, "Am I Obsessed by Bobby?" 235.

21. Clark, "On Being 'The Last Kantian in Nazi Germany,'" 169.

22. Levinas, "Interview," in *Animal Philosophy*, ed. Calarco and Atterton, 49.

23. The most significant exception that I have seen is Deborah Bird Rose, who in a chapter responding to Levinas devotes several pages to the dogs of Exodus in *Wild Dog Dreaming: Love and Extinction* (Charlottesville: University of Virginia Press, 2011), 31–36. I want to thank Kate Rigby for calling Rose's work to my attention.

24. See, for example, Heather A. McKay, "Through the Eyes of Horses: Representation of the Horse Family in the Hebrew Bible," in *Sense and Sensitivity: Essays on Reading the Bible in Memory of Robert Carroll*, ed. Philip R. Davies and Alastair G. Hunter (London: Sheffield Academic Press, 2002), 127–41; Brent Strawn, *What Is Stronger Than a Lion? Leonine Image and Metaphor in the Hebrew Bible and the Ancient Near East* (Fribourg/Göttingen: Academic Press/Vandenhoeck and Ruprecht, 2006); Tova L. Forti, *Animal Imagery in the Book of Proverbs* (Leiden: Brill, 2008); Kenneth Way, *Donkeys in the Biblical World: Ceremony and Symbol* (Winona Lake, Ind.: Eisenbrauns, 2011); Deborah O'Daniel Cantrell, *The Horseman of Israel: Horses and Chariotry in Monarchic Israel (Ninth–Eighth Centuries B.C.E.)* (Winona Lake, Ind.: Eisenbrauns, 2011). With the partial exception of McKay, who engages briefly questions of animal rights and animal perspective, most of these recent works are strictly historical-critical in their orientation and ignore the contemporary emergence of something like a subfield of interdisciplinary animal studies. Nevertheless, they are helpful resources, which indicate collectively that animals are being taken more seriously within conventional biblical scholarship.

25. See, e.g., Edwin Firmage, "The Biblical Dietary Laws and the Concept of Holiness," in *Studies in the Pentateuch*, ed. J. Emerton (Leiden: Brill, 1990), 177–208; Jacob Milgrom, *Leviticus 1–16: A New Translation with Introduction and Commentary* (New York: Doubleday, 1991), 643–742; and Walter Houston, *Purity and Monotheism: Clean and Unclean Animals in Biblical Law* (Sheffield: Sheffield Academic Press, 1993). An important touchstone for all studies on this topic continues to be Mary Douglas, *Purity and Danger: An Analysis of the Concepts of Pollution and Taboo* (London: Routledge and Kegan Paul, 1966). For an earlier attempt of my own to engage the laws on clean and unclean animals in the context of a queer reading of the Bible, see Ken Stone, *Practicing Safer Texts: Food, Sex and Bible in Queer Perspective* (London: T&T Clark, 2005), 46–67.

26. See, for example, the New Century Bible commentary by J. P. Hyatt, *Exodus* (Grand Rapids, Mich.: Eerdmans, 1980), 130, 245.

27. Derrida, *Animal That Therefore I Am*, 114.

28. Clark, "On Being 'The Last Kantian in Nazi Germany,'" 193.

29. Ibid.

30. Borowski, *Every Living Thing*, 135.

31. D. Winton Thomas, "ĸᴇʟᴇʙʜ 'Dog': Its Origin and Some Usages of It in the Old Testament," *Vetus Testamentum* 10, no. 4 (1960): 414.

32. Some of the conclusions reached by Thomas about the negative attitude taken in the Hebrew Bible toward dogs have recently been challenged by Geoffrey David Miller, "Attitudes toward Dogs in Ancient Israel: A Reassessment," *Journal for the Study of the Old Testament* 32, no. 4 (2008): 487–500. The supposed negative biblical attitude is, however, accepted as a starting point by Joshua Schwartz, "Dogs in Jewish Society in the Second Temple Period and in the Time of the Mishnah and Talmud," *Journal of Jewish Studies* 55, no. 2 (2004): 246–77.

33. Houston, *Purity and Monotheism*, 190. Cf. Elaine Adler Goodfriend, "Could *keleb* in Deuteronomy 23:19 Actually Refer to a Canine?" in *Pomegranates and Golden Bells: Studies in Biblical, Jewish and Near Eastern Ritual, Law, and Literature in Honor of Jacob Milgrom*, ed. David P. Wright, David Noel Freedman, and Avi Hurvitz (Winona Lake, Ind.: Eisenbrauns, 1995), 388–92.

34. On the significance of this distinction for biblical representations of animals, see Gene M. Tucker, "The Peaceable Kingdom and a Covenant with the Wild Animals," in *God Who Creates: Essays in Honor of W. Sibley Towner*, ed. William P. Brown and S. Dean McBride (Grand Rapids, Mich.: Eerdmans, 2000), 215–25; idem, "Rain on a Land Where No One Lives: The Hebrew Bible on the Environment," *Journal of Biblical Literature* 116, no. 1 (1997): 3–17.

35. Susan McHugh, *Dog* (London: Reaktion Books, 2004), 7–8.

36. See Darcy F. Morey, *Dogs: Domestication and the Development of a Social Bond* (Cambridge: Cambridge University Press, 2010); Adam Miklósi, *Dog Behaviour, Evolution, and Cognition* (Oxford: Oxford University Press, 2007); Juliet Clutton-Brock, "Origins of the Dog: Domestication and Early History," in *The Domestic Dog: Its Evolution, Behaviour, and Interactions with People*, ed. James Serpell (Cambridge: Cambridge University Press, 1996), 7–20.

37. Raymond Coppinger and Lorna Coppinger, *Dogs: A New Understanding of Canine Origin, Behavior, and Evolution* (Chicago: University of Chicago Press, 2001).

38. See, e.g., Mary Douglas, *Purity and Danger: An Analysis of the Concepts of Pollution and Taboo* (London: Routledge, 1966).

39. See, e.g., Jon D. Levenson, *The Death and Resurrection of the Beloved Son: The Transformation of Child Sacrifice in Judaism and Christianity* (New Haven: Yale University Press, 1995), esp. 1–24; Francesca Stavrakopoulou, *King Manasseh and Child Sacrifice: Biblical Distortions of Historical Realities* (Berlin: Walter de Gruyter, 2004).

40. Derrida, *Animal That Therefore I Am*, 115.

41. Ibid., 110.

42. Ibid., 101.

43. Derrida, "Eating Well," 279.

44. Derrida, *Animal That Therefore I Am*, 278.

45. Ibid., 280.

46. Ibid., 281.

47. See, for example, David Wood, *"Comment ne pas manger*—Deconstruction and Humanism," in *Animal Others: On Ethics, Ontology, and Animal Life*, ed. H. Peter Steeves (Albany: State University of New York Press, 1999), 15–35; and the response to Wood by Matthew Calarco, "Deconstruction Is Not Vegetarianism: Humanism, Subjectivity, and Animal Ethics," *Continental Philosophy Review* 37, no. 2 (2004): 175–201. Cf. Calarco, *Zoographies*, 126–36.

48. For a recent attempt to sort through some of the possible reasons for the donkey's unusual status, see Way, *Donkeys in the Biblical World*, 178–83.

49. I explore this story further in my essay "Wittgenstein's Lion and Balaam's Ass: Talking with Others in Numbers 22–25," in *The Bible and Posthumanism*, ed. Jennifer Koosed, Semeia Studies 74 (Atlanta: Society of Biblical Literature, 2013).

50. See, e.g., Charles F. Fensham, "The Dog in Ex. XI 7," *Vetus Testamentum* 16, no. 4 (1966): 504–7.

51. Schwartz, "Dogs in Jewish Society in the Second Temple Period," 261–62.

52. McHugh, *Dog*, 42.

53. For a useful discussion of the implications of Darwin's theories for our understanding of the relationships between humans and other animals, see James Rachels, *Created from Animals: The Moral Implications of Darwinism* (New York: Oxford University Press, 1990).

54. For one influential critique, see Robert Allen Warrior, "Canaanites, Cowboys, and Indians: Deliverance, Conquest, and Liberation Theology Today," in *The Postmodern Bible Reader*, ed. David Jobling, Tina Pippin, and Ronald Schleifer (Oxford: Blackwell, 2001), 188–94.

DEVOURING THE HUMAN: DIGESTION OF A CORPOREAL SOTERIOLOGY | ERIKA MURPHY

1. Hélène Cixous, *Stigmata: Escaping Texts* (New York: Routledge, 2005), 258.

2. Stephen D. Moore, *God's Gym: Divine Male Bodies of the Bible* (New York: Routledge, 1996), 113.

3. Cixous, *Stigmata*, 258.

4. Hugh S. Pyper, "'Job the Dog': Helene Cixous on Wounds, Scars, and the Biblical Text," *Biblical Interpretation* 11, no. 3–4 (2003): 440.

5. Cixous, *Stigmata*, 259.

6. Ibid., 261.

7. Ibid., 252.

8. Ibid., 250.

9. For more on the historical context of the dichotomies between materiality / transcendence, see Virginia Burrus, *"Begotten, Not Made": Conceiving Manhood in Late Antiquity* (Stanford, Calif.: Stanford University Press, 2000). Burrus points out, for example, how Athanasius's attempt to separate Christ's transcendence from his materiality in "On the Incarnation of the Word," is "unveiled as a lie" but also "heavily reinscribes the irreducible difference of divinity" (44).

10. Craig S. Keener, *The Gospel of John: A Commentary* (Peabody, Mass.: Hendrickson, 2003), 1:694–95.

11. Stephen D. Moore, *Poststructuralism and the New Testament: Derrida and Foucault at the Foot of the Cross* (Minneapolis: Fortress Press, 1994), 58.

12. Ibid., 58–59.

13. Ibid., 59.

14. Virginia Burrus, *Saving Shame: Martyrs, Saints, and Other Abject Subjects* (Philadelphia: University of Pennsylvania Press, 2008), 50.

15. Ibid.

16. Moore, *God's Gym*, 39.

17. Hélène Cixous, "Extreme Fidelity," in *Writing Differences: Readings from the Seminar of Hélène Cixous*, ed. Susan Sellers (New York: St. Martin's Press, 1988), 16.

18. Pyper, "'Job the Dog,'" 447.

19. Ibid.

20. Shelly Rambo, *Spirit and Trauma: A Theology of Remaining* (Louisville, Ky.: Westminster John Knox Press, 2010), 8–9.

21. Ibid., 6.

22. Sharon V. Betcher, *Spirit and the Politics of Disablement* (Minneapolis: Fortress Press, 2007), 66.

23. Jacques Derrida, "Typewriter Ribbon: Limited Inc (2)," in *Without Alibi*, trans. and ed. Peggy Kamuf (Stanford, Calif.: Stanford University Press, 2002), 104.

24. Burrus, *Saving Shame*, 49–50.

25. Cixous, *Stigmata*, 123.

26. Ibid., 19.

27. Ibid., 21

28. Ibid., 19.

29. Pyper, "'Job the Dog,'" 445.

30. Moore, *God's Gym*, 4.

31. Ibid.

32. Ibid.

33. Cixous, *Stigmata*, 21.

34. Ibid., 250.

35. Hélène Cixous, *Three Steps on the Ladder of Writing*, trans. Susan Sellers and Sarah Cornell (New York: Columbia University Press, 1994), 48.

36. Derrida, "Typewriter Ribbon," 135.

THE MICROBES AND PNEUMA THAT THEREFORE I AM | DENISE KIMBER BUELL

This chapter is revised from a paper presented at "Divinanimality: Creaturely Theology, The Eleventh Transdisciplinary Theological Colloquium," Drew Theological School, September 29–October 2, 2011. My sincere thanks to Stephen Moore and Catherine Keller for the invitation to participate in this galvanizing colloquium, to Mayra Rivera Rivera for her insightful response to the paper, to the other participants for their stimulating contributions, and to James Grzelak, Melanie Johnson-DeBaufre, Jason Josephson, and Stephen Moore for their valuable comments on drafts of this chapter.

1. Juliana Spahr, "Poem Written after September 11, 2001," in *this connection of everyone with lungs: poems* (Berkeley: University of California Press, 2005), 4.

2. And it is not only humans who breathed in the wreckage of the twin towers but also pigeons, seagulls, dogs, cats, and other nonhuman animals.

3. Nancy Tuana, "Viscous Porosity: Witnessing Katrina," in *Material Feminisms*, ed. Stacy Alaimo and Susan Hekman (Bloomington: Indiana University Press, 2008), 198.

4. The colloquium for which this essay was originally crafted took as its organizing principle an exploration of "divinanimality" and "creaturely theology." As the conference materials state: "Human-animal relations are emerging as an ever more important focus for academic engagement with the more-than-human world. The heterogeneous academic field that has resulted has attracted various (non-synonymous) names, including 'animal studies,' 'animality studies,' 'posthuman animality studies,' and 'zoocriticism.' The Eleventh Drew Transdisciplinary Theological Colloquium will attempt to triangulate these vital reflections on humanity and animality with reflections on divinity. The resources for a 'creaturely theology' are considerable. All Christian scripture and most Christian theology predates the epochal Cartesian realignment of human-animal relations in terms absolutely oppositional and hierarchical, as do Jewish and Muslim traditions. Prior to the Cartesian revolution in philosophy, post-humanist zoocritics are claiming, there were no 'animals' in the modern sense, and hence no 'humans' either. 'We have never been human,' Donna Haraway hyperbolically but incisively insists *(When Species Meet)*. A contemporary crea-

turely theology might begin with the recognition that the concepts of the human and the animal inherited from the Enlightenment are best construed as the epiphenomenal products of a particular historical moment—albeit the formative moment for almost every aspect of western culture, including the academic discipline of theology itself—bracketed by a pre- and posthumanism that think the human/animal distinction differently, and hence, potentially, the divine/human/animal distinction in addition" (http://depts.drew.edu/tsfac/colloquium/2011/).

5. I understand part of the impulse in animal studies and within post- and transhumanism to be a critique of understandings and practices of subjectivity, agency, and being that are seen to have had devastating results such as oppression among humans (racism, sexism, heterosexism, genocide, imperialism), destruction of many nonhuman species and their habitats, and poisoning of the environment. The privileging of the human as a species viewed as both distinctive and superior, the notion that agency is ideally characterized by autonomy and voluntary capacity to effect change in the world, that only certain varieties of humans are capable of such agency—all these have been challenged in important ways. One strand of critique has redefined "otherness" to ward off the dangerous effects of claiming to know, speak for, and thus assimilate or kill the "other," whether that be human or nonhuman animal others. Protecting alterity is especially central to the philosophical project of Emmanuel Levinas, for example. And as many readers will know, the title of this essay is adapted from Jacques Derrida's late meditation, "The Animal That Therefore I Am (More to Follow)," trans. David Wills, *Critical Inquiry* 28, no. 2 (2002): 369–418; republished in *The Animal That Therefore I Am*, trans. David Wills (New York: Fordham University Press, 2008), 1–53. Derrida is also concerned to protect alterity. From a different perspective, protecting the alterity of divinity has been a feature of much Christian theology—a goal that has been challenged by some feminist theologians whose work resonates with some of the ideas in this essay. I am thinking here specifically of the work of Laurel Schneider and Mayra Rivera Rivera, in addition to the pathbreaking work of Catherine Keller. See, e.g., Laurel Schneider, *Re-Imagining the Divine: Confronting the Backlash Against Feminist Theology* (Cleveland: Pilgrim, 1998), and *Beyond Monotheism: A Theology of Multiplicity* (New York: Routledge, 2008); Mayra Rivera, *The Touch of Transcendence: A Postcolonial Theology of God* (Louisville, Ky.: Westminster/John Knox, 2007); Catherine Keller, *On the Mystery: Discerning Divinity in Process* (Minneapolis: Fortress, 2008).

6. The neologism "intra-action" underscores the position that processes produce actors and not simply that, as interaction implies, already distinct actors come

together to act. Intra-action has been especially developed by Karen Barad; see her *Meeting the Universe Halfway: Quantum Physics and the Entanglement of Matter and Meaning* (Durham, N.C.: Duke University Press, 2007).

7. Stacy Alaimo, *Bodily Natures: Science, Environment, and the Material Self* (Bloomington: Indiana University Press, 2010); Karen Barad, *Meeting the Universe Halfway* (Durham, N.C.: Duke University Press, 2007); Donna Haraway, "A Cyborg Manifesto: Science, Technology, and Socialist-Feminism in the Late Twentieth-Century," in *Simians, Cyborgs, and Women: The Reinvention of Nature* (New York: Routledge, 1991); Donna Haraway, "The Promises of Monsters: A Regenerative Politics for Inappropriate/d Others," in *Cultural Studies*, ed. Lawrence Grossberg, Cary Nelson, and Paula A. Treichler (New York: Routledge, 1992), 295–337; Donna Haraway, *Modest_Witness@Second_Millenium.Female Man©_Meets_OncoMouse™: Feminism and Technoscience* (New York: Routledge, 1997); Donna Haraway, *When Species Meet*, Posthumanities 3 (Minneapolis: University of Minnesota Press, 2008); Myra Hird, *The Origins of Sociable Life: Evolution after Science Studies* (London: Palgrave Macmillan, 2009); Vicki Kirby, *Telling Flesh: The Substance of the Corporeal* (New York: Routledge, 1997); Tuana, "Viscous Porosity," 188–213; and Elizabeth A. Wilson, *Psychosomatic: Feminism and the Neurological Body* (Durham, N.C.: Duke University Press, 2004).

8. See the last section of the essay for further discussion.

9. See also Alaimo, *Bodily Natures*, 14–15; and Tuana, "Viscous Porosity."

10. My approach in this essay builds on my past and current work in some respects, while also being quite exploratory and experimental in other ways. For related discussions of the notion of haunting as an alternative to linear historical narrative and ally to theological analyses, see Denise Kimber Buell, "Cyborg Memories: An Impure History of Jesus," *Biblical Interpretation* 18, no. 4–5 (2010): 313–41; and Denise Kimber Buell, "God's Own People: Specters of Race, Ethnicity, and Gender in Early Christian Studies," in *Prejudice and Christian Beginnings: Investigating Race, Gender, and Ethnicity in Early Christian Studies*, ed. Elisabeth Schüssler Fiorenza and Laura Nasrallah (Minneapolis: Fortress Press, 2009), 159–90; for a consideration of agency, see Denise Kimber Buell, "Cyborg Memories"; "Imagining Human Transformation in the Context of Invisible Powers: Instrumental Agency in Second-Century Treatments of Conversion," in *Metamorphoses: Resurrection, Body and Transformative Practices in Early Christianity*, ed. Turid Karlsen Seim and Jorunn Økland, Ekstasis: Religious Experience from Antiquity to the Middle Ages 1 (Berlin: Walter de Gruyter Press, 2009), 249–70; and Denise Kimber Buell, "The Afterlife Is Not Dead: Spiritualism, Postcolonial Theory, and Early Christian Studies," *Church History* 78, no. 4 (December 2009): 862–72.

11. Alaimo writes: "Potent ethical and political possibilities emerge from the literal contact zone between human corporeality and more-than-human nature. Imagining human corporeality as trans-corporeality, in which the human is always intermeshed with the more-than-human world, underlines the extent to which the substance of the human is ultimately inseparable from 'the environment.' . . . Thinking across bodies may catalyze the recognition that the environment, which is too often imagined as inert, empty space or as a resource for human use, is, in fact, a world of fleshy beings with their own needs, claims, and actions. By emphasizing the movement across bodies, trans-corporeality reveals the interchanges and interconnections between various bodily natures" (*Bodily Natures*, 2). See also Alaimo's insightful analysis of additional examples of pneumatic transcorporeal interactions, notably of the inhalation of "natural" materials such as silicon dust created from mining, which in turn produce bodies that are not simply vulnerable but are simultaneously classed and raced bodies (chap. 2).

12. "Viscosity is neither fluid nor solid but intermediate between them. Attention to the porosity of interactions helps to undermine the notion that distinctions, as important as they might be in particular contexts, signify a natural or unchanging boundary, a natural kind. At the same time, 'viscosity' retains an emphasis on resistance to changing form, thereby a more helpful image than 'fluidity,' which is too likely to promote a notion of open possibilities and to overlook sites of resistance and opposition or attention to the complex ways in which material agency is often involved in interactions, including, but not limited to human agency" (Tuana, "Viscous Porosity," 193–94). Both Alaimo and Tuana attend to the transcorporeal effects of chemical agents such as silicone (Alaimo) and PCV (Tuana), analyzing their effects in the larger context of practices such as mining and the plastics industry as they interact with class, race, geology, and weather, compellingly illustrating the interconnectedness of "nature" with "culture."

13. Tuana, "Viscous Porosity," 199–200, my emphasis.

14. Spahr, "Poem Written after September 11, 2001," 3.

15. Sara Ahmed, *Strange Encounters: Embodied Others in Post-Coloniality* (London: Routledge, 2000), 143–44. From a very different grounding in physics, Karen Barad makes a similar point in *Meeting the Universe Halfway*.

16. See, e.g., Haraway, "The Promises of Monsters"; Kirby, *Telling Flesh*; and Wilson, *Psychosomatic*—each of whom differently articulates challenges to the binaries of nature/culture, biological/social, material/semiotic.

17. See also Alaimo, who offers a similar kind of caution (*Bodily Natures*, 9–11, 15–17).

18. Juliana Spahr's most recent collection of poems and essays contains pieces that disrupt this anthropocentrism. See Juliana Spahr, *Well Then Here Now* (Boston: David R. Godine, 2011), 55–93, 124–33.

19. See also Carol Newsom, "Common Ground: An Ecological Reading of Genesis 2–3," in *The Earth Story in Genesis*, ed. Norman C. Habel and Shirley Wurst (Cleveland: Pilgrim/Sheffield: Sheffield Academic Press, 2000), 65. In the first creation account, it appears that the "breath of life" may not be unique to humans (see Gen. 1:30), but rather the fact that humans are created in the divine image (Gen. 1:26) and are given dominion over "every living thing" (Gen. 1:28; see also 1:26).

20. In the second creation account, pneuma/ruah is not the only means by which the text marks the difference between humans and nonhumans; Adam's naming of other living creatures (Gen. 2:19–20) has also been understood in this light.

21. For an excellent discussion of ancient views toward animals, see Ingvild Saelid Gilhus, *Animals, Gods, and Humans: Changing Attitudes to Animals in Greek, Roman, and Early Christian Ideas* (New York: Routledge, 2006).

22. "Given this, to discuss the particular modes of encounter (rather than particular others), is also to open the encounter up, *to fail to grasp it*. We have a temporal movement from the now to the not yet. We could ask, not only what made this encounter possible (its historicity), but also what does it make possible, what futures might it open up? At the same time, we have a spatial movement from here to there. We need to ask, not only how did we arrive here, at this particular place, but how is this arrival linked to other places, to an elsewhere that is not simply absent or present? We also need to consider how the *here-ness* of this encounter might affect *where we might yet be going*. To describe, not the other, but the mode of encounter in which I am faced with an other, is hence not to hold the other in place, or to turn her into a theme, a concept or thing. Rather it is to account for the conditions of possibility of being faced by her in such a way that she ceases to be fully present in the moment of the face to face, a non-present-ness which, at one and the same time, opens out the possibility of facing something other than this other, of something that may surprise the one who faces, and the one who is faced (the not yet and the elsewhere)" (Ahmed, *Strange Encounters*, 145).

23. Jacques Derrida, *Specters of Marx: The State of the Debt, the Work of Mourning, and the New International*, trans. Peggy Kamuf (1993; New York: Routledge, 1994), 16. See further discussion in Buell, "God's Own People," 164–71. In what follows, I draw on Christian texts without respect to canonical boundaries and

do not privilege resources that have become retrospectively claimed as ortho-dox. Although most contemporary forms of Christianity may privilege texts that became canonical, the process of canon formation is itself part of the inheritance of the Christian tradition; any thoughtful engagement with Chris-tian theology in the present must either reaffirm or question this inheritance by filtering, sifting, and criticizing—clearly, there are far more texts than those that became canonical that constitute the overall legacy of Christianity. See also Denise Kimber Buell, "Canons Unbound," in *Feminist Biblical Interpretation in the 20th Century*, vol. 20 of *The Bible and Women: An Encyclopaedia of Exegesis and Cultural History*, ed. Elisabeth Schüssler Fiorenza (Atlanta: SBL,2011–).

24. Similarly, in his first letter to the Corinthians, Paul distinguishes between spiri-tual and unspiritual humans (1 Cor. 2:14), addressing his audience as those who have "received not the spirit of the world [*pneuma tou kosmou*] but the *pneuma* from God" (1 Cor. 2:12), which Paul equates with having the "mind [*nous*] of Christ" (2:16) (even as he chides them for not yet having developed themselves to become spiritual). For further analysis of the meaning and significance of pneuma in Paul's writings, see Troels Engberg-Pedersen, *Cosmology and Self in the Apostle Paul: The Material Spirit* (Oxford: Oxford University Press, 2010).

25. See, e.g., "But you are not in the flesh, you are in the spirit, if in fact the spirit of God dwells in you. Anyone who does not have the spirit of Christ does not belong to him. But if Christ is in you, although your bodies are dead because of sin, your spirits are alive because of righteousness. If the spirit of the one who raised Jesus from the dead dwells in you, the one who raised Christ Jesus from the dead will give life to your mortal bodies also through the spirit which dwells in you" (Rom. 8:9–11, RSV).

26. See Caroline Johnson Hodge, *If Sons, Then Heirs: A Study of Kinship and Ethnic-ity in the Letters of Paul* (Oxford: Oxford University Press, 2007), 72–76.

27. For this text, these rulers are the archons, including the creator god Yaltaboath, the imperfect offspring of Sophia, a power of the perfect, heavenly realm, and Yaltaboath's minions (themselves imperfect copies of the various powers of the heavenly realm).

28. The contrast between types of pneuma in the *Apocryphon of John* is reminis-cent of the "elemental powers" Paul contrasts with the God whose gospel he preaches. It is not clear, though, that the author of the *Apocryphon of John* knows any Pauline correspondence. But another text discovered at Nag Ham-madi, *The Reality of the Rulers* (or *Hypostasis of the Archons*), is explicitly framed to interpret the evil powers mentioned in the Pauline letter to the Ephesians, which echoes the contrast between divine and elemental powers: "For we are

not contending against flesh and blood, but against the principalities, against the powers, against the world rulers of this present darkness, against the spiritual hosts of wickedness in the heavenly places" (Eph. 6:12, RSV).

29. See Ismo Dunderberg's helpful discussion of these terms and their ancient field of meanings, especially as enacted in Valentinian writings: *Beyond Gnosticism: Myth, Lifestyle, and Society in the School of Valentinus* (New York: Columbia University Press, 2008), 124–28.

30. For further discussion of this relational model as it plays out in early Christian discussions of conversion and agency, see Buell, "Imagining Human Transformation." For an excellent reading and historical analysis of the *Apocryphon of John*, see Karen L. King, *The Secret Revelation of John* (Cambridge, Mass.: Harvard University Press, 2006).

31. All discussed in Buell, "Imagining Human Transformation."

32. Linda Nash, *Inescapable Ecologies: A History of Environment, Disease, and Knowledge* (Berkeley: University of California Press, 2006), 24–25.

33. Ibid., 25.

34. Ibid., 48.

35. Bruno Latour, *The Pasteurization of France*, trans. Alan Sheridan and John Law (Cambridge, Mass.: Harvard University Press, 1988), 35.

36. Ibid., 37.

37. Louis Capitan, "Le rôle des microbes dans la société," *Revue Scientifique* 10, no. 3 (1894): 292. Cited ibid., 37.

38. Latour, *Pasteurization*, 37. The internal quotation is from G. Sternberg, "Les bactéries," *Revue Scientifique* 16, no. 3 (1889): 328.

39. Latour, *Pasteurization*, 38–39.

40. "We must remember that the period was full of people who turned themselves into the spokesmen for dangerous, obscure forces that must now be taken into account. The hygienists were not alone in inventing new forces. There were those who manipulated the fairy electricity, those who set up leagues for colonization, for the development of gymnastic clubs, for the promotion of the telephone, radio, or X-rays. The radical party, for instance, gained ground everywhere by forcing the traditional agents of the social game to take account of the dangerous laboring classes, whose actions and intentions were so little known. But it is with Freud that the resemblance is greatest. Like Freud, Pasteur found treasure, not in the parapraxes and trifles of everyday life, but in decay and refuse. Both announced that they were speaking in the name of invisible, rejected, terribly dangerous forces that must be listened to if civilization was not to collapse. Like the psychoanalysts, the Pasteurians set them-

selves up as exclusive interpreters of populations to which no one else had access" (ibid., 39–40).

41. In *The Corinthian Body*, Dale Martin analyzes Paul's arguments about pneuma in the Corinthian correspondence as belonging within what he calls an "invasion etiology" of disease, whereby "the body is construed as a closed but penetrable entity that remains healthy by fending off hostile forces and protecting its boundaries. Disease is caused by alien forces, either personal agents (for example, demons or gods) or impersonal but harmful materials (for example, germs, pollutants, or 'tiny animals'), that invade the body" (*The Corinthian Body* [New Haven: Yale University Press, 1995], 143–44). Although Martin also make the connection between Paul's arguments and nineteenth-century discourse about microbes, his analysis is limited by framing Paul's arguments in terms of views of illness and health instead of more broadly in terms of ontology. In addition, as I have argued elsewhere (Buell, "Imagining Human Transformation in the Context of Invisible Powers") and as is reinforced by Romans 8:9–11, Paul's arguments assume the necessary penetrability of the body in his texts, exhorting readers to make themselves the instrumental agents of divine pneuma and not of demonic powers. Thus even health is not about protecting one's closed boundaries but negotiating one's inevitable porousness "correctly."

42. See, e.g., David Frankfurter, "Beyond Magic and Superstition," in *A People's History of Early Christianity*, vol. 2: *Late Ancient Christianity*, ed. Virginia Burrus (Minneapolis: Fortress Press, 2005), 255–84; and AnneMarie Luijendijk, *Forbidden Oracles? The Gospel of the Lots of Mary*, Studien und Texte zu Antike und Christentum (Tübingen: Mohr Siebeck, 2014).

43. *New York Times*, August 28, 2011, Arts, 18.

44. Cited in Lori Hinnant, "Roma Trapped in Misery as France Demolishes Camps," Associated Press release, August 15, 2012, mercurynews.com (and posted to other sites, including *The Huffington Post*).

45. Kim Willsher, "France's Deportation of Roma Shown to Be illegal in Leaked Memo, Say Critics," September 13, 2010, guardian.co.uk.

46. This perspective disturbingly echoes much earlier European tropes about Roma. Miriam Eliav-Feldon has demonstrated that Roma were widely characterized in early modern Europe as agents of disease and disruption warranting expulsion and extermination as "vermin" infesting the body politic. She argues that this association of Roma with vermin explains why "Gypsies were the sole target of organized manhunts in Germany, Switzerland, and the Netherlands from the late sixteenth century into the eighteenth century" (Mir-

iam Eliav-Feldon, "Vagrants or Vermin? Attitudes towards Gypsies in Early Modern Europe," in *The Origins of Racism in the West*, ed. Miriam Eliav-Feldon, Benjamin Isaac, and Joseph Ziegler [Cambridge: Cambridge University Press, 2009], 291).

47. Bruno Latour, *We Have Never Been Modern*, trans. Catherine Porter (Cambridge, Mass.: Harvard University Press, 1993), 10–11.

48. See Alaimo, *Bodily Natures*, chaps. 2–5 for extensive discussion.

49. In addition to the use of these oils with special properties, this text also states that those who have been "set apart for baptism," catechumens near the end of their period of instruction, shall be exorcised both by unspecified persons laying hands upon them (perhaps their sponsors, also mentioned in this portion of the text) and specifically by the bishop (see Apostolic Tradition 20.1–4; 7–8); although traditionally attributed to Hippolytus of Rome and dated to the early third century C.E., most scholars doubt that Hippolytus compiled this work. For an accessible English translation, see *The Apostolic Tradition of Hippolytus*, trans. and introduced by Burton Scott Easton (1934; Cambridge: Cambridge University Press, 1962).

50. Translation by Wesley Isenberg, in *The Coptic Gnostic Library: A Complete Edition of the Nag Hammadi Codices* (1989; Leiden: Brill, 2000), 2:173.

51. English translation slightly modified from Robert Pierce Casey, *The Excerpta ex Theodoto of Clement of Alexandria*, Studies and Documents 1 (London: Christophers, 1934), 40–91 (other English translations are available online through www.earlychristianwritings.com). See also Paul F. Bradshaw, *The Search for the Origins of Christian Worship: Sources and Methods for the study of Early Liturgy*, 2nd ed. (Oxford: Oxford University Press, 2002), 144–70; and Henry Ansgar Kelly, *The Devil at Baptism: Ritual, Theology, and Drama* (Ithaca, N.Y.: Cornell University Press, 1985).

52. Alaimo, *Bodily Natures*, 12.

53. Ibid., 13.

54. "There are two trees growing in Paradise. The one bears [animals], the other bears humans. Adam [ate] from the tree which bore animals. [He] became an animal and he brought forth animals. For this reason the children of Adam worship [animals]. The tree [. . .] fruit is [. . .] increased [. . .] ate the [. . .] fruit of the [. . .] bears humans, [. . .] human. [. . . .] God created humans. [. . . humans] create God. That is the way it is in the world—humans make gods and worship their creation. It would be fitting for the gods to worship humans!" (*Gospel of Philip*, 71.22–72.4).

55. Caroline Walker Bynum, *The Resurrection of the Body* (New York: Columbia University Press, 1995), 39.

56. Ibid., 39.

57. I cannot help thinking of plasticized products here—imagining the Christian body as having become plasticized and thus simultaneously transformed and resistant to decomposition.

58. Hird, *Origins of Sociable Life*, 137.

59. Ibid.

60. Tuana, "Viscous Porosity," 198.

61. Haraway, *When Species Meet*, 3.

62. Hird, *Origins of Sociable Life*, 136.

63. K. B. D'Angelo, "Microbes 'R' Us," final research paper for Women's Gender Sexuality Studies 402 (Transformations and Entanglements: Identity and Agency) (May 2012, unpublished), 6.

64. Ibid., 6. Citation from Joshua Lederberg, "Infectious History," *Science*, n.s., 288, no. 5464 (2000): 287–93.

65. For example, we still must reckon with how to inherit sayings such as these two: "Blessed is the lion which becomes human when consumed by a human and cursed is the human whom the lion consumes and the lion becomes human" (*Gospel of Thomas*, 7); and "One who drinks from my mouth will become like me. I myself shall become them, and the things that are hidden will be revealed to them" (*Gospel of Thomas*, 108). These sayings speak about ingestion in terms that suggest that the encounter that is eating or drinking results in a transformation: The lion might become human in the process of being eaten by a human *or* by eating a human. Neither saying specifies a mechanism of transformation parallel to the symbiotic function of microbes in digestion. If there is a functional equivalent, it is something along the lines of "the living" force that is being incorporated itself accomplishing this change: "The one who lives from the living one will not see death" (*Gospel of Thomas*, 111). The contrast between the blessing and curse in saying 7 depict the "human" as properly the consumer of the lion, while raising the question of whether the direction of transformation turns not so much on the act of consumption as the status of the consumer and consumed. Otherwise, we might expect to read that the human who consumes a lion becomes lion-like. (Does the lion not benefit from consuming a human?) Saying 108 seems to put the "one who drinks" in the position of the consuming lion of saying 7; that is, the one who drinks becomes like the beverage. The second part of the saying explains this process in terms of the beverage turning into the one who drinks. But in this case, Jesus is not the one receiving the blessing, as the lion does in saying 7, but instead the emphasis is on the benefit to the drinker, who will now be receiving what has previously been hidden. Once again, I am inclined to

correlate the emphasis with an understanding of status distinctions between consumer and consumed even as porousness between them is also the point of the encounter.

If I want to claim the *Gospel of Thomas* as useful in some way for developing a creaturely theology, I have to question this implication about a hierarchical distinction between the lion and the human. What happens if I read the text through the lens that the lion and the human are the products of relational encounters, not ontologically fixed entities that have relations? This lens permits a reading of the gospel's acknowledgment of the possibilities of transformation without accepting that "lion" is a less desirable outcome of the intra-action here described as consumption. Should I be any less troubled about a distinction between the Jesus to whom these sayings are attributed and the one who might drink from his mouth?

66. Haraway, *When Species Meet*, 31.

67. Spahr, "Poem Written after September 11, 2001," 10.

THE APOPHATIC ANIMAL: TOWARD A NEGATIVE ZOOTHEOLOGICAL *IMAGO DEI* | JACOB J. ERICKSON

1. Jacques Derrida, *The Animal That Therefore I Am* (New York: Fordham University Press, 2008), 6.

2. See Judith Butler's use of the theme of "undoing" in many of her later works, especially *Precarious Life: The Powers of Mourning and Violence* (New York: Verso, 2004). See also Judith Butler, *Giving an Account of Oneself* (New York: Fordham University Press, 2005). Elizabeth Grosz's recent work deploys the phrase differently, using it particularly for ecological exploration. See Elizabeth Grosz, *Becoming Undone: Darwinian Reflections on Life, Politics, and Art* (Durham, N.C.: Duke University Press, 2011).

3. Max Oelschlaeger. *The Idea of Wilderness* (New Haven, Conn.: Yale University Press, 1991), 1. The concept of "wilderness" is a complicated one in ecological meditations. "Wilderness" is, in the United States, a particular political designation of land that has, in ecological theory, elicited a number of responses. I am bracketing those "wilderness" debates for the theopoetics of this paper. They are, however, implicated together. See especially William Cronon's classic essay, "The Trouble with Wilderness," in *Uncommon Ground: Rethinking the Human Place in Nature*, ed. William Cronon (New York: W. W. Norton, 1995), 69–90.

4. Larry L. Rasmussen. *Earth Community, Earth Ethics* (Maryknoll, N.Y.: Orbis Books, 1996), 189.

5. Ian A. McFarland, *The Divine Image: Envisioning the Invisible God* (Minneapolis: Fortress Press, 2005), 2.

6. Ibid.

7. Ibid., 3–4. On page 4 he writes, "In short, Christ alone is truly the image of God."

8. And many other Genesis narratives. For the peculiar intertwinings of Derrida's biblical interpretation see, for example, Matthew Chrulew's essay "Feline Divinanimality: Derrida and the Discourse of Species in Genesis," *Bible and Critical Theory* 2, no. 2 (2006): 18.1–18:22.

9. Derrida, *Animal That Therefore I Am*, 16.

10. Ibid., 4.

11. Ibid., 18.

12. Ibid., 17.

13. Ibid.

14. Ibid.

15. Ibid., 34.

16. Ibid., 23.

17. Ibid., 29.

18. Ibid., 12.

19. Donna J. Haraway, *When Species Meet* (Minneapolis: University of Minnesota Press, 2008), 20.

20. Ibid., 22.

21. I mean this queer pleasure in a very literal sense. We need to, like Stacy Alaimo, rethink the possibility of queer animals and queer naturecultures. See *Queer Ecologies: Sex, Nature, Politics, Desire*, ed. Catriona Mortimer-Sandilands and Bruce Erickson (Bloomington: Indiana University Press, 2010).

22. A particular example is cooperative dolphin and human fishing that occurs in Laguna, Santa Catarina, Brazil. Dolphins drive the fish to fishermen and signal when the fisherman are to cast their nets. These companion species work and play together for the benefit of food.

23. See, for example, Alfred Crosby's now classic work, *The Columbian Exchange: Biological and Cultural Consequences of 1492* (Westport, Conn.: Greenwood, 2003).

24. Derrida, *Animal That Therefore I Am*, 31.

25. Sharon Betcher, "Grounding the Spirit: An Ecofeminist Pneumatology," in *Ecospirit: Religions and Philosophies for the Earth*, ed. Laurel Kearns and Catherine Keller (New York: Fordham University Press, 2007), 334–35.

26. It's important here to note I'm not considering Spirit underneath a binary of life and death. Dying is a part of the process of living for all creatures, and Spirit is in the midst of this process. See Shelly Rambo's articulation of the "middle Spirit" in her *Spirit and Trauma: A Theology of Remaining* (Louisville, Ky.: Westminster John Knox Press, 2010).

27. Wangari Maathai, *Replenishing the Earth: Spiritual Values for Healing Ourselves and the World* (New York: Doubleday, 2010), 89. Maathai's words here might intimate a sort of "back to nature" argument. I am not advocating that sort of line of thought, but rather a sensuous attentiveness to the mysterious exposures of the chaos of life.

28. See Karl Barth, *Church Dogmatics IV:I: The Doctrine of Reconciliation* (New York: T&T Clark, 1956), 157–210.

29. Hans Urs von Balthasar, *Heart of the World* (San Francisco: Ignatius Press, 1974), 210.

30. Ibid., 215.

31. Ibid., 210.

32. Stacy Alaimo, *Bodily Natures: Science, Environment, and the Material Self* (Bloomington: Indiana University Press, 2010), 2.

33. John 3:8, NRSV.

34. Anne Primavesi, *Cultivating Unity within the Biodiversity of God* (Salem, Ore.: Polebridge Press, 2011), 10.

35. Ibid.

36. Jean-Christophe Bailly, *The Animal Side*, trans. Catherine Porter (New York: Fordham University Press, 2011), 46.

37. Ibid.

38. Ibid., 47.

39. Cronon, "Trouble with Wilderness," 88.

40. Terra Rowe, "John Muir's Aesth/Ethics: A Postmodern, Postcolonial Interpretation of Muir, Wilderness Preservation, and the Transcendent In Nature." Unpublished paper, quoted with permission from the author.

41. In consonance with Sharon Betcher's critique of pneumatology, this conception of the Spirit thinks through our created reality and not out of it, and "will have nothing much to do with ideals, perfections, and whole(some)ness." See *Spirit and the Politics of Disablement* (Minneapolis: Fortress Press, 2007), 4.

42. I strongly resonate, in this regard, to Denise Buell's contribution to this book.

THE DIVINANIMALITY OF LORD SEQUOIA | TERRA S. ROWE

1. Richard Cartwright Austin, *Baptized into Wilderness: A Christian Perspective on John Muir* (Abingdon, Va.: Creekside Press, 1991), 3.

2. Donna J. Haraway, *When Species Meet* (Minneapolis: University of Minnesota Press, 2008), 5–6. Messmates are another name for her "companion species": "Human and nonhuman animals are companion species, messmates at table, eating together" (301). In an essay titled "Cyborgs to Companion Species" Har-

away sums up what she means by companion species as "a four-part composition, in which co-constitution, finitude, impurity, and complexity are what is" (363). She also explains in "Cyborgs to Companion Species" that, as Clifford exemplifies, "companion species can consist of artifacts, organisms, technologies, or other humans. . . . They are not substitutes for other things, they are not surrogates for theory, they are 'not here just to think with'—they are here to live with" (362). Donna Haraway, "Cyborgs to Companion Species: Reconfiguring Kinship in Technoscience," in *The Animals Reader: The Essential Classical and Contemporary Writings*, ed. Linda Kalof and Amy Fitzgerald (New York: Berg, 2007), 362–74.

3. Haraway, *When Species Meet*, 3–5.

4. Ibid., 216, for Haraway's definition of "contact zones."

5. Jacques Derrida, *The Animal That Therefore I Am*, ed. Marie-Louise Mallet, trans. David Wood (New York: Fordham University Press, 2008), 12.

6. Andrew Linzey provides a critique of Liberation Theology's Christology in "Liberation Theology for Animals," in his *Animal Theology* (Urbana: University of Illinois Press, 1995), 62–75.

7. Examples especially, but not exhaustively, include Sallie McFague, Ivone Gebara, and Catherine Keller. These ecotheologians are troubled by the anthropocentrism of incarnation and so, like Schneider—as we will see later—avoid Christocentric incarnation.

8. This approach remains problematic since, as McFague uncritically writes: "In Jesus we see the presence of God, and that God's presence is embodied, paradigmatically, in a mere human being" (Sally McFague, "An Ecological Christology," in *Christianity and Ecology: Seeking the Well-Being of Earth and Humans*, ed. Dieter T. Hessel and Rosemary Radford Ruether [Cambridge, Mass.: Harvard University Press, 2000], 34). A human body is still the ruling paradigm for the way that God is embodied in the world. Ivone Gebara emphasizes Jesus as metaphor for God's presence in the world. She writes, "Along with McFague, I believe that to affirm the incarnation, or the bodiliness, of the divine does not necessarily require that Jesus have some unique metaphysical character. . . . For this reason, the incarnation, the presence of the greatest of mysteries in our flesh, is more than Jesus of Nazareth. In this sense, we could say that Jesus is for us a metaphor of the divine presence, the unfathomable mystery, the unutterable in the human flesh in which we all are included" (Ivone Gebara, *Longing for Running Water: Ecofeminism and Liberation* [Minneapolis: Fortress Press, 1999], 185). Gebara here sacrifices the particularity of God's entering into creation, broadening incarnation to sacralize all embodied life. A more

recent example is Anne Primavesi, *Cultivating Unity within the Biodiversity of God* (Salem, Ore.: Polebridge Press, 2011). Primavesi here adapts John Dominic Crossan's parabolic Jesus for her theology of biodiversity.

9. Process thought, such as that of Catherine Keller in *Face of the Deep: A Theology of Becoming* (New York: Routledge, 2003), provides another alternative. I admire that this approach doesn't squander the gift of the divine entering into the muck of creation by making it into a metaphor or parable. What this approach lacks, from my perspective, is particularity: that God shows up in a special way in a particular time and place and not only in a general, universally creative way. God enters into muck and flesh in particular times and places, and those times and places are unlikely for their seeming God-forsakeness (Golgotha, for example)—this is the scandalous nature of incarnation that I want to emphasize.

10. Laurel C. Schneider, *Beyond Monotheism: A Theology of Multiplicity* (New York: Routledge, 2008), 4.

11. Derrida, *Animal That Therefore I Am*, 132.

12. The feminist theologian and philosopher Mary Daly famously insisted in *Beyond God the Father* (Boston: Beacon Press, 1973): "If God is male, then male is God."

13. Joseph Sittler, "The Role of Negation in Faith," in his *The Care of the Earth* (Minneapolis: Fortress Press, 2004), 22.

14. Sittler suggests that Christocentrism is to blame, but also calls it "one of our greatest virtues." Joseph Sittler, *Gravity and Grace: Reflections and Provocations* (Minneapolis: Fortress, 2005), 7.

15. Ibid., 3.

16. Ibid.

17. Ibid., 44.

18. Sittler moves grace to the everyday, the mundane, or the worldly. It is not a state or quality but an "occasion" or event. He references Alfred North Whitehead's critique of simple location here in *Essays on Nature and Grace* (Philadelphia: Fortress Press, 1972), 87. See note 23 for more information with reference to "in, with, and under."

19. See Dieter T. Hessel and Rosemary Radford Ruether, "Introduction: Current Thought on Christianity and Ecology" in *Christianity and Ecology*: "Ecotheology first surfaced noticeably in North America through the Faith-Man-Nature Group convened by Philip Joranson in 1963 with support from the National Council of Churches. That initiative was stimulated by pioneering thinkers, such as Joseph Sittler, whose 1961 speech to the World Council of Churches

called for earthy Christology and greater emphasis on cosmic redemption" (xxxiv).

20. Sittler, "Called to Unity," *Ecumenical Review* 14, no. 2 (1962): 177–87.

21. Paul Santmire, "Studying the Doctrine of Creation," *Dialog* 21 (Summer 1982): 199. Cited in Steven Bouma-Prediger, *The Greening of Theology: The Ecological Models of Radford Ruether, Joseph Sittler, and Jürgen Moltmann* (Atlanta: American Academy of Religion, 1995), 63.

22. Joseph Sittler, "The Sittler Speeches," in *Center for the Study of Campus Ministry Yearbook 1977–78*, ed. Phil Schroeder (Valparaiso, Ind.: Valparaiso University, 1978), 43.

23. "In, with, and under" is a common descriptor of Luther's position on Christ's presence in sacramental bread, wine, and water. In his *Large Catechism* Luther writes, under the heading "Of the Sacrament of the Altar," that the sacrament is "the true body and blood of our Lord Jesus Christ, in and under the bread and wine, which we Christians are commanded by Christ's word to eat and drink. . . . The sacrament is bread and wine, but not mere bread and wine such as are ordinarily served at the table. Rather, it is bread and wine within God's Word and bound to it" (*The Book of Concord: The Confessions of the Evangelical Lutheran Church*, ed. Robert Kolb and Timothy J. Wengert, trans. Charles Arand et al. [Minneapolis: Fortress Press, 2000] 467). Luther's position on Christ's presence in the sacraments was different from both Roman Catholic and Calvinist positions. Luther, unlike Calvin, held the Roman Catholic insistence of the "real presence" of Christ in the sacramental elements. However, instead of transubstantiation he suggested consubstantiation, which is likely what the "with" in the above phrase references. Also the German word usually translated as *"under"* is *unter* which does not imply a lesser materiality, but can also be translated as "among."

24. Bouma-Prediger, *Greening of Theology*, 62. Citing Conrad Simonson, *The Christology of the Faith and Order Movement* (Leiden: Brill, 1972), 94.

25. Sittler is in good company as someone whose ecotheology is undermined by a remnant humanism. Stephen Moore's insightful essay on David Rhoads and Donald Michie's *Mark as Story* is a similar example. Moore argues that their characterization of Jesus is rooted in humanism and thus Descartes's hierarchical dualism between human and animal. Rhoads has elsewhere done significant work for the cause of care for the earth, but Moore points out the inconsistency between Rhoads's ecological concerns and his interpretation of Christ. Stephen D. Moore, "Why There Are No Humans or Animals in the Gospel of Mark," in *Mark as Story: Retrospect and Prospect*, ed. Kelly R. Iver-

son and Christopher W. Skinner (Atlanta: Society of Biblical Literature, 2011), 71–93.

26. Derrida writes in "Circumfession" that he can "quite rightly pass for an atheist." Geoffrey Bennington and Jacques Derrida, "Circumfession," in *Jacques Derrida*, trans. Geoffrey Bennington (Chicago: University of Chicago Press, 1999), 155. John D. Caputo notes the ambiguity of this comment and asks Derrida to remark further on it in *Deconstruction in a Nutshell: A Conversation with Jacques Derrida*, ed. John D. Caputo (New York: Fordham University Press, 1997), 20.

27. Jacques Derrida and Elisabeth Roudinesco, "Violence against Animals," in *For What Tomorrow . . . : A Dialogue*, trans. Jeff Fort (Stanford, Calif.: Stanford University Press, 2004), 62–63.

28. Derrida explains, "Descartes will, with all due rigor, do without his definition of the human in the combined terms of animality and rationality, of man as rational animal. There is in his gesture a moment of rupture with respect to the tradition, a rupture for which Descartes is not given credit often enough" (*Animal That Therefore I Am*, 71). On Aristotle, see Aristotle, "The History of Animals," in *The Animals Reader: The Essential Classical and Contemporary Writings*, ed. Linda Kalof and Amy Fitzgerald (New York: Berg, 2007), 5–7.

29. Moore, "Why There Are No Humans or Animals in the Gospel of Mark," 80.

30. Ibid.

31. Derrida, *Animal That Therefore I Am*, 5.

32. Ibid., 9.

33. Ibid., 11. See also 29: "The animal looks at us, and we are naked before it. Thinking perhaps begins there."

34. Jacques Derrida, "The Gift of Death," in *The Gift of Death and Literature in Secret*, trans. David Wills (Chicago: University of Chicago Press, 2008), 60.

35. Ibid., 78.

36. Ibid., 83.

37. Simon Critchley writes, "The alleged ethical turn of Derrida's thinking might be viewed simply as a return to Levinas, one of the major influences on the development of his thinking." Conversely, Critchley goes on to add, "It is fair to say that in the English-speaking world many people came to Levinas through the astonishing popularity of the work of Derrida. The turn to Levinas was motivated by the question of whether deconstruction . . . had any ethical status." Simon Critchley, introduction to *The Cambridge Companion to Levinas*, ed. Simon Critchley and Robert Bernasconi (Cambridge: Cambridge University Press, 2002), 3–4.

38. Derrida, "Gift of Death," 84.

39. Derrida, *Animal That Therefore I Am*, 119.

40. See Gayatri Chakravorty Spivak's comments on the Derridean trace: "Derrida's trace is the mark of the absence of a presence, an always already absent present, of the lack at the origin that is the condition of thought and experience." Spivak, Translator's Preface to Jacques Derrida, *Of Grammatology*, trans. Gayatri Chakravorty Spivak (Baltimore: Johns Hopkins University Press, 1974), xvii.

41. Derrida, *Animal That Therefore I Am*, 68. The reference to Descartes in the title of these lectures and in themes such as this become clearer when read as "The Animal that *ergo sum*." This reference is also clearer in Derrida's original French. Derrida is here playing on the French *je suis* which can mean both "I am" and "I follow."

42. Ibid., 131.

43. Ibid., 132.

44. "The Chimaera was said to be 'invincible,' of a divine race and in no way human . . . : a lion in front, a serpent behind, a goat in the middle, its breath spouting frightening bursts of flamboyant flame. . . . As we shall understand, that is not how Descartes describes the Chimera whose existence has to be excluded at the moment of 'I think therefore I am,' in part four of the *Discourse on Method* ('we can distinctly imagine a lion's head on a goat's body without having to conclude from this that a chimera exists in the world')" (ibid., 46).

45. Leonard Lawlor explains that for Heidegger, "In order to be world-forming, in order to have an understanding of the world [*Weltverstehen*], we must have access to the 'as such' of beings. And to have access to the 'as such' of beings, we must question our own being." To Heidegger it is clear animals lack this ability. Lawlor goes on to explain that to have access to death, and not merely "perish" as animals do, one must also question one's own being. "Animals Have No Hand: An Essay on Animality in Derrida," *New Centennial Review* 7, no. 2 (2007): 51.

46. Derrida, *Animal That Therefore I Am*, 131.

47. Ibid., 132. This is precisely what makes animal "rights" so problematic. The concept of rights has been founded on the Cartesian subject, which was founded on the exclusion of the animal.

48. Ibid., 160. The full quote on the final page is as follows: "Hence the strategy in question would consist in pluralizing and varying the 'as such,' and, instead of simply giving speech back to the animal, or giving to the animal what the human deprives it of, as it were, in marking that the human is, in a way, similarly 'deprived,' by means of a privation that is not a privation, and that there is no pure and simple 'as such.' There you have it. That would presume a radical

reinterpretation of what is living, naturally, but not in terms of the 'essence of the living,' of the 'essence of the animal.'"

49. Ibid., 29.

50. Ibid.

51. Haraway, *When Species Meet*, 19.

52. Ibid., 20.

53. "Companion species can consist of artifacts, organisms, technologies, or other humans. . . . They are not substitutes for other things, they are not surrogates for theory, they are not here just to think with—they are here to live with" ("Cyborgs to Companion Species," 362). Haraway is referencing Lévi-Strauss here, who opined, "Species are chosen as totems 'not because they are 'good to eat' but because they are 'good to think'" (Claude Lévi-Strauss, "The Totemic Illusion," in Kalof and Fitzgerald *The Animals Reader*, 262.

54. Derrida, *Animal That Therefore I Am*, 10.

55. Haraway, *When Species Meet*, 4. With more time and space I would also expand on Haraway's dependence on the work of the physicist, feminist, and philosopher (as well as Haraway's former advisee), Karen Barad. See Karen Barad, *Meeting the Universe Halfway: Quantum Physics and the Entanglement of Matter and Meaning* (Durham, N.C.: Duke University Press, 2007). According to Barad, we are interdependent even at what we view as the foundation of our independence and differentiation—our ability to make responsible decisions and be held accountable for those decisions. We are only ever, as Barad says, "intra-acting," rather than interacting, which implies separate entities affecting each other only externally and preexisting the relation with another. Resonance with Haraway's description of "Clifford" is not by chance. Haraway makes explicit use of Barad's "intra-action" throughout *When Species Meet*.

56. Ibid., 42.

57. Ibid.

58. Ibid., 3–4.

59. Ibid.

60. Laurel C. Schneider, *Beyond Monotheism: A Theology of Multiplicity* (New York: Routledge, 2008), 5.

61. Ibid., 175.

62. Ibid., 172.

63. Ibid.

64. Ibid., 175.

65. My use of the "figure" is informed more by Haraway than by Derrida, who rejects the potential assumption that his cat is a figure or metaphor of a cat

and not an actual, living, cat whose singularity defies conceptualization (*Animal*, 6). Haraway's use of "figure," in contrast, is a "chimerical vision," which "collect[s] the people through their invitation to inhabit the corporeal story told in their lineaments." "Figures," she continues, "are not representations or didactic illustrations, but rather material-semiotic nodes or knots in which diverse bodies and meanings coshape one another." These figures encompass both "imagined possibility" and "fierce and ordinary reality" (*When Species Meet*, 4). Like Haraway's figures, Christ is a material-semiotic knot of the divine—who imagines possibilities—and a particular piece at a particular time of our "fierce and ordinary reality."

66. This interpretation is not meant to be exclusive of other religions or other traditions that don't recognize Christ as Christians do. It is merely a way of making sense of the call of the neighbor on us toward responsiveness and responsibility from a Christian perspective. More to the point, it is an attempt to make sense of and radicalize Christian ethical impulses such as that of Martin Luther, who insisted that the gift of grace in Christ overflows the bounds of the individual human and on to their neighbors so that Christians should be "little Christs" to their neighbors. See Luther's "Freedom of a Christian," in *Martin Luther's Basic Theological Writings*, ed. Timothy Lull (Minneapolis: Fortress, 1989), 619–20: "As our heavenly Father has in Christ freely come to our aid, we also ought freely to help our neighbor through our body and its works, and each one should become as it were a Christ to the other that we may be Christs to one another and Christ may be the same in all."

67. Laurie Shannon notes the correspondence between the modern conceptualization of the animal/human binary (a shift from a more fluid premodern continuum of "creatures") and the disappearance of wilderness space: "'The disappearance of the more protean creatures into the abstract nominalizations of *animal, the animal*, and *animals* parallels livestock's banishment to a clandestine, dystopian world of industrial food production, where the unspeakable conditions of life depend on invisibility. It mirrors, too, the increasing confinement of wildlife in preserves as wild spaces disappear with alarming speed" (Laurie Shannon, "The Eight Animals in Shakespeare; or, Before the Human," *PMLA* 124, no. 2 [2009]: 477, as quoted in Moore, "Why There Are No Humans or Animals in the Gospel of Mark," 87).

ANIMAL CALLS | KATE RIGBY

This essay is dedicated to Bishop Neville Chynoweth (1922–2011), in loving memory of his wise parish ministry, brilliant jazz piano improvisation, and deep fellow-feeling for animals (human and otherwise).

1. Jacques Derrida, "The Animal That Therefore I Am (More to Follow)," trans. David Wills *Critical Inquiry* 28, no. 2 (2002): 400.

2. Laura Hobgood-Oster, *Holy Dogs and Asses: Animals in the Christian Tradition* (Urbana: University of Illinois Press, 2008).

3. Bruno Latour, *We Have Never Been Modern* (Cambridge, Mass.: Harvard University Press, 1993).

4. Val Plumwood, *Environmental Culture: The Ecological Crisis of Reason* (London: Routledge, 2002), 97–122.

5. A. D. Hope, "Tasmanian Magpies," in *Cross-Country: A Book of Australian Verse*, ed. John Barnes and Brian McFarlane (Richmond, Vic.: Heinemann, 1984), 109–10.

6. Donna Haraway, *When Species Meet* (Minneapolis: University of Minnesota Press, 2008), 20.

7. Jacques Derrida, *The Animal That Therefore I Am*, trans. David Wills, ed. Marie-Louise Mallet (New York: Fordham University Press, 2008).

8. Matthew Calarco, *Zoographies: The Question of the Animal from Heidegger to Derrida* (New York: Columbia University Press, 2008), 149.

9. Plumwood, *Environmental Culture*, 165.

10. In one of her last essays, Plumwood articulated a philosophy of human-animal relationship in death, which helpfully provided instruction to her friends as to how to arrange her burial. See the posthumous publication, *The Eye of the Crocodile*, ed. Lorraine Sharron (Canberra: ANU E-Press, 2012).

11. Unless otherwise stated, all biblical quotations are from *The New Oxford Annotated Bible: New Revised Standard Version with the Apocrypha* (Oxford: Oxford University Press, 2007).

12. Sue Wesson, *Murni Dhungang Jirra: Living in the Illawarra*. Introduction online at http://www.environment.nsw.gov.au/resources/cultureheritage/illawarra AboriginalResourceUseIntroduction.pdf, p. 6.

13. Gisela Kaplan, *Australian Magpie: Biology and Behaviour of an Unusual Songbird* (Collingwood, Vic.: CSIRO Publishing, 2008), 108.

14. Deborah Bird Rose, *Wild Dog Dreaming* (Charlottesville: University of Virginia Press, 2011), 138–41.

15. See, e.g., Jesper Hoffmeyer, *Signs of Meaning in the Universe* (Bloomington: Indiana University Press, 1993), and Robert S. Corrington, *Ecstatic Naturalism: Signs of the World* (Bloomington: Indiana University Press, 1994).

16. Maurice Merleau-Ponty, *Nature: Course Notes from the Collége de France*, trans. Robert Vallier, ed. Dominique Séglard (Evanston, Ill.: Northwestern University Press, 2003).

17. Jean-Louis Chrétien, *The Call and the Response*, trans. Anne A. Davenport (New York: Fordham University Press, 2004).

18. This deistic tendency in some contemporary ecotheology is questioned, e.g., by Stanley Hauerwas and John Berkman in "A Trinitarian Theology of the 'Chief End' of 'All Flesh,'" in *Good News for Animals? Christian Approaches to Animal Well-Being*, ed. Charles Pinches and Jay B. McDaniel (Eugene, Ore.: Wipf and Stock, 1993), 62–74.

19. Karen Barad, *Meeting the Universe Halfway: Quantum Physics and the Entanglement of Matter and Meaning* (Durham, N.C.: Duke University Press, 2007). The term *intra-active* was coined by Barad to refer to mutually constitutive interactions.

20. Catherine Keller, *On the Mystery: Discerning Divinity in Process* (Minneapolis: Fortress Press, 2008), 153.

21. James Hatley, "The Anarchical Goodness of Creation: Monotheism in Another's Voice," in *Facing Nature*, ed. William Edelglass, James Hatley, and Christian Diehm (Pittsburgh: Duquesne University Press, 2012), 264.

22. Pinches and McDaniel, eds., *Good News for Animals?*

23. Roderic Dunkerley, *Beyond the Gospels* (Harmondsworth: Penguin, 1961), 143–44.

24. In his *Discourse on Method*, Descartes ties the lifting of ethical constraints on animal experimentation to the alleged inability of animals "to show that they are thinking what they are saying," which, in his analysis, proved "that they have no intelligence at all, and that it is nature which acts in them according to the disposition of their organs. In the same way a clock, consisting only of wheels and springs, can count the hours and measure the time more accurately than we can with all our wisdom" (quoted in Hobgood-Oster, *Holy Dogs and Asses*, 36).

25. The "strange stranger" is how Timothy Morton translates Derrida's *arrivant*, with a view to challenging the anthropocentric limitation of Levinasian ethics. Timothy Morton, "Coexistence and Coexistents: Ecology without a World," in *Ecocritical Theory: New European Approaches*, ed. Axel Goodbody and Kate Rigby (Charlottesville: University of Virginia Press, 2011), 325–50.

26. Anne Elvey, *The Matter of the Text: Material Engagements between Luke and the Five Senses* (Sheffield, Eng.: Sheffield Phoenix Press, 2011), 82.

27. Ibid.

28. Max Scheler, "Fellow Feeling, Benevolence, Forms and Kinds of Love," in *On Feeling, Valuing, Knowing: Selected Writings*, ed. and intro. Harold Bershady (Chicago: University of Chicago Press, 1993) 69–81.

29. Elvey, *Materiality of the Text*, 161.

30. Mick Smith, "Dis(appearance): Earth, Ethics and Apparently (In)significant Others," in *Unloved Others: Death of the Disregarded in the Time of Extinctions*, ed. Deborah Bird Rose and Thom van Dooren, special issue, *Australian Humanities Review* 50 (2011): 37–39.

31. Mary Oliver, *Truro Bear and Other Adventures: Poems and Essays* (Boston: Beacon Press, 2008), 61–62.

32. Mary Oliver, *What Do We Know: Poems and Prose Poems* (Cambridge, Mass.: Da Capo, 2002), 21.

33. Milan Kundera, *The Unbearable Lightness of Being*, trans. Michael Henry Heim (London: Faber & Faber, 1984), 289.

34. Rose, *Wild Dog Dreaming*, 146. The embedded quote is from Brent Dowe and Trevor McNaughton's song, "By the Rivers of Babylon."

35. Robyn Eckersley, "Beyond Human Racism," *Environmental Values* 7, no. 2 (1998): 165–82.

36. Robert S. Corrington, *A Semiotic Theory of Theology and Philosophy* (Cambridge: Cambridge University Press, 2000), 18–20. On the unconscious in Schelling's *Naturphilosophie*, see also Kate Rigby, *Topographies of the Sacred: The Poetics of Place in European Romanticism* (Charlottesville: University of Virginia Press, 2004), 38–45 and 80.

37. Wendy Wheeler, *The Whole Creature: Complexity, Biosemiotics and the Evolution of Culture* (London: Lawrence & Wishart, 2006). Peirce coined the term *abduction* to refer to insights that are based neither on induction or deduction, but that arise from unconscious or preconscious levels of recognition.

38. Marija Gimbutas, *The Civilization of the Goddess* (San Francisco: Harper SanFrancisco, 1991).

39. Mark I. Wallace, "Sacred-Land Theology: Green Spirit, Deconstruction, and the Question of Idolatry in Contemporary Earthen Christianity," in *Ecospirit: Religions and Philosophies for the Earth*, ed. Laurel Kearns and Catherine Keller (New York: Fordham University Press, 2007), 291–314.

40. Martin Buber, "Prophecy, Apocalyptic, and the Historical Hour," in *Pointing the Way: Collected Essays*, trans. Maurice Friedman (London: Routledge and Kegan Paul, 1957), 192–208. See Catherine Keller's *Apocalypse Now and Then: A Feminist Guide to the End of the World* (Boston: Beacon Press, 1996) for a far more detailed discussion of varieties of the apocalyptic. On the prophetic imagination in the context of ecocatastrophe, see also Kate Rigby, "Writing in the Anthropocene: Idle Chatter or Ecoprophetic Witness?" *Australian Humanities Review*, no. 47 (2009), online at http://www.australianhumanitiesreview.org/archive/Issue-November-2009/rigby.html.

41. Terry Eagleton, *After Theory* (London: Penguin, 2004), 175.

42. Deborah Bird Rose, "On History, Trees, and Ethical Proximity," *Postcolonial Studies* 11, no. 2 (2008): 165.

43. Walter Brueggeman, *The Prophetic Imagination*, 2nd ed. (Minneapolis: Fortress Press, 2001).

44. I am grateful to Val Billingham for alerting me to the significance of this figure in Jeremiah, and for pointing out that the Hebrew word commonly translated as "mourns" can also mean "dry up," as examined in depth in her doctoral dissertation, "The Earth Mourns/Dries Up in Jeremiah 4: 23–28: A Literary Analysis Viewed through the Heuristic Lens of an Ecologically Oriented Symbiotic Relationship" (PhD diss., Melbourne College of Divinity, 2010). I am also indebted to my own DMin student at Melbourne College of Divinity, Janet Morgan, for her conceptualization of ecoprophetic imagination and ministry in her doctoral dissertation, "Earth's Cry: Prophetic Ministry in a More-Than-Human World" (DMin diss., Melbourne College of Divinity, 2010).

45. On "penitential witness" see James Hatley, "Blaspheming Humans: Levinasian Politics and *The Cove*," *Environmental Philosophy* 8, no. 2 (2011): 16–20.

46. Judith Wright, *Collected Poems* (Sydney: HarperCollins, 1994), 219–20.

47. Veronica Brady, *South of My Days. A Biography of Judith Wright* (Sydney: HarperCollins, 1998); Jennifer Coralie, "Resonance, Reconnection, Reparation: Judith Wright's Radical 'Green' Writing Project" (PhD diss., Monash University, 2011).

48. Lawrence Troster, "Hearing the Outcry of Mute Things: Towards a Jewish Creation Theology," in Kearns and Keller, eds., *Ecospirit*, 352.

LITTLE BIRD IN MY PRAYING HANDS: RAINER MARIA RILKE AND GOD'S ANIMAL BODY | BEATRICE MAROVICH

1. Rainer Maria Rilke, *Stories of God*, trans. Michael H. Kohn (Boston: Shambhala, 2003), 4.

2. Ibid.

3. Ibid., 6.

4. Ibid., 7.

5. Rainer Maria Rilke, *Stories of God*, trans. M. D. Herter Norton, 3rd ed. (New York: W. W. Norton, 1992), 31.

6. Rainer Maria Rilke, "The Eighth Elegy," in *Duino Elegies*, trans. C. F. MacIntyre (Berkeley: University of California Press, 1961), 61.

7. Giorgio Agamben, *The Open: Man and Animal*, trans. Kevin Attell (2002; Stanford, Calif: Stanford University Press, 2004), 57.

8. Ibid., 92.

9. Ibid., 58, paraphrasing Heidegger.

10. See Carl Schmitt, *Political Theology: Four Chapters on the Concept of Sovereignty*, trans. George Schwab (1922; Chicago: University of Chicago Press, 2004).

11. Eric L. Santner, *On Creaturely Life: Rilke, Benjamin, Seabald* (Chicago: University of Chicago Press, 2006), 9.

12. Ibid., 21.

13. Ibid., 22.

14. Eric L. Santner, *The Royal Remains: The People's Two Bodies and the Endgames of Sovereignty* (Chicago: University of Chicago Press, 2011), 59.

15. Michael Naas, *Derrida from Now On* (New York: Fordham University Press, 2008), 143.

16. Significantly, however, this divinity does *not* appear to be Christological. Numerous commentators have noted that Rilke was opposed to the theological role of Christ as mediator. F. W. van Heerikuizen quotes a 1900 passage from one of Rilke's diaries (written several years before *Stories of God*): Especially for young people, "Christ the great danger, the far-too-near, the concealer-of-God, they grow used to seeking the divine within the measure of the human. They enervate themselves with the human and later freeze in the keen air of the heights of eternity. They stray among Christ, the Virgin Mary and the saints. They lose themselves among figures and voices." See F. W. van Heerikuizen, *Rainer Maria Rilke: His Life and Work* (London: Routledge, 1951), 356.

17. Jacques Derrida, *The Animal That Therefore I Am*, trans. David Wills (New York: Fordham University Press, 2008), 132.

18. Jacques Derrida, *The Beast and the Sovereign*, vol. 1, trans, Geoffrey Bennington (Chicago: University of Chicago Press, 2009), 13.

19. Ibid., 17.

20. Ibid.

21. Ibid., 28.

22. Ibid., 41.

23. Ibid., 42.

24. Rainer Maria Rilke, *The Book of Hours: Prayers to a Lowly God*, trans. Annemarie S. Kidder (Evanston, Ill.: Northwestern University Press, 2001), 27.

25. Ibid., 43.

26. Ibid., 45.

27. Ibid., 27.

28. Ibid., 33.

29. Ibid., 75.

30. Isabelle Stengers, *Cosmopolitics I*, trans. Robert Bononno (Minneapolis: University of Minnesota Press, 2010), 20–21.

31. Rilke, *Book of Hours*, 159.

32. Ibid., 57.

33. Ibid., 109.

34. Ibid., 47.

35. Ibid.

THE LOGOS OF GOD AND THE END OF HUMANITY: GIORGIO AGAMBEN AND THE GOSPEL OF JOHN ON ANIMALITY AS LIGHT AND LIFE | ERIC DARYL MEYER

1. See the formulation of "the question of the animal" in Matthew Calarco, *Zoographies: The Question of the Animal from Heidegger to Derrida* (New York: Columbia University Press, 2008), 1–6.

2. Consider Justin Martyr's *Apologies*, for example, or Clement of Alexandria's *Paedagogos*.

3. Athanasius of Alexandria, *De incarnatione verbi dei*, §§3–4, see also §5. This and all subsequent translations are my own. Text: *Contra Gentes and De Incarnatione*, ed. Robert Thomson (Oxford: Clarendon Press, 1971).

4. John McGuckin, *Saint Gregory of Nazianzus: An Intellectual Biography* (Crestwood, N.Y.: St. Vladimir's Seminary Press, 2001), 337–43.

5. John 1:9; Gregory of Nazianzus, *Orat.* 39.1. Text: *Grégoire de Nazianze: Discours 38–41*, ed. Claudio Moreschini, trans. Paul Gallay, *Sources Chrétiennes*, vol. 358 (Paris: Éditions du Cerf, 1990).

6. John 1:4.

7. Gregory of Nazianzus, *Orat.* 39.10.

8. See ibid., 28.2 for a particularly poignant example.

9. Ibid., 39.11.

10. Ibid., 39.8.

11. Ibid., 39.10.

12. Giorgio Agamben, *Homo Sacer: Sovereign Power and Bare Life*, trans. Daniel Heller-Roazen (Stanford, Calif.: Stanford University Press, 1998), 8; translation of idem, *Homo Sacer: Il potere sovrano e la nuda vita* (Torino: Einaudi, 1995).

13. Ibid., 2, 7–8.

14. Ibid., 1, 8–9, cf. 66. In particular, Agamben seems to have utterly confused James Gordon Finlayson, who finds Agamben's distinction "abstract" and labors to understand "what it amounts to concretely" ("'Bare Life' and Politics in Agamben's Reading of Aristotle," *Review of Politics* 72, no. 1 [2010]: 99). Finlayson mistakenly believes that Agamben posits an unambiguously oppositional and exclusive relationship between *zōē* and *bios* when, in fact, Agamben is precisely

interested in the ways in which bare life is concretely included in the opera-
tions of political life, while being distinguished (and thus "excluded"). When
Finlayson finally offers the "correct" reading of Aristotle, which he thinks that
Agamben has bungled so badly, his reading exactly corroborates Agamben's
understanding. Finlayson's distinction between "natural life" and "political
life" (111) is exactly the distinction between zōē and bios that Agamben analyzes.
A similar misunderstanding of the function of the zōē / bios distinction within
Agamben's text underlies a significant portion of Derrida's biting critique of
Homo Sacer. Derrida suggests that Agamben is laboring toward an "absolutely
rigorous" distinction and that he "puts his money on the concept of 'bare life,'
which he identifies with zōē, in opposition to bios" (Jacques Derrida, The Beast
and the Sovereign, trans. Geoffrey Bennington [Chicago: University of Chicago
Press, 2009], 1:325–26). Conceding that Agamben's reading of Aristotle is tenuous, Derrida uncharacteristically misreads Agamben's larger aims. Agamben
is overwhelmingly concerned with the constitutive co-implication of zōē and
bios—and the way that Western politics relies on the appearance of an oppositional relation between the two. Agamben does not endorse zōē over bios;
his argument calls for a suspension of the operation in which the two are distinguished (Agamben, Homo Sacer, 90, 181–82, 188). Andrew Norris correctly
parses Agamben's terminological shift, and, as Norris notes, the careful and
charitable reader does indeed find that the tension is "superficial" rather than
ultimately detrimental to Agamben's project (Andrew Norris, "Giorgio Agamben and the Politics of the Living Dead," Diacritics 30, no. 4 [2000]: 45n17).

15. Agamben, Homo Sacer, 182; see also 83.

16. Ibid., 28–29, 83, 109, 181.

17. Ibid., 102, 126–35. Cf. Hannah Arendt, Eichmann in Jerusalem: A Report on the
Banality of Evil (New York: Penguin Books, 1994), 150–205, esp. 157–58.

18. Agamben, Homo Sacer, 122–23, 127, 133; see also Norris, "Politics of the Living
Dead," 51.

19. Matthew Calarco is exactly correct to note that every figure Agamben uses to
represent the new politics he seeks is essentially human, whether the refugee,
the "whatever singularity," or the Musselmann. Calarco, "On the Borders of
Language and Death: Agamben and the Question of the Animal," Philosophy
Today 44, no. 2 (2000): 96–97. Calarco's criticism is only overcome, I believe, by
reading Agamben's oeuvre in light of The Open. Calarco himself recognizes
this broadening in Agamben's work in Zoographies, 90–103.

20. Jacques Derrida, The Animal That Therefore I Am, ed. Marie Louise Mallet, trans.
David Wills (New York: Fordham University Press, 2008); idem, Beast and the
Sovereign, vol. 1.

21. Giorgio Agamben, *The Open: Man and Animal*, trans. Kevin Attell (Stanford, Calif.: Stanford University Press, 2004). I am not the first to read *The Open* as the completion of the logic of *Homo Sacer*. See Martin Puchner, "Performing the Open: Actors, Animals, Philosophers," *Drama Review* 51, no. 1 (2007): 24.

22. Strikingly, Althusser refers to ideology as a logos in which "we live and move and have our being." Louis Althusser, *On Ideology* (New York: Verso, 2008), 44–51; see also 34–35.

23. Agamben, *Open*, 21, 26, 37–38, 78–80.

24. Ibid., 37–38. Leland de la Durantaye marks this fine parsing of the inner logic of distinctions as Agamben's "signature gesture." Leland de la Durantaye, "The Suspended Substantive: On Animals and Men in Giorgio Agamben's *The Open*," *Diacritics* 33, no. 2 (2003): 7.

25. Agamben, *Open*, 15–16.

26. Derrida, *Beast and the Sovereign*, 1:324–34.

27. Agamben claims as much in *The Open*; see Agamben, *Homo Sacer*, 6, 88–90 with *The Open*, 80.

28. Derrida, *Beast and the Sovereign*, 1:326. It seems that Derrida never commented publicly on *The Open*, the text of Agamben's in which I see the greatest affinity between their treatments of animals/animality. There is no mention of Agamben in *The Beast and the Sovereign*, vol. 2, trans. Geoffrey Bennington (Chicago: University of Chicago Press, 2011).

29. Session 13 of the seminar "Beast and the Sovereign" offers an extended discussion on the inseparability of human logos from political sovereignty; *The Beast and the Sovereign*, 1:346–49.

30. Agamben, *Open*, 76–77. Aaron Bell also reads Agamben and Derrida as converging on the production of "humanity" and human subjectivity. Aaron Bell, "The Dialectic of Anthropocentrism," in *Critical Theory and Animal Liberation*, ed. John Sanbonmatsu (Lanham Md.: Rowman and Littlefield, 2011), 166–67.

31. Derrida, *Animal*, 87, 102, 138–39.

32. For example, ibid., 33, 62.

33. Ibid., 12.

34. Calarco criticizes Derrida for maintaining the human-animal distinction *at all*, arguing that the human-animal distinction in any form underwrites inexcusable regimes of experimentation, eradication, encroachment, confinement, display, slaughter, and consumption (*Zoographies*, 137). However, to deny outright the human-animal distinction would be impossible for Derrida, for two reasons: First, as Calarco recognizes, such a denial would flatten and obscure real differences among many species, including humans, rather than multiplying those differences along a thousand different frontiers (see Derrida,

Animal, 31, 92). Second, and more important, Calarco overestimates the degree to which it is possible to leave behind the human-animal distinction in an act of the will or as a concerted program of thought. If Derrida's analysis is correct (and Calarco relies heavily on it), then the human-animal distinction structures human subjectivity, will, and consciousness. There is, as it were, no exit—especially not as a matter of personal choice. Calarco's dismissal of Agamben's religious categories similarly leaves him in a voluntaristic optimism. Both the gaze of the animal in Derrida and Agamben's invocation of a messianic Shabbat function as sites of transcendence that signal the end of humanity as we currently inhabit it, not a latent potentiality that we might choose to actualize (see Derrida, *Animal*, 132).

35. Agamben, *Open*, 92. Kryzstof Ziarek's thesis that Agamben remains mired in anthropocentrism and humanism (traps that Heidegger purportedly eludes) rests on a misunderstanding of Agamben's notion of *inoperativity* ("After Humanism: Agamben and Heidegger," *South Atlantic Quarterly* 107, no. 1 [2008]: 189–90). Inoperativity is more than not-knowing or refraining from entering the order of knowledge with regard to differences between human beings and animals (see Agamben's development of the concept in *The Coming Community*, trans. Michael Hardt [Minneapolis: University of Minnesota Press, 1993], or idem., *Nudities*, trans. David Kishik and Stefan Pedatella [Stanford, Calif.: Stanford University Press, 2011], esp. 43–45). Inoperativity is a different mode of subjectivity and agency altogether, dependent on Agamben's immanent messianism and linked to his reliance on Benjamin. See Lorenzo Chiesa and Frank Ruda, "The Event of Language as Force of Life: Agamben's Linguistic Vitalism," *Angelaki: Journal of the Theoretical Humanities* 16, no. 3 (2011): 171–73, for a more accurately nuanced understanding of Agamben's notion of inoperativity.

36. The *imago dei* is the other linchpin of anthropological exceptionalism. Kathryn Tanner, *Christ the Key* (Cambridge: Cambridge University Press, 2010), 1–57, provides a slightly more open account of the *imago dei*.

37. I mean to invoke the form of Barth's understanding of election more than the precise substance.

38. This construction inverts the hierarchy found in Athanasius's famous dictum in *De incarnatione*, §54.

39. The thirteenth-century manuscript miniature with which Agamben frames *The Open* is a helpful illustration of what I mean to invoke here. In it, a number of figures are seated at the Messianic banquet, the long-awaited "Day of the LORD." All the figures at the table are human in form except that on their

shoulders they bear the heads of various animals—an eagle, an ass, an ox, a lion, a leopard. Whatever unimaginable mode of subjectivity belongs to such blessed creatures, it signals a profound difference from our own current self-understanding. Agamben, *Open*, 1–3, 92.

40. Giorgio Agamben, *The Kingdom and the Glory: For a Theological Genealogy of Economy and Government*, trans. Lorenzo Chiessa and Matteo Mandarini (Stanford, Calif: Stanford University Press, 2011), xiii, 259.

ANZALDÚA'S ANIMAL ABYSS: *MESTIZAJE* AND THE LATE ANCIENT IMAGINATION | AN YOUNTAE AND PETER ANTHONY MENA

1. This is one of the many nonsynonymous names given to the emerging fields of academic inquiry into human-animal relations and the nonhuman world. Others include animality studies, animal studies, posthuman studies, and zoocriticism.

2. Cary Wolfe, *Animal Rites: American Culture, the Discourse of Species, and Posthumanist Theory* (Chicago: University of Chicago Press, 2003), 8.

3. Gloria Anzaldúa, *Borderlands/La Frontera: The New Mestiza* (San Francisco: Aunt Lute, 1987).

4. Gloria Anzaldúa, "To(o) Queer the Writer: Loca, escritoria y chicana," in *Inversions: Writing by Dykes, Queers and Lesbians*, ed. Betsy Warland (Vancouver: Press Gang, 1991), 253.

5. Anzaldúa, *Borderlands*, 19.

6. Ibid., 27.

7. Ibid., 28.

8. Sonia Saldívar-Hull, introduction to the second edition (1999) of *Borderlands*, 2.

9. Anzaldúa, *Borderlands*, 48.

10. Ibid.

11. Neel Ahuja, "Postcolonial Critique in a Multispecies World," *PMLA* 124, no. 2 (2009): 558.

12. I use the term "borderlands" as Anzaldúa understands it—applicable to spaces where "two or more cultures edge each other."

13. Anzaldúa, *Borderlands*, 76.

14. Ibid., 77.

15. Ibid., 80.

16. Patricia Cox Miller, "Jerome's Centaur: A Hyper-Icon of the Desert," *Journal of Early Christian Studies* 4 (1996): 209–33; Virginia Burrus, "Wyschogrod's Hand:

Saints, Animality, and the Labor of Love," *Philosophy Today* 55, no. 4 (2011): 412–21.

17. The desert imaginary has been discussed variously by several scholars of late antiquity. See, for example, Antoine Guillaumont, "La conception du désert chez les moines d'Egypt," *Revue de l'histoire des religions* 188, no. 1 (1975): 3–21; Robert Markus, *The End of Ancient Christianity* (Cambridge: Cambridge University Press, 1990); idem, "How on Earth Could Places Become Holy? Origins of the Christian Idea of Holy Places," *Journal of Early Christian Studies* 2, no. 3 (1994): 257–71; Paul Harvey, "Saints and Satyrs: Jerome the Scholar at Work," *Athenaeum* 86, no. 1 (1998): 35–56; James Goehring, *Ascetics, Society, and the Desert: Studies in Early Egyptian Monasticism* (Harrisburg: Trinity Press International, 1999); and idem, "The Dark Side of Landscape: Ideology and Power in the Christian Myth of the Desert," in *The Cultural Turn in Late Ancient Studies: Gender, Asceticism, and Historiography*, ed. Dale Martin and Patricia Cox Miller (Durham, N.C.: Duke University Press, 2005), 136–49.

18. The translation of this Latin work used in this essay is that of W. H. Fremantle, G. Lewis, and W. G. Martley in *Nicene and Post-Nicene Fathers*, 2nd series, vol. 6, ed. Philip Schaff and Henry Wace (Buffalo, N.Y.: Christian Literature, 1893). Revised and edited for New Advent by Kevin Knight.

19. Virginia Burrus, *The Sex Lives of Saints: An Erotics of Ancient Hagiography* (Philadelphia: University of Pennsylvania Press, 2004), 25.

20. Miller, "Jerome's Centaur," 218.

21. Burrus, *Sex Lives*, 29.

22. Miller, "Jerome's Centaur," 229, emphasis added.

23. Rebecca Lyman, "Origen as Ascetic Theologian: Orthodoxy and Authority in the Fourth-Century Church," in *Origeniana septima: Origenes in den Auseinandersetzungen des 4. Jahrhunderts*, ed. W. A. Bienert and U. Kühneweg (Leuven: Leuven University Press, 1999), 187.

24. Both Žižek's Schellingian-Lacanian construction of the subject and Catherine Malabou's reading of Hegelian dialectics through the notion of plasticity reflect the recent philosophical tendency to read the notion of freedom in tandem with the negativity of the abyss. See Slavoj Žižek, *The Abyss of Freedom/ Ages of the World* (Ann Arbor: University of Michigan Press, 1997); Catherine Malabou, *The Future of Hegel: Plasticity, Temporality, and Dialectic* (New York: Routledge, 2005).

25. See Homi K. Bhabha, *The Location of Culture* (New York: Routledge, 1994).

26. Gilles Deleuze and Félix Guattari. *A Thousand Plateaus: Capitalism and Schizophrenia* (Minneapolis: University of Minnesota, 1987); Rosi Braidotti, *Meta-*

morphoses: Toward a Materialist Theory of Becoming (Cambridge: Polity Press, 2005).

27. Braidotti, *Metamorphoses*, 57.

28. Ibid., 127.

29. Jacques Derrida, *The Animal That Therefore I Am*, ed. Marie-Louise Mallet, trans. David Wills (New York: Fordham University Press, 2008).

30. Braidotti, *Metamorphoses*, 56.

31. Anzaldúa, *Borderlands*, 101.

32. Ibid., 104–5.

33. Adrian Johnston, *Žižek's Ontology: A Transcendental Materialist Theory of Subjectivity* (Evanston, Ill.: Northwestern University Press, 2008), 102–6.

34. Anzaldúa, *Borderlands*, 48.

35. Ibid., 57.

36. Robert Young, *White Mythologies: Writing History and the West* (New York: Routledge, 1990), 152.

37. Eleanor Ty and Donald Goellnicht warn against the danger of postethnic validation of hybridity that upholds the naturalized expansion of unregulated capital at the global level. They attest that the notions of hybridity and diaspora, when reified as a racialized commodity to advertise borderless and globally themed products, implicitly serve the consumption habits and economic interests of a transnational capitalist class. See Eleanor Ty and Donald Goellnicht, *Asian North American Identities: Beyond the Hyphen* (Bloomington: Indiana University Press, 2004), 26.

38. Slavoj Žižek, *The Ticklish Subject: The Absent Centre of Political Ontology* (London: Verso, 1999), 212.

39. Johnston, *Žižek's Ontology*, 92.

40. Ibid.

41. Ibid., 106.

42. Judith Butler, "Finishing, Starting," in *Derrida and the Time of the Political*, ed. Pheng Cheah and Suzanne Guerlac (Durham, N.C.: Duke University Press, 2009), 298.

43. Nelson Maldonado-Torres, "On the Coloniality of Being: Contributions to the Development of a Concept," *Cultural Studies* 21, nos. 2–3 (2007): 240–70.

44. Anzaldúa, *Borderlands*, 72.

45. Ibid.

46. By dialectical synthesis, I do not mean to invoke a finalized form of subjectivity/substance. Rather, as Mark C. Taylor has remarked, the core of Hegelian dialectic is "infinite restlessness." It does not progress toward a teleological

end in which its grand goal of a static, totalized subjectivity will be achieved. Rather, it is a ceaseless negation of any sense of completeness. See Mark C. Taylor, "Infinite Restlessness," in *Hegel and the Infinite: Religion, Politics, and Dialectic*, ed. Slavoj Žižek, Clayton Crockett, and Creston Davis (New York: Columbia University Press, 2011) 91–114.

47. Ibid., 97.

48. Slavoj Žižek, *The Sublime Object of Ideology* (London: Verso, 1989), xxix.

49. Jon Mills, *The Unconscious Abyss: Hegel's Anticipation of Psychoanalysis* (Albany: State University of New York Press, 2002), 12.

50. Alexandre Kojève, *Introduction to the Reading of Hegel: Lectures on the Phenomenology of Spirit*, trans. James H. Nichols, Jr. (Ithaca, N.Y.: Cornell University Press, 1980), 3.

51. Katrin Pahl, "The Way of Despair," in Žižek et al, eds., *Hegel and the Infinite*, 142.

52. G. W. F. Hegel, *Phenomenology of Spirit*, trans. A. V. Miller (Oxford: Clarendon Press, 1977), 49; Pahl, "The Way of Despair," 142.

53. Anzaldúa, *Borderlands*, 72.

54. Braidotti, *Metamorphoses*, 127.

55. Anzaldúa, *Borderlands*, 73

56. Ibid., 100.

57. Bhabha, *The Location of Culture*, 160.

DANIEL'S ANIMAL APOCALYPSE | JENNIFER L. KOOSED AND ROBERT PAUL SEESENGOOD

1. We start, as well, with a sincere "thank you" extended to the administration, faculty, students, and staff of Drew Theological School for their exceptional hospitality, as well as to our fellow members of the colloquium for their questions, corrections, and ideas.

2. Jacques Derrida, *The Animal That Therefore I Am*, trans. David Wills (New York: Fordham University Press, 2008), 160.

3. The summer we were reading the book of Daniel, the final Harry Potter movie was released, at times tempting us to write a very different essay.

4. Our primary reading companions have been Danna Nolan Fewell, *Circle of Sovereignty: Plotting Politics in the Book of Daniel* (Nashville: Abingdon, 1991); John E. Goldingay, *Daniel*, Word Biblical Commentary 30 (Dallas: Word Books, 1989); Louis F. Hartman and Alexander A. Di Lella, *The Book of Daniel*, Anchor Bible Commentary 23 (Garden City, N.Y.: Doubleday, 1978); James A. Montgomery, *A Critical and Exegetical Commentary on the Book of Daniel*, International

Critical Commentary (Edinburgh: T&T Clark, 1926); and W. Sibley Towner, *Daniel*, Interpretation (Atlanta: John Knox Press, 1984).

5. Our dating of Daniel and our definition of "apocalypse" all arise from John J. Collins, *The Apocalyptic Imagination: An Introduction to Jewish Apocalyptic Literature*, 2nd ed. (Grand Rapids: Eerdmans, 1998), 85–115.

6. Derrida, *Animal*, 132.

7. The Aramaic of this passage is unclear. An alternate translation could be that Nebuchadnezzar develops feathers and talons like an eagle (though apparently an herbivorous one).

8. Fewell, *Circle*, 75.

9. Montgomery, *Daniel*, 225–30.

10. E. Cassin, "Daniel dans la 'fosse' aux lions," *Revue de l'histoire des religions* 139, no. 2 (1951): 129–61.

11. Hartman and Di Lella, *Daniel*, 199.

12. Fewell, *Circle*, 114.

13. Jacques Derrida's *The Beast and the Sovereign*, ed. Michel Lisse, Marie-Louise Mallet, and Ginette Michaud; trans. Geoffrey Bennington (Chicago: University of Chicago Press, 2009), 1:97–135.

14. Collins, *Apocalyptic Imagination*, 98.

15. Another historical inaccuracy. Belshazzar was son of Nabonidus and never king. See Lawrence M. Wills, "Daniel," in *The Jewish Study Bible*, ed. Adele Berlin and Marc Zvi Brettler (New York: Oxford, 2004), 1640–65. Note also page 1655: "The depiction of the end of time in apocalyptic visions is often similar to biblical depictions of the beginning of time, that is, creation. The sea monsters here are paralleled in many stories of creation (Gen. ch. 1; Job 26.12–13; Pss. 33.6–7; 74.12–14; Isa. 27.1)."

16. Goldingay, *Daniel*, 148–49. His reference here is to P. A. Porter, *Metaphors and Monsters: A Literary Critical Study of Daniel 7 and 8*, Coniectanea biblica, Old Testament Series 20 (Lund: Gleerup, 1983).

17. Ibid., 150.

18. Hartman and Di Lella simply title the pericope "Vision of Four Beasts and the Man."

19. Antiochus's outrage, in 1 and 2 Maccabees, was improper sacrifice of improper animals at the temple. Given the connections between animal sacrifice and slaughter of animals for food, the vegetarian challenge of Daniel 1 is awakened.

20. Or angel/messenger. In Daniel, unlike other biblical texts, angels are named. This one, Gabriel ("Man of God") reminds us of the "one like the son of man" in chapter 7.

21. Hartman and Di Lella, *Daniel*, 230.

22. Fewell, *Circle*, 120. Hartman and Di Lella, *Daniel*, 233–34 note that there are also astrological overtones: Persia was associated with Ares (the Ram), and Alexander was a purported Capricorn.

23. For extensive discussion of the "appalling abomination," particularly its interpretation (which we affirm) as Antiochus's offering of a swine to Zeus on the Temple altar, see Hartman and Di Lella, *Daniel*, 252–53 and their treatment of 1 Macc. 1:54 and 2 Macc. 6:2. As noted in Towner, *Daniel*, 116, the story is "a theological interpretation of history written after most of that history had already transpired and is designed to give the reader some purchase on the events which lay immediately ahead."

24. For example, see his discussion of his cat (Derrida, *Animal*, 6).

25. Derrida accomplishes his survey of animals in Western literature more or less successfully, depending on one's evaluation. For example, Donna Haraway's primary critique of Derrida is that he "came right to the edge of respect" but was "sidetracked." He writes convincingly and movingly of the crimes committed against animals and the ways in which philosophy has erected great barriers separating the human from the animal, but he never comes back to his cat. "But with his cat, Derrida failed a simple obligation of companion species; he did not become curious about what the cat might actually be doing, feeling, thinking, or perhaps making available to him in looking back at him that morning." Donna J. Haraway, *When Species Meet* (Minneapolis: University of Minnesota Press, 2008), 20.

26. Derrida, *Animal*, 111; for further discussion see 105–12 (on Levinas), and 143–60 (on Heidegger).

27. This tendency becomes even more acute in apocalyptic literature intermediate between Daniel and the Revelation to John. Note, for example, the allegory and systems of dominance inherent in the "Animal Apocalypse" traditions associated with Enoch.

28. For example, see Deborah Rose Bird, *Wild Dog Dreaming: Love and Extinction* (Charlottesville: University of Virgina Press, 2011) for the self-identification of Australian Aboriginal peoples with the dingo in their own creation theology versus the ways in which Australian colonizers employed (and employ) the same strategy for the purposes of annihilating both.

29. Giorgio Agamben, *The Open: Man and Animal* (Stanford, Calif.: Stanford University Press, 2004), 3.

30. Ibid., 19.

31. Ibid., 21.

32. Towner, *Daniel*, 120.

33. Haraway, *Species*, 77–78.

34. Ibid., 80; See also Derrida, *Animal*, 48.

35. Derrida, *Animal*, 48.

36. Haraway, *Species*, 88.

ECOTHEROLOGY | STEPHEN D. MOORE

1. Jacques Derrida, *The Beast and the Sovereign*, ed. Michel Lisse et al.; trans. Geoffrey Bennington, Seminars of Jacques Derrida 1 (Chicago: University of Chicago Press, 2009), 1:24.

2. The Seminars series promises to run to forty-three volumes (see Geoffrey Bennington et al., "General Introduction to the French Edition," in Derrida, *Beast and the Sovereign*, 1:ix).

3. See also Jacques Derrida, *The Beast and the Sovereign*, ed. Michel Lisse et al.; trans. Geoffrey Bennington, Seminars of Jacques Derrida 1 (Chicago: University of Chicago Press, 2011), vol. 2.

4. Jacques Derrida, *The Animal That Therefore I Am*, ed. Marie-Louise Mallet; trans. David Wills, Perspectives in Continental Philosophy (New York: Fordham University Press, 2008).

5. The English translation of the Bible used in this essay (but frequently modified) is the New Revised Standard Version.

6. Cf. Ingvild Saelid Gilhus, *Animals, Gods and Humans: Changing Attitudes to Animals in Greek, Roman and Early Christian Ideas* (New York: Routledge, 2006), 177: "John, the author of Revelation, did not intend to say anything about real animals."

7. Colleen Glenney Boggs, "Emily Dickinson's Animal Pedagogies," *PMLA* 124, no. 2 (2009): 535. Cf. Derrida, *Animal That Therefore I Am*, 37: "We know the history of fabulization and how it remains an anthropomorphic taming, a moralizing subjection, a domestication. Always a discourse *of* man, on man."

8. Graham Huggan and Helen Tiffin, *Postcolonial Ecocriticism: Literature, Animals, Environment* (New York: Routledge, 2010), 173.

9. For this term, see Akira Mizuta Lippit, "Magnetic Animal: Derrida, Wildlife, Animetaphor," *Modern Language Notes* 113, no. 5 (1998): 1111–25; idem, *Electric Animal: Toward a Rhetoric of Wildlife* (Minneapolis: University of Minnesota Press, 2000), 162–98.

10. See, for example, Stephen D. Moore, *God's Gym: Divine Male Bodies of the Bible* (New York: Routledge, 1996), 117–38; idem, *God's Beauty Parlor: And Other Queer Spaces in and around the Bible*, Contraversions: Jews and Other Differences (Stanford, Calif.: Stanford University Press, 2001), 175–99 passim.

11. Rosi Braidotti, too, cautions against "the metaphoric habit of composing a sort of moral and cognitive bestiary in which animals refer to values, norms, and

morals," as in "the nobleness of eagles, the deceit of foxes, or the humility of lambs." Instead, she urges "a neoliteral relation to animals. . . . The old metaphoric dimension has been overridden by a new mode of relation. Animals are no longer the signifying system that props up humans' self-projections and moral aspirations. . . . They have, rather, started to be approached literally, as entities framed by code systems of their own" ("Animals, Anomalies, and Inorganic Others," *PMLA* 124, no. 2 [2009]: 527–28).

12. How does one ascertain such a "fact"? By utterly unscientific means. Typing "Obama Beast Revelation" into the Google search box on January 12, 2013. yielded around 4,640,000 hits, while typing the same words into the YouTube search box yielded around 3,670 hits.

13. See Amarnath Amarasingam, "Baracknophobia and the Paranoid Style: Visions of Obama as the Anti-Christ on the World Wide Web," in *Network Apocalypse: Visions of the End in an Age of Internet Media*, ed. Robert Glenn Howard, The Bible in the Modern World 36 (Sheffield, UK: Sheffield Phoenix Press, 2011), 96–123. According to a 2009 survey cited by Amarasingam, 24 percent of young voters in my (now) home state of New Jersey "believed Obama to be the Antichrist" (ibid., 97).

14. Derrida, *Beast and the Sovereign*, 1:25. Derrida is in transit from his passing reference to "all the beasts from John's Revelation, which clearly present themselves as political or polemological figures, the reading of which would merit more than one seminar" (24), to his analysis of Thomas Hobbes's *Leviathan*, that archetypal work of political theory from 1651, whose argument Derrida paraphrases as follows: "So the state is a sort of robot, an animal monster, which . . . is stronger . . . than natural man. Like a gigantic prosthesis designed to amplify . . . the power of . . . the living man that it protects, that it serves, but like a dead machine, or even a machine of death" (28).

15. Another animal, too, lurks within this Beast. The Beast is, more specifically, a Sea Beast ("And I saw a beast rising out of the sea" [Rev. 13:1]) as distinct from a Land Beast ("Then I saw another beast that rose out of the earth" [13:11]), and concerning this beastly duo David E. Aune observes: "These two beasts clearly reflect the Jewish myth of Leviathan, the female monster from the sea, and Behemoth, the male monster from the desert" (*Revelation 6–16*, Word Biblical Commentary 52B [Nashville: Thomas Nelson, 1998], 728; cf. 728–29, 732).

16. Derrida, *Animal That Therefore I Am*, 41.

17. Ibid., 34. To say "animal" in the singular, then, is to utter "an asininity [*bêtise*]" (ibid., 31). This Revelation does and does not do. On the one hand, it presents us with the specificity of the Lamb. On the other hand, it presents us with the nonspecificity of the Beast.

18. Derrida, *Beast and the Sovereign*, 1:17.

19. See Rev. 6:4, 8; 8:9, 11; 9:15, 18; 11:13; 14:19–20; 16:2–10, 18–21; 19:11–21; 20:9, 15; 21:8.

20. Derrida, *Beast and the Sovereign*, 1:17.

21. Ibid., 18.

22. Elsewhere I have argued Revelation's hybridity out of the matrix of post-colonial theory; see my *Empire and Apocalypse: Postcolonialism and the New Testament*, The Bible in the Modern World 12 (Sheffield, UK: Sheffield Phoenix Press, 2006), 115–18.

23. Unless the anonymous interjections in 11:12 ("Come up here!") and 16:17 ("It is done!") are attributed to God as well. Further on this near-aphasia, see Moore, *God's Gym*, 121–23.

24. Derrida, *Beast and the Sovereign*, 1:57. Derrida is glossing Hobbes here, and articulating a stereotype of bestiality that he also wishes to problematize: "this place of nonresponse that is commonly and dogmatically called bestiality, divinity, or death" (ibid). Derrida concludes a lengthy analysis of *Robinson Crusoe* in *The Beast and the Sovereign*, vol. 2, by noting: "What Robinson thinks of his parrot Poll is pretty much what Descartes, Kant, Heidegger, Lacan, and so very many others, think of all animals incapable of a true responsible and responding speech" (2:278; see also 2:260).

25. Notwithstanding the phrase *tēn ōdēn tou arniou* in Revelation 15:3a. Most contemporary commentators translate the phrase as "the song about the lamb" (objective genitive) rather than as "the song of [i.e., sung by] the lamb" (subjective genitive).

26. Derrida, *Animal That Therefore I Am*, 64.

27. The dictum "cruelty implies humanity" (as opposed to animality) is Lacan's. See Jacques Lacan, *Écrits: The First Complete Edition in English*, trans. Bruce Fink (New York: Norton, 2006), 120. Derrida discusses (and dissects) this dictum in volume 1 of *The Beast and the Sovereign* (1:97, 102–11). He returns to the paradoxical humanity of inhumanity in volume 2 (2:140–41).

28. Feminist scholarship on Revelation has been drawn repeatedly and irresistibly to this female figure. For a sampling of such work, see Tina Pippin, "The Heroine and the Whore: The Apocalypse of John in Feminist Perspective," in *From Every People and Nation: The Book of Revelation in Intercultural Perspective*, ed. David Rhoads (Minneapolis: Fortress Press, 2005), 127–46; Elisabeth Schüssler Fiorenza, *The Power of the Word: Scripture and the Rhetoric of Empire* (Minneapolis: Fortress Press, 2007), 130–47; Caroline Vander Stichele, "Re-membering the Whore: The Fate of Babylon according to Revelation 17.16," in *A Feminist Companion to the Apocalypse of John*, ed. Amy-Jill Levine with Maria Mayo Robbins,

Feminist Companion to the New Testament and Early Christian Writings 13 (New York: T&T Clark, 2009), 106–20; Jennifer A. Glancy and Stephen D. Moore, "How Typical a Roman Prostitute Is Revelation's 'Great Whore'?" *Journal of Biblical Literature* 130, no. 3 (2011): 543–62; and Lynn R. Huber, "Gazing at the Whore: Reading Revelation Queerly," in *Bible Trouble: Queer Readings at the Boundaries of Biblical Scholarship*, ed. Teresa J. Hornsby and Ken Stone, Semeia Studies 67 (Atlanta: Society of Biblical Literature, 2011), 301–20.

29. Susan McHugh, *Animal Stories: Narrating across Species Lines*, Posthumanities 15 (Minneapolis: University of Minnesota Press, 2011), 117.

30. Ibid., 132–33.

31. On the city's gates are inscribed the names of the twelve tribes of Israel (Rev. 21:12), and on the foundations of its wall are inscribed the names of the twelve apostles (12:14; cf. Eph. 2:19–20). The twelve jewels that adorn the foundations correspond to the twelve jewels on the breastplate of the high priest (Rev. 21:19–20; cf. Exod. 28:15–21; 39:8–14). This in turn evokes Revelation's description elsewhere of the redeemed as a company of priests (1:6; 5:10; 20:6). The Bride herself likewise appears to be a symbol for the redeemed (cf. 2 Cor. 11:2; Eph. 5:23–32): the "fine linen, bright and pure" in which she is arrayed is glossed as "the righteous deeds of the saints" (Rev. 19:8). For more on this commonplace construal of the city and the Bride, see Robert H. Gundry, "The New Jerusalem: People as Place, Not Place for People," in his *The Old Is Better: New Testament Essays in Support of Traditional Interpretations*, Wissenschaftliche Untersuchungen zum Neuen Testament 178 (Tübingen: Mohr Siebeck, 2005), 399–412.

32. Nevertheless, this husband-wife relationship is implicitly a master-slave relationship, because the Lamb's relationship to the redeemed is explicitly that of a slave owner. The terms *slave* and *slaves* (*doulos/douloi*) are used fourteen times in Revelation (1:1; 2:20; 6:11; 7:3; 10:7; 11:18; 15:3; 19:2, 5, 10; 22:3, 6, 9) for those who serve God or Jesus—and each time the term is euphemistically rendered as "servant(s)" in every major contemporary English translation.

33. For further analysis of this paradox, see Stephen D. Moore, "Ruminations on Revelation's Ruminant, Quadrupedal Christ; or, The Even-Toed Ungulate That Therefore I Am," in *The Bible and Posthumanism*, ed. Jennifer Koosed, Semeia Studies 74 (Atlanta: Society of Biblical Literature, 2014), 301–26.

34. For a resourceful reading of this one word, see Jorunn Økland, "Why Can't the Heavenly Miss Jerusalem Just Shut Up?" in Caroline Vander Stichele and Todd Penner, eds., *Her Master's Tools? Feminist and Postcolonial Engagements of Historical-Critical Discourse*, Global Perspectives on Biblical Scholarship 9 (Atlanta: Society of Biblical Literature, 2005), especially 327–32.

35. The work of Barbara R. Rossing is especially representative of this approach to Revelation and ecology. See, for example, her "River of Life in God's New Jerusalem: An Ecological Vision for Earth's Future," in *Christianity and Ecology*, ed. Rosemary Radford Ruether and Dieter T. Hessel, Religions of the World and Ecology 3 (Cambridge: Harvard Center for World Religions, 1999), 205–24; and "For the Healing of the World: Reading Revelation Ecologically," in *From Every People and Nation*, ed. Rhoads, 165–82. See also Duncan Reid, "Setting Aside the Ladder to Heaven: Revelation 21:1–22:5 from the Perspective of the Earth," in *Readings from the Perspective of Earth*, ed. Norman C. Habel, Earth Bible 1 (Sheffield, UK: Sheffield Academic Press, 2000), especially 243–44; Harry O. Maier, "There's a New World Coming! Reading the Apocalypse in the Shadow of the Canadian Rockies," in *The Earth Story in the New Testament*, ed. Norman C. Habel and Vicki Balabanski, Earth Bible 5 (Sheffield, UK: Sheffield Academic Press, 2002), 177–79; Richard Bauckham, *The Bible and Ecology: Rediscovering the Community of Creation* (Waco, Texas: Baylor University Press, 2010), 174–78; and Mark Bredin, *The Ecology of the New Testament: Creation, Re-creation, and the Environment* (Colorado Springs: Biblica, 2010), 172–77. Many other such examples could be listed.

36. Attention to the size of the heavenly city has been all but absent from ecocritical, ecotheological, and ecojustice work on Revelation. The notable exceptions are Thomas W. Martin, "The City as Salvific Space: Heterotopic Place and Environmental Ethics in the New Jerusalem," *SBL Forum* 7, no. 2 (2009): http://www.sbl-site.org/publications/article.aspx?ArticleId=801; and David G. Horrell, *The Bible and the Environment: Towards a Critical Ecological Biblical Theology* (London: Equinox, 2010), 100–101. Like the scholars listed in note 35, however, Martin's perspective on the heavenly city through most of his colorful and intriguing article is overwhelmingly positive. Horrell's brief analysis of the city is far more critical.

37. Michael Wise, Martin Abegg Jr., and Edward Cook, eds. and trans., *The Dead Sea Scrolls: A New Translation*, 2nd ed. (New York: HarperCollins, 2005), 558. The editors remark of the dimensions of the visionary city in this fragmentary text: "This new Jerusalem would have been larger than any ancient city and could only have been built by divine intervention" (558). Or modern technology. At just under 250 square miles, it would have been fractionally smaller than El Paso, Texas, and one-twentieth the size of Tokyo.

38. David E. Aune, *Revelation 17–22*, Word Biblical Commentary 52C (Nashville: Thomas Nelson, 1998), 1162.

39. For instance, gargantuan stature was frequently imputed to gods, angels, and other heavenly beings in the ancient Near East. As Wesley Williams phrases it,

"While the gods possessed an anthropoid or human-like form, this form was also in a fundamental way unlike that of humans in that it was transcendent, either in size, beauty, the substance of which it was composed, or all three" ("A Body Unlike Bodies: Transcendent Anthropomorphism in Ancient Semitic Tradition and Early Islam," *Journal of the American Oriental Society* 129, no. 1 [2009]: 20). Gigantic angels are a frequent feature of ancient Jewish apocalyptic literature (and not unknown in Revelation either: see especially 10:1–10).

40. Aune, *Revelation 17–22*, 1161.

41. Derrida, *Beast and the Sovereign*, 1:257.

42. Carolyn Merchant, *Reinventing Eden: The Fate of Nature in Western Culture* (New York: Routledge, 2003), 157–58.

43. Ibid., 158.

44. Ibid.

45. "Dead mall" is the technical term for a commercially failing or shut-down shopping mall.

46. Directed by Sam Green and Carrie Lozano, Lucky Hat Entertainment, 2009.

47. Derrida, *Animal That Therefore I Am*, 101.

48. Revelation 11:18 reads: "The nations raged, but your wrath has come, and the time for judging the dead, for rewarding your slaves, the prophets and saints and all who fear your name, . . . and for destroying those who destroy the earth." Rossing plausibly identifies the destroyers of the earth as imperial Rome; see Barbara R. Rossing, "Alas for Earth! Lament and Resistance in Revelation 12," in *The Earth Story in the New Testament*, ed. Habel and Balabanski, 180–92. See also Maier, "There's a New World Coming!" 176.

49. Derrida, *Animal That Therefore I Am*, 101–2.

50. At least one scholar has argued that literal, not metaphorical, dogs are in view here: "Because dogs were regarded as purificatory animals among both Greeks and Romans, and because Revelation 22:14 refers to purification by washing, Revelation 22:14–15 might well have been heard by Asian audiences as a polemic against pagan purificatory rites, especially those related to the cult of Hecate" (Rick Strelan, "'Outside are the dogs and the sorcerers . . .': Revelation 22:15," *Biblical Theology Bulletin* 33, no. 4 [2003]: 148).

51. See, for example, Joan Massyngberde Ford, *Revelation*, Anchor Bible 38 (Garden City, N.Y.: Doubleday, 1975), 345; Bruce M. Metzger, *Breaking the Code: Understanding the Book of Revelation* (Nashville: Abingdon Press, 1993), 106; Robert L. Thomas, *Revelation 8–22: An Exegetical Commentary*, Wycliffe Exegetical Commentary (Chicago: Moody Press, 1995), 507; Robert H. Mounce, *The Book of Revelation*, 2nd ed., The New International Commentary on the New

Testament (Grand Rapids, Mich.: Eerdmans, 1998), 408; Aune, *Revelation 17–22*, 1222–23.

52. See G. K. Beale, *The Book of Revelation: A Commentary on the Greek Text*, The New International Greek New Testament Commentary (Grand Rapids, Mich.: Eerdmans, 1999), 1141: "The despicability of the godless is emphasized, since dogs are regarded as despised creatures throughout Scripture." Cf. Ian Boxall, *The Revelation of Saint John*, Black's New Testament Commentaries 18 (London: A. & C. Black, 2006), 317: The word "dogs" refers "to despised groups, including evildoers."

53. Beale, *Book of Revelation*, 1141.

54. Aune, *Revelation 17–22*, 1223. Cf. Stephen S. Smalley, *The Revelation to John: A Commentary on the Greek Text of the Apocalypse* (Downers Grove, Ill.: InterVarsity Press, 2005), 574: "Dogs are associated with habits which are unsavory."

55. Ben Witherington III, *Revelation*, The New Cambridge Bible Commentary (Cambridge: Cambridge University Press, 2003), 282. Cf. G. B. Caird, *The Revelation of Saint John*, Black's New Testament Commentaries 19 (London: A. & C. Black, 1966), 285: "The dogs . . . are here defined as those heathen who are indelibly marked with the qualities of the monster and the whore."

56. Mounce, *The Book of Revelation*, 394

57. Heinrich Kraft, *Die Offenbarung des Johannes*, Handbuch zum Neuen Testament 16A (Tübingen: J. C. B. Mohr [Paul Siebeck], 1974), 280.

58. Derrida, *Animal That Therefore I Am*, 102.

59. Beale argues: "That 'they will serve *him* [*latreusousin autō*—22:3b]' likely does not refer only to God or only to the Lamb. The two are conceived so much as a unity that the singular pronoun can refer to both" (*The Book of Revelation*, 1113, his emphasis). Thomas B. Slater changes the "him" to a "them" in his paraphrase of the passage—"God and the Lamb . . . will provide the highest quality of life possible and the servants of God will worship them . . ." (*Christ and Community: A Socio-Historical Study of the Christology of Revelation*, Journal for the Study of the New Testament, Supplements 178 [Sheffield, UK: Sheffield Academic Press, 1999], 200)—and cites the commentaries of J. P. M. Sweet, Gerhard A. Krodel, Leon Morris, Robert H. Mounce, and George Eldon Ladd in support of his reading.

60. Thomas R. Schreiner's assessment is typical: "Even though Revelation is an apocalyptic work, the Christology is astonishingly explicit and high. Indeed, the Christology is analogous to that in the Gospel of John. Jesus as the Lamb is on the same plane as God and is worshiped as a divine being. . . . Just as God is the Alpha and Omega and the first and the last, so too Jesus is the Alpha and

Omega and the first and the last" (*New Testament Theology: Magnifying God in Christ* [Grand Rapids, Mich.: Baker Academic, 2008], 430).

61. And in a book that is notably fastidious about proper and improper objects of worship (see 19:10; 22:8–9; cf. 9:20; 13:4, 8, 12, 15; 14:9–11; 16:2; 19:20–21; 20:4).

AND SAY THE ANIMAL REALLY RESPONDED: SPEAKING ANIMALS IN THE HISTORY OF CHRISTIANITY | LAURA HOBGOOD-OSTER

The title is taken from Jacques Derrida, "And Say the Animal Responded," trans. David Wills, in *Zoontologies: The Question of the Animal*, ed. Cary Wolfe (Minneapolis: University of Minnesota Press, 2003), 121–46, reprinted in Jacques Derrida, *The Animal That Therefore I Am*, trans. David Wills (New York: Fordham University Press, 2008), 119–40.

1. Donna J. Haraway, *When Species Meet* (Minneapolis: University of Minnesota Press, 2007), 19–20.

2. Derrida, *Animal That Therefore I Am*, 132.

3. Marc Hauser, Noam Chomsky, and W. T. Finch, "The Faculty of Language: What Is It, Who Has It, and How Did It Evolve?" *Science* (November 22, 2002): 1569–70.

4. David Buttrick, *Homiletic: Moves and Structures* (Philadelphia: Fortress Press, 1987), 5–6. The author was the professor of homiletics when I was a divinity graduate student at Vanderbilt University.

5. The Word in Christianity includes Hellenistic and Jewish concepts of the Spirit of God. The Logos / Word is not the same as "word"; rather it points to Jesus as the incarnation of God. However, the myriad connections between this idea, a focus on the written text and an eventual focus on preaching and analyzing scripture as the primary way to understand the tradition conflate in such as way to make "words" central to Christian practice and belief.

6. This is not to deny the centrality of words and the analysis of scripture in other traditions. Islam and Judaism also focus on the word.

7. Most notably, the Society of Friends does not recognize sacraments or focus on formalized preaching per se.

8. David Lotz, "Sola Scriptura: Luther on Biblical Authority," *Interpretation* (July 1, 1981): 261–62.

9. As quoted in Belden Lane, *Ravished by Beauty: The Surprising Legacy of Reformed Spirituality* (New York: Oxford University Press, 2011), 80.

10. Harry Stout, *The New England Soul: Preaching and Religious Culture in Colonial New England* (New York: Oxford University Press, 1986), 3–4.

11. Buttrick, *Homiletic*, 173–75.

12. Lynn White Jr., "The Historical Roots of Our Ecologic Crisis," *Science* 155, no. 3767 (1967): 1203–7.

13. For an interesting analysis of Numbers 22 see Basil Herring, "Speaking of Man and Beast," *Judaism* 28, no. 2 (1979): 169–76.

14. J. K. Elliott, ed., *The Apocryphal New Testament* (Oxford: Clarendon Press, 1999), 408–9.

15. This, of course, is the same Paul who proclaims that women should keep silence in church.

16. Fragmentary texts make up this apocryphal Act. This particular account with the lion is from the Ethiopic text and is quoted in Tamas Adamik, "The Baptized Lion in the Acts of Paul," in *The Apocryphal Acts of Paul and Thecla*, ed. Jan N. Bremmer (Kampen, The Netherlands: Kok Pharos, 1996), 61.

17. Haraway, *When Species Meet*, 20.

18. Elliott, ed., *Apocryphal New Testament*, 378–79.

19. Haraway, *When Species Meet*, 21–22.

20. John Berger, "Why Look at Animals?" in his *About Looking* (New York: Pantheon, 1980), 3–28.

21. Haraway, *When Species Meet*, 27.

SO MANY FACES: GOD, HUMANS, AND ANIMALS | JAY McDANIEL AND J. AARON SIMMONS

1. Matthew Calarco and Peter Atterton, eds., *Animal Philosophy: Essential Readings in Continental Thought* (London: Continuum, 2004).

2. For just a few of the more prominent examples, see Matthew Calarco, *Zoographies: The Question of the Animal from Heidegger to Derrida* (New York: Columbia University Press, 2008); Kelly Oliver, *Animal Lessons: How They Teach Us to Be Human* (New York: Columbia University Press, 2009); Anne Emmanuelle Berger and Marta Segarra, eds., *Demenageries: Thinking (of) Animals after Derrida* (Amsterdam: Rodopi Press, 2011).

3. Calarco and Atterton, *Animal Philosophy*, xii.

4. For example, see Adèle Thorens, "Peter Singer et 'La liberation animale': une approache critique autour de la notion de 'spécisme,'" *Revue de Theologie et de Philosophie* 136, no. 2 (2004): 140–65.

5. Emmanuel Levinas, *Totality and Infinity: An Essay on Exteriority*, trans. Alphonso Lingis (Pittsburgh: Duquesne University Press, 1969), and *Otherwise Than Being, or Beyond Essence*, trans. Alphonso Lingis (Pittsburgh: Duquesne University Press, 1997).

6. For good attempts to think through how Levinasian Otherism might stand as a resource for environmental philosophy broadly construed, see William Edelglass, James Hatley, and Christian Diehm, eds., *Facing Nature: Levinas and Environmental Thought* (Pittsburgh: Duquesne University Press, 2012). Importantly, many of the essays in that volume are either critical of some of the seeming limitations of Levinasian philosophy in that direction or are willing to address objections regarding anthropocentric ethics, etc.

7. Emmanuel Levinas, *Difficult Freedom: Essays on Judaism*, trans. Sean Hand (Baltimore: Johns Hopkins University Press, 1990). For considerations of this text, see John Llewelyn, "Where to Cut: '*Boucherie*' and '*Delikatessen*,'" *Research in Phenomenology* 40, no. 2 (2010): 161–87; Bob Plant, "Welcoming Dogs: Levinas and 'the Animal' Question," *Philosophy and Social Criticism* 37, no. 1 (2011): 49–71.

8. Diane Perpich, "Scarce Resources: Levinas, Animals, and the Environment," in *Facing Nature*, ed. Edelglass, Hatley, and Diehm, 67–94.

9. David Wood, *The Step Back: Ethics and Politics after Deconstruction* (Albany: State University of New York Press, 2002), 135.

10. Jacques Derrida, *The Animal That Therefore I Am*, ed. Marie-Louise Mallet, trans. David Wills (New York: Fordham University Press, 2008).

11. For engagements with Derrida on this issue, see Gerald L. Burns, "Derrida's Cat (Who Am I?)," *Research in Phenomenology* 38, no. 3 (2008): 404–23; Llewelyn, "Where to Cut"; Leonard Lawlor, "Waiting and Lateness: The Context, Implications, and Basic Argumentation of Derrida's 'Awaiting (at) the Arrival' in *Aporias*," *Research in Phenomenology* 38, no. 3 (2008): 392–403, and "This Is Not Sufficient: The Question of Animals in Derrida," *Symposium: Canadian Journal of Continental Philosophy* 11, no. 1 (2007): 79–100; Nathan Van Camp, "Negotiating the Anthropological Limit: Derrida, Stiegler, and the Question of the 'Animal,'" *Between the Species: A Journal of Ethics* 14, no. 1 (2011): 57–80; Michael Naas, "Derrida's Flair (For the Animals to Follow . . .)," *Research in Phenomenology* 40, no. 2 (2010): 219–42; Tracy Colony, "Epimetheus Bound: Stiegler on Derrida, Life, and the Technological Condition," *Research in Phenomenology* 41, no. 1 (2011): 72–89; Ted Toadvine, "Life beyond Biologism," *Research in Phenomenology* 40, no. 2 (2010): 243–66.

12. Wood, *Step Back*.

13. See Jacques Derrida, "'Eating Well,' or the Calculation of the Subject: An Interview with Jacques Derrida," in *Who Comes After the Subject?* ed. Eduardo Cadava, Peter Connor, and Jean-Luc Nancy (New York: Routledge, 1991), 96–119; See also Matthew Calarco, "Deconstruction Is Not Vegetarianism: Humanism,

Subjectivity, and Animal Ethics," *Continental Philosophy Review* 37, no. 2 (2004): 175–201.

14. See Calarco, "Deconstruction Is Not Vegetarianism."

15. See Richmond West, "Can We Really Cope with Creatures? 'Dasein' and Animality in Heidegger," *Contemporary Philosophy* 20, no. 1–2 (1998): 38–44.

16. See J. Aaron Simmons, *God and the Other: Ethics and Politics after the Theological Turn* (Bloomington: Indiana University Press, 2011), chap. 12.

17. Calarco and Atterton, *Animal Philosophy*, xiii.

18. Charles S. Brown and Ted Toadvine, eds., *Eco-Phenomenology: Back to the Earth Itself* (Albany: State University of New York Press, 2003).

19. Wood, *Step Back*; David Wood, *Thinking After Heidegger* (Cambridge: Polity Press, 2005).

20. John Llewelyn, *Seeing through God: A Geophenomenology* (Bloomington: Indiana University Press, 2004); John Llewelyn, "Am I Obsessed by Bobby? (Humanism of the Other Animal)," in *Re-Reading Levinas*, ed. Robert Bernasconi and Simon Critchley (Bloomington: Indiana University Press, 1991), 234–45.

21. Edelglass, Hatley, and Diehm, eds., *Facing Nature*.

22. Youru Wang, ed., *Deconstruction and the Ethical in Asian Thought* (New York: Routledge, 2007).

23. For just a few examples, see the essays in Edelglass, Hatley, and Diehm, eds., *Facing Nature*.

24. John B. Cobb Jr., *Sustainability: Economics, Ecology and Justice* (Eugene, Ore.: Wipf and Stock, 2007). See also Herman E. Daly and John B. Cobb Jr., *For the Common Good: Redirecting the Economy toward Community, the Environment, and a Sustainable Future* (Boston: Beacon Press, 1994).

25. Clare Palmer, *Animal Ethics in Context* (New York: Columbia University Press, 2010), and *Environmental Ethics and Process Thinking* (Oxford: Clarendon Press, 1998).

26. For example, see Perpich, *Scarce Resources*; Simmons, *God and the Other*; Christian Diehm, "Ethics and Natural History: Levinas and Other-Than-Human," *Environmental Philosophy* 3, no. 2 (2006): 34–43; Lisa Guenther, "'Le flair animal': Levinas and the Possibility of Animal Friendship," *PhaenEx: Journal of Existential and Phenomenological Theory and Culture* 2, no. 2 (2007): 216–38; Peter Atterton, "Levinas and Our Moral Responsibility toward Other Animals," *Inquiry: An Interdisciplinary Journal of Philosophy* 54, no. 6 (2011): 633–49; Plant, "Welcoming Dogs."

27. See J. Aaron Simmons and Jay McDaniel, "Levinas and Whitehead: Notes toward a Conversation to Come," *Process Studies* 40, no. 1 (2011): 25–53.

28. Jay McDaniel, "A Response to Deckers," *Journal of Animal Ethics* 1, no. 1 (2011): 93–95.

29. We are indebted to James Dow for the insights and references in this paragraph and the next.

30. Robert Lurz, ed., *The Philosophy of Animal Minds* (Cambridge: Cambridge University Press, 2009); Susan Hurley and Matthew Nudds, *Rational Animals?* (Oxford: Oxford University Press, 2006); Jose Luis Bermúdez, *Thinking without Words* (Oxford: Oxford University Press, 2003); Michael Tomasello and Josep Call, *Primate Cognition* (Oxford: Oxford University Press, 1997).

31. Donald Davidson, "Thought and Talk," in *Inquiries into Truth and Interpretation* (Oxford: Clarendon Press, 1984), 155–79.

32. Robert Lurz, "The Philosophy of Animal Minds: An Introduction," in *The Philosophy of Animal Minds*, ed. Lurz, 7–8.

33. For more on the relationship between theory and data, see Nicholas Wolterstorff, *Reason within the Bounds of Religion*, 2nd ed. (Grand Rapids: William B. Eerdmans, 1984).

34. Jacques Derrida, *The Gift of Death*, trans. David Wills (Chicago: University of Chicago Press, 1995).

35. J. Aaron Simmons and Bruce Ellis Benson, *The New Phenomenology: A Philosophical Introduction* (London: Bloomsbury, 2013).

36. This leads some process thinkers and continental philosophers to believe that vegetarianism—or perhaps veganism—is the only viable option when it comes to eating. But an animal ethic must be about more than eating, and the following mandates, proposed by the Humane Society of the United States, seem helpful. They are endorsed by Birch and Cobb in *The Liberation of Life*.

37. Importantly, the authors of this essay have different views on exactly how to work out such implications as it relates to theology, philosophy of religion, and ethical existence.

38. For more on sensibility in Levinas, see John Drabinski, *Sensibility and Singularity: The Problem of Phenomenology in Levinas* (Albany: State University of New York Press, 2001).

39. Levinas, *Totality and Infinity*, 51.

40. Alfred North Whitehead, *Process and Reality*, corrected edition, ed. David Ray Griffin and Donald W. Sherburne (New York: Macmillan, 1979), 342–51. Illustrative of creatures experiencing God is the following: "He is the lure for feeling, the eternal urge of desire. His particular relevance to each creative act, as it arises from its own conditioned standpoint in the world, constitutes him the initial 'object of desire' establishing the initial phase of each subjective aim" (344).

41. For example, Derrida, *Gift of Death*, 69.

42. Ibid, 82.

43. Emmanuel Levinas, *Basic Philosophical Writings*, ed., Adriaan Peperzak, Simon Critchley, and Robert Bernasconi (Bloomington: Indiana University Press, 1996), 6.

44. Whitehead, *Process and Reality*, 349: "The consequent nature of God is the fulfillment of his experience by his reception of the multiple freedom of actuality into the harmony of his own actualization." When we say that God "hears" prayers we mean that God prehends, and thus receives into the divine life, the self-creative yet relational feelings of creaturely events. God feels their feelings.

45. See Simmons, *God and the Other*.

A SPIRITUAL DEMOCRACY OF ALL GOD'S CREATURES: ECOTHEOLOGY AND THE ANIMALS OF LYNN WHITE JR. | MATTHEW T. RILEY

1. White's father, a Presbyterian minister and professor of Christian social ethics at San Francisco Theological Seminary, was popularly known as "Lynn White" and he published under the name of "Lynn Townsend White." To avoid confusion, I will refer to Lynn Townsend White, jr., by his full name where it is practical to do so. It should also be noted that he preferred that his name be spelled with a lowercase "j" in "jr." In honor of his wishes, I will refrain from capitalizing "jr." in the body and notes of this text where I am able. In the interest of veracity, I also preserve the use of the lowercase "j" in the titles of publications when the original author has done the same. For an example of this practice, see "University Professor Lynn White, jr., 'Renaissance Man' for All Seasons," *UCLA Weekly* 3, no. 14 (1973): 4.

2. Lynn Townsend White, jr., "The Historical Roots of Our Ecologic Crisis," *Science* 155, no. 3767 (1967): 1203–7. Although it is perhaps one of the most cited articles in the entire field of religion and ecology, the title of White's 1967 article is frequently misspelled. In researching this chapter, I conducted an informal survey of more than two hundred books and articles and found that more than half of those examined altered the title of "The Historical Roots of Our Ecologic Crisis" in some way. Although a variety of errors exist, the most common iteration is to list the title as "The Historical Roots of Our Ecological Crisis." Other misspellings including changing "Historical" to "Historic," replacing "Ecologic" with "Environmental," and substituting "the" for "Our." See, for example: Whitney A. Bauman, Richard R. Bohannon II, and Kevin J. O'Brien, "The Tensions and Promises of Religion and Ecology's Past, Present,

and Future," in *Inherited Land: The Changing Grounds of Religion and Ecology*, ed. Whitney A. Bauman, Richard R. Bohannon II, and Kevin J. O'Brien (Eugene, Ore.: Wipf and Stock, 2011), 2n5, 17; Willis Jenkins, "After Lynn White: Religious Ethics and Environmental Problems," *Journal of Religious Ethics* 37, no. 2 (2009): 309; and Laurel Kearns, "The Context of Eco-theology," in *The Blackwell Companion to Modern Theology*, ed. Gareth Jones (Malden, Mass.: Wiley-Blackwell, 2004), 484.

3. In addition to being frequently cited as the spark that ignited the study of eco-theology, White's thesis is also credited as being *the* formative paper in environmental ethics as well as one of the founding documents of the Deep Ecology movement. For more information on the impact that White has had on scholarship on religion and ecology, see Jenkins, "After Lynn White," 285–86; Elspeth Whitney, "History, Lynn White, and Ecotheology," *Environmental Ethics* 15, no. 2 (1993): 158; J. Baird Callicott, *Beyond the Land Ethic: More Essays in Environmental Philosophy* (Albany: State University of New York Press, 1999), 40–41; and Elspeth Whitney, "Christianity and Changing Concepts of Nature: An Historical Perspective," in *Religion and the New Ecology: Environmental Responsibility in a World of Flux*, ed. David M. Lodge and Christopher Hamlin (Notre Dame, Ind.: University of Notre Dame, 2006), 32.

4. White, "Historical Roots," 1206.

5. The most common response to White and his writings in the field of eco-theology by far has been the focus on the biblical notions of dominion and stewardship. "The most common charge," wrote White in observance of this phenomenon, "was that I had ignorantly misunderstood the nature of 'man's dominion' and that it is not an arbitrary rule but rather a stewardship of our fellow creatures for which mankind is responsible to God." Lynn Townsend White, jr., "Continuing the Conversation," in *Western Man and Environmental Ethics: Attitudes toward Nature and Technology*, ed. Ian G. Barbour (Reading, Mass.: Addison-Wesley, 1973), 60. Additionally, Elspeth Whitney, one of the leading experts on White's thought, states that "the great bulk of . . . responses were to one particular aspect of White's argument, his claim in 'Roots' that Christianity inculcated a specifically 'exploitative' attitude towards nature" and that most argued that Christianity was more accurately interpreted as "a care-taking or stewardship relationship to the natural world." Elspeth Whitney, "White, Lynn (1907–1987)—Thesis of," in *The Encyclopedia of Religion and Nature*, vol. 2, ed. Bron Taylor (New York: Continuum, 2008), 1736. See also Kearns, "Context of Eco-theology," 467–68, and Ben A. Minteer and Robert E. Manning, "An Appraisal of the Critique of Anthropocentrism and Three

Lesser Known Themes in Lynn White's 'The Historical Roots of Our Ecologic Crisis,'" *Organization & Environment* 18, no. 2 (June 2005): 163–76.

6. For two excellent attempts to recover White's legacy and to reform scholarly responses to him, see Jenkins, "After Lynn White," and Whitney, "History, Lynn White, and Ecotheology."

7. According to Roderick Nash, "Most critics of Lynn White did not read beyond his 1967 condemnation." Roderick Frazier Nash, *The Rights of Nature: A History of Environmental Ethics* (Madison: University of Wisconsin Press, 1989), 95. On occasion, authors will cite White's follow-up article, "Continuing the Conversation," but this is not a common practice. In-depth readings of White's work on religion and ecology are few and far between. See, for example, Nash, *The Rights of Nature*, and "The Greening of Religion," in *This Sacred Earth: Religion, Nature, Environment*, ed. Roger S. Gottlieb (New York: Routledge, 1996).

8. White employed the term "creatures" in an inclusive way, it should be noted, to indicate not just living animals, but also nonliving entities such as rocks, mountains, and natural processes. See, for example, Lynn Townsend White, jr., "Christians and Nature," *Pacific Theological Review* 7 (Summer 1975): 7; "A Remark from Lynn White, Jr.," *CoEvolution Quarterly* 16 (Winter 1977/78); 108; "The Future of Compassion," *Ecumenical Review* 30 (1978): 105; and "Commentary on St. Francis of Assisi," *Bohemian Club Library Notes* (July 29, 1982): 19.

9. White, "Continuing the Conversation," 61.

10. Historian Bert S. Hall described White as "the founder of all serious modern study" of the history of technology in medieval Europe. Hall also stated that a "reasoned assessment of his public life would certainly conclude that Lynn White was the most widely read and influential medievalist of his generation." Bert S. Hall, "Eloge: Lynn White, Jr., 29 April 1907–30 March 1987," *Isis* 79, no. 3, A Special Issue on Artifact and Experiment (September 1988): 478.

11. For the most extensive bibliography of White's work currently available, see Bert S. Hall, "Lynn Townsend White, Jr. (1907–1987)," *Technology and Culture* 30, no. 1 (January 1989): 194–213.

12. Lynn Townsend White, jr., "What Accelerated Technological Progress in the Western Middle Ages?" in *Scientific Change: Historical Studies in the Intellectual, Social, and Technical Conditions for Scientific Discovery and Technical Invention, from Antiquity to the Present*, ed. Alistair C. Crombie (New York: Basic Books, 1963), 272–91.

13. Ibid., 283. Also see Lynn Townsend White, jr., "Technology and Invention in the Middle Ages," *Speculum* 15, no. 2 (1940): 156.

14. See, for instance, the articles gathered in Lynn Townsend White, jr., *Machina Ex Deo: Essays in the Dynamism of Western Culture* (Cambridge, Mass.: MIT Press, 1968), and *Medieval Religion and Technology: Collected Essays* (Berkeley: University of California Press, 1978).

15. For examples, see Lynn Townsend White, jr., "Presbyterians and the Intellectual Worship of God," *Presbyterian Outlook* 138, no. 25 (1956): 5; "The Medieval Meeting of East and West," *Journal of the Blaisdell Institute* 7, no. 2 (1972): 21; "A Jewish Option in Modern America," pamphlet, commencement address (Los Angeles: Hebrew Union College—Jewish Institute of Religion, June 12, 1964), 5; and Hall, "Eloge," 480.

16. Lynn Townsend White, jr., "The Social Responsibility of Scholarship: History: Is Clio a Tutelary Muse?" *Journal of Higher Education* 32, no. 7 (1961): 357–61.

17. Ibid., 359.

18. Ibid.

19. Lynn Townsend White, jr., "Medieval Technology: Transfers and Spinoffs," *The First Annual Rolf Buchdahl Lecture on Science, Technology and Values* (Raleigh, N.C.: Division of University Studies, North Carolina State University, November 3, 1981), 5. White was dedicated to the hypothesis that theological ideas and religious values lay at the root of Western thought. "Theological controversy," he proclaimed, "is the basic form of all disagreements." Lynn Townsend White, jr., "A Renegade Calvinist Looks at Methodist Theology and Education," speech, MacMurray College. Box 2—Speeches and Articles, File 57, Lynn Townsend White, jr., Special Collections, F. W. Olin Library, Mills College (n.d.).

20. Hall, "Lynn Townsend White, Jr.," 195.

21. Ibid., 198.

22. See, for example, Lynn Townsend White, jr., "A Climate of Courage: Loneliness, the Great Disease of the Twentieth Century," *Vital Speeches of the Day* 21 (March 1, 1955): 1075–77; "The Crisis in Democratic Leadership: Importance of the Individual Must Not Be Denied," *Vital Speeches of the Day* 10 (August 15, 1944): 655–59; and "The American Subversion: The Fundamental Worth of Every Human Being," *Vital Speeches of the Day* 11 (October 1, 1945): 755–57.

23. Lynn Townsend White, jr., *Educating Our Daughters: A Challenge to the Colleges* (New York: Harper, 1950). White wrote a number of other short texts on women's education. For a more complete list, consult Hall, "Lynn Townsend White, Jr."

24. See, for example, White, *Educating Our Daughters*, 125.

25. Lynn Townsend White, jr., *Minding the Earth* (MTE-6, audio cassette; Berkeley, Calif.: Strong Center, New Dimensions Foundation, n.d.).

26. See, for instance, Laura Hobgood-Oster, *The Friends We Keep: Unleashing Christianity's Compassion for Animals* (Waco, Texas: Baylor University Press, 2010), 107; and Ernst M. Conradie, "What on Earth Is an Ecological Hermeneutics? Some Broad Parameters," in *Ecological Hermeneutics: Biblical, Historical, and Theological Perspectives*, ed. David G. Horrell, Cherryl Hunt, Christopher Southgate, and Francesca Stavrakopoulou (New York: T&T Clark, 2010), 295–314.

27. Lynn Townsend White, jr., "History and Horseshoe Nails," in *The Historian's Workshop*, ed. L. P. Curtis, Jr. (New York: Alfred A. Knopf, 1970), 60.

28. I translate White's statement as follows: "I have a naturally theological mind" (ibid.). Despite White's assertions that he was not a theologian, he was aware of his own propensity for theological thinking. "I am not a theologian," White admitted, "although I do have *the knack*." Lynn Townsend White, jr., "Christian Materialism," unknown format, Box 16, "bibliographies, no date, general," 21 index cards, "Lynn Townsend White Papers, 1937–1985," Collection 1541, Department of Special Collections, Charles E. Young Research Library, University of California, Los Angeles (n.d), 12.

29. White, "Continuing the Conversation," 55. White's "theology of ecology," as I argue later in this essay, is that Christianity needs to move beyond notions of dominion and stewardship to a "third legitimately Biblical position, that Man is part of a democracy of all God's creatures, organic and inorganic, each praising his Maker according to the law of its being" and that this point of view requires that humans extend compassion and courtesy to other animals both as autonomous, rights-bearing beings as well as co-worshippers of God. White, "A Remark," 108.

30. White, "Continuing the Conversation," 55.

31. Ibid.

32. Interestingly, the connection between religious ideas and values and ecology, here specifically in reference to the treatment of animals, occurred to White only "later, after [he] had read Max Weber" (ibid., 55). Although many have compared the work of White to that of Max Weber, White's self-admitted intellectual indebtedness to Weber remains largely unexamined and undocumented by scholars in the field of religion and ecology. I explore White's use of Weber's thought further in my dissertation and elsewhere.

33. White, "Continuing the Conversation," 58.

34. White, "Historical Roots," 1203.

35. It should be noted that White did feel that Christianity, especially in the West, was most likely the prime shaper of the current environmental crisis. But he was also careful to point out that he did not subscribe to a monocausal view of history. Although he argued strongly that Christianity was most likely the

chief source of values and ideas that led to the ecological crisis, he acknowledged that other causal factors, in other places and during other time periods, could generate values and ideas that could have led to similar results (see "Continuing the Conversation," 58). Furthermore, he was quite clear in his assertion that although he felt religious ideas were a primary shaper of history, he did not think that all negative attitudes toward the environment came from religious values. In his words, "No sensible person could maintain that all ecologic damage is, or has been, rooted in religious attitudes" ("Continuing the Conversation," 57). See also White, "Historical Roots," 1206.

36. See, for instance, Norman C. Habel and Shirley Wurst, *The Earth Story in Genesis* (Sheffield: Sheffield Academic Press, 2000), and Kearns, "Context for Eco-Theology." For an excellent discussion of the term *dominion* as it appears in Genesis, see Theodore Hiebert's "Rethinking Dominion Theology," *Direction* 25, no. 2 (1996): 16–25.

37. White, "Continuing the Conversation," 63.

38. Ibid., 62.

39. Lynn Townsend White, jr., "Snake Nests and Icons: Some Observations on Theology and Ecology," *Anticipation: Christian Social Thought in Future Perspective* 10 (February 1972): 37.

40. White, "Continuing the Conversation," 61.

41. White, "Historical Roots," 1207. White proposed Saint Francis as the "patron saint for ecologists" in the closing line of "Historical Roots" in 1967. Twelve years later, Pope John Paul II named Saint Francis as the first patron saint of ecology. However, it should be noted that White was neither the first to nominate Saint Francis, nor did he acknowledge a causal link between his suggestion in "Historical Roots" and the 1979 papal proclamation. When asked if his suggestion had reached the pope, White replied, in his usual jocular style: "I'm not sure that my nomination reached the Vatican directly" (White, *Minding the Earth*). Also see Nash, "Greening of Religion," 199. Additionally, it should be of interest to scholars engaging with White's thesis that White was writing about Saint Francis's revolutionary religious thought and notion of a "democracy of all God's creatures" as early as 1947, at least two decades before the publication of "Historical Roots." See, for example, Lynn Townsend White, jr., "Natural Science and Naturalistic Art in the Middle Ages," *American Historical Review* 52 (1947): 433, and Nash, "Greening of Religion," 221n3.

42. White, "Historical Roots," 1207.

43. Ibid.

44. Ernest S. Feenstra, Lynn Townsend White, jr., Renato Baserga, Cesare Emilani, and Shale Niskin, "Christian Impact on Ecology," *Science* 156, no. 3776 (1967): 738.

45. White, "Future of Compassion," 106.

46. White, "Continuing the Conversation," 63.

47. Ibid., 61.

48. White, "Remark," 108.

49. Ibid.; White, "Continuing the Conversation," 61; White, "Historical Roots," 1206; White, "Christian Impact on Ecology," 738; White, "Commentary on St. Francis," 19; White, "Future of Compassion," 105; and White, "Snake Nests," 37.

50. In a letter written in 1984, for instance, he explained that the length and depth of his argument was restricted by the time allocated to him for his speech. "The time limitation was strict," he stated, "and on a topic like that much had to be omitted." Lynn Townsend White, jr., personal letter, 24 July, 1984 cited in Mary Aline Duitsman, "Ecology and Theology: Christian Responses to Lynn White Jr.," PhD diss., California State University, Northridge, May 1987), 15. Additionally, in the *Minding the Earth* audio interview, when asked where he got his inspiration for "Historical Roots," White did not characterize his argument as thorough or fully developed. In his words, "I just sat down and wrote that speech out of my head (there being no other source available)." This tendency to publish his thoughts, even as he was in the midst of developing them, was noted in his eulogy by Hall. When summarizing White's scholarly contributions, Hall described White's 1967 thesis as one of many "evolving ideas" that he built on over time. Hall, "Eloge," 480.

51. Hall, "Lynn Townsend White," 198.

52. White, "Historical Roots," 1207.

53. Ibid. and White, "Commentary on St. Francis," 19.

54. White, "Christians and Nature," 11.

55. White, "Snake Nests," 37.

56. White, "Christians and Nature," 11.

57. Ibid., 10.

58. Nash, "Greening of Religion," 200.

59. See White, "Commentary on St. Francis," 19.

60. White, "Christians and Nature," 7.

61. White, "Continuing the Conversation," 61.

62. See, for example, White, "Christians and Nature," 10; Lynn Townsend White, jr., "Dynamo and Virgin Reconsidered," *American Scholar* 27, no. 2 (Spring 1958): 194; and White, "Presbyterians and the Intellectual Worship of God," 7.

63. White, "Presbyterians and the Intellectual Worship of God," 7. See also White, "Future of Compassion," 106.

64. White, "Dynamo and Virgin Reconsidered," 194.

65. White, "Commentary on St. Francis," 19.

66. White, "Presbyterians and the Intellectual Worship of God," 7; White, "Christians and Nature," 9–10; and White, "Continuing the Conversation," 62.

67. White, "Continuing the Conversation," 62.

68. Ibid.

69. White, "Future of Compassion," 106, 109; White, "Presbyterians and the Intellectual Worship of God," 7; White, "Christians and Nature," 9; and White, "Continuing the Conversation," 62.

70. White, "Continuing the Conversation," 62.

71. Ibid., 63.

72. Ibid.

73. Ibid.

74. White, "Future of Compassion," 109.

75. Ibid., 106.

76. Ibid., 107.

77. Ibid., 106.

78. Ibid., 104.

79. Ibid., 108–9.

80. Ibid., 105.

81. Ibid., 107. Flourishing together and extending compassion and courtesy to other creatures, however, do not require that the rights of humans be heedlessly denied. Indeed, as should be evident in the example just given, White is careful to pay attention to human needs as well. He noted, in "Snake Nests and Icons," that simply extending rights and compassion to other creatures can still lead to ethical conundrums for humans. Some forms of Hinduism and Buddhism, he mused, may serve as examples of the way in which Christian thought might eventually respect other animals and creatures as individuals. But even the most exemplary forms of religious concern for animals can lead to unexpected dilemmas. Speaking of the widespread human suffering and poverty that he and his wife observed on a visit to Calcutta, he recalled that "we yearned to take the sacred cows that were blocking the traffic and turn them into hamburgers to feed the city's refugees! People are part of nature too," he continued, "the other creatures don't have all the rights" (White, "Snake Nests," 36–37).

82. White, "Future of Compassion," 107.

83. Ibid.

84. Ibid.

85. Ibid., 109.

86. Ibid., 108.

87. White, "Historical Roots," 1207.

88. White, "Continuing the Conversation," 61.

EPILOGUE. ANIMALS AND ANIMALITY: REFLECTIONS ON THE ART OF JAN HARRISON | JAY McDANIEL

The conference "Divinanimality: Creaturely Theology" (Drew Theological School, 2011) on which this volume is based featured the art of Jan Harrison (http://www.janharrison.net). The remarks that follow are a culling from conversations at the conference, as interpreted with help from Whitehead's philosophy. They were originally published online in *Jesus Jazz and Buddhism*: http://www.jesusjazzbuddhism.org/animals-and-animality.html.

1. See, for example, Jea Sophia Oh, *A Postcolonial Theology of Life: Planetarity East and West* (Louisville, Ky.: Sopher Press, 2011).

2. See, for example, Jacques Derrida, *The Animal That Therefore I Am*, ed. Marie-Louise Mallet; trans. David Wills, Perspectives in Continental Philosophy (New York: Fordham University Press, 2008), 9.

3. Jan Harrison performs "Animal Tongues" while wearing animal masks of her own creation. See (and hear) http://www.janharrison.net/videos -performance-animal-tongues- (accessed 2/11/13).

4. Jan Harrison, "Artist's Statement": http://www.janharrison.net/artist-s-state ment (accessed 2/11/13).

5. See Catherine Keller and Laurel Schneider, eds., *Polydoxy: Theology of Multiplicity and Relation* (New York: Routledge, 2011).

CONTRIBUTORS

AN YOUNTAE is a PhD candidate in Theological and Philosophical Studies at Drew University. His research focuses on exploring the theological possibilities at the boundaries between different philosophical discourses, including continental philosophy, Latin American/Caribbean decolonial thinking, critical theory of race and gender, and theopoetics.

DENISE KIMBER BUELL is Professor of Religion at Williams College and a member of its Women's, Gender, and Sexuality Studies Program. Her work appears in multiple articles as well as in *Making Christians: Clement of Alexandria and the Rhetoric of Legitimacy* (Princeton University Press, 1999) and *Why This New Race: Ethnic Reasoning in Early Christianity* (Columbia University Press, 2005). Her current book-length project relates to the essay in this volume.

JACOB J. ERICKSON is a PhD candidate in Theological and Philosophical Studies at Drew University, Visiting Instructor of Religion at St. Olaf College, and Ecotheologian in Residence at Mercy Seat Lutheran Church in Minneapolis. His dissertation, "A Theopoetics of the Earth," constructs an ecotheology of planetary conviviality—life together in the midst of creaturely difference—attentive to the challenges of global warming.

LAURA HOBGOOD-OSTER is Paden Chair and Professor of Religion and Environmental Studies at Southwestern University. Her most recent publications are *A Dog's History of the World* (Baylor University Press, 2014),

The Friends We Keep: Unleashing Christianity's Compassion for Animals (Baylor University Press, 2010), and *Holy Dogs and Asses: Animals in the Christian Tradition* (University of Illinois Press, 2008). She teaches courses in the history of the Christian tradition and on animals and religion. Currently, she serves as president of the International Society for the Study of Religion, Nature, and Culture.

LAUREL KEARNS is Associate Professor of Sociology and Religion and Environmental Studies at Drew University. Her research is focused on religious, particularly Christian, involvement in environmental issues, nature spirituality, environmental justice, and religious responses to climate change. She is co-editor with Catherine Keller of *Ecospirit: Religions and Philosophies for the Earth* (Fordham University Press, 2007), and author of many articles and essays.

JENNIFER L. KOOSED is Associate Professor and Chair of Religious Studies at Albright College in Reading, Pennsylvania. She is the author of *(Per) mutations of Qohelet: Reading the Body in the Book* (Bloomsbury, 2006) and *Gleaning Ruth: A Biblical Heroine and Her Afterlives* (University of South Carolina Press, 2011). She is also the editor of *The Bible and Posthumanism* (Society of Biblical Literature, 2014).

BEATRICE MAROVICH is a PhD candidate in Theological and Philosophical Studies at Drew University. Her dissertation, currently titled "Dream of the Creature: Religion, Ethics, and Interspecies Kinship," examines the figure of the creature as what she calls a "theological relic" in an attempt to discern whether, in the conflicted figural dynamics of creaturely life, there might be a latent form of ethical reflection.

GLEN A. MAZIS is Professor of Philosophy and Humanities at Penn State Harrisburg. He is the author of *Emotion and Embodiment: Fragile Ontology* (Peter Lang, 1993); *The Trickster, Magician and Grieving Man: Reconnecting Men with Earth* (Bear & Company, 1994); *Earthbodies: Rediscovering Our Planetary Senses* (State University of New York Press, 2002); and *Humans, Animals, Machines: Blurring Boundaries* (State University of New York Press, 2008). His *The Depth of the Face of the World: Silence, Ethics, Imagination and Time* is forthcoming from Fordham University Press.

JAY McDANIEL is Director of the Steel Center for the Study of Religion and Philosophy at Hendrix College and editor of the online magazine *Jesus Jazz and Buddhism*. Author of ten books and with much experience in being mentored by animals, he is also co-editor of *Good News for Animals? Christian Approaches to Animal Well-Being* (Wipf and Stock, 2008). He is especially interested in the sense of kinship that is possible with animals and wants to consider relations between kinship, alterity, and poetics (understood as seeking wisdom for daily life).

PETER ANTHONY MENA is a PhD candidate in Historical Studies at Drew University. His work focuses on the history of Christianity in late antiquity, and his research interests include women's, gender, sexuality studies, and interdisciplinary approaches to the study of Latina/o identities in the United States. His current work applies theories of space articulated by Gloria Anzaldúa in order to interpret Christian hagiographies in late antiquity.

ERIC DARYL MEYER is a PhD candidate in the Theology Department at Fordham University. His current research examines the formative conceptual role of the human-animal distinction within Christian theological anthropology as it emerges in tensions and contradictions between human animality and "proper" humanity.

STEPHEN D. MOORE is Professor of New Testament Studies at the Theological School, Drew University. He has written or co-written and edited or co-edited around twenty volumes, most recently *The Invention of the Biblical Scholar: A Critical Manifesto*, with Yvonne Sherwood (Fortress, 2011). His book-in-progress is *The Bodybuilder, the Sex Worker, and the Sheep: Untold Tales from the Book of Revelation* (Society of Biblical Literature, forthcoming).

ERIKA MURPHY received her PhD in Theological and Philosophical Studies from Drew University in 2013. Her dissertation, "Inhabiting God's Wounds: Rediscovering the Wisdom of Vulnerability," is an exploration of the possibilities of bodily and psychic vulnerability in humanity and divinity.

KATE RIGBY is Professor of Environmental Humanities at Monash University. She is a Fellow of the Australian Academy of the Humanities and of the Alexander von Humboldt Foundation. Her research ranges across German studies, European philosophy, literature and religion, and culture and ecology. Among her publications are *Topographies of the Sacred: The Poetics of Place in European Romanticism* (University of Virginia Press, 2004), and *Ecocritical Theory: New European Approaches* (co-edited, University of Virginia Press, 2011).

MATTHEW T. RILEY is a PhD candidate at Drew University. He is currently a Research Associate at the Forum on Religion and Ecology at Yale University and an Instructor at Yale's Interdisciplinary Center for Bioethics. His dissertation research focuses on Max Weber's social theory, the development of religiously inspired environmental ethics and ecotheology, and the work of Lynn T. White Jr.

TERRA S. ROWE received an MA in Diaconal Ministry from Wartburg Theological Seminary and an STM from the Lutheran Theological Seminary at Philadelphia. She is currently a PhD candidate in Theological and Philosophical Studies at Drew University. Her research interests include incarnation and embodiment, posthumanism, and Lutheran ecotheology—particularly intersections of ecology, economy, and the Protestant tradition.

ROBERT PAUL SEESENGOOD is Associate Professor of Religious Studies and Chair of Classical Languages at Albright College in Reading, Pennsylvania. His work includes *Competing Identities: The Athlete and the Gladiator in Early Christian Literature* (T&T Clark, 2006), *Paul: A Brief History* (Wiley-Blackwell, 2010), and, with Jennifer L. Koosed, *Jesse's Lineage: The Legendary Lives of David, Jesus, and Jesse James* (Bloomsbury, 2012).

J. AARON SIMMONS is Assistant Professor of Philosophy at Furman University. Specializing in postmodern philosophy of religion and political philosophy, he is the author of *God and the Other: Ethics and Politics after the Theological Turn* (Indiana University Press, 2011), coauthor of *The New Phenomenology: A Philosophical Introduction* (Bloomsbury, 2013), and co-editor of *Reexamining Deconstruction and Determinate Religion: Toward a Religion* *with Religion* (Duquesne University Press, 2012) and *Kierkegaard and Levinas: Ethics, Politics, and Religion* (Indiana University Press, 2008).

KEN STONE is Professor of Bible, Culture and Hermeneutics and Academic Dean at Chicago Theological Seminary. He is the author of *Practicing Safer Texts: Food, Sex, and Bible in Queer Perspective* (T&T Clark, 2005) and *Sex, Honor and Power in the Deuteronomistic History* (Sheffield Academic Press, 1996), and the editor of *Queer Commentary and the Hebrew Bible* (Sheffield Academic Press, 2001) and (with Teresa J. Hornsby) *Bible Trouble: Queer Reading at the Boundaries of Biblical Scholarship* (Society of Biblical Literature, 2011).

INDEX

TRANSDISCIPLINARY THEOLOGICAL COLLOQUIA

Laurel Kearns and Catherine Keller, eds., *Ecospirit: Religions and Philosophies for the Earth*.

Virginia Burrus and Catherine Keller, eds., *Toward a Theology of Eros: Transfiguring Passion at the Limits of Discipline*.

Ada María Isasi-Díaz and Eduardo Mendieta, eds., *Decolonizing Epistemologies: Latina/o Theology and Philosophy*.

Stephen D. Moore and Mayra Rivera, eds., *Planetary Loves: Spivak, Postcoloniality, and Theology*.

Chris Boesel and Catherine Keller, eds., *Apophatic Bodies: Negative Theology, Incarnation, and Relationality*.

Chris Boesel and S. Wesley Ariarajah, eds., *Divine Multiplicity: Trinities, Diversities, and the Nature of Relation*.

Stephen D. Moore, ed., *Divinanimality: Animal Theory, Creaturely Theology*. Foreword by Laurel Kearns.